GEORGE BANCROFT

George Bancroft in Berlin

GEORGE BANCROFT

The Intellectual as Democrat

LILIAN HANDLIN

A Cornelia & Michael Bessie Book

HARPER & ROW, PUBLISHERS, New York
Cambridge, Philadelphia, San Francisco, London
Mexico City, São Paulo, Singapore, Sydney

Grateful acknowledgment is made for permission to reprint:

Quotations from documents in the Aaron Bancroft and George Bancroft papers from the Manuscripts Collection, Aaron Bancroft Papers, Rare Books and Manuscripts Division, The New York Public Library, Astor, Lenox and Tilden Foundations.

Frontispiece: Oil by Gustav Richter. Courtesy of the Harvard University Portrait Collection— Bequest of George Bancroft.

FIRST EDITION

Designer: Sidney Feinberg

This book is set in 10½-point Bembo. It was composed by TriStar Graphics, Minneapolis, Minnesota, and printed and bound by R. R. Donnelley, Harrisonburg.

Library of Congress Cataloging in Publication Data

Handlin, Lilian.
   George Bancroft, the intellectual as Democrat.

   "A Cornelia & Michael Bessie book."
   Includes bibliographical references and index.
   1. Bancroft, George, 1800–1891. 2. United States—History—1815–1861. 3. Diplomats—United States—Biography. I. Title.
E340.B2H36   1984   973.8′092′4   83–49057
ISBN 0–06–039033–6

---

84 85 86 87 88 10 9 8 7 6 5 4 3 2 1

To Oscar
for learning and love

CONTENTS

The History

ACKNOWLEDGMENTS

The Bancroft Papers at the Massachusetts Historical Society constitute the core of the sources relied on in writing this volume; and it is a pleasure to record my indebtedness to the staff of the Society and to its director, Louis L. Tucker, who gave generously of their time and knowledge. I am also grateful to the staffs of the New York Public Library, Manuscripts Collection, the Library of Congress, the Boston Public Library, the Harvard University Archives, the Houghton and Widener Libraries of Harvard University, the Cornell University Archives, and the American Antiquarian Society for permission to use their rich holdings which shed light on Bancroft and his contemporaries.

Thanks are also due to Laura Margolis and Antonia Gabor for their good-natured patience as the manuscript took shape, and to the indefatigable editors at Harper & Row, Beena Kamlani and Mary Jane Alexander.

I would also like to express my gratitude to my teachers, professors Frank A. Warren and Michael Wreszin of Queens College. Professors Yehoshua Arieli and Arieh Goren of the Hebrew University of Jerusalem taught me much about the American past and encouraged and inspired me over the years. To my husband, who read the manuscript at various stages and made insightful suggestions as to both substance and form, my debt is greatest. Whatever is good in the book is to his credit. The errors are all my own.

FOREWORD

George Bancroft was a man of letters and politician, a moralist and diplomat, occasionally a prophet and often, in appearance, a reformer. Before turning to history he tried poetry; when that failed, education. Denied a university appointment, he shifted to banking and politics. In a life span that began at the dawn of one century and ended on the verge of another, he acquired the reputation of strident nationalist, firm believer in progress, worshiper of the popular will, and great romantic historian. He thereby became a controversial figure, so that contemporaries suggested he lacked "qualities of a higher order" and classed him among the "canting twaddlers." Bancroft's careers expose the fundamental problems of men of letters in American society—their status and legitimacy, the connection between the study and the marketplace, the role of ideas in a democracy, as well as the pitfalls that await self-proclaimed custodians of culture.[1]

This study traces the relationship between what the historian wrote and what the politician or observer did. In a century when intellect in the United States usually took the conservative side, Bancroft seemed to swim against the current. His responses were the products of their historical context; the century's shifting political climate, its changing economic patterns, territorial expansion, Civil War, and Reconstruction shaped his reactions. A participant and opinion maker, a commentator, social critic, recorder of the past, and popular leader, Bancroft felt the influence of his time and place, and though he occasionally hoped to transcend them both, the effort failed. The twists and turns of his life therefore offer insights into the forces that also operated on his contemporaries.[2]

Never a visionary or a dreamer, Bancroft remained what he became in early manhood—a pliable learner. Worcester, where he was born, and Cambridge, where he received the bulk of his education, early shaped his outlook; everything else was only a thin layer of rhetoric that barely covered the hard core of concepts already acquired. Neither a Göttingen doctorate nor the major intellectual developments of his century altered the dutiful son of Aaron Bancroft, the studious pupil of Benjamin Abbot at Phillips Exeter, and the loyal student of Andrews Norton and John Thornton Kirkland at Harvard. The future author of learned articles on European thinkers, who claimed acquaintanceship with Kant, Goethe, and Herder and was regarded as a major transmitter of German romanticism to America, held fast to his own brand of moral philosophy. And if facile adoption of a basically foreign terminology made him appear something of a transcendentalist, he was not.

Nor was Bancroft, in his writings and politics, a radical social critic or politician, either a Jeffersonian democrat or a full-fledged Jacksonian. In fact he upheld most orthodoxies, rebelling against his native environment neither in thought nor in civic activities, and it was one of the sadder aspects of his life that he and his contemporaries never conceded how closely their views matched. Bancroft's dislike for shouting with the multitudes was not the superficial reaction of a born aristocrat (which he was not) nor that of a Brahmin disdaining the people. Rather it was the outgrowth of a profoundly traditional orientation which, in its last phases, found him worshiping institutions with the best reactionaries of his generation.

Bancroft soon regretted the early ebullience of his faith in the inner workings of democracy as guarantee of national progress. Ultimately he rested the future of the United States on the Constitution adopted, he believed, to spare the people the anarchy he and his contemporaries regarded as a prelude to tyranny. Fearful of "those treasons of the ballot box" whenever a society fell victim to mobs, Bancroft shared with his political opponents a veneration for regulated liberty founded on positive institutions sanctioned by history. Therefore, on intellectual and practical grounds, he vociferously defended the status quo when it seemed endangered by declamations about abstract rights, by wild innovations, and by dreaming speculators. He had little use for the "unwritten higher law, interpreted by individual conscience" and clung to those "drags and anchors" that checked rapid progress. The interest in history became a veneration for the past because of the experience, caution, and wisdom with which it shackled the present.[3]

The philosophical democrat, which Bancroft unquestionably was, constructed an elaborate theory to prove that the mechanics of American communal life in effect canceled out the fears of those who anticipated either anarchy or despotism as the natural end of self-rule. Concepts derived from early Unitarianism and from moral philosophy made Bancroft appear a progressive optimist, but a closer inspection reveals a very qualified and cautious view of human development and certainly no worshiper of vox populi, which, Bancroft's experience proved, was emphatically not always vox dei.

His vision rested on an abstraction—the people, whom he thought he knew, from Worcester, Springfield, and Boston, as well as from his study of the American past. Well before Tocqueville, Bancroft concluded that they were a conservative force, their nonrevolutionary character paradoxical in a nation proud of its heritage as the vanguard of humanity. He found them always cautious in the face of change, hesitant about reforms, slow to be swayed by new ideas, and remarkably set in their ways. That conclusion formed the crux of Bancroft's democratic philosophy and underscored its relevance to the times, because it reassured some about the safety of the status quo while cautioning others bent on immediate drastic change.

He provided countless historical instances to show the danger of opting for "the simple genuine self against the world," branding as reckless visionaries those who labeled history the mere "story agreed upon by posterity" and who bemoaned the rubbish accumulated before the portals of nature. Bancroft, the antirevolutionary recorder of America's glorious revolution, took comfort in the way the past bound the present and offset the hot haste and din of his times. The great fortune of the United States and the chief evidence of God's love was the unique revolution that spared it future convulsions. The colonies "took their point of departure from the world as it was," refused "to overthrow all traditional inequalities," and, guided by experience, produced the world's most conservative polity, sufficiently strong to dampen individualistic impulses and preserve a community of thought and will.[4]

This profoundly anti-individualist orientation accounted for Bancroft's conservative political persuasion and qualified his faith in the mass. A politician trying to come to terms with the world around him, his inherited perceptions clashed with new realities. He saw man as his Puritan ancestors had—faulty, prone to error, shortsighted, occasionally cruel, grasping, and greedy—a disturbing perception in a society growing more democratic. But a metaphysical dualism, grounded for Bancroft

in moral philosophy, offered hope. Another side to the human character—the soul, reason, or conscience—tied the individual to the infinite
and enabled man on occasion to rise above himself. To succeed in this
arduous and uncertain effort, the individual needed the support of the
whole; only thus could he bring his higher faculties into play and triumph over his negative character. Society did not always reach the right
decisions; but the likelihood of approximating the correct choice was
greater when man submerged his selfishness in the multitude of other
selfishnesses, thereby canceling out their influence.

"The people" could be trusted in politics as in everything else; for
their judgment, Bancroft was fond of saying, was the nearest approxima-
tion to the voice of reason, the whisper of universal conscience, the
immediate revelation of God to man, all of which was utterly impossible
to the individual standing alone. "The individual is often lost, Providence never disowns the race." In an era when some called for self-
reliance, extolled Man, and worshiped those who broke the shackles of
custom, Bancroft resolutely marched the other way.[5]

Bancroft's career also revealed the conservative cast of his politics.
Concerned with dignifying labor and moral culture, he rarely bothered
with particulars and offered few prescriptions for societal ills. Since
human history was in effect the clash between "the fanatics for conservatism" and the "enthusiasts for ideal freedom," progress was defined as
the attempt to bring "the established order into nearer harmony with the
eternal law of justice." How this was to be translated into legislation or
governmental acts Bancroft did not say. Instead he focused on moral
reform, a nebulous, undefined construct that made for good orations but
little programmatic content. Not much more was needed, he believed, in
a country where, except for a few easily disposed-of maladjustments,
social equality was a fact of life and no one in his right mind wanted
economic equality as well. All men were created equal and all were equal
in their mortality; what happened in between, however blatantly unequal, was part of God's design. The dangers of contemporary life
stemmed more from opulence than from poverty—and Bancroft's cure
was to balance the influence of wealth with the influence of numbers.
The less affluent, being in the majority, were presumed to have the best
interests of society at heart since, unlike a narrowly circumscribed elite,
they were not blinded by possessions.[6]

The historian traced the uniqueness of the United States to the adoption of popular sovereignty as the central feature of its life early on in
national evolution. This spectacular development he illustrated in twelve
volumes written in the course of a lifetime and very much influenced by

the circumstances of their composition. The guiding theme, however, remained the same: all "events" or facts corresponded to a divine idea. Nothing changed without God's will; the world knew no catastrophic collapses; and no state of nature ever demanded from man a totally fresh start. This organic theory of evolution (derived from moral philosophy much more than from a German education) made the past crucial to the understanding of the present and also guaranteed that nothing that was ever passed away completely. The interconnectedness of all things under providential supervision promised an inner core of sameness and only the superficial appeared new. Hence the writer, politician, and theorist could read contemporary events serenely, secure in the knowledge that no individual or group could throw this cosmic process out of gear.[7]

That was the ultimate message of the *History* and the source of its appeal to readers for many years. The public, enamored by its prose as well as by its ideas, read an immensely reassuring account, to which nationalism, progressive vision, and libertarian inclinations were merely incidental. Over and over again, Bancroft told his contemporaries that, in spite of appearances to the contrary, they lived in a stable society not easily upset by caprice, visionary theories, or mistaken notions of right and wrong. That message also appeared in lectures, political tracts, speeches, and orations. When Bancroft harnessed his knowledge of history and managerial skills to reinforce it, he rose on the Democratic Party ladder and became one of the more distinctive men of letters of his day.

A basically religious outlook sustained lifelong views. Having grown up in economic deprivation amidst endless theological squabbles, Bancroft did not unclasp tenets of belief that were his anchor of stability as a child and young man. Early Unitarianism, his true intellectual background, in spite of its anti-Calvinist, more optimistic evaluation of human nature and view of a benevolent deity, also assumed that the believer was prone to sin and needed guidance and restraint. "No man that lives has not sinned," Bancroft stated; the individual always required grace and redemption, his life on earth a season of labor in preparation for eternity, his lot predetermined—if no longer by original sin, then by his own inadequacies. This made man's perfectibility very much conditional; the communion between his soul and the infinite was never perfect, and remained hedged in by mundane reality. Only arrogant pretenders propagating dangerous falsehoods argued otherwise. Bancroft, whose political career began with an assault on all "infidels," discovered toward the end of the century that some theorists regarded religion as the opiate of the people, "but an instrument of government in the hands

of their oppressors," rather than "the poor man's consolation and defence." This rejection of religion was for Bancroft tantamount to racial
suicide, a cosmic impossibility. Modern civilization was built on the interconnectedness between the human and the divine, in its Christian
form; those who discarded the central means of knowledge abandoned
all hope of understanding mankind. Revelation, the moral law, and objective standards of judgment, not a reliance on the senses or intuitions,
were the tests by which to judge anything in a universe where God's
justice was overwhelming and His superintendence a guarantee that
truth was one and indivisible, and evil always defeated itself.[8]

The twentieth century would have defined Bancroft as an intellectual, a term that became popular only late in the nineteenth century. His
contemporaries called him a man of letters, one of a larger group who
shared a concern for society and believed that learning obliged them to
speak out on public issues. Occasionally such individuals eschewed direct
political involvement, and left their drawing rooms, offices, or studies
not to mingle with the mob but to guide it through written or oral
exhortations. Others opted for a more direct role, presenting themselves
as candidates for office. Critics charged them at times with prostituting
their sacred trusts for influence and self-gratification, but society rewarded this broadening of professional concerns with power and office.
Still other men of letters exploited the political process for a particular
reform and exhorted contemporaries to countenance fundamental
changes in line with higher truths, universal laws, or supreme values of
which they were the custodians. At various periods of his life Bancroft
straddled these diverse relationships between letters and politics.

Living in an era when the connection between scholarship and the
marketplace was intimate enough to allow an American with a German
Ph.D. to run for governor of Massachusetts and become a spokesman for
territorial expansion, he successfully seized the opportunities that came
his way. In so doing Bancroft behaved as intellectuals did then and still
do now, exploiting images and symbols to define political identities,
popularize programs, and broaden the social and cultural imagination of
his generation. But he also paid a price, since the very versatility and
adaptability to pressures that advanced his careers also subverted his talents. Atrophied critical faculties, credulity, incessant rationalization, and
selective visions—the penalties of a seemingly charmed existence—reduced an able man and great historian to one of the lesser luminaries of
the era. Therein lies the ultimate significance of his career.

Preparation

I

THE MINISTER'S SON

STANDING on board the American ship *Belle,* watching the Staten Island shoreline glide by, George Bancroft, twenty-two years old and newly arrived from Europe, experienced mixed sensations. This was the moment for which he had long waited. He was almost home. Behind him were a Worcester childhood, two years at the Phillips Exeter Academy, a Harvard A.B. and M.A., and a turbulent European adventure. What lay ahead he did not know.

Sight of the Jersey shore in the moonlight restored confidence, and as the vessel neared the wharf uncertainty dissolved only to revive during the trip from New York to Worcester. The United States was "a country not formed after the higher laws of beauty"; it was not the land of romance; no picturesque ruins enlivened the landscape. This was the nation of sober manners, restraint, and propriety. Could a young man returning from warmer latitudes fit in after encountering the passionate Lord Byron, the immortal but also immoral Goethe; a youth who had walked the streets of Paris with Washington Irving, dined with Lafayette, and earned the praise of Alexander von Humboldt?[1]

Reassuring faces greeted the traveler near the family farm. These were the people he cherished—his aging parents, Aaron and Lucretia Bancroft, and a small flock of sisters. Several days later in Cambridge he called on Andrews Norton, John Thornton Kirkland, and Edward Everett, the benefactors who had made Europe possible. The two small groups represented what he valued most, his family and his education. For their sake, as much as his own, he had left the United States in the hope of returning a knowledgeable and proud contributor to the intellectual and social life of New England.

3

Dressed in foreign garb—silk shirt, velveteen trousers, and yellow gloves—and sporting a small beard, George mumbled French and German phrases where good English words applied and planted kisses all around, violating the laws of self-restraint and polite society. He gushed forth plans and stories, expounding his dreams and hopes in a strange concoction of unreal expectations, hardheaded calculations, misunderstood ideas, and sheer exuberance. Andrews Norton, for four years the recipient of fawning letters which implied that he was the sole source of his protégé's hopes and happiness, grew increasingly cool. When the young man returned to Worcester he found a note full of rebukes. Visitors from Cambridge also brought disturbing news—Norton was telling his colleagues that Bancroft would never do as a Harvard tutor or clergyman.

Aware that a man of influence was actively undermining his prospects, Bancroft fired back a self-righteous and indignant message, alternately bemoaning his misfortune and standing up for his rights. How can you do this to me, now that I need you most, he wailed. "Your views of my chances are unjust and your prophecies of my poor success ill founded." But in the short run, Norton, not Bancroft, proved the better prophet.[2]

These incidents were emblematic of a career. Although Bancroft spent his long adult life far removed from the universe of his childhood, losing along the way some of its narrowness and provincialism, attraction to and repulsion from his native environment shaped his life. Basic traits and attitudes acquired on a Worcester farm remained permanently fixed notwithstanding a multiplicity of challenges. He could not altogether shake off that heritage, however much his generation determined to abandon set intellectual assumptions of their childhood universe. Since the conflict between acceptance and rejection evoked tensions not easily subdued, Bancroft's efforts to bridge the gaps shaped the early years of his life.

Worcester eventually remembered Aaron Bancroft as a kind and gentle person, frequently seen in the street as he hurried from the Second Parish meetinghouse to his other obligations—a stooped figure, curiosity shining in small eyes set in a wrinkled face, always meticulously dressed, the last man in town to wear smallclothes and a three-cornered hat. His fame had spread far beyond the confines of the town in which he lived for more than fifty years and where he gained respect for his public spirit and for his contributions to the community's welfare. But it had not always been so.

The future clergyman, born in 1755, was the son of a reputable farmer in Reading, Massachusetts, a fifth-generation American, of English Puritan ancestry. Aaron early determined not to follow his father's calling and chose the ministry, graduating from Harvard in 1778. But he found it difficult to settle in a parish and, restless, received permission from the Massachusetts Executive Council to go to Nova Scotia as a missionary. A short apprenticeship in theology, a college education marred by the Revolutionary War, the Bible and a few other books were his only equipment for three years on the frontier, in an environment of religious ferment, fanaticism, and disorder. In Yarmouth, Annapolis, and Horton, confronting human nature in the raw, the young man formed his lifelong attachment to rational religion which alone could triumph over mysticism, intolerance, and bigotry.[3]

In 1783 he came to Worcester, as a temporary substitute for the ailing Reverend Thaddeus Maccarty. That semirural community, emerging from the war, struggled not quite peaceably with new problems. Joseph Allen, Joseph Wheeler, and Isaiah Thomas formed the Revolutionary Committee of Inspection, Correspondence and Safety, charged with ferreting out hidden enemies. The town meeting still debated the sorry state of education, appropriated some funds, and appointed committees. Swine yoked and ringed wandered about except near the school, while heavy fines punished those who damaged trees planted for shade or ornament. Worcester would not pay Dr. John Campbell for attending the late John Wait, whose wife and children received support from Fitchburg, where they lived; let Fitchburg take care of the bills. Nevertheless the stingy town agreed to re-cover the cushion in the pulpit, and most people believed that the spirit of Christian charity reigned. In 1783 forty-nine inhabitants cast their votes for the wealthy and popular John Hancock to be the next governor of the state, while only eight voted for the equally wealthy but less popular James Bowdoin.

New roads were evidence of economic growth but Lincoln Street remained the main thoroughfare over which stages and coaches rambled to Boston, bringing the mail from Philadelphia after a three-week delay. Nearby would rise the imposing Antiquarian Hall, built by Isaiah Thomas as depository for materials in American history. The brick courthouse would shelter the Second Parish until it built its own church. On court days the town seethed with excitement as people came from far away and local jockeys used Main Street as a race course until discouraged by heavy fines. The Exchange Coffee House, kept by Samuel B. Thomas, identifiable by his white hat and green spectacles, hosted important visitors, while Ephraim Mower, town selectman, later representative to the General Court, and a strong supporter of the young minister, kept a hotel of lesser quality.[4]

In the fifty years Aaron Bancroft lived there the town did not change much. Though the population increased from around 2,000 in 1783 to 4,172 in 1830, the community retained many eighteenth-century ways. People complained that Worcester was losing its rustic charm, yet the houses were still far enough apart to accommodate gardens and vegetable plots. Four homes had pianos, but no one would come from Boston to tune them for less than four dollars. Rather than pay the twelve-and-a-half-cent rate to send a letter to the state capital, frugal inhabitants used private travelers or teamsters. Whenever the merchant Stephen Salisbury thought of going to Boston, people prepared letters for him to take along. Only one mantua maker resided in Worcester, and servants were a problem, as always and everywhere.[5]

Few inhabitants were wealthy, although some made a pretense to high rank. Levi Lincoln had a splendid farm, a garden, and a pond, but he had carpeted only one room in his house; painted board floors were good enough for the others. The equally well-to-do Stephen Salisbury ran a dry-goods store, spending his days behind the counter and the nights in an adjoining room. Daniel Waldo, one of his competitors, owned the first chaise in Worcester, which earned him the reputation of an extravagant aristocrat. He was also one of the town's chief religious troublemakers.

Social friction paralleled the town's complicated ecclesiastical history. The congregation had dismissed one pastor for playing practical jokes, only to choose a successor who battled the revivalist party. Maccarty in turn approved of the Great Awakening and while at Kingston had invited George Whitefield to preach, upon which angered parishioners had boarded up the meetinghouse doors. When Maccarty came to Worcester, he had the support of the town's conservative believers, who chose him over Jonathan Mayhew by a vote of 44 to 2. Despite this vote of confidence, John Adams remembered constant parish disputes and noted the dislike of some for Maccarty's loud threats of divine chastisement and execrations of carnal, unregenerate rebels against God.

The minister's life mirrored the difficulties of his flock. Harsh economic conditions made existence a constant struggle. Father of fifteen, Maccarty buried eight of his children in infancy. And perennial doctrinal disputes lessened his effectiveness. The inscription on his wife's tomb read appropriately "Remember Death," while he chose another austere epitaph for himself: "The law was given by Moses, but grace and truth came by Christ." That grace and truth, he believed, enabled him to sit atop this small religious volcano for almost forty years. Never again would the First Parish, which Aaron Bancroft came to serve, experience such continuity.[6]

At Maccarty's death in 1784, the church, contrary to custom, refused to bestow succession on his substitute. Efforts to settle the dispute amicably failed, while "heat, contention and unchristian struggle for a major vote" mounted. For a while Bancroft threatened to go elsewhere, while petitioners informed the town that "perfect unanimity to wait for it will be wait for ever." "The majority of our inhabitants," said the exasperated chairman of one parish committee, "are rabid Calvinists, the petitioners are rank Arminians." When a few more committees got nowhere after months of bickering, Bancroft led an exodus of sixty-seven members from the established church and founded the Second Congregational society.[7]

On a raw Wednesday in February 1786, the Reverend Zabdiel Adams of Lunenburg extended the right hand of fellowship and the Reverend Thomas Barnard of Salem preached the ordination sermon. The congregation, unable to find more suitable quarters, held the ceremony in a private home. Just as the town refused the use of public facilities, so few Massachusetts clergymen wished a relationship with the Worcester minister. But Adams had defended another local minister against a discontented community while Barnard was also known for tolerance. "I never heard you preach a sermon on the Trinity," a parishioner once told him. "No," Barnard replied, "and you never will," thus rebuking an effort to enforce uniformity and fetter the minds of believers. The followers of Bancroft concurred.[8]

In Worcester, the issue was not Unitarianism but the doctrine its opponents called Arminian (using the name as a term of derision)—the belief that all men could earn salvation, as distinct from the Calvinist insistence that some were predestined for damnation. What this meant exactly Bancroft did not know, and it took him fifty years to work out the meaning of the New or Practical Christianity he espoused. But his simple creed, which stressed the usefulness of faith for the development of man's Christian nature, was enough of a departure from orthodoxy to divide the parish; the majority of believers held to the original Trinitarian covenant signed in 1746, and adhered to the Westminster confession because "the prevalency of sin dwelleth in us." Their covenant, renewed in 1815, upheld the doctrine of election and affirmed that "every individual of the human race is, by connection with the first man and in consequence of his apostasy, natively dead in trespasses and sins, at enmity with God and must be regenerate in heart and sanctified by the agency of the Holy Ghost in order to attain final salvation."[9]

Aaron Bancroft confronted Congregationalists for whom salvation was emphatically not a do-it-yourself business. To the Arminian argument that salvation by grace as the sole means of redemption left no proper role for human effort and responsibility, the Congregationalists had an age-old response. With Samuel Willard, they declared the condition of faith to be "connex and consequent," not "antecedent and Meritorious"; God made clear what He expected of the believer, and that had to be performed even if only through His spirit. For His glory, God determined man's redemption and foreordained all the means to it.[10]

These views had never been congenial to Aaron Bancroft. The Westminster confession had appalled him even in his childhood when he read every Saturday from Samuel Willard's *Compleat Body of Divinity*. He never accepted the Calvinist doctrine of human nature, and early on searched the Scriptures for a truer meaning of human destiny. He emerged in early manhood a qualified believer in the goodness of man, but also in his susceptibility to sin. Under the influence of Jonathan Mayhew and Charles Chauncey, he was willing to assist at the ordination of Unitarian James Freeman at King's Chapel in Boston when other clergy refused. While his opponents held fast to the pale version of their forefathers' creed, Bancroft and his followers moved on.

Their intellectual lineage stretched back to the seventeenth century when the ideas of Jacob Arminius, the Dutch modifier of high Calvinism, spread to England and later to the colonies. None of Aaron Bancroft's arguments were new. That the Scripture did not prove divine reprobation of mankind, that some were condemned only because they rejected the light, that the Bible in fact promised salvation to all, that the orthodox made God into an unrighteous respecter of persons whose concept of justice was strange indeed, had all been expounded and defended for decades.

This theology assumed that faith involved the continuous evolution of inherent qualities in the pilgrimage to God. Personal virtue, moral rectitude, and Christian behavior were its only outward manifestations. An essentially moral Deity ruled the universe, known not only because God consented to reveal Himself through the Law and nature, but also because of man's sense of right. Grace was an internal state that people earned through faculties variously and often inconsistently defined as reason, soul, conscience, or the sense of right, terms hardly synonymous but all expressing an inborn capacity to distinguish right from wrong. For the majority of the town's believers, this was heresy.[11]

Rejecting mechanistic determinism, Aaron Bancroft made his focal point Christian liberty, defined as the free will to fulfill divine commandments, central among which was imitation of Christ's perfection, as a duty to self, society, and God. Persuasion, reasonable argument, and independent judgment were the requirements of faith. "Divine clemency, the moral agency of man, the sufficiency of scriptures, the right of private judgment, the adaptation of the terms of acceptance to human power, and the certainty of salvation to all who sought Divine assistance and proved their faith by their works" summarized Bancroft's theology. "By their fruits ye shall know them" was one of his favorite quotations.[12]

Aaron Bancroft, thus rebelling against Calvinism, nevertheless retained much of his forefathers' faith. Orthodoxy too discouraged passivity on the part of either the elect or the reprobate. Aaron Bancroft's definition of faith was not so far removed from Samuel Willard's antidote to resignation. "Strive to enter" was Christ's advice and Willard's prescription. "If you find your hearts moved with an apprehension of your great misery," Willard added, "be not discouraged, you are in a fair way to be one of that little flock; Christ hath said, if you come to him, he will not cast you off."[13]

This faith, rebellious in part, yet deeply indebted to that against which it rebelled, framed Aaron Bancroft's outlook as the poor ostracized Arminian preacher became an honorary Harvard D.D. and president of the American Unitarian Association. That the definitions were fluid and imprecise troubled neither him nor his congregation when they signed their simple covenant in 1786. Conscious of the seriousness of their step, they withstood pressures, threats, and suits. That year one churchgoer cast a vote for Aaron Bancroft to be the next lieutenant governor, unaware that the state constitution excluded clergy from officeholding. Without knowing it, the schismatic rebel was on his way to respectability and establishing a new orthodoxy.

While the larger community preferred complicated creeds and confessions, Bancroft and his followers believed that their faith made them better Christians and better citizens. The church would play a role in their lives as a moral guide, stressing ethical conduct and purity of motives, while leaving the choice of dogma to each enlightened believer. With the arrogance common to embattled reformers, they thought they had all the answers and had resolved all problems. If only the town would free them from the general ministerial taxes, they would prove the error of opposition charges of apostasy and lapsarianism. Aaron Bancroft knew that a reasonable creature became a Christian not only through divine persuasiveness, but also through inner illumination and preparation. When he and his followers disputed with the orthodox the extent of the preparatory work required, they drew upon the writings of such Puritan stalwarts as Perkins and Ames for respectability.

Respectability was important to Bancroft's congregation, whose members were indistinguishable from their opponents except in religious beliefs. Among them were farmers and mechanics, as well as professional and business types—some patriots, others former loyalists, and many pillars of the community, including Levi Lincoln, later Jefferson's attorney general, and Nathaniel Paine, later judge of probate. Isaiah Thomas joined, as did a tanner, a woolen manufacturer, a clockmaker, a physician, and the county treasurer. So too did one of Maccarty's sons, and Stephen Salisbury and his son. Madam Salisbury preferred to remain in the First Parish, where she caused endless problems. Bancroft's parishioners differed in their politics as in their possessions, but all considered themselves solid citizens and supporters of the standing order.[14]

The year of the formation of Bancroft's church was also the year of his marriage to Lucretia Chandler, daughter of Judge John Chandler, known as Tory John. The family had once been well off, wealthy, and respected, holding crown offices, its portraits painted by John Smibert. Driven away when the Revolution exposed his English sympathies, Judge Chandler took refuge in London, his property confiscated, his fortune wiped out. The family remained behind. When several of her brothers joined the Second Parish, Lucretia, then twenty-eight years old and still single, followed.

She had been tried in so many ways, Lucretia later told one of her daughters, that she had learned there was "no certainty in riches." She wanted a quiet life with a clergyman, and though her family disapproved, chose a pastor with whom life was anything but quiet. It remained the "first object of her life to see him happy" and she never quite understood why he found her attractive—she "a child of nature—unfortunate in being bred without the least culture of mind." A cheerful disposition left her always ready for gaiety and amusement; perhaps the overly serious young minister found in her a welcome contrast. And she remained his source of strength and joy.[15]

Their income at first was small, strained by thirteen pregnancies and support of Aaron's aged mother. Lucretia scrimped and saved, took in boarders, and attended fully to the sphere of woman's duties and enjoyments. She gladly joined her husband in visiting the sick, befriended his students, and took food to the needy when there was not enough at home. Her children ever remembered her as a pillar of strength. They also recalled the imperceptible division of duties between husband and wife, and tried to follow the pattern in their own lives; none ever became interested in women's rights and all regarded their parents' marital relations as an ideal to be cherished.[16]

There was no help in the house, even though Lucretia's mother had once had a full staff and a special servant to look after the linens and lace. The early years were particularly difficult, for even after the parish dispute quieted, the town excused some from the payment of ministerial taxes and collections due did not always arrive. Farmers paid in goods of fluctuating value, and the Bancroft family depended on charitable parishioners for fuel and food. Breakfast and supper consisted of "rye bread toasted, the fragments of cold coffee boiled and put on milk." Count Rumford's paper on feeding the poor came in handy, with advice on "boiling potatoes so as to be eaten as bread," recipes for the use of barley and hominy in making "cheap soup," and suggestions for "a cheap pudding." Lucretia was frequently ill, and later felt that only Christian fortitude and the solicitude of her husband helped her survive.[17]

Despite its simplicity and occasional poverty, the Bancroft household became one of the community's favorite meeting places. As Aaron's reputation for fairness, honesty, and decency spread, curiosity attracted strangers who had heard of his gracious hospitality and pleasant conversation. When court was in session, lawyers and judges dropped by. Sunday evenings devoted to intimate friends and parishioners were later recalled as spiritual feasts. Those bored by more serious subjects found their host ever ready for backgammon or chess. Amidst incessant controversies, which Bancroft disliked but could not escape, no one ever impugned his motives. His most stubborn opponents conceded his respect for other people's opinions, even if they had no respect for his.[18]

As writer, educator, editor, and historian, his connections were extensive. Sermons appeared in the *Liberal Preacher,* the *Christian Monitor,* and the *Unitarian Advocate.* The *Western Messenger* brought out the "Moral Power of Christianity," and Isaiah Thomas printed numerous discourses by Bancroft. Joseph Allen, Nathaniel Thayer, and Samuel May, all members of the Worcester Association of Ministers, of which

Bancroft became presiding officer, opened out wider circles of acquaintance. William Emerson, father of Ralph, was a friend, as was John Thornton Kirkland, later president of Harvard. Several sermons published in 1822 elicited praise, including a highly laudatory note from John Adams. And on numerous occasions Bancroft resolved disputes between clergymen and their congregations.[19]

In 1812, with Isaish Thomas, Harrison G. Otis, Nathaniel Paine, and others, he petitioned the state legislature for incorporation of the American Antiquarian Society, and then served for years as its vice president. "The decline as well as the rise of nations is the course of nature," the petition declared. "Like causes produce like effects, and, in some distant period a decline may be the state of our country." A voluntary organization devoted to knowledge would be a weapon to stave off the inevitable. Aaron Bancroft lent his support.[20]

Josiah Quincy, DeWitt Clinton, James Winthrop, and Edward Dwight of Springfield were also members, and at the biannual meetings, in Boston or Worcester, Bancroft saw some of the leading New England men of letters. He met others, as a member of the American Academy of Arts and Sciences. A trustee of the Leicester Academy, and for a while its president, Bancroft also cultivated those who wished to further education in the region, and he was one of the town's leading school supervisors. His interest in missionary activity brought him the vice presidency of the Worcester and Middlesex Missionary Society.

Definitive answers were hard to come by. Bancroft's reading and his small private library reflected a never ending desire, conveyed to his offspring, to attain that certitude faith gave his forefathers. The past was not all superstition and ignorance. Aaron did not dismiss out of hand ideas that no longer appealed to him. John Locke's *The Reasonableness of Christianity* could show his children that religious rationalism need not lead to deism or skepticism, while Samuel Clarke, the Anglican theologian, transmitted the enlightenment spirit. Ebenezer Gay's moderately liberal arguments stressed beliefs anyone could undogmatically accept, and supplemented William Law's devotional and mystical writings, the sermons of Jonathan Mayhew and Charles Chauncy, the works of John Tillotson, and Richard Price's exposition of the power of reason in making moral judgments. Even Calvinism became more comprehensible through Isaac Watts, Richard Baxter, and Philip Doddridge. The boys and girls could also dip into the classics and *Guy Mannering.* The *Christian Monitor, Christian Observer,* and other newspapers kept abreast of current developments.

This seemingly fluid tolerance, broad-mindedness, and pragmatic approach faded with the years as Aaron Bancroft felt increasingly out of step with the times. He took satisfaction in his own growing respectability, but also observed the strange fruits of his early rebellion. "I have outlived my generation," he declared in his farewell sermon in 1836, preached after fifty years in the ministry, "and in the midst of society may be considered a solitary man." The relaxation of religious dogmas had enabled many to preserve their faith, but looser standards also bred an unseemly passion for novelty, and many a minister succumbed to "refined sentiments and polished style," telling his congregation what it wanted to hear, not what it should be taught. Man-made tests of Christian character supplanted appeals to biblical authority. Speculative opinions led to divisions on the slightest provocation, so that uncertainty of tenure discouraged young men contemplating a clerical career. Neither a scholar nor a particularly eloquent preacher, Bancroft was satisfied with his own Christianity but could not understand why a later generation wanted more.[21]

Year by year his conservatism became more pronounced. He feared the insidious effects of divisive opinions that threatened the social order, while always maintaining that his own views were not one of their causes. He had shuddered at Daniel Shays's uprising, especially since critics blamed it on Arminian notions of self-determination. As Worcester County seethed in 1786 and 1787 and debtors organized to repossess goods taken by constables, the courts closed and armed bands overran the countryside. The militia refused to suppress the rebellion, while Isaiah Thomas converted his *Spy* to the *Worcester Magazine* in protest against a tax, even though he, like Bancroft's other parishioners, had no sympathy for the embattled farmers. Disorderly proceedings and government by mobs seemed signs of general social breakdown.[22]

In this feverish atmosphere some people had regarded Bancroft's parish as but another instance of the disregard for authority. A voluntary association, lacking the sanction of civil government, was a dangerous innovation. Multiplication of such associations would drain the community's ability to maintain any minister properly, spread eccentric notions, and undermine social unity. Partly in response to these accusations, Bancroft and most of his followers came out squarely on the side of law and order. Then and later, he labored to explain the differences between destructive movements like that of Shays, and secession from the First Parish Church or, for that matter, the American Revolution.

He then urged his congregation to steer clear of politics and concentrate on leading a holy life. Fearing that the spirit of liberty might get out of hand, his sermons treated social and economic injustice as acts of God punishing a sinful society, while distinguishing between the redress of unjust regulations and radical social disturbances. His parishioners found this message persuasive, having heard it countless times before.

The difference between just protest and radical disturbance was one of emphasis, for Bancroft did not threaten wayward sinners with divine wrath, but instead reminded them that they were subject to "the regular operation of the established laws of the natural as well as the moral Kingdom."[23] In spite of his milder faith, Aaron Bancroft, more indebted to his predecessors than he liked to acknowledge, was no radical. He detested metaphysical niceties and had little use for the merely learned preacher whose arrogance, pretentiousness, and condescension antagonized the revolutionary generation. But he was also wary of merely evangelical ministers whose enthusiasms frequently cloaked an anti-authoritarian and anti-institutional message. He therefore spent a great deal of effort trying to convince others that Arminianism and Shays's Rebellion were very distinct developments.

At the same time his open social vision denoted a measure of political liberality. He reserved absolute perfection for a time beyond history; ambiguity would always mark man's life in this world. But he blurred the distinction between the elect and the damned because he would not ascribe that ambiguity directly to Adam's fall. Personal calamities and afflictions were not therefore necessarily punishments for incorrigible impenitence. The sins of society Bancroft sometimes decried were the sins of the whole, not of a portion of the community. He neither castigated the lower classes nor praised the pillars of the social order, but admonished all for pride, for the desire to lead an easy life, and for the quest for luxury. He attacked no one for trying to climb, since personal advancement was the very essence of the American experience; and his own rise to respectability and eminence proved the elasticity of society.

But the desire of some to rush the process left the republican experiment uncommonly prone to instability. As a steward of the public culture, Bancroft determined to fend off assaults on constituted authorities and root out mistaken notions about the American past, salvaging along the way the central role of faith. The short and turbulent national history, which began in war and revolution, made the task necessary. Those events, he intended to prove, involved no upheaval at all, but had left intact society, the role of the clergy, and the duties of rulers and ruled. Recency of experience and the lack of tradition, of customary modes of action and of established institutions, exposed people to error. The pulpit was one way to recall them to righteousness, secular writings another. Bancroft's biography of Washington and numerous historical illustrations in his sermons harnessed the American past to the cause of social stability. Rather than delivering jeremiads, he chose history to argue his message. His son would do the same.

Biography was an edifying educational tool and since time immemorial had inculcated patterns of meritorious action among the people and their leaders. Bancroft, in spite of his spotty formal education, knew his Plutarch and Thucydides. Revolutionary history was particularly useful because of its peculiar balance between freedom and order. In 1806 when Aaron Bancroft applied his precise and dry prose to simplifying John Marshall's biography, George Washington had already become the embodiment of Cincinnatus and Joshua, leading a self-sacrificing, sober, industrious, and pious people in its battle for liberty. But the results of that struggle were still controversial, and here the clergyman's warning was clear: the Revolution did not sanction lawlessness, and its heritage would survive only if the present generation exhibited the sturdy self-denying courage and discipline of its predecessors.[24]

Bancroft did not hide the blemishes of the revolutionary generation. Inexperienced leaders who then surprised the world by their abilities nevertheless made costly mistakes. After an initial period of fervent patriotism, people changed allegiances according to who seemed to be winning. And plenty of instances showed the pitfalls of improvisation. The states, for instance, pursued their own interests rather than the general good, while human nature then too was fallible and sinful. No one reading Bancroft's book could miss its conclusion. What was permissible in the chaos of 1776 was impermissible by 1800; what worked in 1783 would fail two decades later.

These and other warnings did not produce the desired effect. Nevertheless Bancroft's search for order continued, if not by the old methods then by appeals to sincerity and emphasis on morality, righteous living, self-control, honesty, and just dealings. Unhappily, unrest persisted. Clergymen quarreled with their parishes over doctrines, salaries, contracts, and personal privileges, while constant squabbles in the First Parish disgraced all religion. People moved around and parcels of land in Worcester changed hands all the time; everyone seemed discontented, searching for something without knowing what. At the same time, the political order appeared increasingly corrupt, factions abounded, and characters were besmirched, while no one seemed to respect authority.

The passing years revealed the insufficiency of moral appeals and forced Aaron Bancroft, like other ministers, to reassess his views.[25]

Never a confirmed believer in deferential politics and more tolerant of change than others, Bancroft was too liberal to argue that people know their place or show proper manners of subordination. Since society could not rely on external constraints for stability, inner constraints—voluntarily imposed, self-generated, and guided by enlightened ministers—had to replace the civil actions that in the past punished breaches of moral conduct. Guidance would flow from educational, moral, and Christian societies, appropriate for this enlightened age. This was the faith of a man genuinely convinced that whoever "acts agreeably to the dictates of his conscience, which he has endeavored to enlighten, will have the approbation of his own mind, and may rest in the persuasion that God will accept him though his judgment be erroneous."[26]

The sermon entitled "The Importance of Attending to Our Own Salvation" was a frank call on each individual to take matters into his own hands, submit to divine commandments, and attend to "the momentous business of salvation." Cautious enough to add that merit alone was insufficient, Bancroft nonetheless stressed that the "progressive improvement" man could make in his "Christian life" was helpful in checking "forbidden practices," the pursuit of "vicious pleasures," in fact all transgressions dangerous to the social order.[27]

Not all ministers agreed, and some vented their fury by charging Bancroft with radicalism and doctrines that left nothing sacred. Bancroft, less appalled by a wayward citizenry than by erroneous leadership, replied in kind. The orthodox clergymen blindly undermined everyone's authority by their obstinacy and their intemperate rantings. Stubborn ministers, exciting their attendants' itching ears, turned religion into a passion, promoting enthusiasm and animal instincts. Some of society's moral guardians were more to blame for the devotional shortcomings of their flocks than the people themselves.

One way out of the impasse was clearly to restrict the power of the clergy to the areas of their proper concern. Bancroft welcomed disestablishment, which released the church from controversial political issues that were not its business anyway. Without state support, the clergy could no longer hide behind habitual deference and neglect their duties. Strengthened by subjection to the wishes of the parish, with persuasion his chief weapon, the minister would earn authority by his personal character. In terms reminiscent of Roger Williams's *Bloudy Tenent of Persecution,* Bancroft argued that an alliance with the state corrupted both church and believer. Neither civil laws nor sanctions could elicit faith, but only man's free choice to behave like a Christian.

Lest, however, his position be misinterpreted as advocating a complete divorce between formal religion and daily life, Bancroft preached forcefully on the necessity for making faith a guide to action. He reminded his listeners that the responsibilities of this world and the next were one, that God could not be served on the Sabbath while Mammon received his dues for the rest of the week. But religion was a personal interest, "and no human being, in concerns purely religious, may interfere between God and the souls of men."[28]

Bancroft also opposed the professional centralization by which his more orthodox colleagues sought to resolve their difficulties. Such organizations were factious and a source of instability, much like the new political groupings. Troubles rose when ministers tried to lord it over their flocks and hungered for power. The Worcester Association and the other ministerial organizations he joined were community oriented, locally based, concerned with immediate guidance for parish difficulties, not with the formulation of creeds or imposition of dogma.

While Aaron Bancroft was its president, the American Unitarian Association confined itself to publishing and distributing religious tracts, collecting money for the widows and orphans of deceased ministers, preaching to the sick and the poor, encouraging Sunday schools, and relieving indebted churches of financial burdens. Through teaching and persuasion, its members fought the public's fondness for such matters of ephemeral importance as politics. Hostile to the revival spirit, which Bancroft deemed unreasonable, extravagant, and ruinous, the Association resisted the consuming flames of irrationality regardless of sectarian differences.[29]

A Federalist more by habit than conviction, the minister did not make the political shifts that marked his son's career. Yet Aaron Bancroft's definition of man as a moral being lessened the fears of human nature, and several members of his parish were prominent Jeffersonians while others in later years voted for Democrats. A benevolent and rational character disposed to obey the impulses of his better nature made man a worthy citizen of a democratic republic. Political authority was a regulatory agency mediating among different interests and demands. The sovereign people were sinful and fallible, but capable of self-government.

Bancroft rarely made his opinion known on current political issues, unlike his violently anti-Jeffersonian rival in the First Parish. But his election sermon when Caleb Strong became governor of Massachusetts

in May 1801 called the Republicans, the great sophists of the day, dangerous because they did not take account of the dissocial passions of man.
The choice of the hour was between the certain blessings of civil freedom and social order as against the fanaticism of ideal liberty and equality.
The people, rising above factional disputes and party spirit and uniting in
morality, religiosity, and reason, could guarantee that God's promise to
America would continue to unfold.[30]

Such tirades were exceptional. A minister who assumed that the state
no longer required concerted religious support had no need to threaten
the people. A republican society could tolerate more than one political
persuasion just as a community could profit from more than one parish.
Bancroft paid lip service to Federalist doctrine but also condemned clerical political involvement. Jeffersonian Calvinists who joined battle with
Arminian Federalists only confused their parishioners. Levi Lincoln
merely repeated Bancroft's admonitions when he wrote to Jefferson in
disgust at ministers who converted their pulpits into founts of party
rantings. The Second Parish was different.

Not politics but education and morality were the minister's proper
province. In this turbulent society, where the tumult of the marketplace
and the spirit of worldliness forever distracted the public, education
would further rational religion and enhance cohesiveness. The relaxation
of social and religious controls threw the individual back upon his own
judgment and increased the importance of shaping proper modes of
thought. However, Worcester, like many other New England towns,
preferred to pay fines rather than provide appropriate schools, and while
several of Bancroft's parishioners banded together to form a more proper
establishment in 1787, their interest waned when their children grew
up. As late as 1823 Bancroft reported on the sorry state of local education.[31]

Into this environment George was born on October 3, 1800, the
fourth son and eighth child of Aaron and Lucretia Bancroft. In spite of
the parents' homage to Christian liberty, they stressed important certain-
ties about God, man, and society and reared their children strictly. The
father's mixture of liberal and conservative sentiments left little doubt
about right and wrong, while the mother, burdened with recurrent pregnancies and a household full of children, lacking the means to meet
expenses, and often exhausted and ill, made demands of her own. A deep
religious experience was no longer requisite to righteous living, but the
emphasis on morality and self-discipline imposed other restraints.

George spent his early years on the farm, a mile and a half from the town center. Later he styled himself a wild boy, the scourge of the neighborhood, an imp who tempted others into mischief. A nearby river provided endless amusement, swimming and rafting in the summer, skating in the winter. On fine fall days the surrounding area turned its colors, and the hills shimmered in the clear light of the brisk New England autumn. The youth read local history in the landscape; and he often heard tales of the Revolutionary War begun and fought in far-off Boston, Lexington, and Concord. Special occasions brought fondly remembered trips to nearby communities, nestling in the changing countryside.

The beauty of that countryside masked hard lives; the rugged terrain let none forget man's lot in life. Yet cultivation of the soil, Aaron Bancroft's sermons explained, promoted serenity of mind and purity of manners. A sober yeomanry, he believed, composed the strength and sinew of the nation, performing a special mission for society. But the children also saw the less idyllic aspects of country life and the hard work necessary for survival. Knowing the hazards and uncertainties of husbandry, none chose a life close to the soil; each in his or her own way tried to escape its burdens, since social mobility meant not only growing respectability but also physical removal from the place of one's birth.

A commonplace in Aaron Bancroft's sermons was the view of childhood as a distinct period of the life cycle. "Youth is the season in which the seeds of moral habits must be sown that will not only yield pleasant products in earth, but also ripen into the incorruptible fruits of heaven." Parents, admonished to teach their offspring that religion was "not a matter for the closet only, but also for the scenes of active life," also learned that this was the time "to discipline human passions and to accumulate a fund of resolutions and patience which may be sufficient for the conflicts and trials of active life." The key to future success, Aaron Bancroft informed his parishioners, was self-control, restraint, and obedience.[32]

Confined rural households fostered such habits. The Bancrofts moved several times to meet growing family needs, but the child remained under adult supervision. A divine constitution in the natural order of things vested parents with absolute authority, which they occasionally delegated to older siblings. Aaron and Lucretia knew that exuberant youngsters would resist, revealing feelings so destructive of order, peace, and happiness that they had to be subdued early. George was to be governed before he was guided, amidst crowded surroundings, where someone was always ill, a horror to the parents who had already buried one child before George was born. Brother Thomas, four years old in 1800, was clearly different, although no one was sure why. With their mother suffering from maladies of her own, the children were taught to place mutual respect and common needs above their own wishes and to value order and self-restraint.

Governing sometimes required punishment, but in the Bancroft home reasoning preceded the use of the rod. In this the mother shared parental tasks; and Aaron regarded Lucretia's role as vastly more important than his own. She ministered to the wants of the children, tried to imbue them with her own piety, sheltered them from the rough-and-tumble of the world, and prepared them to be worthy members of the community. Watching their parents' never-ending struggle to make ends meet, they learned the value of money and work. For the rest of his life George remembered his parents' kindness and prudence, their tender love for each other, and those frequent moments of Christian resignation when death tested the strength of their convictions. Life was neither fun nor games, but a season of trials.[33]

This attitude deeply affected George's brothers and sisters, and some later blamed their parents for instilling a gloomy outlook on life, suspicious of joys and anticipating affliction as a matter of course. While Aaron and Lucretia were always recalled as figures of courage and determination to be revered and emulated, not all the children lived up to their expectations. Of those who survived, only two—George and Eliza, future wife of Governor and Senator John Davis—succeeded. Henry, who died at the age of thirty, left the sea to help on the family farm but lacked ambition or drive. John Chandler chose the sea as his vocation, but was almost a Calvinist in his faith and worried deeply about his own nothingness in the face of divine perfection. Anna died in her twenties, never having left the family home. Sarah married when she was in her thirties, only to die soon after the wedding. Caroline survived for a year, Charles for two months, and Dolly Ward for only two weeks. The others led hard, unstable, and often tragic existences. Mary never married and moved from household to household, existing always on the edge of poverty. Lucretia, the brightest, married late, never had children of her own, and died alone, separated from her bankrupt and profligate husband. Jane, wed to an Italian refugee despite parental doubts about the suitability of the match, died of yellow fever in New Orleans.

The effort to bear burdens with the stoicism of their parents hardened the children's character, and bred independence, resourcefulness, and pessimism. Yet positive influences of which George was less conscious were equally important. "I who seek instruction everywhere, know that controversy winnows truth" was an often repeated statement, a variant of what his father had also said.[34] The intellectual turbulence of Aaron Bancroft's life matched that of his son. Factionalism in religion was as difficult to combat as in politics, for both involved deeply held norms that no reasoning could alter. Aaron Bancroft, faced with discontented parishioners, placed his faith in education, sermons, and growing enlightenment, only to doubt their efficacy at the end of his life. His son would do the same, even if his frames of reference were larger and the stakes more consequential.

The intellectual kinship between father and son spilled over into George's concern for society and letters. The perception of man as inherently good and moral became the foundation of a democratic persuasion, and mass participation in politics was seen as an antidote to the dissocial passions against which Aaron Bancroft spoke, and of which his son also disapproved. George's intellectual horizons would be considerably broader than his father's; but if his language lost some of its religious derivation, it retained a moral tone, employing a set of ethical terms buttressed by faith. In later years George would transform religiously derived precepts into social values, finding the framework of sermons useful for orations, making the usual catechism of the church the basis for political outlook.

Aaron Bancroft also became a symbolic figure for his son, a living example of the way in which man controlled his destiny, became an agent of change, and helped disseminate new ideas. In order to sustain himself and his family during the difficult years, Aaron developed and passed on to his children a certain self-righteousness, a stubborn adherence to independently evolved ideas, coupled with constant self-evaluation and thirst for knowledge. In this often faulty world, "the candid and impartial exercise of the faculties of the mind" and an "honest zeal for truth" were the keys to advancement and the shields against misfortune.[35]

Lucretia and George were the children most infected with the idea that education could remedy the shortcomings of human nature and of sinful society. The two enjoyed Aaron's instruction at home and participated in Sunday school teaching. For a year Alfred Wright, an itinerant pedagogue, stopped by to teach them, their siblings, and other children. Later the brother and sister trudged to Nelson's school, two miles away—a one-story building, cold in the winter, hot in the summer. For Lucretia, this was the end of formal schooling.

George's lot was different. By the time he was eleven he had exhausted the learning available in Worcester. Since he proved studious, serious, and able, Aaron Bancroft decided to give him the opportunities he himself had lacked. Lucretia was equally deserving, but there was not enough money to send both of them away, and family needs predetermined her lot. George was chosen for a better future than life on the farm could promise. Aaron Bancroft's religious leanings and George's inclinations made the academy at Exeter, New Hampshire, the only reasonable selection.

Founded by John Phillips to instruct youth in conventional academic subjects, the school aimed to encourage industry, science, and morality, and to guide in the great and real business of life. Few parents yet considered such training away from home necessary. Only one other boy from Worcester attended; even those aiming for a college degree, like some of Bancroft's playmates, would pass Harvard's entrance examination without formal preparation.

Benjamin Abbot had been principal of Exeter since 1788, an acquaintance of George's father from Harvard days, a scholar and gentleman, who tried to reshape the academy to the model of Eton. If students later prided themselves on the Americanness of the school, that was entirely due to Abbot's fine sense of what was appropriate for the young republic. He infused the institution with a sense of purpose, and a spirit of kindness, mutual respect, understanding for youthful foibles, and attention to individual needs. His wards remembered him as intelligent and compassionate, concerned for their well-being, administering discipline without humiliation. And Abbot's common sense compensated for his unfamiliarity with the latest educational theories.[36]

In 1811, those theories and the needs of a growing society had relaxed the hold of classical subjects on the curriculum. A drift to the physical and moral sciences made room for courses in chemistry and natural philosophy, as well as in modern and United States history. An English department of sorts taught grammar, punctuation, and prosody; its head, the professor of mathematics and natural philosophy, served also as pastor of the town's Second Congregational church.

The academy's religious climate was decidedly liberal. The Board of Trustees included several Arminians, and Abbot himself showed such leanings. Still, Exeter was a Christian institution unwilling to leave its pupils without clear guidance, for everyone knew that the child was God's creature but also Satan's prey. No longer considered little vipers destined for damnation, the boys nonetheless had to learn how to save their souls. The school emphasized attendance at chapel, Bible reading, and the proper manifestations of faith.

Exeter students came from all parts of the union, with poor children of promise especially welcome. Tuition was three dollars a quarter, but the school provided scholarships for the needy. In its varied population, awkward country boys mingled with heirs to West India fortunes. Daniel Webster was a member of the class of 1796, Edward Everett was there in 1807, and Jared Sparks and John G. Palfrey were around when Bancroft entered. Inequalities of wealth and the uneven ages of the pupils created a mixed student body which was remarkably peaceful and disciplined.

Their preceptors and teachers were neither brilliant scholars nor prominent pedagogues; frequent turnovers in staff indicated how confining and wearying the profession could be. Hosea Hildreth, father of a future historian, headed the English department, memorable for his irony and wit. Hildreth, for years, straddled, the orthodox deeming his leanings too Unitarian, while the Unitarians thought him too orthodox, but he frequently exchanged pulpits with other ministers and his congregation in Exeter found nothing wrong with his views. A firm disciplinarian, he kept the students in line, before abandoning both school and pulpit for temperance reform. Henry Ware, Jr., fresh out of Harvard, was another of Bancroft's instructors, typical of young New Englanders not yet settled in their lives who taught for a while until something more interesting came up. With the help of three others, Hildreth and Ware took their charges through the appropriate Greek and Latin texts, English writing exercises, a smattering of science and moral propositions, judged sufficient preparation for the years ahead. Many pupils never demanded more and left the academy to enter directly into the professions.

Frequently reminded that he was a charity case, George never forgot his parents' admonition—to be grateful and to make the most of his good fortune. He knew himself to be bright, able, and diligent, worthy of aid; if not more brilliant than others, certainly hardworking and steady. But the strings attached created an unwelcome sense of dependence, and with it the seeds of an emotional conflict that would mark his personality for years. The desire to please and to prove worthy of confidence meant following advice that at times conflicted with other impulses. Living all the time up to expectations stifled creativity and bred submissive acceptance.

George adjusted as best he could without complaints and with very little self-indulgence. A son of Aaron Bancroft could do no less; life was a serious business, and George embarked on his educational pilgrimage ready to face the world in earnest. For a while loneliness overshadowed the excitement of Exeter's challenges, and the eleven-year-old buried problems under hard work, striking one visitor, who dropped by in October 1811, as uncommonly serious and intelligent. A few months later Aaron Bancroft read of George's scholarly accomplishments with satisfaction. Students were ranked according to merit and, although most were older than he, his name headed the list. The structured life of the academy also helped submerge unresolved conflicts. The school stressed distinctions obtained by merit, and Bancroft, the poor scholar, found achievement a way of showing gratitude.[37]

For two years Abbot guided his ward along the course deemed the best preparation for Harvard. George shared with the principal a love for Cicero and Horace, and listened to the schoolmaster terrify the classroom with thunderous denunciations of Catiline. Grammar and prosody, roots and rules, were crammed into the heads of would-be fools, and Bancroft's knowledge of the classics expanded. In the second year he won a prize of four dollars, converted into a scholarship, for distinction in "construing and parsing the Greek and Latin languages." Instead of the money came a set of books—*Elements of Criticism,* judged appropriate for students of advanced standing. Abbot informed his friend in Worcester that he wished for more boys like George.[38]

Lord Kames's *Elements* was then the standard rhetoric text in the United States, a product of the Scottish enlightenment, published originally in 1762. George later learned much more about that intellectual movement, but what he read at Exeter sounded neither strange nor new, for Kames in various diluted versions provided the underpinning of late-eighteenth-century American ideas about human psychology, the relationship between art and nature, the uses of language, writing conventions, poetry, drama, music, and gardening—the last-named also a fine art with social connotations. To students bent on becoming men of taste, Kames held out the promise that everyone potentially could acquire refinement in the fine arts.[39]

But, Kames wrote (and the Exeter masters concurred), only those who did not depend on bodily labor for their existence could realize that potential. George Bancroft, the future democrat, did not know whether that was indeed the case, but in 1813 he hoped that an easier way to make a living awaited him. And he fully agreed with the theme of an article by a classmate—intense application to study not detrimental to health.

Frequent reminders at Exeter left no doubt that idleness and dissipation were not the road to fame. Bells announced the beginning of the schoolday, with prayer in the study room, followed by tutoring in English composition and classes in Latin and Greek, in mathematics, logic, geography, and philosophy, with ancient history for the more advanced students. In the fall the boys spent free hours at football and pranks; newcomers who failed to climb a bare post had their faces scrubbed. At the welcome sight of the season's first snow, they left facial imprints in the slush; and when the rivers froze there was skating and sledding. The spring brought cricket and foot races. The school's rhetorical society had its own library, but George lacked the one-dollar membership fee. He did join the Washington Whites, a semimilitary company formed in honor of the first president. Edward Everett and Lewis Cass had been members also, and Bancroft too paraded in a fancy uniform, escorting trustees on Exhibition Day from the main building to the principal's house, carrying an ancient rifle and enjoying the attention.

The Reverend Nathan Parker, a native of Reading and now a resident of Portsmouth, provided a home for George during vacations, when the more affluent students returned to their parents. Parker had lived in Worcester and had studied divinity under Aaron Bancroft, who later preached his ordination sermon at the South Parish in Portsmouth. For two years Parker served as substitute father for his friend's son.[40]

Portsmouth, larger than Worcester, an old seaport where ships laden with West Indian goods discharged their cargoes, held much to attract the boy's attention, and George relished the town's atmosphere and broad horizons. In 1812 he observed a real fire engine, and the next year heard about a great conflagration the engine failed to extinguish. Equally exciting was the wreck of the schooner *Granville,* which lost its cargo of raisins and lemons. On July 4, 1812, Bancroft heard an oration by Daniel Webster, one of the town's prominent lawyers. Webster castigated the Madison administration for the war just declared against England. Aaron Bancroft would have approved and so, for the moment, did his son.

The faraway war did not intrude seriously upon the boy's consciousness, although the economic side effects worsened the family's financial affairs. Nor did it mar Bancroft's final period at Exeter. In August 1813 he enjoyed the graduation ceremonies by participating in a dialogue and acting in a staged siege of Colchester. He also contributed to "The Philosopher" discourses. After the valedictory address, delivered by another student, a small orchestra played the "Oporto," ending the first phases of the minister's son's preparation for the business of life.

That business, as Abbot reminded his students, involved public service and the stewardship of morals. Thrift, hard work, self-discipline, and proper views were the starting points for all future careers. Conformity was not a choice but an essential ingredient of approved behavior in such small communities as Worcester and Exeter, which frowned upon eccentricity, outrageous notions, and novelty. Without knowing it, George Bancroft, the budding man of letters, had acquired some key facets of his adult mind.

II

❦

HARVARD

IN THE SUMMER of 1813, when George Bancroft arrived, Harvard Yard nestled amidst the pastures, orchards, and scattered houses of a sparsely settled village. University Hall, erected in 1815, would extend the Yard to the east, but the college center still lay between Harvard and Massachusetts halls, with Holworthy and Holden Chapel in the north and Wadsworth House, the president's home, in the south. Cambridge existed in rural isolation; trips to Boston, a few miles away, required preparation and were not undertaken lightly. Beyond the college buildings were the First Parish meetinghouse, several taverns, and Harvard Square. The Brattle Estate remained one of the local showplaces, serving also as a student lodging house. Everywhere the smell of manure reminded the scholars of the cows on the common and the sheep in the muddy alleys.[1]

John Thornton Kirkland, Harvard's president since 1810, administered the institution with the help of the Corporation, which included a Lowell, a Channing, a Phillips, and a Gore. Once a minister of the South Church, his cavalier delivery gave rise to the rumor that he dashed off his witty and terse sermons on the backs of envelopes. Such frivolities only cloaked his sense of duty, which balanced self-righteousness with understanding of the desirable and attainable. His religious liberalism was aesthetic rather than doctrinal; bored by abstract philosophy, he detested controversy. A slippery Federalist whose tastes ran to literature and conviviality, neither narrow-minded nor a pedant, Kirkland knew all there was to know about being a Christian preacher and a gentleman. George Bancroft discovered in him a more mature Benjamin Abbot.[2]

Kirkland became one of the best-loved presidents in the college's

27

history, for Bancroft "first in manners, first in liberal scholarship, first in
the mastery of English style and first in the direction of thought and
culture." George also thought that "no one knew better how to deal
with his fellow men." Kirkland was not a serious scholar, but he recognized talent in others and fostered its growth. Students appreciated his
unfailing helpfulness, sympathy with their foibles, and willingness to
tolerate harmless pranks. The president flatteringly remembered their
names and many hoped to live up to the confidence he placed in them, in
itself a recognition that rank, stations, and positions were fluid in an
increasingly free society. They heartily agreed when he told them that
their Harvard education was designed not to train grammarians or math-
ematicians, but to prepare men for life.[3]

The university, as Kirkland envisioned it, would ready young men
for the professions, but also foster letters and learning. His staff would
not transmit knowledge by rote to blind disciples but would "give an
impulse to [the students'] reason" without controlling it, and would encourage creativity—within limits. By producing liberal Christians and
gentlemen, much like the president himself, Harvard would counterbal-
ance the mercantile obsessions of American culture which Kirkland and
his colleagues deplored.[4]

Liberal Christians and gentlemen believed in "the right of every man
to the liberty not incompatible with the liberty of another," venerated
John Adams, detested factions, and watched uneasily "the seeds of parties
. . . sown deep and thick in the soil of liberty." Their college education
would lead to "a faithful discharge of . . . duty as men, as Christians and
as citizens, according to the means in [their] power and the stations and
relations in which [they] are placed." Reference to those stations did not
imply a rigid hierarchical order; ambitious youngsters, of worthy but
impoverished background, accepted such statements with no sense of
limited possibilities.[5]

The staff saddled with carrying out this mission was brilliant when
compared with that of Kirkland's predecessors. It restructured the course
of studies, raised standards of scholarship, added permanent professor-
ships and new buildings, and expanded the library. His critics grumbled
that Kirkland had no sense of money, could not manage accounts, and
kept sloppy records; but he reminded them that he was president, not
steward or treasurer, and diplomatically tried to cajole into agreement his
instructors, the students, the larger community, and the state legislature,
still a source of revenue.

Always on the lookout for poor deserving scholars, Kirkland provided them with money and they, eager to please, respectful and studious, rarely made trouble. But not all the students were what the president wanted them to be. Many seemed lazy and, when not in class, spent their time carousing, drinking, and smoking, their minds, some thought, in perpetual stupor. Critics charged that Kirkland's geniality contributed to disorders, forgetting that under sterner presidents the college had been as unruly. Joseph Cogswell, Bancroft's future friend, attributed misbehavior to the feeling of utter freedom experienced by youths released from parental control. Others blamed boring courses and pedantic instructors for frustrations vented in rioting. Those like Jedidiah Morse who opposed Harvard's Unitarian drift linked the declining reputation of the college to its abandonment of orthodoxy. The desire of Bancroft and others in later years to reform the college sprang partly from the belief that Harvard had no right to refer to itself as the university in Cambridge when in fact it was more like a glorified boarding school then an institution of higher learning.[6]

When not faced with disciplinary problems, the president spent his time fending off the grievances of the underpaid and overworked staff, which resented spending its time policing rather than teaching. Henry Ware, Levi Hedge, Sidney Willard, Andrews Norton, and other pillars of the college claimed that they could not support families on what Kirkland paid, or that their expenses outdistanced their incomes. At the same time their duties precluded outside employment. They grumbled that if the president could raise funds for building, he ought to consider their purses as well.[7]

Kirkland did, although mutterings about inadequate compensation continued while college enrollment fluctuated. Harvard offered few scholarly surprises in its structured four-year course of studies. Classical languages, readings in Livy and Horace, backed by Robert Adam's *Roman Antiquities,* balanced by Hugo Grotius's *The Truths of Christian Religion* and Griesbach's edition of the New Testament, as well as plane geometry and algebra, occupied the freshman year. Sophomores continued Greek and Latin, read Cicero, and struggled with mathematics. Juniors encountered logic, moral philosophy, Tacitus, Homer, and more advanced science courses. And seniors studied philosophy, William Paley's *Evidences of Christianity,* and Joseph Butler's *Analogy.*[8]

The curriculum aimed to provide more than mere knowledge to shape modes of thought. The emphasis on analytical methods showed the relationship of evidence to judgment and put dampers on imagination and enthusiasm, propensities with dire consequences. Ideally, the four years thus spent left the student mentally balanced, self-reliant, and trained in disciplined obedience, a synonym for self-control in an era that defined insanity as want of control over feelings. Well grounded in the classics, with a smattering of religious instruction, a Harvard graduate acquired a proper general outlook, a rational world view, and an eminently reasonable faith.[9]

These goals were appropriate to the larger world of which the college was a part. No one questioned the importance of learning; but an excess unfortunately bred perfectionist certainty in the infinite improvement of man, and the radical speculations of unfettered intellects were assumed to produce a disastrous outcome, as in the French Revolution. A proper education would subdue pride and fight atheism through knowledge and faith, the two barriers against fanaticism and superstition. To shore up knowledge, the curriculum drew upon John Locke to show that reason was the appropriate guide of life; and, since unaided reason was inadequate, the faculty backed up Kirkland's faith with references to man's innate moral sense drawn from the philosophers of the Scottish enlightenment. In the face of endemic social conflicts, Harvard thus armed the student against demagogues likely to exploit baser instincts.

The college succeeded. Even the putative rebels of later years owed it more than they acknowledged.

Aaron Bancroft's liberal Christianity foreordained Harvard College as the next step of George's education. Once more the family strained its resources; and help from Kirkland and from an uncle spared the lad the need to earn money while he attended, as many students did. Once more consciousness of his obligation to others preyed on his mind; consumed for four years by the passion for self-improvement, he developed the personality appropriate to the poor scholar—serious in demeanor and sober in attitude. He became something of a prig, remembered by his classmates chiefly as someone never noticed. His teachers considered him just the kind of graduate Harvard hoped to produce.

In the summer of 1813, George became a member in good standing of the Harvard class of 1817. Having exhibited sufficient knowledge of Latin and Greek, Sallust, a bit of Cicero, mathematics, and geography, he handed the president a certificate of good moral character, paid a bond to the college steward, and signed a statement promising to obey the regulations. Kirkland wished George well, gave him a copy of the college laws, and inquired about his old friend Aaron Bancroft.

Stringent college rules reflected years of experience in restraining rambunctious pupils. Unlike the fellows who studied the regulations to discover those easiest to evade, George obeyed to the letter. He neither swore nor fought, did not lie, rarely quarreled, and conducted himself at all times with modesty and civility. He never appeared in women's clothing, shunned the Cambridge taverns, and neither gambled nor played cards. At thirteen, he was younger than most members of his class, and his short stature and quiet demeanor, a certain shyness and diffidence of manners, also set him apart. He early determined what the college would do for him, ignored whatever might divert him from his goals, and concentrated on his work to the exclusion of almost everything else. The charity scholar, aware of his good fortune, wasted no time in unseemly diversions.

If the crisis of adolescence descended on him, there is no record of it. Whatever doubts, passions, and insecurities he may have suffered remained hidden even from himself. Harvard was the first step toward earning a living; unlike some classmates, he could rely upon no family fortune. Scholarship one day might open possibilities to compensate for lack of funds; in the meantime, frugality and self-denial were imperative, encouraging introversion and quiescence, all very different from the personality of a man who would later be remembered for his voluble and nervous temperament, the chatty and outgoing individual who liked to be the center of attention and often was.

Since money was scarce, accommodations had to be cheap. For the first year Bancroft roomed at Captain Dana's; the simple fare and crowded conditions made occasional evenings at President Kirkland's house a welcome relief. His roommate was Stephen Salisbury of Worcester, whose adjustment was both more painful and more enjoyable. The son of a well-to-do merchant, Bancroft's chum had more money to spend, worried about his attire, and treated college as a necessary duty to be enjoyed whenever possible. While Salisbury skated on the river, went snowballing, skipped rope, and took dancing lessons, Bancroft wrote in his diary how foolish such diversions were. But Salisbury often expressed his homesickness, something Bancroft never did. And George kept to himself any envy he may have felt of his chum's clothes, spending money, and extracurricular activities. More absorbing were the hours spent with Professor John Farrar, so admirable in his total devotion to science.[10]

The college's threat to restrict students' trips to Boston bothered Bancroft less than Salisbury, who had aunts and uncles in town. Such excursions required money, which George did not have, and, as he often pointed out to his friend, good moral Christian work provided all the diversion needed. Since Salisbury remained unpersuaded, George found another roommate for his sophomore year—a good scholar, very quiet, also deaf in one ear. While Stephen began a war of attrition through the mails to convince his parents that he needed a suite all to himself, Bancroft continued to room at the college during his junior and senior years until the last few months, when he lived as a divinity student in the home of Levi Hedge. There was nothing unusual about that arrangement—professors frequently augmented their income by taking in boarders.

Nor did the other methods students invented to drain off excess energy attract George. The great 1815 rebellion left him unmoved. Sufficiently self-reliant not to be swept away by the mob, Aaron Bancroft's son believed that the authorities were right to send away anyone who persisted in missing recitations. Government had to be obeyed; rules and regulations existed for students' benefit. Those who believed that he was ingratiating himself with the administration derisively nicknamed him Sir George and Dr. Bancroft. For the rest of his life he remembered their ridicule, and when people insisted on calling him Doctor—even though they had a right to—he would angrily reply that George Bancroft was his name, good enough for him. But election to Phi Beta Kappa, high marks on English compositions, and praise from Kirkland compensated for slights.[11]

Praise from parents and tutors meant a great deal to Bancroft. Since students received no formal grades, exhibitions and college exercises demonstrated their learning and scholarly rank tested their character and respectability; these provided vindications of trust and justifications for support. When in June 1814 freshmen prepared to exhibit their acquired knowledge before the Corporation and everyone's nerves were on edge, Bancroft worked doubly hard while his friends eyed each other anxiously for signs of deteriorating health. A few believed themselves the most overworked class in Harvard's history. Stephen Salisbury tried to hide his insecurity by worrying about his outfit—inadequate for the occasion; a toothache and the ague also kept him from studying. George, equally insecure, vented his fears in redoubled application.

The exercises passed well before an impressive assembly, increasing Bancroft's self-confidence. Aaron and Lucretia Bancroft came from Worcester and agreed that George acquitted himself well. The young man, still short and childish-looking, relished the praise. Like others, he listened attentively as Harrison Gray Otis cautioned the students not to consider going to Oxford or Edinburgh. They had more to learn in

Cambridge; many a member of the class of 1817 sadly agreed, and for the time being Bancroft had no intention of going anywhere.

"Every man must wear his skin to market," Kirkland used to say, by which he meant, Bancroft thought, that "one is worth not more than others think he is." Since the students seemed very early to have sized up Bancroft's worth, he craved the company of his elders. Their opinions were different and judgments more consequential. Several he had known from their stays in Worcester, others were familiar by name. Through Kirkland, he met the community's intellectual pillars—John Pickering, Alexander H. Everett, William Tudor, Jr., and Harrison Gray Otis. The kindness of Andrews Norton brought acquaintance with the small circle engaged in publishing the *General Repository and Christian Review*. Occasional invitations to small suppers in town were significant indications that social barriers did not exclude a boy from Worcester.[12]

George was fined only once during his college career, for improper attitude at public worship, but he appealed and won. Shuffling feet or whispers during the sermon were nothing compared to the audacity of William H. Miller, a classmate rusticated to Medford for having disturbed the peace and injured the reputation of society by riding a horse up the stairs to a preceptor's door. Such acts did not command Bancroft's respect; they clashed with the solemnity, dignity, and respectability of professors whom he imitated. While Thorndike, the most notorious rake of the class, was suspended for giving midnight parties, Bancroft wrote his exercises, dabbled with poetry, furthered his moral reading, and made no secret of his contempt.[13]

The curriculum to which Bancroft devoted so much attention was designed to thwart the Millers and Thorndikes of this world by fostering self-cultivation and growth, thus shaping well-balanced characters able, by self-improvement, to face life's challenges. Emphasis on the right of private judgment placed great responsibility on the believer, while a free society imposed duties and obligations upon citizens. Bancroft's mentors assumed that the right education would impart to the students a predisposition to accept of their own choice the divine commandments without the restraints formerly imposed by an impure faith.

Moral philosophy, inherited from Europe but altered by decades of American political and religious conflict, defined the intellectual climate of the college and shaped its instruction.[14] Moral philosophy provided citizens in a well-ordered republic "the foundation that supports the whole superstructure of society" and showed, independent of revelation, the applicability to life of Christian truths. Its subcategories included knowledge "of the mind, the means of moral and intellectual improvement, the social nature, duties and destination of man." Grounded in Lockean rationalism and Scottish common sense, it infused the teaching of classics, mathematics, and the sciences, as well as biblical criticism, civil polity, and natural and revealed theology.[15]

That philosophy generated a progressive and optimistic, but also cautious, outlook. It did not extol man's innate goodness or his inner capacity to discover God, but neither did it limit knowledge to sense impressions or exclude intuition. The impact on George Bancroft was overwhelming. The peculiar mixture of ebullient visions and realistic calculations, of surface radicalism and deep conservatism, that characterized the Democratic Whig Bancroft later became was partly the outcome of his Harvard education.

Levi Hedge, professor of logic, taught the fundamental methods of cognition, derived from Locke's *Essay on Understanding,* but embellished with emotionally appealing concepts of innate moral sense. Hedge's *Elements of Logick* summarized his message. By the term logic, he meant the entire realm of human thought and knowledge, which served religion by sustaining proofs of faith and validated all rational activity. What he had to say sounded vaguely familiar to George, for the professor expounded in a scholarly fashion that for which Aaron Bancroft had groped and that which had been made more explicit at Exeter. Logic was an eminently reasonable decision-making method, designed to guide students' judgments—which was just what it did for the boy.[16]

Having spent fourteen years writing his book, Hedge welcomed no hint that it needed improvement; and Bancroft felt none was needed. Like his fellow students, he recited its sentences verbatim without additional explanation, since the arguments spoke for themselves. But the purpose was not dogmatic; Hedge did not expect Bancroft to go through life repeating his rules. Through memorization, the student assimilated logical methods and formed acceptable modes of thought he could later adapt to his individual needs. The ability to distinguish between judgments based on intuitive and those based on deductive evidence, the awareness that chance merely denoted ignorance of cause, and the realization that analysis was the best method of acquiring natural knowledge shaped a logical mind.

The course taught George to think systematically. Here he learned that some evidence stemmed from common sense, from the structure of the mind as created by God. Moral evidence called for logical deductions from accepted premises, reinforced by empirical and sensory data allowing man to trust his judgments about the real world. The various ways of handling data, further subdivided into induction, analogy, and reasoning on facts, influenced him for years to come, since the three subcategories proved as useful in writing history as in composing political speeches. When Bancroft later sprinkled his pronouncements with terms like mutual affections, internal senses, and intuitive evidence, he was but recalling his logical training that no rival system would obliterate.

Hedge possessed no great philosophical acumen or sophistication, but he grasped and tenaciously maintained a few central ideas drawn from the Scottish enlightenment. Some knowledge derived from a priori principles that no reasonable man denied; and therefore the innate awareness of the difference between good and evil did not depend on external stimuli. Bancroft, vastly impressed by these propositions, plowed through the course's supplementary readings—Thomas Reid's *Essay on the Intellectual Powers of Man,* Isaac Watts's *Logick,* Dugald Stewart's *Elements of the Philosophy of the Mind,* and James Beattie's *Essay on Truth.*

Henry Ware, Sr., Levi Frisbie, and Andrews Norton applied these epistemological precepts to more specific fields. Having identified the faculties that help the individual distinguish right from wrong and enable even the untutored mind to see eternal truths and make correct choices, they tutored their students in understanding the relationship between appropriate logic and the diverse spheres of their lives.

Henry Ware, Sr.,'s appointment in 1805 as Hollis Professor of Divinity had been a clear sign of Harvard's drift to liberal Christianity. Married three times and the father of nineteen children, Ware trusted the wisdom of Providence to an extent that astonished acquaintances. His rigid self-control, much admired by Bancroft, enabled him to bear without any sign of emotion the drowning of a son, before his very eyes. Logical, sensitive, and moderate, he seemed to some unimaginative and to others too rounded and free from angles to be easily grasped.[17]

The Hollis professor accepted religion on faith and also because it was rationally plausible. He harmonized natural and revealed religion, the God of Newton and of the Bible. His course taught Bancroft that religious assertions, evaluated by secular knowledge, provided rational evidence for the existence and attributes of God because all natural phenomena were products of divine power. From the course George also discovered the intellectual underpinnings of his own father's faith, made academically respectable and relevant.

In Ware's thought, established laws guided the moral, like the natural, world. Within each person a moral sense heard the divine voice commanding obedience; reason, feeling, and ultimately God assured man that the law of cause and effect was fully operational. Everything that happened occurred by necessity, the links of which stretched back to the ultimate cause; and all was for the best. Even what appeared evil proved on closer inspection good. Divine Providence, which man could not question, arranged individual actions. To the central ethical question— Why should man promote the general good?—Ware gave Richard Price's answer. Not only God's will, but an invariable and universal sense of right determined the human response. Bancroft, like William Ellery Channing and others, read Price on morality, found Ware's exposition sufficient, and did not need the German idealists to be saved from Locke. Deeply impressed, he dutifully repeated the verbiage heard in the classroom. Years later, when he began to write his *History of the United States,* he did not have to search for a framework. Ware and Hedge supplied the philosophy that shaped the volumes while also transmitting, in a new form, the old New England heritage in which God was visible in history and the historian was the Lord's scribe.

Bancroft read with delight one of the major texts for Ware's course, William Paley's *Natural Theology,* its lessons reinforced by Joseph S. Buckminster, whose fame hovered over the Yard. Since God's providences revealed themselves in the universe, revelation was but natural reason enlarged by direct communication. Bancroft also read Ralph Cudworth's *True Intellectual System of the Universe,* Joseph Butler's *The Analogy of Religion, Natural and Revealed,* and Samuel Clarke's *Demonstrations of the Being and Attributes of God.* Whether or not Bancroft was aware of the fine distinctions these books made, Ware made sure that the students did not misunderstand the correct conclusions—revelation came from rational experience, from the clear evidence of divine intervention in history; and, in the words of Levi Hedge illustrating one form of logic, all good Christians will be saved—all good Christians have sinned—therefore some who have sinned will be saved.[18]

Levi Frisbie, Alford Professor of Natural Religion, Moral Philosophy and Civil Polity, dealt with the social and political realms. He too expected correct methods of thought to counter the dangerous implications of the speculative philosophies of Hobbes, Rousseau, and Godwin. That trio of theorists forever repelled Bancroft, who held their insidious teachings in part responsible for the disasters of the French Revolution. As against them, Frisbie consoled himself with Cudworth, Butler, and Stewart, whose moral philosophy was certain, rational, and simple—not metaphysical, irrational, or complicated.[19]

Faith in man's benevolent (social) affections, Frisbie explained to his classes, made possible an intellectually satisfying adjustment to the novel American democratic society. Reid, Stewart, Richard Price, and Paley had described how those affections, regulated by conscience, amplified the capacity for virtue. Common and moral sense were the two facets of the same faculty; and benevolent affections properly applied were the mainstays of Christian existence. Frisbie would not follow Joseph Butler and Samuel Clarke, who assumed that man's social nature, capacity to empathize, and feeling for right and wrong were purely reasonable responses. The Harvard philosopher argued that feelings rather than rational propositions conducted the individual "to the proper end of his being; the highest perfection, dignity and happiness of his own nature, and the widest display of the glory of his creator."[20]

Since not all people were blessed with the knowledge to cut through metaphysical subtleties and since reason was not a faculty uniformly developed in all, Frisbie took "an enlarged view of the objects of governments"; malevolent as well as benevolent affections influenced mankind. Students had to exercise their reason and invigorate their understanding—knowledge could be acquired at any time, but wisdom had to become an early habit.[21]

The learned professor had some sharp words to say about the American political situation. But the frenzied fears aroused by the War of 1812 had subsided, and derogatory references to Jacobins and corrupt human nature were mostly ritual. The pessimism of Fisher Ames gave way to the resigned acquiescence of Kirkland and Frisbie, which would one day flower in the enthusiastic acceptance of George Bancroft. His teachers did not condone relaxed standards. On the contrary, the more they adjusted to unwelcome realities, the more they tried to offset the insidious side effects, observing uneasily that men mastering their own destiny could act out either benevolent or less benevolent passions. It was a tribute to Frisbie and his colleagues that their work bore the desirable fruit with Bancroft and most of his classmates; none ever considered himself a rebel.

Andrews Norton, one of the younger instructors, early became George's friend and protector. Medium in height, pallid in complexion, and mild in countenance, Norton possessed by reputation the sharpest brain in the Yard. Sensitive and refined, he wrote lyrical poems, enjoyed good literature, edited an important journal, ran the university library, and taught. Some students found his humor amusing, but most considered him aloof, inaccessible, and impatient. This precise, deeply religious scholar had convinced himself that knowledge rendered the faith he held dear immune to human criticism. For a time few quarreled with him, and certainly not Bancroft, who long aspired to be a younger version of his revered tutor.[22]

Norton's lectures related Hedge's doctrines about evidential reasoning to the Bible, showing the compatibility of faith and reason. Facts, empirical evidence, confirmed the historical authenticity of the Bible and proved God's intervention in human affairs. Faith, repeated one of Bancroft's classmates, dutifully recalling what he had learned, was but "an assent to the truth on the testimony of another, in whose veracity we have confidence of the senses and of self acknowledged truths." In applying moral philosophy to biblical criticism, anything reminiscent of "technical theology" was discarded as rubbish, that had too long buried "the internal evidence of the truth of religion." Theology as a science coincided with the judgments of unprejudiced reason, and the man of plain good sense would reach the same conclusions as the trained scholar. In Norton's classes Bancroft saw Calvin's ghost laid low and heard the same sentiments that had moved his father to split the Worcester parish years earlier.[23]

In defense of this outlook Norton would one day oppose new forms of infidelity that grew out of intuitional epistemological premises. For the rest of his life he clung to the belief that Christianity was a divinely ordained faith, resting on unique revelations. That belief his pupil never abandoned either. In later years the younger generation regarded Norton as a standpat conservative; but Bancroft remembered him for his courageous opposition to orthodoxy, for his religious liberalism, his broad vision of biblical analysis, his attention to contexts of time and culture, as well as for linguistic skills.[24]

Moral philosophy absorbed from Ware, Hedge, Frisbie, and Norton provided Bancroft an anchor of stability and solace, answering inner needs, quieting doubt, and assuring approval. It colored practically everything George wrote while at Harvard, from early exercises to fully developed essays. The necessity of revelation, a favorite topic, employed Hedge's logic against the pride of secular philosophy, which provided no answers to such imponderables as the death of young men and the immortality of the soul. Emerson, in his junior year, found in imagination one answer to emotional difficulties and determined to roam the universe intellectually; Bancroft concentrated on moral philosophy and the less imagination the better.

All those sermons he had heard about death and the wages of sin fostered fears in the insecure and introverted adolescent. Consciousness of debts to family and duties toward parents and society bred a morbid outlook, frowning on frivolities and loftily rejecting worldly vanities. The death of brother Henry was a blow; hard as he tried, George could find nothing more consoling for his parents than the wish that the gospel would help them meet yet another dispensation of Providence. And as he fretted over the fate of his siblings and his obligations as a son and brother, George concluded that the world was a barren place, full of woe, in which, were it not for faith and friendship, despair would reign, as it sometimes did in his own mind.[25]

The conclusions found their way into essays written by a boy desperate to live up to his own and other people's expectations. Man could be lazy, sinful, greedy, and ambitious; to his sorrow, George found himself guilty on all counts. The remedy was logical dissection of one's faults, just as Hedge advised. A short paper on the difficulty of beginnings urged application and consistency, needed to overcome shortcomings, while the sad effects of self-doubt yielded to hard work. Indecision, another malady, led to idleness, intemperance, and vice; George put himself on guard. Aware that he possessed a more than ordinary share of ambition, he gratefully concluded that, directed to honorable ends, it could be a force for positive good.[26]

For Exhibition Day in his junior year (1816), Bancroft tackled a more controversial sentiment. On that occasion, his friend Stephen Salisbury, as befitted the son of a merchant, discussed the values of promptness, prudence, and perseverance. Samuel J. May, future minister and abolitionist, examined the effects of increased publication of science and literature, while Asa Cummings, about to become an orthodox preacher, dealt with Locke's metaphysical researches. Bancroft's English oration treated the effect of enthusiasm on happiness. The son of a minister who steadfastly opposed religious revivals and preached forcefully against fanaticism knew the problems. Norton too argued that passions unsettled the personality and the social order. But others considered some enthusiasm in devotion desirable. Appropriately, Bancroft straddled—a little enthusiasm was conducive to happiness, an excess destructive. Enthusiasm that interfered with sober judgment clouded man's reason, but as backing for commitment it offset indifference. Kirkland, who had the unfortunate task of hearing the students' papers twice (no one trusted them to speak unsupervised), with customary tolerance thought it good.[27]

Had Ware, Frisbie, Hedge, and Norton heard the paper, they would have agreed. An enthusiast was someone who allowed passions to subvert the moral sense, just as Bancroft implied. Norton saw enthusiasm behind worthless revivalist conversions, as opposed to the prolonged character development he favored. Defined by William Ellery Channing as a disproportionate strength of feeling and emotion, which interfered with judgment, enthusiasm implied irresponsibility and lack of logic; Bancroft said as much and for the rest of his life had little sympathy for any of its practitioners, social or religious.

His second English oration, delivered a year later, also showed him absorbing moral philosophy and grasping for self-justification—while John sent home money earned at sea, George studied at others' expense. The essay expounded the benefits of intellectual as opposed to material pursuits to prove the legitimacy of his own work. The man who engaged "in the study of the mind . . . feels himself elevated above the common sphere of mankind. He lives in an upper world and contemplates with calm indifference the labours of ordinary man, as of inferior beings." "The majestic eagle," soaring above mundane concerns, dealt with the more elevated aspects of reality. George's teachers did not intend to create intellectual snobs, and none dismissed agricultural or commercial endeavors as of no value. But they did believe that while all pursuits were equally worthy, some were more so than others; Bancroft, the budding man of letters, agreed.[28]

Moral philosophy also influenced the classics still central to the Harvard curriculum. John Snelling Popkin—Old Pop—for years made students unhappy in Greek recitations. Tall, erect, with a ruddy complexion, this shy man, somewhat of a recluse, reputed to be the greatest hypochondriac in the Yard, lived to a ripe old age. Bancroft, as well prepared in Greek as most entering freshmen, found his classes orderly and instructive if not exciting. For Latin he went first to Levi Hedge and then to Edward Everett, about to take up the Brattle Church pulpit.

The recitations in Greek and Latin emphasized grammar as the key to ancient literature, rather than life in antiquity. As students parsed and construed, to the neglect of all else, they were told that Greek was a wonderfully pliable language, made like the yielding wax, fit to receive an impression of everything which can be conceived by the mind. But the struggle with vocabulary and derivations hid the beauty of the language. Since there were no easily accessible lexicons, Greek words were traced through Latin definitions which frequently had several English meanings, while resourceful students inherited their predecessors' translations, already worked out, only to see them confiscated by the instructors. Two textbooks—Adam's *Roman Antiquities* and John Potter's *Antiquities of Greece*—supplied general, dry, grim, and dogmatic background. Adam demonstrated from the constitution of Roman government the effects of aristocratic domination, and warned against democratic licentiousness and oligarchic tyranny. Potter concentrated on facts without reference to social and political life.[29]

Nevertheless, every cultivated gentleman knew that classics shaped tastes, disciplined the mind, and offered models of republican virtue and honor. Incessant translation, emphasizing precision and accuracy, molded writing abilities, and the use of metaphors and similes informed the student's ornate style. No matter how frequently admonished that long sentences and overblown descriptions were clumsy ways to hide confused thoughts, at commencement and class day exercises many an orator imitated Cicero. Bancroft's college oratory, grandiloquent and florid, owed much to the classics. This was not a handicap. Later on that style of writing, studded with classical allusions, Homeric digressions, and philosophizing, enormously increased his popularity.

A blistering article published in Scotland blamed the sorry state of the classics at Harvard on teachers who subverted "the most powerful means of intellectual regeneration" and left their students' minds "in a state of hopeless insensibility." The faculty did not know what to do with the ore it mined, and, bent on practical, utilitarian purposes, neglected aesthetics in the classics. In response, the *North American Review* defended Popkin, Everett, and Hedge. Grammar and rules would always be boring; no one considered the classics impractical; and, anyway, English and Scottish universities also left much to be desired.[30]

The *North American Review* did not mention what George also knew—despite their glory, the ancients were suspect. Moral philosophy inherited, along with the ancient Christian admiration for classical literature, the regret that all ancient thinkers were, alas, born before revelation. The *Monthly Anthology*, which Bancroft read, blasted their unbounded skepticism and want of religious references. Harvard students, instructed to appreciate Locke and Bacon more than the remnants of learning from the Lyceum and the Academy, learned—from teachers who shied away from superseded metaphysics and the rage for mythology—to detest syllogisms and to venerate reasoning by induction.[31]

As a result, youths left college with stereotypical impressions—Sparta, one later recalled, was the archetype of brute force, full of "bullies and boxers, thieves and fighters"; Athens was where some worthies lived; and Rome was all warriors, great art, and the law. One of Bancroft's

chums pitied Homer for having lived in a barbaric period, before the
birth of urbanity and refinement. Homer could be tender, sublime, terri-
fying, and sentimental, but also disgusting, ridiculous, and, worst of all,
boring. The encounter between Glaucus and Diomedes in the *Iliad* clearly
reflected the poet's inadequacies. In the midst of a tedious battle scene,
Homer, unable to liven up the action, broke the narrative by an irrelevant meeting between two fierce enemies who did not move the plot
along by trying to slaughter each other, but inquired instead about their
respective genealogies.[32]

George was more charitable. The classics immunized citizens against
demagogues, but since the ancient writers were all heathens, their mythology "was a pool of pollution." Agamemnon committed the most
beastly crime by sacrificing his virgin daughter to propitiate horrible
gods; and the altars of Diana "smoked with human gore." Ancient reli-
gions and, by implication, some ancient literature corrupted the heart,
"vitiated the imagination," and sanctified vile deeds.[33] Years later Andrews Norton expressed similar strictures, judging Homer not morally
elevating and deciding that classical poets made poor literature.

Science and mathematics, another integral part of the curriculum,
also buttressed the theology defined by moral philosophy. Astronomy,
Newtonian physics, and Euclidean geometry proved that the rationally
organized universe reflected the pure reason of its creator, while Hedge's
Logick showed how "extensive observation and comparison of particulars" as well as "laborious induction" could further scientific comprehension. William Enfield's text, *Institutes of Natural Philosophy*, investi-
gated the laws of nature by experiment and observation without
reference to metaphysical speculations, which were regarded as little
more than unsuccessful efforts to extend the boundaries of human
knowledge beyond the reach of human faculties. Ralph Waldo Emerson
a few years later detested Enfield; Bancroft did not. Both had to master
him.[34]

John Farrar, Hollis Professor of Mathematics and Natural Philosophy, exemplified the place of science in the Harvard curriculum. The
son of a farmer, he studied divinity and initially taught Greek. He was a
solid lecturer and a competent translator and astronomer. George, who
admired his devotion and even temper and his effectiveness as a tutor, did
well in astronomy and mathematics.[35] There was simplicity, elegance,
and certainty in the way Hedge's logic applied demonstrative reason to
mathematics, its subject perfectly defined, its properties necessary and
immutable. The Newtonian universe, clearly expounded, provided suffi-

cient and acceptable answers to all queries. For the rest of his life Bancroft retained a view of science molded by his Harvard mentors, maintaining a gentlemanly interest in the latest discoveries always interpreted in the light of moral philosophy. He became a great admirer of Louis Agassiz, who upheld this tradition, and an opponent of Darwinian evolutionary theories, with their unacceptable conclusions.

A year before Bancroft arrived in Cambridge, the always turbulent literary atmosphere of Boston quivered at the publication of George B. English's *Grounds of Christianity Examined,* greeted by many as the latest form of infidelity. Edward Everett soon replied, convincing those already converted, while the reviewer in the *General Repository and Review,* in disposing of English's erroneous doctrines, went on to define the rules of literary evaluation, similar to those George acquired at Harvard. Among English's sins were "a more than common share of imagination, strength of conception, undisciplined warmth of feeling and force," and deceitful propensities. How much better were "slow and patient attention," the avoidance of first impressions, and keeping the "mind in a state of doubt and deliberation." The *North American Review* said the same while disposing of Byron's *Childe Harold.* A society that demanded an observance of arbitrary forms of decorum made the rules of taste and literary criticism additional pillars of the social order.[36]

As against English and Byron, Bostonians juxtaposed Edward Everett, like Bancroft a product of the moral philosophy school. Dignified, moderate, self-controlled, Everett based his arguments on Paley and Butler, who, the *Christian Disciple* smugly noted, "have never been answered and never even been attempted to be answered." His reasoning, in short, was comfortable in its familiarity. Everyone knew that pondering old truths was preferable to the absorption of new ideas, which were like a "troop of pretty performers who glide along with the most elegant imbecility, till a stroke of adversity confounds them." Literature that escaped reality was dangerous, prejudicial to the interests of society, bred a generation of smatterers, and inflamed the passions for novelty.[37]

Perusing old issues of the *Monthly Anthology,* or reading Norton's *General Repository and Review* and the *North American Review,* Bancroft found these distinctions repeatedly asserted. Baneful works filled the reader's mind with unreal portrayals of life, beguiling him from sobriety, sense of duty, and enjoyment of the actual. Separated from the realm of the understood, the imaginative—the hidden and the mysterious—was dangerous because impossible to assimilate under existing categories of thought. As Hedge's and Frisbie's student, he carried the common sense philosophy into aesthetics. [38]

Too young to have listened to him, George heard from others the Reverend Joseph S. Buckminster's message that good literature was the ally of the pulpit and the schools. Religion and morality provided the standard by which to evaluate novels, poetry, historical writing, travel accounts, and philosophical treatises. Bancroft, after reading Buckminster's sermons, approved the preference for "a practical philosophy" over "speculations . . . of very little value except as connected with practice." The young Harvard man repeated what he had been taught—fiction, however truthful, that left "an impression unfavorable to a healthful state of thought and feeling" was "peculiarly dangerous to the finest minds and most susceptible hearts." [39]

The admonitions of Kirkland, Norton, Frisbie, and Hedge cut him off from alternative aesthetic modes. In the course of a long and varied life, his propensity for moral philosophy and literature resisted every assault; neither idealism nor romanticism ever shook his youthful assumptions. "Moral writings are the parent of instruction," an 1815 essay declared; novels were alluring but dangerous. Six years later, in a vastly different setting, where neither moral philosophy nor moral literature mattered, Bancroft noted with satisfaction that one of his sisters read no novels. They "spoil the relish for better things and weaken the mind." [40]

Literature could be a force for good when its moral influence and religious didacticism were wholesome. While Bancroft's Harvard mentors delighted in the *Edinburgh Review's* attacks on Goethe and "the German sentimentalists," they welcomed authors who met their standards, as Maria Edgeworth and Walter Scott did. Bancroft read them with relish and cautiously admitted that something could be said in favor of imaginative works. For Kirkland the Great Maria's writings were a sort of essence of common sense, terms of praise in New England. Frisbie and Norton styled her the Tacitus of fiction, for her realistic portrayal of character, in which virtue never ennobled vice. She taught reliance on the purely rational powers of the mind, denigrating emotions, imagination, and intuition as unsafe guides to life. The *Monthly Anthology* found among her "sterling qualities" harmony, purity, the arousal of pleasant sensations, and ridicule of "the high sublime of deep absurd in the late fashionable philosophistical metaphysical French system of morality." By 1817 Edgeworth's *Belinda, Ennui, Patronage, Leonora,* and *Castle Rackrent* were popular in the United States and delighted Bancroft.[41]

Walter Scott was well known in America even before the Waverley novels became the rage. Already in 1806, the *Monthly Anthology* had pointed to his *Lay of the Last Minstrel* as the model of proper poetry— balancing noble passions, realistic in its presentation of vice and virtue, respecting the beautiful and the sublime, not too arousing for the imagination, full of simple and genuine pathos. When *Guy Mannering* appeared in the United States, Aaron Bancroft procured a copy for his children. The Waverley novels, Edward Everett thought, overshadowed all other works of fiction. *Rob Roy,* reprinted in 1818, drew crowds to the doors of the Philadelphia publishers.[42]

Scott, reviewers explained, did not invent; his fiction dealt with authentic truths and was superior to ordinary historical works for the portrayal of daily life, for the description of men and women as they actually were, and for connecting public acts and private lives, national temper and a country's mind. One reviewer suggested that future historians of the United States derive from Scott precisely that kind of insight and descriptive capacity needed to bring America's past to life. This style of fiction, employed to flesh out the moral philosophy, provided the ingredients of Bancroft's later success as a historian.

When, in his senior year, Bancroft entered the Bowdoin Prize essay contest, some of the themes pervasive to his education had already fused in his mind. The liberty of moral agents, the peculiar genius of Shakespeare, and a comparison between ancient and modern historians were among the topics he could have chosen. John Hubbard Williams picked the Shakespearean theme, portrayed the Bard as the child of nature who triumphed in part because he lacked a good education. Had he gone to Harvard, the writer implied, English drama would have been the poorer for it. John Everett's comparison of ancient and modern drama showed how efficiently his tutors demolished Voltaire. Bancroft made the least controversial choice—the use and necessity of revelation, beginning the never ending quest for pattern in chaos. Since morality demanded certainty, ethical systems not grounded in divine authority were deficient. This in turn meant that natural religion without revelation could not evoke the idea of a just God. "The eye of reason may perhaps catch a glimpse of the glory of God but it can be seen clearly and distinctly only through the medium of revelation." Even "ancient philosophy could never have been redeemed from worse than Egyptian darkness but by revelation from above." Luckily, moral philosophy resolved all uncertainties, a conclusion never questioned in the course of his long life.[43]

He restated that conclusion, in slightly different form, as his under-graduate career came to an end. Commencement day, the last Wednes-day in August, was one of the Commonwealth's great annual celebra-tions. Visitors, alumni, parents, and siblings flocked into town, and the Boston newspapers published the order of exercises. Banks closed as did the Customhouse, and merchants locked up their stores. The sheriff of Middlesex County with two justices of the peace and a dozen officers maintained order. Without envy Bancroft observed the frantic last-minute preparations by Salisbury, whose parents for weeks had planned a great party for the occasion.

The day passed peacefully. George S. Bulfinch, class poet, spoke of nature, the source of poetic inspiration, while the once rebellious Francis William Winthrop considered the effects of revolutions on the advance-ment of the human mind. Bancroft delivered the English oration, an honor indicative of his class standing. He spoke on the dignity and phi-losophy of the mind, which the *Boston Advertiser* judged "a remarkable unison of neat and florid styles . . . delivered with much energy and propriety."[44]

Having practiced for weeks, he felt sure of himself and of what he had to say. Still somewhat small for his age and trying to cut an impres-sive figure, George lifted himself on his toes and spoke in a high, shrill voice. The oration, climax of four years of study, restated the theories of moral philosophy in simple terms. "Character, both moral and intellec-tual, depends almost entirely on education." The "creation of balanced faculties" in man was a direct product of the philosophy of the mind, to which Locke had cut "a path straight and narrow through the forest of metaphysics." At the age of seventeen, assessing his Harvard education, Bancroft found it morally satisfactory, intellectually solid, and rationally acceptable.[45]

The class of 1817 produced its share of lawyers, politicians, scientists, and reformers, none of whom in the end attained Bancroft's fame. Samuel A. Eliot, later his friend, became a distinguished public figure, but had a wealthy father to back his pursuits. Caleb Cushing, the son of a China merchant, interested in astronomy but not in orderly behavior, studied law, tutored at Harvard and, for a while Bancroft's rival for honors, would become a political adversary in years to come. John H. Cobb turned to biology and Moses Kelley Emerson to medicine. Asa Cum-mings, who waited on tables and taught school to finance his education, abandoned Harvard's liberalism to become an orthodox minister, a path

Alva Woods also followed. George B. Emerson chose education, spreading moral philosophy to the Massachusetts school system. Stephen Salisbury, Jr., went into business, and Samuel J. May, who insisted on wearing an illegal coat much to the chagrin of college authorities, later countenanced more serious infractions in the hope of freeing the slaves.

Bancroft made the most unexceptional choice and decided to become a minister. For the son of a clergyman that seemed proper, and Aaron Bancroft, Kirkland, and Norton gladly concurred. Although he was well aware of the hardships and possible penury of the career, George had no other option. The law, medicine, and business were unattractive, and he lacked the required connections and money. They were also not intellectual enough for his tastes. Life in Cambridge obliterated some of the harsher memories of a Worcester parish, and Bancroft thought his ardor and piety sufficient for the task. He had also seen the regard with which Bostonians, even men of wealth and power, treated ministers. Not everyone could get a glittering post like the Brattle Church pulpit, from which Aaron Bancroft had once delivered a sermon, but even a lesser one was respectable.

For the next six months Bancroft studied for an M.A. degree, the first step toward a ministerial career. The theology school, still in its rudimentary stages, had a loose program, but one whose focus was clear. It fostered divines who, if not overly learned, were intellectual enough for the taste of their parishioners and well equipped for their tasks. The clergy, though poor, shared the leadership of society, as Ware, Frisbie, Norton, and Kirkland reminded their students, and were the chief expounders of the ways of God to man, stewards of public morals, censors of culture, and shepherds of their flocks. The knowledge acquired at Harvard made them educated social arbiters who molded public opinion and community conscience. They would use their influence for the proper goals.

Rereading Butler, Paley, Belsham, and Reid proved tedious, and Bancroft occasionally took respite in Edgeworth and Milton. He also came across Coleridge's *Literary Life and Opinions,* a work so strange that he did not know what to make of it. Rather than work out the challenges of German idealism (which Coleridge transmitted to the English-speaking world), Bancroft reverted to Fordyce, Mason, and Burnett—all textbooks for future divines—and studied the art of preaching. To make men wiser and better, techniques of persuasion and reasoning were legitimately applied, and Bancroft carefully noted the ones most suitable for a New England audience. Since its attention span was short and its reasoning slow and cumbersome, simplicity, clarity, unity of design, and animated but measured delivery were crucial. He was not at all sure that this indeed would be his chosen vocation, but, as it turned out, the skills necessary to move men to virtue proved useful in other ways as well.[46]

Doctrinally, Bancroft was as sound and conservative in his theological views as his instructors. Under the further guidance of Norton and Ware, he progressed in the requisite studies toward the M.A. degree. The Bible was divided into sections and lists of books provided as commentaries. A smattering of philology accompanied textual criticism, and subjects for particular attention included the major issues of Christian dogma. Historical background included readings of Mosheim, Eusebius, and Fleury, with some instruction in the meaning of pastoral office. While Bancroft's friend John Palfrey, proctor of Massachusetts Hall, slept with two pistols in fear of student attack, Bancroft was rereading Everett's *Defense,* the history of ancient Jews, and other edifying books. Life in the house of Levi Hedge was pleasant and the months passed away peacefully, interrupted only by occasional duties, none of them strenuous. They would have been more enjoyable had Bancroft been sure that he had made the right choice. Since he was not, doubts, insecurities, and unresolved questions remained.[47]

The years at Harvard, with their hardships and inner fears, were not among the happiest in Bancroft's life. Unlike others who looked upon their years at the college as a lost golden age, Bancroft regarded them as a preparatory stage full of difficulties and anxieties. Later on he was tempted to belittle their significance. But his New England education shaped his mind, character, and personality in more ways than he was willing to admit. Intellectually, morally, and to a surprising extent politically too, he was what his instructors had made him.

The certitudes of that education derived from the tenets of moral philosophy; all Bancroft's future learning involved adaptation and assimilation through its categories. Moral philosophy dissolved conflicts occasioned by foreign ideas, by awakened curiosity, by desire for knowledge, and by constant self-examination. Told to sharpen his senses, to observe, to classify and catalog all newly acquired information in a systematic fashion, he developed an orderly mind. His lifelong habit of strict attention, long working hours, and training of the mind owed much to his time at Cambridge.

There too he acquired his basic conservatism and frequent intolerance. The stress on association, on imitation, on the assimilation of novelty only in so far as it related to concepts already grasped, bred set ways of thinking. Induction furthered the assumption that things would happen in the future as they had occurred in the past. The analytic method was preferable to the synthetic one, Hedge had said. Taking objects or ideas apart was the only way to grasp their essence. But the reduction of complex phenomena to their elementary parts as a way of approaching an unknown quantity could result in its effectual destruction.

The anti-intellectual strand in moral philosophy proved equally influential. In spite of the devotion to reason, to a process of comparing and discussing, and discriminating and sifting, there was also a basic contempt for hairsplitting, technicalities, and argumentation. Hedge was proud of having made logic plain and comprehensible, Norton cautioned against metaphysical speculations, and Frisbie hoped to rescue the essence of a proper outlook on life by disposing of irrelevancies. Christian behavior mattered more than quarrelsome dogmas. Common sense, to be sure, was not enough; learning was also needed, and Ware and Hedge made sure their students realized the difference between an untutored reason and that of a Harvard graduate. But they preferred memory over creativity; recollections, past and safe, made direct contact with reality, with something that had actually occurred, while imagination conjured up the unreal. As Hedge's *Logick* explained, imagination might be useful for wit and imagery, but not as a learning tool.[48]

The usefulness of learning was very much on the agenda for American men of letters—important for Bancroft too, when he eventually joined their ranks. One of the more impressive lectures he heard in the college (and often reread afterward) was Levi Frisbie's discourse in November 1817. That address summarized the central tenets of moral philosophy and their relevance. Since moral philosophy had "a practical influence upon the character and prospects of society," its practitioners were to steer away from trivialities and concentrate on broadcasting unvarnished truths, enlightening conscience, advancing moral fitness. Those who labored "to unfold the principles and ends of moral action" had to put them to good use. Bancroft would try to heed Frisbie's call.[49]

Bancroft never questioned this guide to life. The framework of thought fashioned at Harvard withstood future challenges. In the coming years, he, like some of his fellow students, propagated moral philosophy among ever widening circles, bringing its benefits even to those not fortunate enough to have attended the university at Cambridge. The outlook then filtered down into society from the pulpit, through articles, books, and orations spreading an interpretation of the promise of American life that validated existing arrangements but also anticipated improvement and progress. Even Bancroft's political career, determined as it was by contemporary exigencies and realities, rested on an intellectual response largely the product of his formal education.

Of course, any deviation from the pattern of moral philosophy called the whole structure into question. So long as Bancroft remained in Harvard's intellectual universe, the problem did not exist. But a new setting in Europe produced enough intellectual turmoil to force a re-examination of fundamental premises. It was a tribute to the persuasiveness of his instructors that the result in time brought him back to the very premises he so dutifully absorbed in Cambridge.

III

INNOCENT ABROAD

At the end of 1817, while still a divinity student, Bancroft learned that his formal education might continue beyond Harvard's confines, a highly unusual suggestion that created new uncertainties. In the difficult time that followed Bancroft and his studies suffered. As he tried to make up his mind, the interest in theology waned; Goethe, Schiller, and the Swiss poet Gessner replaced Paley, Priestley, Butler, and Willard's Hebrew grammar. For the next few months Bancroft plowed through German works, with the aid of Ludwig's *Dictionary,* while considering the proposition that he transfer to the Georgia Augusta University of Göttingen.[1]

The adventure was not essential for his education, Bancroft well knew. Many worthy New England ministers never left their country and some assumed that no solid divine needed foreign trimmings. Nor did he ignore the complications and hardships the exciting offer involved. But he was willing to disregard its possible consequences; tempted, he decided the proposition was reasonable. The price exacted would haunt him for years to come.

Edward Everett, originator of the idea, was in Europe at the time; impressed by what he saw, he suggested to President Kirkland that someone else follow. Kirkland then raised the issue with the Corporation and with members of the faculty, drawing on the experience of the two Harvard students and one Dartmouth graduate—Edward Everett, Joseph G. Cogswell, and George Ticknor—who all testified to the quality of the Georgia Augusta in Göttingen. Although Kirkland followed their advice, he was never quite sure why. Nor did he ever explain why he singled out Bancroft, since George was neither the brightest nor the most advanced member of his class. But he was safe and sound in ways that counted, and that probably tipped the scales in his favor.

As for the candidate, he had much to think about. Bancroft knew of the spectacular success of Everett and Ticknor; his former Latin tutor was the designated Eliot Professor of Greek Literature, and Ticknor would shortly be offered the Smith chair in languages and belles lettres; neither publicized their doubts about the value of his European education. "Everyday I feel anew," Ticknor told his father, "what a mortifying distance there is between an European and an American scholar." "I am not the least Germanized," Cogswell wrote to a friend, "and yet it appalls me when I think of the difference between an education here and in America."[2] To close the gap became their object and ultimately Bancroft's; none of the travelers, initially at least, bothered to ask if that was all to the good.

Aaron Bancroft, among others, had doubts. The expense was great, and even with Kirkland's generous contribution, Uncle Joseph would have to add a share. The Worcester minister trusted his son but also wondered whether George was experienced enough for a prolonged European stay. The boy was mature beyond his age, hardworking, devout, and levelheaded, but he was also impressionable, and a foreign adventure would test his character in unpredictable ways. Proper Bostonians went to Europe for various reasons but not to become better ministers.

The experience, Aaron Bancroft suggested, might even disqualify a liberal Christian minister, since German theological speculations drifted into metaphysical quibbles contrary to common sense. George might join "the German school," renowned for its sophisms, trifling with human hopes. On other grounds too, the choice was unfortunate. The Germany of Goethe's *Werther,* with its glorifications of suicide, sickly sentimentality, and outrageous immorality, was an improper environment. Yet George Ticknor, Edward Everett, and Joseph G. Cogswell were untainted by infidelity; and Kirkland persisted, as did Levi Hedge, who hoped to send his son Frederic along. On a visit to Boston for a meeting of the Massachusetts Congregational clergy, Aaron Bancroft consulted George Cabot, former pirate and president of the Hartford Convention. Cabot knew the wider world beyond Cambridge, spoke French and Spanish, and believed in the profitability of risk taking, as his fortunes testified. He thought the idea of sending George to Europe a splendid one, and Aaron Bancroft after a few weeks of hesitation gave in. The decision delighted his son.[3]

With characteristic fastidiousness, George prepared for the journey by trying to learn about Germany. Joseph S. Buckminster, Samuel Thatcher, and Moses Stuart of Andover had for years followed intellectual developments there, and Bancroft had heard about Madame de Staël's *De l'Allemagne,* the last chapter of which affirmed in ringing phrases the necessity of strong emotional commitments, hinting of a strange new world. George Ticknor had praised the Georgia Augusta as the fountainhead of all modern knowledge, far outdistancing French and English universities. From the *Monthly Anthology* and the *North American Review,* Bancroft gleaned the impressive results. A short notice in the *Review* sent from Europe by Everett described in detail the university's famous professors, its international student body, and its 200,000-volume library.[4]

The key to this exciting world was the German language; and the only available tutor, self-taught, Professor Sidney Willard, helped Bancroft master basic grammar. Using Solomon Gessner's literary works, George learned much as he had already learned Latin and Greek, through translations. In the same manner he read Schiller's *Don Carlos,* Goethe's *Sorrows of Young Werther,* and other works available in the college library. Gessner proved very attractive; this Swiss-born eighteenth-century poet expressed just the kind of devotion, virtue, and religiosity Bancroft appreciated. He did not consider his *The Death of Abel* dull, as did Lord Byron, who decided that Cain had committed no crime in ridding the world of so drab a fellow as Abel. To the minister's son, Gessner combined appropriate and correct sentiments with florid lines. Goethe's *Werther* was something else again, and Bancroft was properly offended.[5]

Bancroft also acquainted himself with the university's requirements from a copy of Göttingen's bylaws, sent to Kirkland by Cogswell. There were few prerequisites for admission, he was pleased to note, not even an entrance examination, and some regulations were not far different from those memorized for Harvard four years earlier. As for the practical problems of life in Germany, he could deal with those only upon arrival.

The college's generosity resolved the financial issues. From Kirkland and from his own family, George received $700 a year, $500 for school expenses, the rest for travel and entertainment. The grant was sufficient for a scholarly existence, with enough left over to taste other excitements. And Bancroft was appropriately grateful. Once more he was the recipient of charity, which elicited the typical promises to sustain the trust vested in him.

In June the Overseers of Harvard College voted that "Mr. George Bancroft, about to go abroad to pursue his theological studies, be entitled

to receive a moiety of the proceeds of Madam Mary Saltonstall's donation, for the year beginning 1 July, 1818." No one really knew whether
theology would be the purpose of the journey, and this confusion in the
Overseers' vote reflected a general lack of clarity about the trip. Bancroft
was not to study German theology, that much was clear. Everything else
had to wait until he got better acquainted with the offerings of the
Georgia Augusta.[6]

New Englanders who had already made the grand tour of the Continent set the pattern Bancroft followed in 1818. They adapted to their
own needs the English aristocratic concept of travel as a part of education, designed to transform schoolboys into cosmopolitan gentlemen.
Bancroft in some ways resembled his three predecessors who went to
Europe, like the thinking American travelers Margaret Fuller later described, aware of the immense advantage of birth in the New World, yet
enormously curious about the decadent Old. Their preconceived notions
determined what they saw and how they saw it, testing and proving the
durability of their New England education.

The first group of Americans to study in a German university also
inaugurated a new cultural relationship between New England and Europe, to which Bancroft hoped to contribute. It was not his "wish merely
to run through and stare," he decided, but "to collect at every place fresh
information," satisfying curiosity but also contributing to American culture and, most important, acquiring a new status. Very early he defined
himself as a member of "a class of men" with a mission "to guide education and give tone to society, disseminate taste and love of literature,"
giving the United States "the same mental as physical education." Such
phrases, new in his vocabulary, were familiar in those of others—Ticknor, determined to be a scholar rather than a lawyer, Everett, still in
Europe, and Cogswell—budding men of letters seeking knowledge to
sustain their social ambitions.[7]

Unwilling to be overawed by the old culture, the young Americans
tried to gather "every plant that will bear a new climate and a new
culture," picking them "clean, free from noxious insects ... to give
them a fair trial in the New World." "How nobly all good literature
would thrive," George soon sighed, "if we could transplant it to America,
if we could engraft it on a healthy tree, if we could join it to religion."
Aware of the problems such plans entailed, Ticknor, the most intelligent
of the early pilgrims, realized that "good literature" was a misnomer,
that there were only national literatures, springing from native soils, and

intimately associated with national character. Everett and Cogswell too understood that European models in art, literature, and science were not suitable to the New World. Bancroft, however, never quite saw the difficulty.[8]

The four travelers faced common challenges, were astonished at the same accomplishments, met the same people, frequently listened to the same gossip, and were offended by the same characters. They heard similar lectures, were impressed by the variety and depth of German scholarship, and wrote appropriately enthusiastic accounts. All were interested in elementary education and admired the German secondary school for producing pupils properly prepared for the universities. Much of the success of the Georgia Augusta they attributed to the quality of its students.

Since they came from similar backgrounds and carried similar prejudices to Europe, vulgarity, meanness, and irreligion shocked them. Having grown up in a moral environment, imbued from early youth with rigid notions of propriety and correct behavior, they self-righteously found only a few human beings up to their own standards and judged some scholars unworthy of their reputations. Others, great thinkers, were shallow as persons. The determination to be living examples of the best the United States offered bred priggishness and condescension that irritated even the most welcoming hosts. While the four appreciated the freedom of thought that allowed scholarship to flourish, they also wondered whether some censorship would not be a welcome antidote to the evil by-products of extreme latitudinarianism in thinking, speaking, and writing. This ambivalence colored their pronouncements.

Nevertheless Bancroft's experience bore different fruits—ironically so, because he was the most determined of the four not to let the European adventure affect him. Less secure and self-assertive than Ticknor and Everett, he always felt on probation, and, unsure of what education would do for him, rationalized incessantly in his writings home. Ticknor and Everett had solid achievements behind them when they went abroad; at ease, they enjoyed their adventures and absorbed much from them. Bancroft had only a good Harvard record and the confidence of friends and benefactors. He regarded this strange world with the jaundiced view of a superior being cast among colorful and exotic characters, constantly on guard lest the foreignness rub off on him—as in the end it did. Frequent assertions that Old World corruptions would not taint a pure American exposed an inner fear that he might not withstand the challenge.

No other American pilgrim in these years made such comments with such frequency. If their mentors in Cambridge occasionally admonished Ticknor and Everett to safeguard their heritage, they took the warnings in stride. By contrast, Bancroft, obedient and prone to worship authority, endlessly proclaimed his gratitude and loyalty to his benefactors. Curiosity enhanced his awareness, but repeated emphasis on learning only what was worthy of a good New Englander in the long run caused him to miss much more.

Already in Cambridge Bancroft had informed his friends that the German character was inferior to the American and that German theology was full of errors, parroting Andrews Norton, who had argued against "that idolatry of everything that is German" and was writing a book contradicting the findings of Göttingen scholars. If their theology was bad, their classics were better, but classics, Bancroft thought, were not proper preparation for the ministry. Ticknor knew he wanted to be a man of letters, for which philology and literature were appropriate, and was returning to a promised professorship, as was Everett. Their less secure younger friend had no fixed goal in mind, so that his fears and hopes mingled with prejudice and curiosity. He resolved his indecision for the time being by emphasizing a worthy Yankee character, without knowing to what it would lead.[9]

Admonitions on the propriety of remaining true to the values of his heritage from Norton, Kirkland, and Aaron Bancroft sustained George's resolve. "Let not your ambition overcome your prudence . . . do not neglect the means of moral and Christian culture," his father counseled. From Lucretia came a similar plea: "take care my dear George that you do not lose that which your old mother wants to retain." Loss of innocence, brother John warned, was terrible, "an end to your peace forever"; a pure mind and correct Worcester habits were more important than the combined riches of European universities. And the more the point was stressed, the more determined George became to vindicate himself. After two years abroad he would sigh with mock sadness that, though away from Boston all this time, he was yet all too American in his ways of thinking.[10]

But the four years spent in Europe ironically had their effects. Worthy resolves made him ignorant of the true nature of temptation, and while his ways of thinking remained New England's, his manner of expression became foreign. "That enthusiasm, ardor and openness" which attracted the affections of the charming Mrs. Samuel Perkins, whom he, like Everett and Ticknor, considered the ideal of womanhood, could not remain entirely impervious to a prolonged European adventure. A change in behavior, dress, and speech paralleled solid scholarly achievements. And as his self-confidence increased, so did his satisfaction in the new personality he observed in himself. Bancroft saw nothing wrong in becoming more manly, proud, self-assured, and controlled; and he did not doubt that those who greeted him upon return to the United States would approve what had happened.[11]

"The American in Europe," Margaret Fuller later wrote, "if a thinking mind, can only become more American." John Adams disagreed. When Norton and Bancroft visited the old former president in the spring of 1818, Norton introduced his young charge as an American scholar bound for Göttingen. Adams showed little understanding for the young man's feelings—the best education, he announced in a raspy voice and with much vehemence, could be gained at home. Earlier, Jefferson had expressed a similar attitude. "An American coming to Europe for his education, loses in his knowledge, in his morals, in his habits and in his happiness." Bancroft's experience proved them partly right. If he did not lose in knowledge and remained steady in his morals, he became a different person nonetheless. As for happiness, that long remained an unsolved question.[12]

On June 27, 1818, accompanied by Frederic Hedge, George sailed for Europe. Levi Hedge, troubled by his son's unruly behavior, instructed Bancroft to enroll young Frederic, at the lowest possible cost, in a place strict enough to correct his rambunctiousness. During their peaceful voyage Bancroft read Milton and Cowley, made resolutions, and calculated expenses, while the younger boy relished the adventure. In Amsterdam the travelers found Everett's letters of advice and warnings: get used to inconvenience; this was a different world and Dutch cleanliness would soon give way to German filth. He could put up with such tribulations, Bancroft thought, and took refuge from feelings of loneliness, abandonment, and self-pity by withdrawing to recollections of the past. He remembered Cambridge, former friends, and pleasant afternoons with the faculty; and wondered whether anyone still cared where he was. And what was to become of him? "Tomorrow I depart for Germany," he wrote to Norton. "Surely a residence of three years among a new people must change my manners, habits and character." He reassured all his correspondents, but mainly himself, that the change could only be beneficial.[13]

Bancroft and Hedge edged on toward Göttingen in German coaches that hardened them to pain. They worried about Old World unrest, for they heard from other passengers that the town was at war and blood poured through the streets. Georgia Augusta students, unable to obtain redress for their grievances, engaged in pitched battles with the townsfolk, in disturbances surpassing those of Harvard. Only the arrival of troops from Hanover restored quiet. In protest, the students departed en masse, leaving behind vacant rooms.

Bancroft easily found an apartment, in a fine wide street, ignored the unrest without, and the next morning, armed with letters of introduction, called on Professor George Benecke, who lectured in the faculty of philosophy on German and English literature. He had once been Everett's tutor and well remembered the brilliant young American, as did other Europeans. For the next two months, Bancroft spent an hour a day with Benecke, reading and translating, learning grammar and pronunciation. Benecke portrayed the Georgia Augusta as a temple of knowledge, the professors its servants, laboring in the cause of humanity. But Bancroft noted his unwillingness to spend more time than he was paid for. An hour meant an hour, and when it elapsed, he expected the student to leave, even in the middle of a sentence.[14]

Schiller and Goethe replaced Gessner as basic texts, and early encounters with German romantic literature left George unmoved. Bancroft read correctly, but still saw everything from a New Englander's point of view. Goethe's language was perfect but wasted in indecency and immorality, emblematic of the poet who glorified vice, turned prostitutes and profligates into heroes, and ignored purity of thought and loftiness of the soul. His antithesis was Schiller, morally pure, devoted to art, independent in his perceptions, and the master of lyrical and dramatic poetry. Goethe by contrast ignored religion, was a puppet of the high and mighty, led a dissolute private life, and if he was a genius (which Bancroft did not dispute) yet he wrote false and dangerous libels on human nature. Goethe's failure to fulfill his duty Bancroft regarded as a warning against the snares of improper literature. What proper literature consisted of he knew from Harvard.[15]

By the end of September Bancroft's German was adequate for attendance at lectures and he embarked on a grueling schedule—time was short and there was much to learn. He rose in darkness before five, had some coffee, and studied. Breakfast of bread and tea at seven led to a full day of lectures, tutorials, private readings, and preparations, with a break for lunch and a short walk at noon. In the evening, tea, bread, and butter carried him over several more hours of work. Twelve hours of study, as Professor Johann G. Eichhorn told him when they met, was no hardship for a young man. No one ever died of learning, and for a true scholar fifteen hours was the minimum.[16]

Uncertain about what to devote those hours to, Bancroft craved guidance through the vast offerings of the university as he blundered into an unfocused program of courses. "To you may I look for advice to regulate my conduct and studies," he wrote to Everett, only to repeat the same plea in a message to Norton. "What shall I do to be forever known and make the world to come my own?" Everett, pursued through the next year by George's pleading letters, soon lost patience; "every man . . . must finally judge for himself," he replied. In response Bancroft modeled himself on Everett and concentrated on ancient languages and philology. It seemed safest to follow the beaten path, although Everett was to become a professor of Greek at Harvard, while Bancroft in theory still thought of divinity.[17]

For six months Bancroft furthered his knowledge of German and combined classical studies with Oriental languages. Dissen on Demosthenes, Koster on Hebrew grammar, Weckler on Tacitus, and Planck on church history—all were "learned, powerful men . . . men of talent, arduous and miraculous industry," he wrote enthusiastically to his father. They were "superior in this respect to anything we have in America . . . I can take my choice and accordingly I have selected the best. . . ." The mental image of "an intellectual manufactory where a thousand hands," constantly employed, turned out scholarly products did not quite match the young man's ideal of intellectual endeavor, shaped by the Cambridge model. Yet the overwhelming impact of Göttingen eased his doubts and stimulated him to work.[18]

But exertion did not compensate for lack of definite goals. The course of studies remained unsettled, despite frequent reminders that "to pursue anything to advantage, one must form an exact and comprehensive plan." Consultations with professors did not help, only revealed how much there was to learn and how little time he had. Fellow students also showed little understanding, and Bancroft felt very much alone. Unable to decide for himself, he again solicited advice from his correspondents, in the vain hope that they would make up his mind for him.[19]

"The university should enable me, upon returning home to act an useful and an honorable part in society," he wrote to Everett. But how? Kirkland considered the issue settled when his letter of introduction informed Eichhorn that Bancroft would "attend especially to philology, the ancient languages and Oriental literature, that he may thus be qualified to pursue theological studies to the greatest benefit, to give instruction as any opening may occur and invite, and become an accomplished philologian and biblical critic, able to expound and defend the revelation of God." But a respectable foundation in philology required at least three years and in Oriental languages a lifetime. And did Syriac and Arabic really interest anyone in Cambridge? As for defending revelation, that was the last thing students learned from Eichhorn.[20]

Even if one crammed philology the prospect was dismal: at the age of eighty, to produce an octavo volume on the anapaest—not the future an energetic young American envisioned for himself. Nor did Bancroft consider literary pursuits worthwhile—to "weave . . . little webs for the lady's toilette and spin out . . . finely scented stories and poems for the idle and the silly." To Kirkland, who blithely assumed that his ward could come back a philologist and a biblical critic, he explained that in Göttingen he had to choose either one or the other, and even then it remained unclear how proficient he would become.[21]

Stocktaking in the winter of 1819 revealed more confusion. Greater insight into the Bible would strengthen moral philosophy; and the Harvard divinity school could use an instructor well versed in linguistics, George told himself. There was no conflict between what he was learning and what New England needed, since Kirkland's worthy plans for the institution provided "the only certain and effective way of arriving at length at the mind of the people." Let Everett have the field of philology all to himself; was there no corner in the theological department for Bancroft? asked a plaintive letter to the Harvard president.[22]

For the rest of his European stay the pattern remained the same. George solicited approval for what he himself wanted to do, under the guise of begging for advice, without always knowing what he was after. But his anxiety, doubts, and confusions were not a subtle psychological confrontation with German scholarship; they resulted from the very concrete problem of defining the goal of all that hard work, sacrifice, and expense. Worst of all, no one wanted to give him the one thing for which he begged—a firm offer of a university appointment. Consequently he became a victim of fears that led to bewildering changes of directions.[23]

At the start, he studied philology, classical literature, biblical criticism, Arabic, Syriac, and Hebrew on the assumption that all would somehow prove useful to a future schoolmaster, minister, university instructor, and theologian. An even more grueling schedule in the spring of 1819 meant French and Greek, ethnography with A.H.L. Heeren, Eichhorn's lectures on the Old and New testaments, and a philological seminar with Dissen. In the second year Bancroft took more courses with Heeren, also Fiorillo on art history, Blumenbach on natural history, and Bouterwek's lectures on the history of ancient literature, in addition to classical languages, philology, and French. And all the while the final outcome of these efforts remained open-ended.[24]

When George Ticknor went abroad, his father advised him to travel rather in the manner of a clergyman, "to keep in mind the object of . . . [the] journey . . . and never to turn to the right nor to the left viz. to improve in solid science, the arts and literature, and in the knowledge of men." Bancroft too saw Göttingen only as a means of broadening his factual information, of testing ideas previously acquired, and of applying the categories of thought assimilated at Harvard. Since "a home education is one of the greatest blessings in the world and happy is he who enjoys it," Bancroft reasoned, he was proud not to have "lived entirely in Europe," glad that his "better part" was always on the other side of the Atlantic. And he plowed on through the treasures of the Georgia Augusta, never certain why.[25]

His predispositions determined his evaluation of the university. Critical and suspicious, he rarely missed an opportunity to discover inadequacies. Judging the purpose of learning by its utility back home, he remained basically unsympathetic to what the Georgia Augusta offered. Whatever set of lectures he attended, the question uppermost in his mind was the reception their content would meet in New England. Lonely and insecure, Bancroft vented his frustrations in a stream of invective, which denigrated the prodigies of German scholarship, undermined their achievements, and called into question the effectiveness of his own enterprise.

The combination of lectures and tutorials, he decided, was not the best "to quicken talent or cultivate taste." Lectures enabled professors to make bold generalizations; and in tutorials textual analysis revealed at close range how a scholar's mind worked. Yet the disappointing results produced unreflective, closed minds. Students, reduced to note takers, their power of invention dormant, formed an "immense herd of compilers and translators." Taking down every word uttered, they became imitators, whose erudition stemmed from memory. How superior was the Harvard approach, with its effort to make all learning immediately relevant to life![26]

Regarded through the spectacles of moral philosophy, the university community was also a disappointment. Assuming that knowledge, while valuable in itself, was more worthy when useful, Bancroft was astonished to observe its slight impact. A fervent democrat but also a good conservative, he discovered with surprise that in Germany few men of letters lived up to New England notions of the better sort. Frisbie and Norton, the *North American Review* and the *General Repository,* made scholars pillars of the social order, men of taste, morality, and personal excellence, community leaders respected by all for the erudition which gave them understanding, vision, and responsibility as guides of public opinion and censors of ideas. To be mere scholars was not enough. The safety of society required that they give authority to truth, expose fallacious doctrines, and apply sound philosophy to all pursuits—as the Harvard professors did. The Germans, according to Bancroft, failed on all counts.[27]

The roster of crimes and criminals, sins and sinners grew as Bancroft's stay at Göttingen lengthened. Further information only strengthened initial impressions. "Eichhorn does not know there is a church in the city. Blumenbach does not know who preaches there"; and the others were unaware that "there is such a thing as Christianity." A long epistle to Norton on the German attitude toward miracles confirmed what the latter had already guessed. The "German rules of criticism are, in general right tho not unlimitedly right, but their application is sadly wrong."[28]

German scholars, he asserted, violated canons appropriate to men of letters. Disrespect for models, disregard for authorities, efforts to supersede all predecessors and "perfect democracy in the world of knowledge" accounted for their achievements and failures. Bancroft, who rhapsodized over American democracy whenever occasion allowed, in this context used the term democracy in a pejorative sense, implying lack of standards or rules in a chaotic, irreverent world, driven by greed and a desire to advance. His instructors appeared to make scholarship a business, devoid of the sublime, while their specialization resulted in technical works unreadable by the uninitiated and thus of no social consequence. "The learned write for the learned" was Bancroft's judgment— "book worms and of no more everlasting fame than the common herd."[29]

For critical accuracy, the depth, industry, and insight of the Germans had no rivals. Keen competition aroused exertion and hope of success accounted for the large numbers who made their living as scholars. Yet "I know no man with whom I can actually interchange ideas, no man in whose vicinity I seem to breath purity," Bancroft complained. Science and learning became a trade "cultivated merely because one can get a living by it." Lacking morals, pure taste, love of fame, and polished manners, Germans "learn Hebrew because it is better to teach Hebrew than till the earth. A German does not write for immortality but for bread."[30]

With surprise, the minister's son discovered that his venerable professors merely plied a trade. Some time passed, he wrote to Kirkland, before "I could learn to honor them for their erudition without despising them for their vulgarity and their manners." Sons of tailors and watchmakers became lawyers and doctors merely because they did not want to follow their fathers' occupations; yet they did not leave the family mentality behind, and learning did not erase the traits of lowly origins. To call someone a philologian in Germany implied that he came from the lower classes, and theologian was a synonym for vulgar fellow. "Capital tradesmen in their respective lines of business," they remained nothing but purveyors of Greek and Latin, theology and literature. "They neither guide public opinion nor form it," Bancroft wrote, thinking of the role he envisioned for himself; but perhaps that was just as well, considering their low morality and audacious theorizings. "Certainly Göttingen is the best place to gather learning, but I hardly think a man would learn there how to use it properly," he told Kirkland.[31]

In all these strictures, Bancroft echoed the line laid down earlier by Joseph S. Buckminster, William Tudor, and later the *North American Review* circle. Responsible moral leadership was the duty of the learned; utility was the object of scholarship; and the alliance between wealth, intellect, and political power guaranteed the beneficial effects of knowledge. The great failure of the Germans was their inability or unwillingness to rise to this standard.

The Göttingen students also fell short of these sober standards. Young, rough, uncivilized, noisy, wild, unsociable, awkward, slovenly, and unmannerly, they were crude, boorish, stinking, coarse, and dirty. Like their professors, they preferred dark garments which did not show the filth. They lacked religious feelings and laughed at chastity. The worst offenders came from the lower classes, who found vice the cheapest diversion and indulged in the offerings of profligate women. Those from the better families prepared for future careers, took little interest in scholarship and, in this hierarchical society, kept to themselves, leaving the lower orders to their vulgarity. The lack of intercourse among social classes confined "polished manners and . . . quick feelings to the highest orders," unlike America, "where the son of an honest countryman is perhaps most likely to think freely and sublimely."[32]

Paradoxically, this cheering and encouraging conclusion enabled

Bancroft to make more of his stay abroad than the writing of endless complaints implied. It confirmed all his prejudices, proved how correct his Harvard mentors were, and suggested that time spent in Europe might not be so difficult after all. It would be easy to live through this learning adventure without absorbing anything inappropriate and without altering cherished ways of thought.

Only when he reached this conclusion and proved to his own satisfaction the inadequacies of German higher education did Bancroft relax. With Europe so flawed, its dangers diminished. There was no need for the mental adjustments a meaningful absorption of this education would have required, and Bancroft happily missed out on much that he could have learned. His pragmatic bent of mind, his propensity for empirically derived reasonable propositions, his limited capacity for abstraction, and a narrow, fundamentally intolerant perception helped assuage incipient conflicts.

Furthermore, news from home that all was not as it should have been reinforced his resolve. Letters from Cambridge and Worcester reported new obstacles to liberal Christianity in New England. From his father George heard of the revivals in the Northampton district, the wild scenes on the Connecticut River, the fanaticism of the worshipers, and the dreadful possibility that sister Jane might be caught in the snare. The squabbles of the Worcester First Parish also revealed an unsettled religious order, as did the controversy over William Ellery Channing's ordination sermon. Jared Sparks's success in Baltimore was reassuring, but Moses Stuart made plain that Unitarianism would lead to "German naturalism," which Bancroft tried hard to avoid. Even Harvard tottered; Samuel A. Eliot transmitted the gossip about the latest riot in the Yard, and Levi Hedge angrily reported on the wanton destruction of property. All of which made it even more important to maintain the rigidity of a proper outlook.[33]

"I have nothing to do with German theology," Bancroft assured Norton, even as he dutifully took down extensive notes on Eichhorn's lectures. Of his "infidel systems I hear not a word," the Harvard graduate, loyal to "the religion of [his] Fathers," told Kirkland. As for other courses, their content remained tucked away in his mind, for the time being suppressed and unexamined. Only later, long after his return to the United States and after struggling through several careers and experiencing major disappointments, did the fruits of their teachings ripen. And then it turned out that, in spite of his determination to restrict himself to factual knowledge and dry detail, Bancroft had in fact acquired much more than he bargained for.[34]

Meanwhile, he could happily criticize and discard, as with Johann G. Eichhorn's lectures. The great German scholar treated the Bible as a historical document composed at specific times for definite needs and susceptible to evaluation like any other text. Bancroft heard with horror for instance that Isaiah was not the wrathful mouthpiece of an angry God sent to castigate a wayward people, but two clever manipulators of public opinion. The Gospels, Eichhorn claimed, attempted to enforce uniformity of beliefs, their contradictions and inconsistencies reflecting local circumstances. Explicating Genesis, he suggested that guilty conscience rather than divine thunder accounted for the unease of the first pair after they had tasted of the tree of knowledge. The professor doubted that the devil was present in the serpent and refused to take literally the curse upon Adam and Eve.[35]

Cautioned by everyone not to go astray in consequence of evil teachings, Bancroft honestly replied that none of it made an impact on him. The Göttingen theologians in his judgment had not the slightest idea of the subject's sublimity and their lectures lacked moral or religious feelings. "They neither begin with God nor go on with him, and there is a great deal more religion in a few lines of Xenophon than in a whole course of Eichhorn." The professors indulged in such vulgar jokes as "would have disgraced a jail yard or a fishmarket" and treated the Holy Book without respect, laughing at its narratives "as an old wife's tale fit to be believed in the nursery." Worst of all, no one in America, Bancroft wrote, would hire a theologian trained in Germany, although Everett assured him that the cause of liberality was stronger than Bancroft thought.[36]

Bancroft's evaluation of Heeren, Bouterwek, Dissen, and Planck was more charitable. They too were innovators; but a liberal Christian, a follower of Hedge's *Logick,* and a supporter of Frisbie's broad empiricism could attend to their content and enlarge his horizons since their lectures did not touch his innermost sensibilities or deeply held convictions. If he did not know at the time that they would shape his future careers, Bancroft's peripheral interests broadened considerably.

Under the influence of Planck and Heeren, his interest in history expanded. Planck's course on the Catholic Church traced the evolution of dogma, institutions, and ideas to reveal the earthly adaptation of a heavenly doctrine according to Protestant historiography. A.H.L. Heeren, who foreshadowed later romantic historians while remaining heir to the German enlightenment, replaced opinionated evaluations of the past with mechanical laws and a naturalistic frame of reference, a rigid adherence to facts, a perception of each era as an independently valid constellation of factors, and a spiritual conception of humanity and the nation. His lectures, shaped as much by Montesquieu, Adam Smith, and Pierre Bayle as by Herder, combined political and commercial history. A strictly factual, chronological arrangement replaced grand philosophical generalizations, for a correct understanding of an era could arise only from the material itself, not from preconceived notions. Heeren also balanced the attention to material factors by an examination of "the leading ideas" of each age. The state, he asserted, was not a machine that could, like any other, be taken apart and put together again at will, for not only material, but moral powers operated in history.[37]

From him, Bancroft learned the complexities of causality and the technical problems involved in recreating the rich patterns of the past from written documents. Political history expanded to include social and artistic phenomena, while an organic law of human development provided the core for the meaningful organization of diverse events. In Heeren's vision of mankind as a unity, governed by a plan whose outline was visible in the past, Bancroft recognized a theme from his own heritage. The importance of colonies, the effects of climate and material resources, and the interrelations between mother country and its offshoots planted interpretive seeds in the mind of the future historian.

Dissen's lectures on the classics and Friedrich Bouterwek's instruction in modern philology and literature treated language as an expression of culture, the conveyor of the national spirit. Influenced by Friedrich Schlegel's *Geschichte der Alten und Neuen Literatur* and his *Poesie der Griechen und Romer,* texts Bancroft read, they stressed the wholeness of a people's literature and sought its linguistic, sociological, and historical determinants. Bancroft also read Johann G. Herder's *Ideen zur Philosophie der Geschichte der Menschheit,* the source of this approach. To a student raised on Adam and Potter, the Göttingen courses brought a whole era to life, and Bancroft waxed ecstatic over the capacity of his teachers to transform the dead past into a living present. "It is wonderful to see how a learned man can go back into antiquity, how intimately he can commune with her, how he can rest upon her bosom as upon the bosom of a friend whom he has long and intimately known." Dissen's command of the literary texts, of grammatical analysis, of archaeology, geography, and numismatics, opened a new world to the student.[38]

But in the short run at least, the broadening of knowledge amounted at first only to acquisition of factual information. Having read Schiller, Goethe, and Klopstock, and having heard Bouterwek's attempts to place them in historical context, Bancroft claimed to "understand their allusions, their imagery and their philosophy." He exaggerated. He had simply memorized facts. By his own admission, neither course made him think. When he tried to apply this knowledge independently, to evaluate literary figures of the entire world of German scholarship, his categories of criticism had nothing to do with the ideas these professors exemplified. Herder was accused of lacking powers of invention and creativity. Gotthold Ephraim Lessing, a great nationalist (a trait of which Bancroft approved) had only negative merits and added little to the sum of human happiness and intelligence. Klopstock, though admirable, was inferior to Milton; if he regenerated German poetry and flapped his wings sturdily, he failed to soar. Jean Paul Richter was able and original, while Goethe was the mirror of his age—sensual, refined, corrupt. Moral philosophy continued to reign supreme.[39]

While his intellect, he was pleased to note, remained impervious to any influences, other changes were taking place in Bancroft's personality. Placed on the defensive by a strange and bewildering civilization, but refusing to be overly impressed and asserting his native superiority whenever possible, Bancroft maintained his self-confidence by entering this society cautiously. After a while he wrote his sister, "I am by this time . . . become quite accustomed to the Germans and German customs, and were you to see me at present in my German costume, I am afraid you would hardly recognize me . . . I am become quite Germanized." The implication was that the adaptation was superficial, to be discarded at will.[40]

But the costume was necessary to get along in Göttingen. Bancroft turned down the first invitation to a waltz with the prim announcement that no one did such things in America; listening to Andrews Norton in the chapel was vastly preferable to a whirl on the dance floor. Soon, however, he changed his mind, as dances, teas, and gracious dinners in local homes erased a sense of alienation. In the evenings he called on some of his professors, who received him with interest. Madame de Staël had told Ticknor that he was the advance guard of humanity, and even the pope had suggested to Cogswell that soon the New World would dictate to the Old. Similar sentiments comforted Bancroft. When Eichhorn told him how much the English dreaded the United States, suspicion of this controversial figure disappeared. Even the prorector was delighted to see yet another American at the Georgia Augusta.[41]

Mrs. Johann Blumenbach, wife of the naturalist, approved of Levi Frisbie's 1817 discourse—a sign that there was some hope of setting the

Germans on the right intellectual path. A meeting with the highly educated daughter of the scholarly August Ludwig von Schlozer was an
encounter with a female Ph.D., which Bancroft considered unnatural,
and he was glad to hear that she disguised her learning to the point
where no one who did not know her past could credit her with an
education. Sunday parties were still offensive, but George was becoming
more tolerant. During school vacations extensive walking tours were a
welcome release from hard labor, and in the fall of 1819 there were
memorable visits to Jena and Weimar for an encounter with Goethe,
pleasant in chatter, but not enough to alter Bancroft's judgments.[42]

By the end of the summer of 1820 Bancroft looked upon the preced-
ing two years as time well spent. While he still preferred to hear Norton's sermons over the gossip of local parties, the thought of postponing
the joys of the Harvard chapel caused less guilt. The alienated, discontented, and priggish visitor who behaved as if he had come from another
and superior planet had changed into a more open and receptive guest,
who still disapproved of much around him, but who lived with himself
more comfortably.

In September Bancroft's studies at Göttingen were almost over. For a
week he went through the necessary formalities, writing the history of
his life, preparing topics for examination, renting an elegant carriage,
and buying the necessary outfit. The grueling doctoral examination covered Hebrew, Arabic, Greek, and classical literature, with all conversation in Latin. A few days later came the defense of the theses presided
over by the dean of the faculty. The candidate, dressed in smallclothes
and silk stockings, defended himself on a variety of philological questions. A few listeners thought he spoke too dramatically, but this intellectual warfare lasted only half an hour. For an American and therefore a
republican to praise the king and the Duke of Cambridge (as was the
custom) was not easy, but Bancroft survived the ordeal. Then, congratulated by the dean for his achievements, he heard everyone shout "Herr
Doktor, Herr Doktor," and the new title pleased him. After an oath of
honor to the university, Bancroft received the degree of Doctor of Philosophy. The arduous and confining life at Göttingen was over. On
September 11, the newly minted philologist left the Georgia Augusta.[43]

"I go from Göttingen without much regret," he wrote to Kirkland,
while expressing his gratitude for the financial assistance that made his
stay possible. In spite of all his misgivings, Bancroft knew how fortunate
his lot had been; and letters from envious friends back home sharpened
his own appreciation. Though his replies usually reassured correspon-

dents that they exaggerated the benefits of Georgia Augusta, secretly he knew the value of the new education. "I wish to make myself meritorious of my country," he told Norton, as if that would be his way of achieving what Edward Everett and George Ticknor were already doing—"raising the standards of taste and culture" of New England.[44]

In the meantime, he had no intention of going home, even if money, as always, was scarce. He had learned to make do with less, and the Harvard scholarship had gone a long way. But he now determined to stay in Europe for at least another year and soon appealed for more funds. True, the family needed his support, and he hoped that his sisters would not have to work for a living—"it is not the business of women to work for their bread." Yet at least for the time being, their brother did not want to work for a living either, and had no qualms about demanding more family sacrifices. Brother John, in Hamburg while on leave from his ship, advanced fifty pounds, with some not so cheerful advice on the meaninglessness of earthly life. Aaron Bancroft, complaining about a depressed economy, contributed more.[45]

But George nursed plans for a grand European tour (different from his impoverished ventures around Germany during vacations) and wanted much more. In October 1820, college chum Samuel A. Eliot offered to pay the expenses of a joint excursion later in the season. This was not, however, what Bancroft had in mind, since he wanted the money sooner and without supervision. A pleading letter to his father expressed the hope that "a rich friend might be found who would lend me such sums as I need and wait three years for his pay." Travel in Europe, he informed others, was an investment in the future, an assurance of success in life, like the tools of a mechanic and the stock of merchants. "Therefore it is that I wish to have money and at my own free disposal." The Herr Doktor also implied that he was getting tired of strings attached, even though they had been figments of his imagination. His strategy worked. One thousand dollars followed six months later, enabling Bancroft to stay in Europe and do what Everett and Ticknor had done with such signal success—see other parts of the Continent and be seen by whoever was worthy of the sight. For the time being, Samuel Eliot, Sr., bore the expense.[46]

This investment in his future took him first to the University of Berlin, the most progressive institution of higher learning in Germany. Bancroft arrived prepared to be inspired and excited, for he knew that some of the major intellectual figures of the decade were among the teachers, and their courses were supposed to overshadow those at the

Georgia Augusta. That he was about to plunge into another intellectual cesspool compared to Cambridge did not deter him; the survivor of Göttingen's impurities was ready for whatever might come.

The Prussian capital was the first metropolis Bancroft came to know intimately, and it promptly effaced all memories of Boston's glories. The wealthy in Berlin, he discovered with pleasure, were what they were supposed to be, pious, polite, and leaders of society. The elite, at least, lived up to his expectations. Not that "any ideal of humanity" flowered here either, but Bancroft now realized that his youthful notions of mental greatness were unrealistic. "Vain is the search after perfection, vain is the hope of ever seeing our early views and expectations realized." But Berlin came as close to the ideal as possible, and while Göttingen seemed in retrospect conservative, this city seemed innovative, speculative, and idealistic. In Göttingen one memorized dry facts, here one learned to think. Dissen could not rival the brilliance and audacity of Wolf, the classical scholar, even if his morals too were undesirable. The historical insights of Boeckh into daily life in ancient Athens were incomparable, but Hegel was a muddle-headed thinker, his lectures a "display of unintelligible words." For the next six months French and Italian, ancient history, courses in education, and Hegel's lectures occupied Bancroft's time. There were also dancing lessons—"for the sake of wearing off all awkwardness and uncouthness," but also because he liked it and wanted to cut a proper figure in the glittering society opening up to him.[47]

The years in Göttingen soon seemed "like living among the dead . . . Life there almost as solitary as a hermitage." Berlin offered pleasant evenings at the homes of some of his professors, a Christmas celebration, with the first Christmas tree George had ever seen and a merry Sylvester party on the last day of the year. At the salon of Rachel Levy, men of letters and action mingled, her Jewish background, to Bancroft's surprise, no barrier in society. A dinner at the Countess America Bernstorff's led to a long conversation with Sir George Rose, the British minister—a good Christian but too attached to the Church of England, Bancroft thought. Baron Wilhelm von Humboldt, full of good advice, discussed education and gave a book as keepsake to George, who offered his opinion of Goethe—a "little manierirt in style," the two agreed.[48]

A new tone rang through the letters home—of enjoyment, of fresh learning, of earnestness giving way to tolerance and empathy. But the words once more belied reality. Praise of the university's speculative and idealistic philosophy did not imply acceptance. If Berlin made him think, Bancroft made sure that his thinking moved in the right direction. And much of his enthusiasm reflected the previous evening's drawing-room conversation.

"He who has a heart and enthusiasm will, amidst a general depravity of manners, seek out and admire a few grand models of uncorrupted virtue." There had been no such person in Göttingen, but in Berlin Bancroft encountered Friedrich Schleiermacher, the one German thinker about whom he had no reservations. Andrews Norton later considered this theologian the source of the latest form of infidelity; but Bancroft found no adjectives precise enough to express his admiration—a "most learned scholar and acute philosopher," the first pulpit orator in Germany, also a devout and honorable man who preached to the understanding rather than to emotions, "a rational, candid, liberal divine, a most pious and domestic man." Schleiermacher, in Bancroft's view, escaped philosophical quibbles, ignored Kant and Friedrich Schlegel, and kept away from "the mysterious speculations and dreams of the day." The fact that here was an acute and innovative thinker who derived his theory of knowledge from Kant and was much influenced by Friedrich Schlegel was lost on Bancroft. Schleiermacher the great Platonist was deeply involved in just the kind of speculations and dreams that Bancroft detested and it was emblematic of the latter's misunderstanding that he found Schleiermacher compatible with his own beliefs in the free and supernatural agency of God, in forgiveness as mediated through Jesus Christ and his death. Schleiermacher's argument for the centrality of religion in human life evoked echoes in Bancroft's mind of Worcester and Cambridge sermons, something no European had done thus far.[49]

The theologian's call for a religious life produced a lasting impression. Schleiermacher's conviction that religion was an experience, and not just a set of rational and moral doctrines about God, was not far removed, in the youth's mind, from the teachings of the Scottish school. And the corollaries of this approach—the denigration of forms, creeds, and doctrine—could be related to Norton's distaste for metaphysical quibbles. By ignoring the revolutionary assertions that made Schleiermacher the leading romantic theologian of the nineteenth century the dogma was made acceptable. That revelation was a fairy tale, that miracles and inspirations were mere crutches, that the seat of religion was not in reason and conscience were all part of Schleiermacher's teachings that Bancroft did not notice. A religion of the soul, he concluded, was legitimate, even if it implied a transcendence of human knowledge, disregard for rationalism, and support for romantic intuition. In the great German bog of irreligiosity, Schleiermacher made the statement "I am a Christian" his central creed, and in Bancroft's mind was transformed into a New England Unitarian.

Under his influence, which extended to education and the classics, George also gave more thought to a teaching career. All along he had maintained an interest in the local schools, partly because of young Frederic Hedge's problems, which acquainted Bancroft with the better institutions around Göttingen, including Ilfeld, where Hedge suffered mental depressions. The distracted Bancroft, who felt that he was saddled with all the cares of a father before becoming one himself, considered Frederic a "perpetual torment," while Levi Hedge's parsimony and suggestions that the lad go wherever George went only made matters worse.[50]

At the end of 1820 Frederic moved to Schulpforte, where Bancroft visted him occasionally. From a lazy, bored little pest Hedge flowered into a studious, serious scholar. Bancroft attributed the change not only to the merciful end of the initial isolation and loneliness of an American child stuck away at Ilfeld, but also to the competitive spirit of the Schulpforte, its ability to foster learning, its competent teachers, and its combination of exercises, play, and studies. Thrown out of Ilfeld for rudeness, impertinence, and "unverbesserliche Faulheit," from which his removal was insisted upon "mit Möglicher Eile," Frederic was growing up like a man. The Schulpforte had accomplished a near miracle.[51]

Hedge later blamed his difficulties on the Ilfeld pupils, who expected to meet "a copper coloured savage" from America, on bad instruction, and on excessive discipline. The Schulpforte had better teachers, more compatible students, music, dancing, drawing, and swimming, all of which opened to him "a knowledge of what is meant by a life of thought and letters." But in the end Hedge felt that his education would have progressed better had he stayed at home. His German adventure made him one of the more peculiar Harvard students, and most of his theological training was sufficiently American to make Hedge in the future something less than a religious radical.[52]

That he might devote his life to teaching the young was more than Bancroft was willing, honestly, to concede. But perhaps a schoolmastership would serve as a transitional career, a suggestion encouraged by Kirkland, Norton, and Edward Everett, who saw the benefits of training students through methods pioneered at the Schulpforte. That school's success owed much to the Prussian government's subsidy, and Bancroft was aware that no such aid was available in America. He also knew that German gymnasia were the pathways to advancement in the professions and the state bureaucracy, reflecting a level of professionalism still foreign to the United States. But he hoped to tap private resources for an institution that would enable students to graduate with advanced standing in the liberal arts, and for a while refused to dwell on the difficulties he would face. Since the Schulpforte embodied "the mode of educating which Plato has extolled as the perfection of the art," it would surely prove ideal for New England.[53]

Meanwhile Bancroft's stay in Berlin came to a close. Prior to departure he gave a copy of his father's biography of Washington to the great Homeric scholar Wolf, also, to Bancroft's mind, one of his most corrupt and greedy teachers. A round of farewell visits ended with a few hours spent in the company of Schleiermacher, and after an uneasy and restless night George left the city. Several weeks of traveling took him through Leipzig, Weimar, Frankfurt, and Heidelberg, to another chat with Goethe, a stint with the historian Schlosser, and an effort to assess the value of German philosophy, which, to his mind, was on the whole revolting.[54]

Disturbed by his failure to receive any letters (or advice), Bancroft moved on to Paris, "trusting to Providence to feed and clothe" him. He still did not know whether his European stay would be prolonged, or what was expected of him. Unable to decide what to do next, he wallowed in self-pity and wrote plaintive messages to justify his course, at the same time settling in the city for a stay of some duration. A few days later a money order from home altered his mood entirely. The Storrows, friends of Washington Irving, and a small flock of resident Americans took him in, dispelling feelings of loneliness; letters of introduction from German and American friends promised a crowded social schedule.[55]

Joseph S. Buckminster years earlier had cautioned New Englanders that whoever stayed too long in Paris would lose "some of his power and his moral perception will be blunted." In no part of the world were "all the contrivances of sensuality so concentrated." Bancroft bore to France the same Yankee fears and prejudices, while lacking the justification to be there at all. Relieved to discover (as had Ticknor earlier) that this den of iniquity was cleaner than he had anticipated, Bancroft surmounted "ungrounded prejudices and false views" and prepared for a more sympathetic evaluation. True, Catholic superstitions were visible in popular fetes and parades of saints. And after several evenings devoted to reading Jean-Jacques Rousseau's *Confessions* (in French)—their fire, passion, stubborn adherence to truth, and republican sentiments all admirable—moral philosophy asserted itself when Bancroft judged that writer "deficient in the calmness of reason, . . . [a] visionary, wild, romantic," all terms of opprobrium. But France had been America's ally against Great Britain, and that noble gesture deserved to be remembered.[56]

His three months in Paris were interrupted by a short trip to London, where Samuel A. Eliot had just arrived with letters from home. There were Chandlers still living in the British capital, and a visit with his maternal relations might be justified on the grounds of future professional requirements. Having persuaded himself that this additional expense was an investment, George decided to go. As the stagecoach rambled in the dark on its way from Dover, his mind gave way "to reveries and schemes and hopes perhaps never to be realized." Not even the strange landscape could take Bancroft's thoughts away from his problems as the uncertain future and the ever nearing prospect of a return to the United States reawakened feelings of insecurity. Only the sight of a wagon filled with convicts jolted him out of his musings—perhaps London was not as safe as he had been led to believe.[57]

Eliot brought good news from Worcester and Cambridge: all was well. The Chandler relatives were hospitable, eager to meet the young American, all past political disagreements forgotten. A professor from the University of Kentucky, Dr. Caldwell, proved an amiable walking companion, and a Worcester friend, Frederick Paine, added to the enjoyment of the stay. From him Bancroft learned about the farflung empire over which the Perkins brothers presided and for which Paine worked. Bancroft's own brother John was sailing on a Perkins ship, but Paine had no information on his whereabouts.[58]

London proved boring. The weather was bad, and many structures erected for the coronation of George IV were being dismantled. Westminster Abbey was closed and none of the sights were as impressive as those in Paris. Out of curiosity Bancroft went to hear the great Unitarian preacher Belsham. The sermon was dull and monotonous, full of metaphysics and shallow philosophy, confirming American criticism. "Good Christianity is better than bad metaphysics," George thought. All this talk about "the possibility or probability of the soul's being material" did little to quicken religiosity. By the end of August he was back in Paris, cured of Anglophile tendencies. "Of fierce, determined vice England will show a stranger more in a night than France in a month," he wrote to Kirkland.[59]

Abandoning the study habits of the previous two years, George tried to enjoy himself. Visits to literary salons perfected his diction and improved "the art of talking" he so admired in others. Under the guidance of Washington Irving, he explored the city; at several evenings spent in the famous author's apartment on the rue Mont Thabor, near the Tuileries, Irving read selections of his tales to the young visitor. Letters from German friends opened many doors; a round of glittering dinners and fascinating talks expanded Bancroft's knowledge of men. Alexander von Humboldt took him to a session at the Institut de France, where Cuvier and others presented papers. At Benjamin Constant's Bancroft met Lafayette, who a few days later invited the American to his home, where the picture of George Washington adorned one of the walls. During a visit to Albert Gallatin, then minister to France, the amiable son of Madame de Staël regaled the company with news. On the Fourth of July, 1821, all Americans celebrated at a dinner presided over by Lafayette; and there Bancroft raised a toast to France, the land of Minerva.[60]

In Paris as elsewhere, everyone inquired about friends who had visited the city earlier. "I had heard them extolled by the German scholars but that I did not much mind," Bancroft wrote, "because they had seldom the faculty of discriminating character and are wholly without knowledge of man. Not so they who live in Paris." Alexander von Humboldt, the Duc de Broglie, and others spoke highly of Ticknor, Everett, and Cogswell. And who could question their judgment? Reminders of his predecessors' successes contributed to Bancroft's disquiet. Could he leave behind a similar reputation?[61]

Politically, however, the Worcester native found much to dislike. The "childishness of political squabbles" among the aspiring intellectuals was appalling; lacking fixed principles, many allowed themselves to be swayed by either extreme despair or unbounded utopianism. And while it was very exciting to hear inside gossip firsthand, it seemed silly for intelligent men to dissipate their time in idle pursuit of glory and power. Successful European statesmen were but time-serving courtiers, Bancroft sadly concluded. Even Laplace, a rival of the great Newton, revealed himself as grasping and ambitious. "I cease to venerate the author of the *Mécanique Céleste*" who abandoned "his sublime wanderings through the infinity of the universe, worthy of an angel," to play unimportant roles in French politics. Another idol had fallen.[62]

The glitter, intelligence, and worldly manners of Paris did not ease a troubled mind. Nagging fears of the future remained, augmented by guilt. Was he not wasting his time and other people's money? And did the witty conversations and stunning elegance mean anything in a larger context? Still claiming that letters from home were his sole moral support, Bancroft often thought about what he had left behind and worried about his nonexistent contribution to the family's welfare. But not enough to do anything about it, not yet at least. Complaints from friends about their parishes revealed another source of disquiet, the dismal state of the clergy, which the future minister had to take into account. Nor could George forget his brother John—now missing at sea—a gloomy and serious young man, who stressed the meaninglessness of earthly joys, the hardships and uncertainties of life, and concerned himself with plans to expand the farm and help his sisters.[63]

"I can come to no other conclusion than this, to follow boldly wherever destiny may lead me," Bancroft decided. And destiny led to Italy, a choice that lifted his spirits. The journey involved a long and solitary walking tour, occasional meetings with groups of travelers, and encounters along the way with quaint villages, magnificent views, and Nature with a capital *N*. Alone most of the time, Bancroft wrestled with his conscience. He thought and pondered, worried and fretted, waking one morning having decided to be a clergyman, changing his mind a few days later and thinking of a schoolmastership.[64]

"He that doubts in the good feelings of man is a worse skeptic than he who doubts in the being of God," he wrote in his diary. Surely his benefactors would come through once more and grant him the post to which his education entitled him. "Nature has given me strength again . . . I feel myself regaining the vigor of youth," another note read. Then came sad news—Frederick Paine, in Paris, had received letters from Worcester confirming what Bancroft had feared: his brother John was lost at sea. The "weight of reflections which are continually urging themselves on me," Bancroft thought, were enough to make him sink into the ground. For a while he considered going home at once, since with John gone there was no one to help the family financially. But a few days later the mood shifted—"I danced and spouted and sprang about and might well have been taken for a madman." God's will was done, and He demanded that man exclaim, "Creation is fair . . . Hail Heaven." Rather than return to Worcester, Bancroft treated himself to several more months in Europe.[65]

The trip to Italy led through Geneva, where an altercation with a beggar revealed that the American democrat felt it beneath his dignity to share wine with a scruffy-looking fellow. Bancroft could not understand why the latter took offense and despite his own long black beard, worn-out shoes, decaying coat, and exhausted funds, remained aloof. But there were compensations. "When I entered Switzerland," he reported to Norton, "I came with a heavy heart . . . but I have reposed in the bosom of nature and have grown young again." All along the journey, however, he pondered the meaning of death, fervently wishing for a speedy end once his faculties withered and his body grew frail. And his wish was fulfilled—almost seventy years later.[66]

From Geneva Bancroft proceeded through Savoy to the beautiful valley of Chamonix, passed the glaciers of Mont Blanc, the eternal snows of the Jungfrau, and crossed the Grimsel where the Rhône gushed forth from the ice. Rain and muddy soil impeded his progress, but in October he reached Milan and spent a few days looking at the sights. That "calm serenity of spirit" still eluded him, and neither resignation nor happiness could be grasped long enough to stay, but there were enough diversions to wrench Bancroft out of his morbid self-absorption. A letter of introduction from Victor Cousin, the French thinker, opened the doors of several worthies, including Alexander Manzoni, whose daughters charmed the guest. Italian girls were very pretty, with fine forms and languid black eyes. For a while they erased the memory of Mrs. Samuel Perkins from the chaste young man's mind. The food too was a welcome relief from the bread and cheese that had formed Bancroft's fare during his walk. Da Vinci's *Last Supper* was impressive, but "the door cut thru the legs of the Savior can not be viewed without horror."[67]

Traveling south freed Bancroft of some inhibitions, and he tried to experience and enjoy, not always successfully. This, after all, was Italy, darling of the romantics, gay and carefree. Much annoyed an American—from swarms of flies to beggars and ever present signs of despotism, all of which contradicted Bancroft's largely literary expectations. But the paintings, sculpture, and music mattered more. And the Italians were friendlier than the Germans, less stern and forbidding. Everyone was talkative, and George relished the chance to display his halting knowledge of the language. Nevertheless even the blue skies did not ease an inner turmoil. "It is indecision which torments me, uncertainty which prevents me directing my whole attention on any subject whatsoever."[68]

On the road from Milan bothersome Austrian soldiers demanded proof of citizenship. Resistance was vain and recriminations dangerous. "My dislike of despotism and military tyranny was stronger than ever," George wrote after he escaped his pursuers. The little adventure had a salutary effect—for the first time in weeks he slept soundly, undisturbed by nightmares. Providence was watching over him as he made his way through Venice and Florence. At the end of November he arrived in Rome.[69]

None of his predecessors ever forgot their encounter with Rome, the great city of the world. Compared to the still medieval Paris, with its narrow alleys and darkened houses, the ruins of antiquity evoked for Roman visitors the fabulous history of the Empire, the oratory of Cicero, the art of Michelangelo. Even though he had been up late into the night, filling out transit and customs documents, Bancroft rose early on his first free day in town. Here Ticknor had contemplated the great question of decline and fall; Bancroft saw Rome as the capital of Christendom, the place for a mystical experience. St. Peter's evoked wonder and delight, sublime feelings and silent admiration, just the mixture anticipated. Thoughts of the scarlet woman of Babylon faded away. Overwhelmed by the grandeur of the church, he flung himself on his knees in front of the altar to give thanks for his good fortune.[70]

That good fortune included generosity and kindness of benefactors, and the very fact of being alive in a world so full of woe, and yet so wonderful since Rome was a part of it. Leaving St. Peter's, Bancroft had breakfast and read letters. Then he ventured out again, once more overwhelmed by the sights. He visited churches, gaped at the sculptures, pondered the meaning of the ruins and, for several unguarded moments, allowed his imagination to run freely.[71]

Rome was also the center of international society; foreigners from all parts of the Continent made their home here, and the skills which served Bancroft so well in Paris were equally useful in the houses of local notables. The evenings brought elegant meals and glittering conversation and an especially memorable meeting with Napoleon's sister in her richly furnished home. At concerts, "the music was divine." The Chevalier Bunsen proved a welcoming host, commencing a friendship that would last fifty years. And if a bookseller mixed up Boston and Hindustan, the Princess Pauline Borghese was much better informed about America, as were the distinguished guests at her amusing parties.[72]

The young man was also discovering womanhood, and in a new light. Those "ministering angels" who could pour "comfort into a wounded breast" and at whose feet he would worship for the rest of his life were familiar enough from the past. But in their Italian version they were also temptresses and enchanters—as the Princess Borghese proved. The amount of money they needed to live in style was astonishing—$600 a year for dresses was not enough. Their sweetness, grace, dignity, and beauty were a clear snare for impressionable young men. Perhaps to turn his mind away from the disconcerting emotions evoked by these women and by the pictures he saw, Bancroft steered his thoughts to Bonaventura, Thomas à Kempis, and St. John Chrysostom.[73]

The first days of 1822 produced new affirmations, of life over death and of nature over art. Thoughts once more turned to home—"may they preserve their affection for me against the hour of my return," Bancroft prayed. Perhaps the ministry would claim him after all. He would become a kindly divine, enforcing purity of mind and generous feelings rather than declaiming against vices of which few parishioners were guilty. He needed only some further resolutions, he thought, to act and think like a man, to discipline the mind, to be less giddy and enthusiastic and "not inattentive to appearance." He was preparing to come home. "When I think of the time when I ran about Worcester as a boy that knew nothing of Europe but what little may be learned from books . . . I can not but wonder at my own happy destiny."[74]

But the wonder and happy destiny did not amount to anything yet. The more resolutions Bancroft made, the more aware he was of possible difficulties. To forestall future disappointments, he poured his troubles out in letters home. There were "duties to be performed, stations to be filled"—did Andrews Norton know what they were? Did John T. Kirkland? Did his father, now that the family was in mourning? For such a frame of mind the beauties of Italy were a mirage: the country was really rotten, its people cheats, "honor is a thing unknown," their towns terrible. "I am homesick," he candidly admitted, "literally homesick."[75]

Having always maintained "that it is an American's duty to go home and fill up well the wide sphere of active employment opened to him," Bancroft was sure the pulpit was the answer, for a few days at least. But the resolve was halfhearted and, tired of his own indecisiveness, he came to blame others, assuming that his own wishes mattered little, that other men had to decide, and that it was their fault for not having made up their minds. "This is my misfortune," he complained. In fact his parents and mentors agreed to leave the choice to him, which was just what George disliked.[76]

In the middle of February, he set out for Naples and a short excursion to Paestum. Then, after a boat trip to the Gulf of Salerno, he landed in Amalfi, where the police asked to see his passport. Unable to produce the documents (left behind in Rome), Bancroft and three traveling companions were sentenced to two nights in jail. They were free to roam around during the day, but the forced lodgings were filthy and infested with bugs. Eventually the Neapolitan authorities ordered his release. Two weeks later he was back in Rome, beginning his journey home.

While still in Italy Bancroft learned that several professors, led by Ticknor and Everett, planned to reform the university in Cambridge. Public opinion appeared favorable, one correspondent informed him, but

Kirkland ominously dragged his feet. Bancroft's "manly character" would surely be in demand, but circumspection was in order—"what is to be done among us must be done by ourselves, with exceeding caution and discretion," he was warned. There was also confusion about his own plans—while some in Cambridge saw him as a university professor, the certainty that he would become a preacher made the rounds of Worcester. In other circles he was rumored to be establishing a new school. "You will have plenty of good advisers when you get home," a friend wrote, warning against the dangers of undue influence.[77]

Worried about the future and about his reception by his benefactors, Bancroft warned everyone what to expect. "You will remember me, and though my face may be changed, you may find my heart unaltered . . . If when I come peeping my head into your parlour, you smile and look glad to see me near you again, I shall rather look at your face than at the finest picture of Raphael." This to Norton. The response from the restrained and polite professor to a barrage of poetry, introspective musings, and gushings about nature was less than George had hoped for but still acceptable. Norton advised "against expecting immediate reputation . . . and not to care for it." "Indeed I will not," Bancroft resolved. On June 12, he boarded the ship *Belle,* bound for New York.[78]

His educational pilgrimage was over; exposed to the world, to scholarship, and to himself, Bancroft acquired greater self-knowledge and solid learning, became more self-assured and proud. His years abroad were not all that they could have been, for unlike Tennyson's Ulysses, Bancroft never claimed, "I am a part of all that I have met," nor was self-revelation his goal. That stage of life, he had thought all along, had ended when Harvard awarded him a Master of Arts in divinity. He had gained a doctorate, lost no virtue, shed some folly, and acquired much enthusiasm. But nothing had occurred from his point of view to cause him trouble upon return to the United States. He was coming back, in Nathaniel Hawthorne's phrase, with empty pockets, but ready "to begin the world in earnest."[79]

Childhood and youth were also over, the boy had become a man. A tone of cool, casual urbanity mingled with exclamatory phrases and sensuous clauses toward the end of his stay in Europe. The early emotional responses, lashing out at all that seemed strange and therefore dangerous, gave place to calmer, more reasonable judgments, broader sentences, a more flowery metaphorical style, and though a moralistic language remained, it acquired new overtones.

A growing preoccupation with the self, efforts to examine his own emotions and states of being, and introspection were aspects of this transformation. Early responses to novelty were factual and critical, rarely stating what Bancroft felt as opposed to what he thought. Toward the end of his voyages the balance shifted. More secure, proud of his accomplishments, and flattered by attention, his personality changed—not only his appearance, dress, and mode of speech, but also his thinking, the product more of his travels and encounters than of his formal education.

Thrown upon his own resources, plagued by doubts about his career and by financial insecurity, Bancroft believed that he had learned the lessons of self-reliance. "I look within myself and live within myself," he wrote, mingling ideas derived from his European education and New England background. "I would give free course to imagination, create for myself a world of my own"—a highly romantic idea, this. "I would strive to draw my principles and my happiness from myself and build a Paradise in my own soul"—not quite what Harvard students were destined to do. As to manners, "I may come home awkward, I may return with outlandish habits," Bancroft informed Norton, but "if I have odd or improper ways tell me of them plainly and honestly . . . I hope to improve more in the first twelve months at home than I have ever done in a year in Europe." [80]

But like the good moral philosopher he had been trained to be, Bancroft at the same time reminded himself that virtue had its own rewards, that worries about careers and the future were unworthy of the devout and pious. Appearances were deceiving, intuition was not enough, and life was a serious business. He resolved to take as his motto in life, "Be perfect as God is perfect," and was determined to prove himself to all concerned. For the first time he also felt somewhat independent.

At the end of his own European stay Joseph Cogswell had declared that he was more contented with his own society after having seen the Continent. Bancroft, "glad to learn, to observe, to compare, to admire, to be amused," agreed. For rules of conduct, thought, and morality, he remained a true New Englander. Like the fountain of Arethusa which maintained its sweetness amidst the bitter waters of the sea, he had remained pure while passing through the slough of the Old World. He thought he had come to terms with the results of his pilgrimage; it remained to be seen whether others would approve. [81]

IV

FLOUNDERING

THEY DID NOT. The disorientation that had marred Bancroft's European stay continued to haunt him. Failures, altercations, and disappointments turned self-induced doubts into signs of personal inadequacy. The first months at home were "such as I would not wish an enemy to be cursed with," the most "wretched time imaginable," and all through no fault of his own, Bancroft thought. Unable to find a niche, the angry twenty-two-year-old blamed everyone else for his problems; self-righteously stubborn, he wallowed in self-pity. Boston and Cambridge—smug, narrow-minded, intellectually backward, and institutionally conservative—refused to recognize his uniqueness or to grant him the position he deserved.[1]

To reject the world outright was impossible. Here, after all, he intended to prove himself. But a wholehearted embrace was also out of the question, for the powers that be judged him short of the mark. In response Bancroft alternately arraigned and praised, rebelled and conformed, satisfying no one, least of all himself. He became a preacher because everyone expected him to, but while a tutor at Harvard conformity yielded to reform impulses, with disastrous results. A fortuitous though unhappy marriage brought new options, while the beginning of a writing career revealed the pitfalls of intellectual pursuits. It took him almost a decade to realize that he could translate intellectual authority into power through partisan politics and scholarship. The Jacksonian man of letters was then on the threshold of his lifelong career.

George spent the first morning after his arrival in Worcester writing letters to his Boston benefactors. Lest there be any misunderstanding, he informed them all that he was willing to act upon good advice. The days of quiet study were over, the situation now demanded action. "I detest and dread an undecided spirit"—a frank admission of his private difficulties. Kirkland in response summoned him to Cambridge, but his letter was noncommittal and less encouraging than expected. Instructions to consult his own feelings and judgment implied that the pleas for guidance were not bearing the desired results.[2]

What happened was predictable. Bancroft came to Cambridge and stayed for two weeks, dividing his time between the Kirkland and Norton households. Wherever he went, he subjected his listeners to a monologue consisting of plans, schemes, demands, and unrealistic expectations. The combination was distasteful to Norton, somewhat disappointing to the more genial Kirkland, and unbearable to others. It was not so much dress and appearance that gave offense—these, all knew, could be shed easily enough. Bancroft's demands, however, struck his listeners as arrogant, unwarranted, almost insulting. He was after an appointment similar to Everett's and Ticknor's, and a sympathetic consideration of the plans for university reform that he had been hatching. Kirkland took it all in with his customary patience. Norton, however, informed Bancroft that he was a disappointment.[3]

The Dexter professor was "one of those whose bread I ate," Bancroft wailed. "Bitter enough was the taste of it in the belly." "I love . . . I love to receive advice," which was all he thought he wanted. Nor did he consider his proposed reform of Harvard's educational system and his request for a high position in the college outrageous. Norton thought otherwise. Bancroft's enthusiasm, unseemly behavior, and false self-assurance struck him as unbecoming. Unceremoniously he told his guest that he would never be invited again. Only Kirkland remained.[4]

Respectability and happiness, Kirkland gently informed his ward, rested on "stability of character, resulting from a proper union of mind, good principles and intelligence."[5] Bancroft agreed; he had heard this often enough before and thought he met all the requirements. As proof of his intelligence there was a German doctorate, and good principles required that his achievements benefit himself and others. The stability of character was also his, regardless of malicious gossip. The rest of Kirkland's advice Bancroft considered equally worthless. The president reminded his protégé that abstract knowledge was futile but did not suggest how to bridge the gap between the learning acquired in Europe and Harvard's needs in 1822.

Bancroft wanted a high university appointment commensurate with his credentials, which, he assumed, had made him into a person of more importance than his age indicated. In Europe he had been the object of curiosity and attention from men whose achievements put those of some Bostonians to shame; and he had acquitted himself well. The suggestion that he once more sink into the mass of undistinguished Harvard gradu- ates and perform noble but unspectacular social tasks seemed prepos- terous.

The intricate and unarticulated quest for a new status also stemmed from the European experience. To repay his benefactors he wanted to do something special and unique. He chose as his pattern the European men of letters he had met, esteemed by society for scholarly accomplishments and sought out for advice on issues outside their own fields of knowl- edge. Bancroft could not understand why no one took seriously his sug- gestion that Harvard become a different kind of college. Surely his opin- ions had to count for something, given his experience and firsthand knowledge. Norton and other Cambridge worthies thought otherwise.

Behind the incipient conflict lay the ambivalence with which this society treated scholars and intellectuals. The community needed men of letters for various tasks. But such individuals earned a living in other ways and devoted only moments of leisure to scholarly pursuits. George Ticknor, Edward Everett, John T. Kirkland, Caleb Cushing, and others were educated gentlemen with a lively interest in the arts, whose per- sonal wealth or careers as lawyers, ministers, and teachers enabled them to write as an avocation.[6] Bancroft implied that he deserved more.

At the same time, he himself shared the propensity of local society to frown upon people who only dabbled in books, and often expressed his distaste for German scholars who devoted their days to esoteric facts of use to no one but themselves. To prove his competence in philology, Bancroft assumed, was not enough, and he thought everyone else would support him in his quest to make his European acquisitions relevant. But, with few exceptions, no one did. Only a socially useful occupation could bring him respectability and happiness, perhaps allow him to pursue other interests, and gain him the position and social weight his insecure character craved.

As a minister and teacher, Bancroft decided, he might yet attain his goals and prove his detractors wrong. There was no other choice. He had to repay debts, make a living, and assist aging parents and sisters. As ever, money remained the stumbling block, and Bancroft refused to take the road some of his colleagues chose early in their lives—an advantageous marriage. When Kirkland offered him the Greek tutorship, Bancroft accepted; it was better than nothing, and perhaps the start of something more. But it was also galling. Everett and Ticknor had received better treatment, why not he? Perhaps he could improve his position by cutting a good figure in the pulpit. A decade of failures thereupon began.

While performing his chores at Harvard, Bancroft floundered into a halfhearted clerical venture in his determination to be useful and to leave a mark on the community. This was still an acceptable opening for aspiring young men, and one of which Bancroft's mentors approved. But the vocation required ardor, devotion, and a willingness to live frugally, for few parishes paid as handsomely in dollars or in influence as the Brattle Street church where Palfrey now preached and where Edward Everett had earlier been a spectacular success. The career offered few substantive rewards, only great spiritual ones, as its practitioners pointed out. Could a young man ever more desirous of earthly recognition find the trade-off satisfactory? Bancroft's answer was a hesitant maybe.

"Men of letters," Ticknor said in 1816, "can work on their contemporaries only in two ways—as publick teachers or as writers." The statement still held true in 1822, and Bancroft mounted the pulpit as a man of letters acting the teacher under the guise of religion. His self-defined task was to evoke moral affections rather than to subdue sin, to enforce "general purity of mind and high and generous feelings" rather than to "distract attention by . . . declamations against heinous crimes and vices of which mayhap not one of the hearers would be guilty." And he felt peculiarly qualified for the vocation by virtue of his Harvard divinity training, his European education, and his long association with liberal Christianity.[7]

Unitarianism in the 1820s was still largely undefined, its tenets evolving more in opposition to the older Calvinism than as positive affirmations. Not all ministers who shared Bancroft's beliefs called themselves Unitarians; some were liberal reformers of Congregationalism. Optimistic about human nature, they exhorted their flocks to lead pure lives and stressed personal regeneration to defeat evil. Character, they were fond of saying, was more important than doctrine, opening themselves to the charge that they had no creed at all. The church did God's work by example, with each pastor free to choose the best way.[8]

Bancroft preached first in his father's pulpit, then in Bolton, Portsmouth, Boston, and other places around Cambridge. Full of hope, he considered his problems all but solved; engaged in good work, he would soon declare himself a candidate for the ministry. But as the tediousness

of itinerant preaching dawned upon him, he delayed ordination, aware
that it would be easier later to change vocations if there were no need for
a formal resignation. Still, he had set his goals and meant to strive toward
them; also having had his fill of altercations, he tried not to create new
ones. That resolution lasted about a year.

At first, the task seemed easy; Bancroft thought that he knew what
he could accomplish. "In preaching I shall endeavor to be earnest and
impressive rather than oratorical and hope to write sermons that are
serious and evangelical rather than fashionable." No one could quarrel
with that—earnestness and old-fashioned virtues were always in season.[9]
By "pulpit eloquence" he would improve his parishioners through their
own affections. The key terms were character, good morals, and virtue,
"to be fed by reason first, but by imagination also." The goal was formation of religious character, in evocation of "the poetic part of our nature,
and dignified by a proper tempering of reason."[10] The son of Aaron
ignored both the orthodox and the extreme liberals, and fully subscribed
to the tenets of moral philosophy. The appeals to the heart and the head,
the exploitation of moral affections, the stress on character rather than
doctrine, verbal eloquence, restraint, avoidance of enthusiasm—these
had been well inculcated in the Harvard divinity student, and Bancroft
stuck close to the expected path.

But to say "Blest of fathers may I never forget your precepts, may I
never be unmindful of your lessons in religion" was a vow more easily
made in Rome than in Worcester. Those lessons in religion were clearly
superior to European acquisitions, and it was simple enough to denigrate
Eichhorn and higher criticism in the *American Quarterly Review* and thus
sustain the appearance of loyalty to a native creed. Yet Bancroft had also
been deeply moved by Schleiermacher's preachings and wondered
whether at least some of his points were correct. The question whether
the religion of New England as expounded by the first generation of
Unitarians was sufficient to the demands of the new decade plagued him
and other members of his circle.[11]

Typically, Bancroft equivocated. The creed was sound; he had no
quarrel over dogma with his father or with Andrews Norton. But presentation was another matter. Here Bancroft thought a new approach
helpful, although with nothing revolutionary or even reformist in it.
That new approach, expressed in a more ornate style and occasional
poetic musings, was simply another avenue toward approved ends. As for
social implications, Bancroft was unwilling to take unnecessary risks. By
temperament, education, position, and association he took the world as it
was, hoping that personal regeneration would slowly filter through soci-

ety, ameliorating existing evils which were part of creation. Once Edward Everett, Jared Sparks, and others had agreed, but, like Bancroft, they could not long abide this cast of mind and, like him, they left the pulpit for other occupations.[12]

Taking the world as it was did not imply hopeless resignation. Nor did the view of religion as ultimately an exclusive affair between God and the believer suggest a disregard for communal concerns. Bancroft had learned from Schleiermacher that the ethical message of Christianity could be fulfilled only in the social context, where man was responsible, the master of his own destiny. But these concepts coexisted in his mind with the rationalism of his early education, the teachings of moral philosophy, and the trust in the unfathomable wisdom and mercy of God.

Having wrestled with these problems for twelve months, Bancroft in the end came out on the side of orthodoxy. He upheld the essential infallibility of the Scriptures and the supernatural origins of Christianity, a position of which Andrews Norton approved. Enthusiasm for Schleiermacher's preachings did not convince the fledgling minister that an inner light endowed each person with a guide to truth and conscience. Nor did he find in the new theology, based on William Ellery Channing's sermons, the seeds of a different outlook, one that Theodore Parker, George Ripley, and Ralph Waldo Emerson would expand in the next decade into a religion of humanity.

This inner intellectual struggle deprived Bancroft's sermons of a clear focus or consistent point of view. They alternated between affirmation of the faith taught in Harvard divinity courses and a broader, more optimistic outlook that appealed to the soul, stressed man's goodness, and relied less on the Bible than on the whispers of conscience. Confident that reason would always harmonize with revelation, Bancroft did not explore the possibility that it might not. If pressed, he would have affirmed the superiority of revelation.[13]

The orthodox strain in his preaching stressed knowledge, piety, and discipline, the belief in miracles, and the equality of men only in death and salvation. Bancroft called reform programs visionary speculations and efforts to translate the doctrine of man's spirituality into a doctrine of democratic egalitarianism dangerous to society. The voice of the people, proclaimed the future Democrat, was patently not the voice of God. "In the freest government, the voice of the people is sometimes bloodthirsty, often unjust, and always uncertain." Men should strive for the virtuous moral life that alone expressed the perfectibility of believers and to which social or political conditions were incidental.[14]

None of his sermons were political, an omission surprising in a period when, some clergymen complained, parishioners wanted to hear nothing else. Like his father, Bancroft believed that ministers should concentrate on higher problems. He thus ignored the cries that wealth demoralized society, that factions tore it apart, that the people were corrupt and the leaders inept. Some colleagues, railing against Jeffersonian atheism, expounded a socially conservative ideology and bemoaned declining piety. But not Bancroft, except in those rare outbursts against relaxation of standards and visionary schemes that promised man a paradise on earth.

The sermons were unusual only in diverging from the dry rhetorical prose of other Unitarians. Bancroft's literary language employed words more suitable to poetry and fiction than to theology, thereby further distorting his concepts and confusing listeners. Ornate sentences on the dignity of the soul stood side by side with harsh words on human sinfulness and nothingness. Temperamentally insecure and still unsure of his opinions, Bancroft did not know where his allegiances lay. Having read more literature than theology for two years, he employed the only comfortable means of expression and turned sermons into moral discourses, using metaphors and exclamations to compensate for lack of direction.

This poetic style reflected Bancroft's literary bent but moved few to piety; its muddled thought conceded more to fashion than he was willing to admit. One sermon, delivered in Worcester, was falsely rumored to be an essay on love. Similes piled one atop another. "Pleasure is an insect with painted wings," one sermon declared, "that buzzes and sparkles only when in motion; if you hold it fast to examine it, every color vanishes." The preacher's firmly held convictions lacked force among parishioners unconvinced of his sincerity. Congregations judged his manner artificial, different from what they expected, and did not like it.[15]

Furthermore, since he had assiduously avoided doctrinal questions, Bancroft now faced the need to articulate a faith in which he believed but could not quite express. As news of these shortcomings spread, his despair increased. Ralph Waldo Emerson, who heard one sermon at the New South Church, thought it was the work of "an infant Hercules" but still "in need of cutting and pruning." Others were less charitable. They considered the talks unedifying and many an eyebrow rose in response to the homilies.[16]

After twelve months during which Bancroft delivered an average of four sermons a month, he abandoned the endeavor, much to the disappointment of his father, and a little bit to his own, for it would have been a simple and easy solution to the career problem. "I think it better to wage the warfare of learning than of faith. . . . Our country needs good instructors more than good preachers." He set aside "the temptation to lead the easier life of a parochial clergyman," realizing how complicated it could be.[17]

The warfare of learning for the time being meant reform of Harvard College, and Bancroft's tutorial year—typical of the man, some snorted—was another failure; he did not attain his objectives, nor did his status in the community improve. Ignoring the good advice of his friends, with foreseeable consequences, he ran afoul of both students and college authorities. Eliot had pleaded for caution, advocating inoffensive moderation, and Bancroft heard about the difficulties of others when their demands outdistanced the acceptable.[18] He also knew what students were like and had no reason to expect a change since his undergraduate days. Nor did the faculty present a reliable united front. One faction charged that their opponents were destroying the college, while yet another group judged the status quo acceptable, except for a few details. Bancroft supported the radicals, halfheartedly but enough to earn the full measure of abuse that rained upon his friends.

The reformers, headed by George Ticknor, tried to transform an inferior boys' school into an institution of higher learning. They hoped that a reshaped curriculum, elective courses, new subjects, and the lecture system would indeed make Harvard the university in Cambridge. Supported by Edward Everett, Ticknor and others battled Kirkland and the Corporation, as well as faculty members and Overseers, who considered them brash meddlers and innovators out to change what previous generations had found eminently satisfactory. Many students agreed.[19]

Like Ticknor, Bancroft prided himself on common sense and practicality, and he personally had no quarrel with the grip of religious liberalism or moral philosophy on the curriculum. In his view, not the content but the methods needed refurbishing. The existing system, he thought, could easily accommodate changes that were neither radical nor dangerous and that had already been successful elsewhere. Harvard could not be remade into a Göttingen, but there were better ways of teaching Greek than Dr. Popkin's. And Greek it would have to be, for no place was available in the theological school, and Kirkland considered Bancroft's alternative suggestion—a history appointment—superfluous. In the fall of 1822 George became a resident instructor, charged with hearing recitations in Greek, policing dormitories, ferreting out offenders, and disciplining those inept enough to get caught.[20] While his friends tried to restructure the entire university, he, more cautious, concentrated on his classes. He expected some opposition, even in this little sphere, but the results, he hoped, would bear him out.

They did not, and the unpopularity of his endeavors brought fresh disappointments. "Bancroft is making great exertions to teach Greek thoroughly and succeeds," the sympathetic Ticknor noted, but at the cost of alienating the students and exhausting himself. Division of classes into five groups according to ability made some study harder than others and antagonized those branded less able. Efforts to cut the figure of a German Herr Professor in the classroom and assertions that his was the method of true scholarship endeared him to no one. "Thus we do in Germany," the students chanted under the windows of their tutor at night. Like some of his own colleagues, they regarded Bancroft as the unfit bizarre pet of Kirkland's, and they responded with broken windows, classroom disruptions, ridicule, and hostility.[21]

Nonetheless they also learned more Greek than under other tutors, and for a while, in spite of the frustrations, Bancroft consoled himself with the newly found power of his position. "Any week and any day I can dispense honour and disgrace and decide," on the basis of such imponderables as general character and disposition (in addition to talent), who should be demoted to the lower sections. Since the students obviously learned, "my points are all gained," he exulted, "people are aware that my system is the best." And Harvard, he was sure, benefited more thereby than it did from the president's efforts to increase endowment. If only Kirkland would cease pouring money into construction and upgrade the income of teachers, the college would be the better for it.[22]

But Kirkland thought otherwise. Under fire from students and from disaffected instructors, the ever kindly and protective president tried to save the institution by patience and Christian forbearance. Battles in the commons, rowdiness in the Yard, disorder in the classrooms, and interruptions at chapel deprived him of the ability to support his protégé, who consequently felt isolated, unappreciated, and battered. "I have the satisfaction of knowing," Bancroft wrote to Eliot, "that I have carried my points alone unassisted by any cooperation whatsoever," save Ticknor's.[23]

Despondently Bancroft turned to Roger Ascham's *The Scholemaster,* designed to train an aristocracy for its proper political and social functions, as well as to several other English works on education. Sound and interesting as they were, the books offered no guidance. Information about the precariousness of a courtier's career and about the temptations in a royal household did not help quiet a riot in the commons. After a particularly nasty assault that led to the rustication of some students, Bancroft gave up, and the Board of Overseers learned that, in compliance with the wishes of the entire freshman class, instruction in Greek would revert to the customary modes.[24]

The college became for Bancroft "a sick and wearisome place," his state "nothing but trouble, trouble, trouble." The "clamours of scandal and the disputes of the irresolute," wars against the Corporation, faculty antagonism, and unappreciative students, made the year a prolonged misery. Already in the winter he considered alternatives, and when a senior-class rebellion caused the expulsion of forty students and thrust Harvard to the verge of collapse, Bancroft's patience petered out. Stephen Higginson, the college treasurer, had his own interpretation of the young tutor's tribulations. "His manners," he wrote, "style of writing, theology, etc. . . . bad, and as a tutor, only the laughing butt of the college."[25]

Ticknor counseled patience but, since his position differed from Bancroft's, he did not have to follow his own advice. The Smith professorship allowed him to live elsewhere, deliver formal lectures, and supervise language instruction without either parietal responsibilities or the chore of daily recitations. Ticknor could advocate stricter discipline, knowing that implementation would fall on overworked resident tutors like Bancroft. It was easy for Eliot to suggest that hopes for independence were illusory—the son of a rich merchant, he now toured Europe, not, as Bancroft had, on a shoestring, but with an ample bank account. The more George thought about it the surer he became that he ought not waste a Göttingen Ph.D. supervising student attire, keeping the boys from playing billiards at Lechmere Point, and regulating the bells in the Yard.

Social ostracism deepened his unhappiness. The elegant salons of Berlin had no counterpart in Cambridge. Nor was Bancroft as much in demand as he had been in Europe. The young American for whom many doors opened there was regarded as an oddball at home; the community ignored his presence, while his colleagues called "about as often as if . . . [he] were on the Ganges or passed the Stix." Catherine Norton, Samuel A. Eliot's sister, tried to heal the breach with her husband but without success. Were it not for Boston, Bancroft feared he would "grow cold and frozen . . . in Cambridge."[26]

Boston offset some frustrations but was the source of others. The Ticknors were always hospitable, and Catherine Prescott, William Hick-

ling's mother, became a good friend. Gossip, sprightly conversation, intelligent discourse, and a stylish life—the Ticknors, the Prescotts, the
Eliots, and others lived well. Bancroft wanted to be like them, but knew
that his tutorship was not the way to do so. Money as always was a
problem, for though social standing and respectability did not necessarily
depend on wealth, some was needed—to repay loans, establish an independent existence, help the family, and get on in life. Former classmate
George Emerson was getting married, but he could afford to start a
family on a $3,000-a-year salary as a master of a young ladies' school. So
too, rich parents and a growing legal career enabled former mathematics
tutor Caleb Cushing to make a name for himself in politics.

As Bancroft looked around him, all managed except himself. "On
evil days and evil tongues" had he fallen, through no fault of his own.
Everyone else was to blame—parishioners who made the pulpit a burden, students who soured a teaching career. Faced with a declining reputation in a small community where a good name and public opinion
mattered, Bancroft wallowed in self-pity. "There are those" in Cambridge, he thought, "who will not allow a Latin and Greek scholar to be
good for anything." These evasions of responsibility merely masked his
own sorry state; he had yet to prove at what he was truly good.[27]

One other option might bring him all he wanted and independence
as well. Bancroft had long considered the desirability of establishing a
novel educational institution, and in the winter of 1822 he embarked on
the project more seriously. Ticknor's, Everett's, and Kirkland's encouragement showed that there was still some goodwill left. Perhaps they
also wanted him out of the way, for his complaints were wearing out
everyone's patience.

Everett and Ticknor hoped that properly trained applicants would
solve one of Harvard's most serious problems, an undereducated and
overly rambunctious student body. Jared Sparks thought Bancroft
swayed by young dreams but, with his own career in Baltimore floundering, was willing to concede that perhaps the project was worthwhile.
Nathan Parker, however, sorry to hear that the son of Aaron was leaving
the ministry, had doubts and tried to get George for Phillips Exeter,
which sought a replacement for the aging Abbot. But the headmaster-
ship of an established, traditional academy meant new strings and would
not solve Bancroft's problems.[28]

Joseph Cogswell at about the same time arrived at similar conclusions. Like Bancroft, he was unhappy at the college. The Corporation

showed no appreciation for his rearrangement of the library, and his nominal professorship of mineralogy lacked supporting funds. He too listened to Ticknor urge loyalty to reform, but did not believe that their faction had a chance of success. In "a state of mortal discontent" all winter, Cogswell spent many an evening with Bancroft reviewing plans for an academy somewhere in the country. Early in the spring they began to search for a suitable site. Neither had much money and Cogswell, older and more experienced, was more cautious. But Kirkland prevailed on Theodore Lyman, Samuel Eliot, and others to cosign promissory notes. On Round Hill near Northampton, two houses overlooking the Connecticut River were available, cheap. Cogswell and Bancroft rented them as of September 1823, determined to open school a month later.[29]

Both thought they had learned enough from European institutions and their own experiences to know what the United States needed. A visit to Fellenberg's school at Hofwyl near Bern had impressed Cogswell with the pupils' cheerfulness and with the founder's view of learning as recreation. Hofwyl was also self-supporting, but its dictatorial procedures would not be suitable for the United States. On the other hand Pestalozzi's overly democratic methods left his institution in shambles. As a graduate of Exeter, Bancroft knew something about local requirements and was less willing to take chances on inappropriate educational models. In the end the partners compromised and settled on a middle course that tried to combine the best of both worlds—European educational experiments and what young Americans needed. Round Hill owed most of its unique features to Cogswell's vision and his faith in the virtues of manual labor and agriculture, combining studies, moral training, and physical exercise. Bancroft's input came initially on the managerial side—the hiring of faculty, contacts with the local community, supervision, and fund raising.[30]

The focus of their project was practical utility, fostering "the active life" so superior to the contemplative existence of cloistered scholars. Round Hill would give its students all the education that the "exercise of stronger powers" demanded. Competition and exertion would make the school a microcosm of the larger world in which they would one day live. Frequent stimuli and challenges would teach them to survive in an egalitarian society. In a sense, the new academy would apply the teachings of moral philosophy to earlier education.[31]

To publicize the project Bancroft helped Cogswell compose the brochure that advertised the school to prospective parents. Shrewdly written, it appealed to both conservative and progressive instincts. The school's "practical character" would "educate not for an ideal world but for the world as it is." Pupils would become learned but also useful citizens, their education liberal enough to prepare them for various vocations in life. "It is not well to engraft every tree with the same fruit," the prospectus proclaimed, appealing to every mother who by the 1820s was willing to agree that her child was special. The school would discover and satisfy special needs, while enforcing a common morality and definite rules of behavior. To benevolent onlookers, this was "Yankee practicality" at its best.[32]

Bancroft's initial enthusiasm for the project shut out the gloom that had long oppressed him. Craving peace, quiet, and independence, he thought he had found in Round Hill the answer to the disquiet that marred his life. "If I were not restless," he rationalized, "I should not be desirous of improvement, honor and knowledge," all of which Round Hill would provide. There was "no water so tranquil that throwing stones into it did not make waves," which explained the assaults in Cambridge, and why the new endeavor would have a different outcome. Life in the country was a further attraction, for, Bancroft now discovered, he had all along felt a dislike "for the bustle of the world. I like to watch the shouts of the multitudes but had rather not scream with them."[33]

Charges were high—$300 a year at a time when a Harvard student could get by on $175. But to give each pupil full attention, the idealistic young masters limited enrollment, thereby lowering profits. Only boys between nine and twelve years of age were admitted, in the belief that this was the time when character molding produced the most beneficial results. The school would discourage the spirit of emulation, would award prizes only on special occasions, and would encourage the evolution of inborn talents, with full respect for individuality and particular needs.

The costs and the aims of the school determined its character. A few day students came from Northampton, but most pupils were boarders from well-to-do, prominent families moved by progressive ideas, willing to experiment, and delighted to entrust their boys to professional care. The children of Massachusetts Amorys, Appletons, Peabodys, and Sedgwicks mingled with South Carolina Pinckneys, Middletons, and Rutledges as the school's fame spread. Dominick Lynch, Sr., of New York sent his boy to Round Hill and persuaded Samuel Ward, Sr., to enroll Sam, Jr. Brother Henry soon followed. Such was their success that for a while the masters toyed with the idea of moving the school to a larger city. Catherine Prescott for one was delighted when they decided to stay in Northampton, as were most town folk, for Round Hill became one of the valley's major intellectual enterprises.[34]

The day's arrangement gave pupils the minimum time on their own, inhibiting mischievous tendencies. Up at six, they prayed and studied until breakfast at eight. Scheduled games and lessons lasted till nine at night. Every Saturday, weather permitting, hikes into the surrounding countryside allowed the boys to vent some of their energy, while in the summer longer trips, part walking, part riding, provided a diversion. The lads cut their own wood for fire, hunted in the forest for rabbits and birds, and at one time built on the surrounding slopes Croney Village, a small community of their own, soon demolished by Cogswell when forays of its occupants into Northampton for pies and food aroused angered neighbors.[35]

Fearful of elite bias, Bancroft and Cogswell insisted on a rough measure of democracy. Students wore uniforms and had no pocket money. Packages of sweets and preserves from home were confiscated to teach the parents, as much as the students, that no favoritism would be tolerated. But unlike Harvard, which under Kirkland made an effort to aid worthy poor scholars, neither Bancroft nor Cogswell ever tried to recruit pupils who would not otherwise have made it to Round Hill. The idea would have struck them as preposterous; in spite of all protestations to the contrary, an elite education was just that—an education for the elite.

Confident that efficient teaching methods and an excellent staff prepared the school's graduates better than most academies, Bancroft wanted to ensure Round Hillers advanced college standing. Lack of success, he later thought, hastened the school's demise. In spite of Bancroft's close ties to Harvard, Round Hill graduates could not pass automatically into the university. Hoping that Yale would be more pliant, Bancroft asked President Jeremiah Day to admit students to a higher standing and at reduced tuition. But Day, like Kirkland, refused. Round Hill did have four instructors who qualified for teaching at a German university, but this did not count much with college treasurers. Day agreed with Bancroft that students should be examined on their general intelligence and perception, rather than on specific books, but was not sure how that could be done. And while there was some justice in Bancroft's claim that parents should not be required to pay double tuition (one at Round Hill and another at college, where presumably the students would be in part repeating what they had acquired in Northampton), Yale refused to concede.[36]

For the time being the satisfaction of "forming a few of the rising generation to be somewhat more virtuous, more intelligent and more happy than they would otherwise have been" carried Bancroft along. From 25 boys in 1824 the number increased to 69 in 1825, and to 135 in May 1827. But the larger student body did not mean greater profits and involved more work. Cogswell refused to cut corners, especially on the food bill; believing that the students should get all the benefits of country life, he also hired a riding instructor and acquired a number of horses. Growing numbers meant new pressures and tensions, while the tasks seemed to grow more arduous. Some children, Cogswell thought, were "wild as young colts" and required "to be constantly curbed and guided by a very tight rein." Worse, they could be "most unreasonably dull." "Job could not have stood out under such a trial." By 1828 Cogswell complained that "there must be a change ere long or I die." The patience of the ever restless Bancroft gave out much earlier.[37]

In spite of appearances to the contrary, the partners disagreed almost from the beginning—over whom to hire and how to apportion the work load, over whether to paint the floors and how to keep the students from walking away with all the spoons. Differences in age, temperament, and character erupted in annoying disputes, with the more impulsive and speculative Bancroft chafing under the constraints. While Cogswell was often gone on money-raising expeditions, Bancroft was forced to stay behind and run the establishment by himself. Just as often Bancroft stole away to Boston and Worcester, from which a stream of gossipy letters were persistent reminders that Northampton was an isolated small country town, pretty and attractive, but inferior to the metropolis. Friends assumed that Bancroft spent his mornings in meditation and evenings in reflection, which was not true, but that was the way he would have liked it to be, if only Cogswell and the duties of the school were not in the way.[38]

After 1824 Bancroft realized also that he would not grow rich in this enterprise and tried to enlist his older partner in a series of speculative real estate ventures financed with other people's money. Aaron Bancroft approved: George was doing "right to turn . . . [his] exertions to profit . . . Mere literary reputation will not secure independence and provide for wants." Brother Thomas, apprenticed to a mechanic, later to a printer, and yet later to another master, failed in all three and needed help. "What can I do more?" Aaron asked; "in our country can not a young man of health, strength and opportunities earn his bread?" George thought he could, and wanted more. But Cogswell refused. "I prefer appropriating my money, if I have any to appropriate, to putting in order what I possess rather than increasing the number of my rags."[39]

Bancroft was eager to increase the number of his rags because he thought it time to establish a family. "Of all the blessings which ever fall to the lot of man, a virtuous and affectionate wife is one of the most highly valued," he had written some time before. While translating several of Goethe's poems, he feared, half in jest, that the public would consider him a ladies' man. To be a true ladies' man, a friend replied, one had to be a true man—firm, reliable, dignified, devoted to a noble purpose.[40] By 1826 Bancroft thought he had become that person and even if his noble purpose remained vague, he decided to look for a wife.

The search was short, for that spring he met Sarah, daughter of Jonathan Dwight of Springfield, one of the wealthier members of the community whose business interests included several banking enterprises and branch stores, held in lucrative partnership with his Boston-based brother Edmund. Edmund was married to Mary Harrison Eliot, daughter of the merchant Samuel Eliot, and one of Bancroft's benefactors. George knew the Dwights, who impressed him by their standing and social connections. If they lacked the Ticknors' intellectual brilliance, they knew how to make money, which was also attractive. Lucretia considered Sarah the perfect wife for her brother, but did not believe that such a match could take place, for the Dwights moved in a higher circle than the Bancrofts. Several times that summer Bancroft journeyed to Springfield—Sarah was twenty-three, pretty, and vivacious.

The courtship followed the rules of the day. Bancroft first wrote to Sarah's brother, who responded favorably, then wrote to Sarah, and though the proposal must have been expected and George certainly knew what the answer would be, she professed to be caught "entirely unprepared to give a decisive answer." While she did not want to be accused of coquetry, she needed time to think. Two weeks passed while Bancroft waited impatiently. Sarah then expressed herself favorably disposed; but no one, except Bancroft's parents, was to know of the engagement, and George was not to appear in Springfield except accidentally. The letter was signed "your friend," becoming "yours affectionately" a month later. By May he addressed his notes to "dearest Sally," ending them with "one who loves you."[41]

Finally, Sarah's father arrived in Northampton and Bancroft explained his prospects. A tour of the school and Bancroft's arguments persuaded Dwight that, even though the suitor's outlook was uncertain, the young man had drive and ambition. An agreement with Cogswell, George explained, would soon relieve him of most obligations to Round Hill, and free him for other pursuits. No specifics were mentioned, but the prospective father-in-law realized that his daughter's suitor was eager to broaden his horizons. By the time Dwight left for Springfield there was an understanding that Bancroft would devote part of his time to business.

By May 1826 the engagement was public knowledge and as congratulations poured in Bancroft's spirits soared. "Calm down," George Ticknor counseled, no one could be so unsettled and survive; only a quick marriage and the tranquillity of domestic life would quiet his young friend. But the house in which the young couple would live was not ready, and Sarah postponed the wedding till the early spring of 1827.[42]

"Of all the human beings, on you my affections unite and all my hopes," Bancroft wrote to Sarah. For her sake he would, if need be, sacrifice "ambition, love of action, of gain, of pleasure, of honor." In fact he had no intention of doing so, and found the long engagement burdensome. George spent much of his time hanging around the post office waiting for letters from Springfield, terrified at the possibility that Sarah might change her mind and bury his prospects. But these frustrations paled beside the happy life he envisioned, based on a clear understanding of matrimony with which Sarah agreed. The husband's duty was "to manage all external relations, to labor and to win," the wife's "to regulate the empire of the home, to soothe, to cheer." Both had to be gentle, faithful, frank, and affectionate, but the secrets of the kitchen and the mysteries of cupboards and closets were her domain. There was something incongruous about a lady "pursuing public admiration," Bancroft thought, and just in case Sarah had ideas—which she did not—Bancroft told her that no woman could reconcile "domestic and retiring loveliness" with "thirst for public applause."[43]

However, he hoped that his wife would broaden her horizons. The fact that women were unequipped to earn a living was no reason for limiting their interests. George well remembered the salons of Berlin, Paris, and Rome and their erudite, if somewhat forward hostesses. Sarah would never become a Madame de Staël, for Northampton was not ready for such a creature, but she could improve her education. He suggested books and offered guidance. Milton met with his approval—his imagination was always brilliant, although, not having been a member of the Levi Hedge school, his reasoning was unsatisfactory. And William Ellery Channing's essays "would do credit to any writer," Sarah cautiously agreed. Bancroft told her about Dante, and about the poet Felicia Hemans, and at times alluded to his own interests, but never in detail, and Sarah did not press. If they were to share "the elegancies . . . of intellectual delight" she had to know more, and Bancroft tried to hasten the process, talking to her about politics and books, which Sarah enjoyed in moderation.[44]

She was more interested in her future home, which Bancroft busily redecorated. Ever conscious of the woman's sphere, he consulted her through the mails, soliciting her advice but also telling her what would be best, so that the decisions were mostly his. In January 1827 she came to Northampton to inspect what he had done, and a minor quarrel about where to place a mirror showed that she would not accept his judgment as a matter of course. On the matter of the mirror Bancroft relented—"I am gentle enough to be docile," he wrote. But both knew that this was not the case.[45]

He frightened her sometimes, with his stern sense of duty, high demands, introspection, and criticism. His letters, full of ponderous philosophy and gloomy musings and disdain for what Sarah considered the ordinary occupations of life, were, she complained, inappropriate. But Bancroft sought to protect himself against yet another disappointment and also to reveal his inner self to a future wife who did not know much about him. His life, he emphasized, had been an anxious one, with care and labor constant, and very different from her sheltered, comfortable existence. This was a terrible world, with few people to trust. Lest thoughts of future felicities bewilder her she should remember that life meant duties as well as enjoyments. Could one be happy in this imperfect world, he asked, as his mood alternated between ecstasy and fear and joy and foreboding.[46]

By the end of January the house was ready and thoughts of the wedding replaced concerns for another world. The great event took place in March, in the bride's family house in Springfield, after which Bancroft gave a glittering ball in Northampton, where the young couple would live while he continued to teach.

For once he thought his happiness complete. No adjectives seemed adequate to describe Sarah's virtues; gentle and joyous, quiet and cheerful, her affectionate nature dispelled his gloom. "Every situation in life has its cares and perplexities," John T. Kirkland cautioned, but, he added, his young friend was as happy as this earthly existence allowed. The newlyweds toured Worcester and Boston, meeting family and friends, who commented on George's contentment. But Sarah found life in Northampton unpleasant and persisted in going back to Springfield whenever possible, while her husband was increasingly immersed in activities in which she had no part. Her one salvation—children—also delayed in coming.[47]

To free his mind from the cares of wife and school, and also to further his scholarly pursuits, Bancroft began to devote more time to study and writing. His first literary product, a slender volume of poems, published at his own expense, had appeared in 1823 and was dedicated to "the author's benefactor and friend," John Kirkland. Bancroft had been writing poems since his Harvard days, and European travels had provided many unresisted temptations. Some compositions had found their way into letters to Norton from Italy; friends had read others. Imitations of Byron, Goethe, Schiller, and Milton, they exposed a gushing, passionate young man, trying to synthesize and control his emotions by translating them into words.[48]

By his own admission the poems were "unripe and but of little" worth. Public reaction confirmed his judgment. Some "ingenious minds and lively fancies" appreciated his devotion to the ideal but "old and hardened Yankees," unmoved by his words, found them deficient. One friend, please with the effort, hoped that Bancroft would not make a career of it. He did not. His strength lay in prose. Later he posted a standing reward to anyone who brought him a copy of his poems for destruction.[49]

Of more lasting consequence was the decision to translate Heeren's *Reflections on the Politics of Ancient Greece* as a tribute to his teacher and also to replace John Potter in the Harvard curriculum. The manual, Bancroft suggested, would discipline the mind, and foster a thriving national literature. It would mark yet another effort to expand Harvard's intellectual horizons, reflecting the current interest in the Greek revolution. Heeren's dry, precise prose, without ornaments or literary allusions, lent itself to a correct and proper English, vapid and unexciting, but accurate enough.

Bancroft's sustained efforts to promote the text met little success. Aware that publicity was important, he was grateful for Everett's laudatory notice in the *North American Review* and saw to it that copies of the volume reached the right readers. He informed others that lack of proper education meant "ignorance and faithlessness," while appropriate historical knowledge would prevent the victory of demagogues. He also stressed the relevance of Greek history. But few were interested and, with low sales, the volume's influence was negligible. Potter remained the required Harvard text.[50]

Undaunted, Bancroft arranged for a translation of Heeren's *Manual of Ancient History* and suggested that Harvard adopt it in place of Adam's *Roman Antiquities*. "How much better to get a picture of antiquity than a narrow account of Rome!" Would not such a book put "that branch of study on a better footing"? In Holland and Germany everyone read the *Manual.* Ticknor, Everett, and Cogswell agreed, but the book's fate was no different from that of the earlier one. Kirkland did not allow Bancroft to use the Harvard name in an effort to lend the volume greater respectability, and the campaign to teach history in a philosophic spirit disintegrated.[51]

Such obstinacy merely reinforced Bancroft's disappointment with the college. Its authorities were adamant—they had nothing against the books but failed to see how to incorporate them into the curriculum. Potter and Adam had longevity and simplicity in their favor; to use Heeren required more knowledge, and his European fame was irrelevant. Nor were other institutions more responsive—Kingsley at Yale was noncommittal, and while several New York booksellers agreed to accept shipment, this did not guarantee larger sales.[52]

Bancroft's next suggestion also met a cool reception. He proposed to compose a complete manual of world history, part translation, part original, combining Heeren's works on Europe with an original outline on the United States. Even the promise that the four projected volumes would be dedicated to Kirkland elicited no favorable reaction. Having failed to get an appointment as professor of philology, as well as of theology, Bancroft also abandoned the hope of becoming a professor of history. Not even an appeal to members of the Corporation helped. "Our old master Heeren must therefore wait."[53]

Heeren could wait. But the young man in a hurry could not and was eager to try other things. Chafing under the boredom of Round Hill duties and the altercations of married life, Bancroft sought other occupations; and the desire to use his educational advantages and his conception of the man of letters drove him to devote more time to scholarship.

He had been dabbling in literature since 1823, when he published a short notice of Schiller's minor poems in the *North American Review*. A long-standing acquaintance with Jared Sparks, its editor, promised an open forum for whatever he could produce. And because the young author considered himself competent in history, philology, theology, and education, the contributions would cover a broad range of subjects and would help establish an independent scholarly career.

The *Edinburgh Review,* edited by Francis Jeffrey, had set the pattern for American magazines. Although Bancroft bemoaned the slighting tone with which it treated the United States, he admired the *Review*'s moral stance and language, as well as its wide influence and authority.

American critics too wished to be the scourge of authors, upholders of standards, and pillars of intellect and moral certainty. The *North American Review* and the *American Quarterly Review* told the public "what to seek and what to shun, in morals or in intellect." More specifically, they sought to mold an American culture based on moral religious convictions, buttressed by sound political doctrines. This was the tradition of literary evaluation Bancroft followed.[54]

For a long series of articles on European literature and thought, Bancroft drew extensively on his Göttingen lecture notes, but he shied away from pre–romantic critical standards he had encountered in Germany. Upright Bostonians could implicitly trust his judgment even when dealing with not altogether suitable novels or plays because his evaluations remained their own. In full agreement with Judge Joseph Story, Andrews Norton, Edward Everett, and Caleb Cushing, he demanded that literature have educational value appropriate for the community. A Harvard student, steeped in moral philosophy, knew what that value was and what the community needed.

The fate of nations, Ticknor had written, depended on their literature. Bancroft, the preacher and educator, ready to shift his talents in other directions while remaining a steward of public culture, proposed to encourage "the dissemination of the principles of justice, learning and liberty" by examining the intellectual achievements of other nations. Such an evaluation also had universal implications, he believed, since the "voice of America, deciding on the literature of Europe, resembles the voice of posterity more than anything else that is contemporaneous, can do." Ticknor had shown how "corrupt literature" poisoned "the life blood of the people" in France and Spain; Bancroft would demonstrate the influence of literature in Germany, where the results were more encouraging and thus more useful for Americans. "The moral vigor which alone can strive for liberty and honor" had infused Germany with beneficial results and would also accomplish great things at home.[55]

Following Levi Frisbie's agenda for American men of letters, Bancroft appointed himself an overseer of national consciousness and argued that the German model was appropriate because that nation, like the United States, had only recently arrived at self-awareness and, again like the United States, was creating appropriate cultural expressions. German men of letters, fulfilling their mission as guardians of moral life, produced a pattern immediately applicable to the United States. Bancroft ascribed to German men of letters qualities that, while in Europe, he doubted they possessed; but some distortion was legitimate for the readers of the *North American Review* and other magazines. He credited the Germans with deep religious convictions and with relative freedom to pursue a literary vocation. Although Bancroft knew better, he implied that invidious court patronage was absent and that eager readers everywhere spurred men to high achievement. The simple conclusion was that Americans could do the same.[56]

Of course the United States lacked great universities, sizable libraries, and a long tradition of secular learning, but for compensation it had statesmen, liberties "which save us from the dominion of established usage," and a "decidedly more common" general intelligence. The universal love of democracy, buttressed by a free heritage, untouched by the "deluding recollections" of a feudal past, offset the lack of learning. Besides, Europe's cultural achievements paled beside American social conditions, in harmony with the eternal laws of morality. And physical isolation was the nations's salvation—"the ocean divides us from the fashions as well as the commotions of Europe." The United States could learn much from the Germans but "whatever benefits America may receive she will not remain in debt. Thank God! She has never been in debt to Europe."[57]

Little was original in these outbursts of literary patriotism, although the examples Bancroft cited—a fairly complete survey of German thought—were. Andrews Norton had long called for a literature growing out of and perpetuating the country's ideals, under the slogan "we are in advance of the rest of the world." Francis C. Gray had urged American authors to widen their horizons, and Bancroft was showing them why they should. While William E. Channing, Franklin Dexter, William Tudor, Richard Henry Dana, Sr., Theophilus Parsons, and Edward Everett bemoaned America's cultural inadequacies, which they attributed to a revolution that had absorbed the attention of its best minds, Bancroft implied it need not remain so. All decried materialism and the contempt for intellectual endeavor. But Bancroft did not consider those traits inherent in the national character, unlike Dana, who felt that the talent for action was inconsistent with an abstract, idealistic, reflective cast of mind necessary for a literary rebirth. True, escapist attitudes drove readers to Fielding, Smollett, and Richardson rather than to Cotton Mather's *Magnalia Christi Americana,* that antidote for novel-sick minds, but this would change once native writers combined their best qualities in a literature fit for a free society.[58]

The great question, as countless magazine articles pointed out, was the relevance of foreign models for the United States. Against the nationalists Bancroft championed the universalists. Interest in other cultures never deformed a literature, but rather strengthened and defined national character, maintaining originality by liberating the public from provincial prejudices. Truly great works of art were of interest to all. Writers who catered to contemporary prejudices produced books of transient fashion. A great literature both answered local needs and met universal standards.[59]

But Bancroft's standards stemmed from moral philosophy, and while he relied heavily on Bouterwek's lectures, his articles had an unmistakable local imprint. The outcome was curious—Bancroft could not help but admire the German achievements, imagination, and enthusiasm, yet, knowing what they could lead to, he remained skeptical. While praising Germany for being a perfect democracy of letters (precisely what he had found intolerable only a few years earlier), he favored those who, isolated from the world, safeguarded the purity of their endeavors and were saved from general pollution. This too contradicted an earlier outburst, which castigated German scholars for not contributing enough to the society of which they were a part.

Everyone who had something to say could teach at a German university, one article stated; how different from the United States, where (as Bancroft knew by sorry experience) a few men monopolized all the good posts. But after this sneer in Harvard's direction (where, Bancroft implied, people still put their money into masonry rather than instruction), he also took the customary swipe at higher criticism (when carried too far). Much gossip, charming anecdotes, a wealth of biographical details, and attention to context livened up the pages, but the student of Henry Ware, Sr., and Levi Hedge always managed to say the expected. Thus Wieland was accused of yielding unfortunately to his animal nature when he made the birth of an illegitimate child the highlight of an epic. Bancroft said little on the subject of philosophy—a few sentences on Kant, Fichte, Schelling, Hegel, and Jacobi showed only that he was aware of their existence. Herder lacked creativity, Lessing was a better critic than the Schlegels, Novalis was unacceptable though interesting, and Schiller in the end was superior to Goethe, who had suggested that man was not born to be free at the very time, Bancroft emphasized, of the American Revolution. The greatest of German writers thus failed to fulfill the central mission of men of letters—to combine the culture of art with the service of humanity.

These thoughts shaped the numerous articles Bancroft wrote on German ideas, classical learning, physical education, poetry, and history, both ancient and modern. They brought his name before the public and established a literary reputation. At the same time composition was an onerous chore, the pay was low, not all editors were tolerant, and circulations were limited. Yet the desire to reach ever wider audiences, to leave a mark and be useful, drove him on. Thinking he had found a new vocation, Bancroft translated, wrote, and edited tirelessly, rarely passing by a chance to send in yet another article to prove that he could do it. The occupation of letters was as honorable as any other.

Growing recognition and a heavier correspondence testified to other changes. Gone was the quiet, diffident, subservient young man who tried to please and expected guidance. The favorable response to his writings fostered inner strength and a stubbornness that helped him parry, indeed thrive on, attacks whenever a review aroused controversy. He also learned to use newly found weapons for his own good. It was a happy coincidence that Bancroft, taken with the poems of Felicia Hemans, wrote a laudatory review of her works, knowing well that Norton was her American publisher and friend. Mrs. Hemans was grateful. But other authors, whom Bancroft treated more harshly, were not, and he found himself at odds with assertive editors who expected reviewers to bend their views.

"I had as lief cheat a man of money as give him an opinion which I know to be false," Bancroft asserted, a principle with which the editor of the North American Review agreed in theory. Practice was different, and the budding intellectual chafed at the all-pervasive "we" in the articles. "My own personality glimmers through every page," Bancroft complained; "I" was the appropriate pronoun. There was only one mind at work in the article—the author's; to have another mind reign was intolerable—"I value myself too much for that."[60]

A translation of Goethe's poems was read by two clergymen to whom Bancroft prudently submitted his copy prior to publication. If the stewards of public morals approved, he was safe, but Jared Sparks rejected the poems on the grounds that their excesses were inappropriate for disciplined Bostonians. Words like "emotions, love, affection, sympathy, sensations, feelings," as well as flights of fancy and "soft abstractions," he told Bancroft, should be used sparingly; readers wanted sober assessments, not emotional tantrums. But Bancroft had no intention of writing "milk and water thing[s] suitable to the meridian of Salem and Boston." When Sparks altered sections of one essay, he felt that he had "wasted [his] time, my good nature is made a fool of." He was not "a hireling writer or novice" to put up with such treatment. The young man who wished to live in peace with all was learning that even a scholarly career had drawbacks.[61]

Bancroft thought he understood the mission of the *North American Review*. "I owe it to the cause of learning if I speak out at all, to raise my voice, however weak, against perpetuating old abuses the continuance of which the improvement of men two hundred years should have thrown aside." This was the true mission of men of letters, and the only valid standard of judgment was reason and justice. By that he would "stand in good report or ill, in friendship and where friends become enemies." The ultimate test—"the most equitable of all"—was public opinion. Without realizing it, he had found the justification for his actions he would employ for the rest of his life.[62]

To buttress his stand Bancroft defended the respectability of his pursuits. Literature was a profession, like the church or the law. The German universities assembled men of learning, offered them careers of honor and utility, benefiting society by providing "an earnest and speculative character to the common mind," and molding the spirit of the nation. The American republic also had to recognize talent, opening to men of letters "the narrow road of emulation," establishing "the empire of the mind and intelligence, lavishing on genius the highest honor." An egalitarian society which discounted the prestige of ranks and hierarchies ought to bestow preeminence upon those who relied entirely on inner resources for success.[63]

In the United States, Bancroft thought, no one realized how tedious writing was, how lonely and unrewarded its practitioners. To merchants, lawyers, and clergymen, men of letters seemed idlers who lived in poverty in garrets, where they belonged. Identifying himself with those who braved disapproval, poverty, and ridicule for the sake of scholarship, Bancroft extolled the fervid spirit that made them independent of fortune and the world. Their "social occupations" were useful. By keeping "aloof from the din of business" because its harshness, greed, and shallowness clashed with their own sense of mission, they gave "the pursuit of knowledge the ardent love which the world could not satisfy."[64]

Those who tired of the seemingly hopeless struggle cut a ridiculous figure. Far better to stay with their craft than abandon it for the hustle of the marketplace. "Is not Blumenbach, among his collections of skulls, better employed for science and mankind than the ambitious Cuvier has ever been in the Chamber of Deputies?"[65] It was not the function of scholars to become politicians (a veiled slap at several friends who disagreed). The contribution of scholars to a democratic society was infinitely more important; far from being parasites, they were members of the productive classes, men of the people, toiling for their bread as honorably and respectably as others, and in tune with popular needs and emotions.

By showing the interaction between scholarship and society, Bancroft sought to dissolve his own isolation and also demolish charges of an aristocracy of intellect, effeminate and useless. "Poor men, the sons of poor men, children of their work, depending on their own resources, not for fame and influence only but for their bread and clothing know best how to appreciate the worth of naked humanity," he wrote to Sparks. Men of letters and the masses were close allies. Great literature was only the end product of a process begun among "the people," their imagination shaped into recognizable form by the scholars. In Germany men from the lowest classes attained the highest levels and their writings reflected "the moral energy of the people" rising against opposition, overcoming indifference, triumphing over contempt.[66]

There could be no aristocracy of intellect in a republic. Men of letters did not know more than other worthy members of the laboring classes, nor were their judgments inherently superior. In this society, the educated public, exercising its common sense, was the final tribunal. The public, "that invisible, impartial personification of the high culture and authority of the nation," in the end decided on worth. And Bancroft was willing to trust the people's judgment.[67]

The seed of an intellectual outlook that would flower in the next decade gave a distinct quality to that plea. Proximity to the people, Bancroft continued, made all true scholars members of the popular parties of progress, on the pattern of German men of letters who had become watchdogs of the people's liberties and had "awakened the nation to an effort for independence." American men of letters were members of "the laboring classes" and "links in the chain that binds together the great and widely diversified elements of society." They rose "from the general mass" and still belonged to it, claiming "just compensation" because they transmitted knowledge to future generations. As teachers, preachers, writers, and editors, they molded "the moral existence of contemporary millions" by providing the information a developing society required.[68]

This elaborate self-justification, which made letters into a profession, was designed to counteract the hostility Bancroft thought surrounded him. Never one to blame himself, he ascribed all his troubles to an unappreciative society, contemptuous of pure scholarship. And when this plea for the legitimacy of his own pursuits elicited little support, his bitterness increased. Since he could not persuade his contemporaries of the worth of a literary career, he plunged into pursuits more congenial to the community of which he was a part.

The budding man of letters discovered his money-making talents and taste for speculation, for which his new family connections provided a widening field. At first Bancroft became something of an adviser to his father-in-law, passing on information about the state of woolen manu-facturers, about plans to improve navigation on the James River, about anything that could bear on the far flung Dwight interests. Later, in trips to Vermont, New York, Albany, Philadelphia, Washington, and Balti-more, he learned the rudiments of banking, and began several ventures that turned the scholar into a man of means.

While he was always sorry to be away from Sarah, "his dearest puss," his "little angel," such prospects only made his own little world, with its concerns, problems, and boredom, more confining. Sarah shared his dis-enchantment with Northampton and assumed that a move to Springfield, where her family lived, would do them good. Bancroft remained doubt-ful; perhaps he did not want to exchange his hard-won independence for the domination of the Dwights. For the time being he decided to stay in Northampton, while Sarah tried to make him content, but that was not easy, given Bancroft's restlessness, moodiness, and temperament.[69]

It was only a matter of time before Bancroft severed his connections with Round Hill. As he took care of scrapes and bruises and saw to it that pupils had the required number of baths, he was "conscious of sufficient courage to sustain collision with men" rather than "restraining the petu-lance and assisting the weakness of children." While he tried "to labour like a German," his fervent proclamations of loyalty to Round Hill and the teaching of the young ended; the question was how to get out of the arrangement. "At present I am doomed to bear the petulance, restrain the frivolity, mend the tempers, and improve the mind of children," but, he noted hopefully, not for long.[70]

He could not enter the boys' life with relish as Cogswell did. It was Cogswell who went hiking and skating with his wards, who developed close ties to many of them and whom they later remembered as the formative influence of their early years. Several recalled their other in-structor, Bancroft, as a stickler for details and a stern taskmaster. "He seemed to be more earnestly intent on learning for himself than on help-ing others to learn," a student wrote. Others called him the Critter behind his back and whenever possible exploited his shortsightedness in their pranks, crawling about on all fours while Bancroft searched for his misplaced spectacles. Once a pupil threw an overripe watermelon at the wall next to which he stood.[71]

To escape dull recitations and poorly aimed fruit, Bancroft continued to write. Welcomed by Robert Walsh, editor of the *American Quarterly Review,* he published several articles in the Pennsylvania capital, in spite of William H. Prescott's jibe that there were not enough readers in Philadelphia to make it worth his while. He even considered moving there. Rumors of a new university in New York led him to suggest his candidacy—only to be told that the plans were uncertain. The $1,600 annual income from the school was not enough to sustain a growing taste for luxury and scholarly pursuits, even when augmented by Dwight funds. Perhaps Cincinnati needed a new review and publishing house; the West might be the answer—with its rising population, growing real estate values, and opportunities for speculation. But these were idle calculations.[72]

Bancroft's thoughts also drifted to politics, with which literature and scholarship were intertwined. He closely followed Edward Everett's career. As the pitfalls facing the Federalists were the topics of conversation at the Ticknors' and the Prescotts', Bancroft weighed the chances of their opponents. For the time being he remained undecided, while agreeing with his brother-in-law, Congressman John Davis (Eliza's husband), who wrote from Washington that "the darkness seems to increase every moment." Davis was trying to cement an alliance with the West to guard New England from the greedy tyranny of the South. He also worshiped Daniel Webster—"the boasted statesmen of the South are mere pygmies to him."[73]

For some time Bancroft pondered these options. "Public opinion is not with the timid, who can resolve on nothing, nor with the prudent who wait until opportunity deserts them." He now admitted that Everett, who had abandoned Harvard for Congress, had not taken the wrong turn. Political influence could enable Everett to accomplish more in the councils of state than in a classroom. Was not Edmund Burke a scholar and statesman? And had not Bancroft decided that the man of letters should also be the man of action?[74]

When Levi Lyman and the Northampton Board of Selectmen asked him, as one of the town's leading citizens, to deliver the Fourth of July oration in 1826, Bancroft seized the opportunity to voice a message he had considered for some time.

That day was one for stocktaking and soul-searching everywhere. Many speakers commented on the political, social, and economic changes of the previous five decades, trying to tie seemingly divergent threads of growth into a meaningful pattern, aiming to ease the disquiet created by novelty. The economy moved toward larger units of production, marketing, and finance. Population expanded and political leaders of a type unknown to Washington and John Adams took office. Divided churches and disestablishment reflected the breakdown of traditional support for the social order. The presidential difficulties of John Quincy Adams, the tariff debate in Congress, suffrage disputes in New York, and new labor organizations created the impression of a system out of joint. Signs appeared of the vast reform movement by which Americans tried to adjust morally and intellectually to new conditions. And the orators called for a fresh perspective to connect the past with the present, to allay the fear of change, to explain away turbulence, and to recover the promise many thought America had lost. The future could be as glorious as the past.

Bancroft's first political speech attempted to quiet the uncertainty aroused by widening suffrage. By placing seemingly new developments in historical context, he interpreted present disorders as the unfolding of principles inherent in the American way of life. A nation in possession of a regenerate past had nothing to fear from the future. It had only to understand the way in which general principles worked themselves out at the moment.

American history informed many discourses on that special occasion. But other speakers divided on its significance. The more conservative hoped to preserve past achievements, the more radical urged further improvement. The former rejoiced that the glorious revolution was over; the latter expected a renewed unfolding. One side warned of infirmities in human nature, the other asserted that the American setting enabled men to triumph over weaknesses. Some glorified the Constitution and its checks and balances; others recalled the promises of the preamble to the Declaration of Independence.[75]

Bancroft found qualified historical grounds for both positions. To those who worried about America's future he gave a reassuring answer. They lived in a happy society where moral order pervaded all classes, where intelligence and social equality prevailed, and where the plow rested in the hands of its owner. The political system fostered the health of the community, its liberal principles establishing the sovereignty of the people, in whom power resided, theoretically and practically. "The government is a democracy, a determined, uncompromising, democracy, administered by the people or by the people's responsible agents." The nation's prosperity and achievements ran no danger of collapse.[76]

Bancroft also reassured those who hoped for further improvement. "The popular voice is all powerful with us, this is our oracle; this we acknowledge is the voice of God." The people speaking at election time were guided by "the deliberate convictions of mankind, reasoning on the causes of their own happiness." The United States was a "corporation, invested with limited powers for accomplishing specific purposes, based on population, not property," with laws favoring the diffusion of wealth. The government was radical insofar as it aimed to "facilitate the prompt reform of abuses" and essentially leveling insofar as it prohibited hereditary distinctions and discouraged artificial ones. Further reform of remaining abuses was inherent in the American system.[77]

Beneath the quotable slogans lay an organic interpretation of American development that owed little to Bancroft's European education and everything to moral philosophy. Under the cover of panegyrics to freedom and liberty, Bancroft stressed the sentiments of community, the interconnectedness between the past and the present, and the structure of a society growing out of the moral law with a traditional pattern of behavior inherent to the people. "Liberty knows nothing of passion," the dutiful student of Ware and Hedge proclaimed, "she is the daughter of God and dwells in unchanging tranquillity behind his throne." The discipline of passions by higher faculties, the subordination of natural inclinations to the prescriptions of conscience, these precepts of moral philosophy Bancroft thought Americans abundantly observed.[78]

The oration was far from "radical, democratic, levelling and unrighteous," as Bancroft jokingly described it; and the response was uniformly favorable. Levi Lyman approved, and the speech "pleased the country folk mightily." They may have been "too sober and not excitable, attached to hereditary usage and hereditary faith," but that was just what Bancroft exploited. Anne Ticknor applauded, as did her husband, who found little objectionable in this "excellent specimen of liberal democracy." Nothing in the address clashed with accepted notions—indeed a few months later Bancroft wrote to Edward Everett "Provoco ad Populum—the right of appealing to the people is never to be taken from a politician," and on the basis of the speech, no one disputed his judgments.[79]

For the time being Bancroft did not explore further the meaning of his pronouncements. But his public exposure confirmed what he had long suspected—in this period the advantage lay with the orator who could harangue a crowd or convince an assembly by manipulating words and enunciating creeds. Men of letters could thus establish a bridge between the political system and the public, the organization and its constituency. Writing was action. "Literature thrives but in the midst of busy scenes where mind is brought into collision with mind, talent developed by emulation, and rewarded by golden honors and wide distinction." Political contests "quicken natural talents and furnish every facility and every inducement for their display." Gone was the image of the recluse in the garret. "What possible conception can a man in his study form of public popular transactions? What mere student dreams of the manner in which negotiations are conducted by the cabinet? How then can a recluse write philosophic history?" The budding politician and scholar in 1828 called on men of letters to be "conversant with practical life to delineate it accurately." They had to be "tossed upon the stormy ocean of public existence, and see the state driven to and fro by the angry convulsions of opposing interests" before sketching "the realities of the scene." Their mission was to exercise "intellectual powers" in directing "the taste and governing the thoughts of many."[80]

On a personal level the conclusions were clear. "I have to get my living by my wits," Bancroft decided. "I will meet the future as it approaches and shape my course according to the stream on which I sail." To satisfy his needs he would break out of the customary mold. His interests were about to coalesce in a fusion between the past and the future, between history and politics. The clergyman-schoolmaster was on his way to becoming a man of letters and of action. Americans, prosaic in business, like the "Israelites of old" were "a heavy mass . . . yet preceded by a pillar of fire." In 1829 Bancroft aspired to carry the torch, and for new purposes. "We have yet to reduce to practice the principles of our government," he said; "they have not as yet entirely pervaded society." In the next decade he would explore the meaning of those cryptic remarks.[81]

Jacksonian Politics

V

POLITICS AND THE PAST

IN 1834 George Bancroft, formerly of Round Hill, published the first volume of his *History of the United States.* Almost at the same time, local newspapers proclaimed his political allegiance.

There was nothing unusual in either step. New Englanders had been writing history since the first settlement, and political involvement accorded with the duties society envisioned for men of letters. Nonetheless Bancroft's choices were different; they changed his life and shaped the course of the many years left him. In a sense he entered politics to become a better historian, and he wrote history to explain his political career.

The young man who had floundered from one occupation to another then settled on his true vocations. He turned into a historian and politician, the man of letters and intellect, as well as the man of action he had always wanted to be. En route the impoverished schoolmaster acquired some means, and the promise of more; to be the son-in-law of the Dwights paid handsome dividends. The ineffective preacher who would not move his parishioners to piety learned to exploit oratorical talents to sway voters, and the inconsequential reviewer of magazines with limited circulation and influence became a household figure far beyond the confines of his native region.

Accomplishments bred self-confidence, lessened bitterness, and resolved inner tensions. Bancroft became more open to outside influences, less self-righteous, and more tolerant. He adeptly exploited opportunities when the notoriety that had hurt his chances in Boston's circles turned into wider popularity, and the much sought-after independence freed him from financial constraints and from other people's supervision.

Bancroft could have become another able young man, like George Ticknor or Edward Everett, of worthy background who married well and never really worked for a living. Both adopted the values of the group to which education and marriage admitted them and remained loyal to their environment. Ticknor made his oracular pronouncements in exclusive drawing rooms and set himself up as the guardian of a tradition about which ever fewer people cared. Everett, determined to safeguard that same tradition, thought politics the better route, but disappointed many in his decision by squandering his talents in unsuitable callings. Yet he long remained Bancroft's model, with one difference; Everett cast his fortunes with the powers that be, while Bancroft chose what seemed the way of the future. Ultimately his judgment, not Edward Everett's, prevailed.

Radical though his future reputation would be, at the end of the 1820s Bancroft still held highly conventional views. He knew the value of his talent for oracular pronouncements that left an audience free to decide whither the political winds blew. But that talent remain unfocused, confined, for the time being, to vague statements with which no one quarreled. Not much had happened to sharpen his vision. The scurrilous presidential campaign of 1828 had failed to clarify any distinct trends. Politics, said the Boston *Atlas,* was "a confused pestilential and putrefying mixture of a mighty swamp, full of frog like sycophants and crocodile demagogues." To a young man in search of a usable political outlook, the national scene offered little choice.[1]

The most striking feature of local politics as Bancroft then assessed the situation was New England's conservatism. People dissatisfied with the old candidates hesitated to vote for new ones. They supported John Quincy Adams, but the National Republicans aroused little enthusiasm and the Democrats were showing strength. Anyone considering a public career had to take account both of existing discontent and of pervasive inertia. Unable to make up his mind, Bancroft gave his support to the group his friends favored. John Quincy Adams had the right answers, he suggested, but his followers seemed old, out of tune with the times, and badly split amongst themselves.

The alternative, for the time being, remained unpalatable. With few exceptions Yankees rejected the Democratic Party, even though some Essex Junto renegades, like Theodore Lyman, became Jacksonians. But the Boston Democrats were an unappealing and disunited lot, with David Henshaw, John K. Simpson, and Andrew Dunlop (the Statesman Party) forming a solid front against another faction, the Jackson Republicans, which included Henry Orne, William Ingalls, and John P. Boyd, and several committees of correspondence. Henshaw's assertion that monopolies were contrary to the natural rights of man, since a previous generation had no power or right to barter away the privileges and rights of the succeeding, sounded a familiar theme. But other Democratic pronouncements, couched in the familiar Jacksonian slogans, were thus far totally unacceptable to Bancroft. At the same time Edward Everett's re-election to Congress proved that the people could vote for meritorious officeholders and that perhaps Jackson's opponents had a chance. Still a National Republican after the presidential contest, Bancroft did not interpret Adams's "Waterloo defeat" as a sign that the cause was lost. "New England [will] rise with the new party that will be formed," he thought. "If I can in any wise serve you this winter," he told Everett, "don't omit to allow me." The young man who had sided with the merchants in 1824 in their outcry against the tariff bill was in his natural political habitat.[2]

Two years later, in 1830, a local Northampton organization of less respectable antecedents than the National Republicans put Bancroft's name on the ballot, apparently without his knowledge, and elected him to the state legislature. When he declined the seat he pleased but also surprised his brother-in-law, who knew Bancroft's ambitions. Later in the year Bancroft also rejected the suggestions from a Springfield Democratic newspaper and from others that he run for Congress or the state senate.[3]

"A portion of the people . . . may and probably will become corrupt and unjust," Bancroft philosophized, "but with us the great body of citizens is sure of remaining uncontaminated, we have far more to apprehend from the headlong ambition or downright corruption of those who are the depositories of power." Such casual statements, expressed in articles, in conversations at elegant suppers in Boston, and in letters, explained why different political alignments sought his support. Since each group could interpret them in its own favor, Bancroft, between 1828 and 1834, maintained open bridges to National Republicans, former Essex Junto members, nascent Whigs, and all manner of Democrats. Few conservatives publicly questioned the people's virtue and common sense, and references to corruption could apply to the Democratic administration in Washington or to their enemies in Boston. Artisan organizations took heart when a member of the Dwight family openly lauded the wisdom

of the people. Both sides welcomed florid sentences in favor of the existing social and political order whose genius, Bancroft declared, lay in
leaving "everything to find its own natural level, to throw no obstacles
in the way of the free progress of honest industry, to melt all the old
castes of society into one mass . . . and to prevent anything like a privileged order in the state."[4]

None of the early political overtures attracted Bancroft, whose affairs
were still unsettled. Private pursuits for the time being seemed more
urgent; and he saw no future in leading independent splinter groups with
little political clout, especially since people like Alexander H. Everett
judged them disguised Jacksonians with little support in the state. While
not one of the Massachusetts aristocracy, Bancroft did not wish to lend
himself to the demagogic needs of others, and his friends agreed. John
Davis suggested that no good could come from representing the liberal
democracy of Northampton in the Massachusetts General Court. Men of
"such consideration and power in the commonwealth that their opinion
is necessarily felt" thought likewise, among them George Ticknor, Edward Everett, and Jared Sparks. The prospective candidate remained
silent.[5]

Silence reflected a confusion that the next few years failed to dispel;
the very people delighted with his choice were themselves in the thick
of political battles. John Davis, who defined politics as a noisy, brawling,
unprincipled business, which must invite disgust in every well-inclined
mind, nevertheless aspired to ever higher public offices. Edward Everett
had left Harvard for Congress and in spite of his protestations seemed to
enjoy Washington, while counseling for Bancroft devotion to literature
and home life. Joseph Cogswell, in Washington busy selling shares in
Round Hill to members of the Senate, found the capital full of strife and
corruption—but also exhilarating and intellectually stimulating.

Lack of a clear political commitment did not preclude involvement in
the burning issues of the day. Unable to decide where to cast his lot,
Bancroft opted for a more traditional way to make his views known. It
had always been the duty of men of letters to apply knowledge to public
problems; by enlightening readers they could sway votes. The quarrel
between President Jackson and the Bank of the United States offered the
chance to establish a reputation for wisdom, principled opinion—and
availability. By dealing with the issue Bancroft could enunciate cherished economic opinions. When he offered to assess the report of the
House Ways and Means Committee in favor of renewing the Bank's
charter for the *North American Review,* the editor, Alexander H. Everett,
delightedly agreed.

In preparation Bancroft read widely and conducted an extensive correspondence. He familiarized himself with Adam Smith and Jean Baptiste Say, with the fate of the French assignats and of the American continentals, with Austrian currency experiments, and with English banking. Henry Dwight, brother of Bancroft's father-in-law, wrote from Geneva, New York, furnishing proof that the grasping, oppressive, and monopolistic Bank bribed congressmen and abused its authority. The institution was "a caged tyger" [sic] that served only itself, not the government or the community. John Davis did not go that far but also believed in limiting its authority. A monopoly of capital, in the hands of any set of men, however well disposed, was dangerous. When Bancroft made up his mind which side to support, he realized that many would disagree, but since opinions cut across party lines, he assumed there was nothing heretical about his position.[6]

Like most writers, Bancroft identified banking with currency but, unlike some Jacksonians, did not propose to restrict the privilege of issuing paper money to the government. Nor did his article express antipathy to banks or blame those institutions for causing price fluctuations through expansion and contraction of notes. The evils of the United States Bank, Bancroft suavely noted, stemmed from its privileged position, its quasi-monopolistic practices, and its violation of natural laws, the best regulators of business. Competition among banks, Adam Smith had said, was a virtue with wholesome effects. The status of the United States Bank, Bancroft declared, went counter to the community's best interest.

In forty closely printed pages he refuted the arguments of the House Ways and Means Committee report and demanded supervision of the United States Bank, "an opulent institution, enjoying exclusive privilege . . . a capital so immense as to have an almost controlling influence on the money markets of the country." While Bancroft acknowledged the Bank's merit, he thought its defenders exaggerated. "The sun would still rise and set and the day be spent in its usual business and merchandising be bought and sold and bills of exchange negotiated, even without a machine so vast and so very useful as the Bank of the United States."[7]

Furthermore, in defending the Bank, the committee had misinterpreted the facts of economic life and the Constitution of the United States. All banks were subject to the laws of necessity, by which Bancroft meant rules guided "by the immutable principles of competition and liberty." In the final analysis, trade in money was like trade in anything else and "should be left with similar concerns to the jurisdiction of the several states under the guarantees of the Federal Union." The budding banker, with a sizable dowry and other gifts to invest and in the process of embarking on some speculations of his own, was determined to safeguard that competition and liberty which would make or break his own future, as well as that of his relatives and countless others.[8]

The implied advocacy of nonrenewal, with which Bancroft concluded, would restore the natural mechanism temporarily unbalanced by laws harmful to social harmony. This placed him, at least nominally, in the Democratic camp. But at the same time the article was free of Jacksonian vocabulary, lacking the traditional phrases about oppression, moneyed powers, and aristocracies, and tallied closely with what the Bank's non-Democratic opponents said.

But the mere implication, though not spelled out, that renewal of the charter was unnecessary alarmed Alexander H. Everett; the *North American Review* could not take the Democratic side. To pacify readers, contributors, and local opinion, Everett appended a short note stating that Bancroft favored renewal. To the furious author he wrote that nonrenewal would be fatal to the country and added that those not in the know might conclude that Bancroft advocated Jackson's reelection. Bancroft admitted that this was not the case although he was sure the Democrats would win in 1832, regardless of the stand of the *North American Review*. Also, lest he be charged with political deviance, he expressed the hope that in four years "the star of New England" might ascend through "harmony, tact and exertion," consigning the detested Democrats into oblivion. Good National Republicans concurred.[9]

His next step was of the kind that in later life earned him the reputation of an unsavory political manipulator ready to trample on principle. While the new issue of the *North American Review* carried a long statement in support of the Bank, Bancroft sent an offprint of his article to Martin Van Buren, along with a note disclaiming responsibility for the last sentence. In addition he tried to gain further publicity for his views. When Van Buren did not reply, Bancroft transferred his attentions to the *American Quarterly Review,* a Philadelphia publication always ready to print his scholarly reviews. But Robert Walsh, its editor, rejected what he too considered an anti-Bank piece and advised the author to stick to literary issues. Bancroft knew the *Review* favored renewal; what he did not know was that Walsh was reputed to be in the pay of the Bank. William H. Prescott, one of the few aware of Bancroft's overtures to the Democratic heir apparent, watched his friend's "misguided maneuverings" and wondered where he would "break out next."[10]

By the end of 1831 some Bostonians, contrary to his protestations, considered Bancroft a Jacksonian, which unnerved Sarah, who, unlike her husband, detested notoriety and did not relish his newly found fame. She thought that he had angered the friends of the Bank, among them Uncle Edmund Dwight, who told Judge Story, Daniel Webster, and others that Bancroft had written under the direction of his father-in-law to defend the family business. But Bancroft also noted connections between the Dwights and David Henshaw's Commonwealth Bank, as well as the money-making spirit that animated dinner conversations at Uncle Ned's. It was sad that Sarah cried, but she was being overly sensitive. "There is nothing in my position in society to justify the imputation of subversive principles," he reassured her, even if some were bent on enlisting against him the entire anti-Jackson party.[11]

The placid reaction to the article encouraged Bancroft to think that he could continue to play both sides of the issue, remaining a National Republican while endearing himself to the Democrats. A Boston bookseller expressed the wish that he write more and a member of the Harvard Corporation intimated that there might be a teaching appointment for him at the college. Many wanted the Bancrofts to abandon the wilds of Northampton and reside in town. Meanwhile, Bancroft stuck by his views that the Bank violated "the rights of all capitalists, the dictates of justice, the rights of free competition . . . which ought to be held supremely sacred in a land of equal liberty." A man bent on working out his own salvation and enjoying a newly found self-confidence considered such twists and turns essential.[12]

Working out his own salvation meant, in addition to a delicate political balancing act, augmenting the family income. Dwight generosity enabled Bancroft to settle most of his debts, but authorship did not pay. The believer in capitalism and in free competition therefore proceeded to do what his growing taste for speculation, books, and comfortable living demanded. His quick learning ability, theoretical knowledge, shrewdness, and adaptability compensated for his lack of experience and impressed the Dwights. Bancroft began to work for his father-in-law and the family banking interests.[13]

By 1830 the Dwights had already shifted part of their capital west. Henry had founded the Bank of Geneva in 1817, and held shares in other upstate New York banks. The family also controlled the Bank of Michigan in Detroit, and in 1831 decided to look into the Commercial Bank of Lake Erie, in Cleveland, Ohio, an institution heavily indebted to the federal government. It had not transacted business for several years, but it retained a valuable dormant charter. Bancroft was sent to see whether a sizable investment would profitably resurrect the institution.

He arrived in Cleveland in the summer of 1831 and was quickly impressed with the city's growth potential. After meeting the state canal commissioner, the bank's stockholders, and local officials and after extensive consultations by mail with the Dwights, he decided that the venture was worthwhile. A trip to Cincinnati confirmed another Dwight suggestion that a financial institution there would also have a bright future. These and other enterprises that affected the family's wealth promised also to further his own fortunes—the death of Sarah's grandfather transferred a share of the property to her, which Bancroft proceeded to sink into the Cleveland bank.

November took Bancroft to Geneva for further consultations. There arguments over his commission showed that he intended to be more than a mere agent for the family. Bancroft thought that, having done the lion's share of the work, his rewards ought to be greater, while the Dwights, appreciative of his efforts, reminded him that the capital invested was largely theirs. In the end one-fifth of the shares went to Henry Dwight, one-fifth to Henry's brother Jonathan, and one-fifth to Bancroft, with the rest scattered.

The West's boundless speculative opportunities overnight transformed an impoverished schoolmaster into a young man of wealth on the make. Contrary to his own later claims, Dwight generosity and solid advice guided all of his decisions. "And so you have really made a bank," Sarah wrote, when informed of his success, "and from what I learn a very good one too. Father says he is well pleased with your proceedings." Bancroft was too. That dream of independence, if not yet entirely within his grasp, was coming ever closer.[14]

In Cleveland Bancroft also learned that he had become a father. The news was especially welcome because he hoped it would improve Sarah's disposition and the marriage with it. A miscarriage a year earlier had left her gloomy, quarrelsome, and irritable, straining their relationship and encouraging his frequent absence from home. "If the past has been clouded by discontent let us hope the future will not be," he counseled his wife. Sarah in turn promised to be all the things she had not been thus far. She still disliked Northampton, but the baby made a great difference. The "little angel," also named Sarah, was doing well, the happy mother reported. If Bancroft did not come home soon, Sarah would talk before she ever saw her father.[15]

Bancroft came home but only for a short while, then left for Washington, charged with settling the bank's debt to the government. Certainly the capital was a scene of corrupting ambition and sentimental elegance, but he relished every moment of his stay there, for the same forces drove him. A further $1,500 from the Dwights found its way into his account, so that he could cut a handsome figure in local drawing rooms and increase his investments.

Dealing with the Treasury was like running through an obstacle course, he complained, since departments were full of lazy clerks, paid huge salaries for neglecting the public business. But those clerks became the focus of his lobbying efforts as Bancroft exploited all his connections when dealing with the government. He turned even to Robert Walsh, no friend of the administration, for a note to Secretary of the Treasury Levi Woodbury, who found the author of the *North American Review* bank article engaging and promised help. But that did not guarantee a quick response; and Bancroft suspected that the Albany Regency, Van Buren's political organization, was not eager to ease his way. "Indeed I must keep my ground firmly, or secret combinations will defeat my wishes," he confided to his wife.[16]

Still waiting, he received disquieting news—baby Sarah was seriously ill. Dr. Frost was in constant attendance during the daytime, but emetics, blisters, and baths only added to the infant's suffering. Her mother meanwhile lay awake nights distraught. "She is the only one, and given after so many years, and to be called so early," she wrote. On January 11, tear-stained letters went off to the capital. Not fair, Sarah cried. She had lost the one substantive bond to her husband. Lonely, bitter, unanswered, she wondered what sins had brought on this affliction. Above all she wanted her husband home.[17]

Aaron Bancroft tried vainly to console his daughter-in-law—since the baby had died before the age of moral action, no doubt she was in heaven. Bancroft's mother, Lucretia, having often lived through such tragedies, was also sympathetic and supportive. "Sevear indeed I have been tried and I acknowledge to you, it was a work of time before I could say my work was easy and my burthens light." George worried mainly about his wife's mental stability. "It is vain to struggle against the will of Heaven. Let us submit, cheerfully if we can, but at least with resignation," he wrote from the capital. By bearing the suffering, Sarah would make herself worthy of future blessings. She was not to blame for what had happened, and was now the repository of all the love he had to give. "Let the virtues of the woman and wife mitigate the sorrows of the mother."[18]

Meanwhile, with the advice of the Dwights, he decided not to come home, and told her about the exciting life in the capital. The Washington winter dragged on pleasantly, he wrote. John Davis was an instructive guide, a better politician than Edward Everett. An elegant dinner with ex-King Charles X, an informative evening with John Quincy Adams, and meetings with the editor of the *National Intelligencer* provided valuable knowledge about administration maneuverings. On the Hill, Bancroft listened to John Calhoun's dissertations, heard Henry Clay on the tariff, and stayed for Hayne's reply. After Everett's speech in favor of colonizing freed slaves and the description of the evils of bondage by Senator Archer of Virginia, Bancroft concluded nothing could be done about the problem until the southern states themselves undertook emancipatory measures.

At a White House reception, Jackson proved impressive—no western boor, but well-mannered, firm, and sincere. Bancroft heartily agreed when Old Hickory said that American institutions were "based on the virtue of the commonality . . . and that the moment demagogues obtain influence with the people our liberties are destroyed." This Democrat was not the destructive radical some of Bancroft's Boston acquaintances thought. Too bad his dirty, bad-mannered supporters were "the vilest, most promiscuous medly," attacking the food like locusts. Having made his peace with democracy, Bancroft did not believe that one had a right to complain about the kind of people who made it into office. Those who thought otherwise, like his friend George Ticknor, ought to set themselves to the task of improving the level of the electorate and thus assure the choice of more congenial candidates.[19]

Such letters hardly helped Sarah overcome her grief, but they reflected her husband's view of life as a season of tests and labor before eternity. Sarah, who grew up in greater affluence, with its attendant comforts and amenities, disagreed. She became ill and after a while too depressed to write. Only then did Bancroft decide against a trip to Ohio; he would finish his business in the capital and come straight home. But the Calvinist in him still hoped to find her more acquiescent. "It is not my wish to see her draped in the outward garb for sorrow," Bancroft wrote his brother-in-law. But Sarah insisted, and he gave in.[20]

Bancroft returned once his lobbying paid off and the bank was fully operational. Homecoming proved sad, for Sarah's hysteria had mounted. Lucretia tried to help, suggesting that the young woman occupy herself with household tasks, but Sarah remained inconsolable. In early spring her husband left on yet another banking expedition, immersing himself in his work, pleased with accomplishments, his satisfaction marred only by the melancholy letters that followed him to Cleveland. The bank prospered, and even John Davis, a cautious investor, became a shareholder. Come summer, Bancroft promised Sarah, they would spend more time in Springfield. She was pregnant again and in January 1833 their second child, Louisa, would be born.[21]

The success of his enterprises as well as a more settled home life should have brought Bancroft the peace he had not known for years. But the respite was only temporary, for his achievements renewed his determination to be more than a failed preacher, former schoolmaster, and family-business troubleshooter. These activities brought to the surface vaguely perceived desires and emotions that further increased his restlessness. Having found the study of "man in life and conduct" vastly attractive, he regretted days wasted "among books and boys." Confident of his capacity "to mix with the active on even terms," the man of letters concluded that the distinction between scholarship and action did not apply to him.[22]

Action in 1832 meant politics, preferably on the side of the National Republicans, who however had not been notably successful nationally and had failed to court him properly. Bancroft watched with some envy the quick rise of his brother-in-law, now a congressman but harboring gubernatorial ambitions. Edward Everett too had made it and seemed content. Neither of them, Bancroft thought, had abilities he could not match. While his letters from Washington bemoaned the lack of stable principles in a Democratic government, that was not the sum total of his views. The National Republicans were right in their outrage at the President's Bank veto, but Jackson enjoyed overwhelming national strength and hence possessed an appeal his opponents lacked. When Clay, Bancroft's private choice in 1832, carried Massachusetts while the Democrats swept the nation, the difference posed a problem for a budding politician.

For the moment, Bancroft's horizons, though broadened by experiences in the capital and the West, did not extend much beyond New England. He joined Edward Everett and Abbott Lawrence in a scathing attack on the President when the National Republican Party met in Worcester and he stepped forward when a local convention searched around for a suitable congressional candidate from the Northampton district. But the nomination went to someone else. Offended and disappointed, Bancroft made noises to the effect that the Democrats would warmly welcome him, but did not pursue the matter further.[23]

He had by then discovered the American past and for the next two years immersed himself in writing about it. Some time in 1832 Bancroft decided to write a history of the United States; he had dealt halfheartedly with that subject since his return from Europe, and had employed aspects of the nation's heritage to buttress his positions. Several of his friends also dabbled in history, with greater or lesser seriousness—William H. Prescott had begun his *Ferdinand and Isabella* in 1826, and Jared Sparks and Washington Irving were toiling at their own interpretations. None, Bancroft believed, was as well equipped as he. Familiar with European history, he had written reviews on such diverse subjects as the French Revolution and Joseph II of Austria. His German education had covered the ancient world and also the more recent past. Such a perspective afforded him a skill that, once translated into literary form, was bound to be influential and, he hoped, very successful.

Bancroft did not know the exact dimensions of his undertaking. In a flush of optimism he projected a grand design carrying the story of national development down to his own day. To gather material he visited local libraries, ransacked private collections, requested books and advice wherever he could find them, and corresponded with other scholars. The Atheneum and the Massachusetts Historical Society, as well as the Harvard Library, proved valuable. But his work was almost a national enterprise in which historical societies and individuals all over the country helped. Later, extensive footnotes and numerous acknowledgments would testify to his efforts to give his work substance, immediacy, accuracy, and persuasiveness. But since the first volume relied largely on secondary sources, the research presented little difficulty and the product was more derivative than his subsequent writings.[24]

The appraisal of later generations would have been an unpleasant surprise for him. His more generous critics would value his history for its contribution to the national psyche, important for the myth of national origins he artistically articulated. The less sympathetic called it faulty, imprecise, slanted, and doctrinaire. Bancroft never intended his history to be any of the above. Nor did he intend that his first volume, and all the others, cast votes for Jackson. His goal was to correct errors, omissions, and bias, not to augment their number. No one ever wrote American history "with criticism—Kritik," he complained, a judgment somewhat unfair to predecessors on whose books he relied, but true enough in the sense that no one brought to the task the training and insight he did. "I should want leave without respect of persons to speak the truth, to quote paragraphs which are wrong, to set down evidence of error." The integrity of the subject demanded a sober if colorful narrative, with no ancestor worship or self-congratulatory tones, written from a philosophical scientific viewpoint, without political prejudice. The fact that later critics did not think he succeeded does not detract from his efforts. He believed that he had succeeded and for a long time no one quarreled with his assessment.[25]

The writing of his history was in itself a private reform movement, confined to one branch of American letters. Not sure that he was entirely correct (although certain of the worthiness of his mission), Bancroft sent sections to numerous colleagues—ostensibly to ask for advice, but really for assurance that what he had written would withstand the test of time. He heard exactly what he wanted to hear. Judge Joseph Story was delighted, as were James Savage, George Ticknor, and Jared Sparks. John Davis thought no one had ever scrutinized authorities with such care, and Edward Everett provided manuscript materials and also moral encouragement. Having passed the supreme test—that of Boston's men of letters—he was ready to face the public. In June 1834 Volume One was complete. At his own expense Bancroft had the plates set and supervised publication.[26]

That volume, devoted to colonial developments down to the middle of the seventeenth century, laid out the premises upon which the historian intended to continue the story. Concentrating on his native region, he paid a moving tribute to New England, for its services to the nation and humanity, its fear of God and respect for man, liberty, and justice, providing factual documentation for what local orators had been saying for years. In that region, the best of "the industrial classes" bore in their hearts "the undying principles of democratic liberty." The tone was deliberate and expressed the spirit "of democratic independence, of popular liberty" that he had told Sparks "should be infused into our literature. Let Mammon rule in the marts, but not on the holy mountain of letters."[27]

In a short Preface on the state of the union in 1834, Bancroft described a growing society, its territory expanding, its wealth increasing. After centuries of struggle, the government identified with the interests of the people, reason was free to combat error, and even subversive doctrines were tolerated. In that fortunate nation the written Constitution was a living document with a capacity for improvement; popular religion was enlightened, immigrants crowded the shores, and "the principles of liberty, uniting all interests by the operation of equal laws, blended the discordant elements into harmonious union." The book then proceeded to outline the circumstances which, in the seventeenth century, prepared the prosperity and freedom of the nineteenth.[28]

The past thus recorded exposed present inconsistencies. In spite of Bancroft's improbable Preface, other observers believed that the ideals of the founding fathers remained unfulfilled and reality was remote from the Puritan promise. Not harmony but strife, corruption, and factionalism, they thought, characterized the 1830s. Instead of loving liberty, some Americans tried to enslave others—the workers, the artisans, the farmers. Aristocracies sprouted and government aided property rather than freedom through privilege and monopolistic institutions. Religious squabbles and revivals were signs that even faith was no longer secure. The American heritage, instead of being purified, was being corrupted.

"The times are out of joint" was the going phrase, old principles appeared to fall by the wayside, and upstart politicians held center stage. "All things seem to be in a hurry," one bitter commentator noted, "as if there was a universal rush to undo all which infinite toil, cost and bloodshed had perfected, and to plunge madly into the gulf of national destruction." John Davis was horrified at this "decay of public spirit . . . a decline in patriotism," as he pointed to that "creeping spirit of submission abroad. Men everywhere seeking for a participation in the plunder and ready to sing hosannahs to him that holds the key to the granary." Preachers spoke of unsettled times, and Henry Ware, Jr., derided a generation that ceased to revere old customs—"the multitudes are easily made to fancy that constancy is bondage and to suppose that they advance into light in proportion as they recede from their fathers." Charles Sumner worried about riots, conflagrations, bloodshed, and murder, and Joseph Buckingham, Bancroft's friend from the *New England Magazine,* foresaw the day "when popular will shall take the place of law, whether this be by riots and tumults or under the form of judicial proceedings, the grave of our nation's happiness and glory will have been prepared . . . Violence will become the common means of self defense, and our only refuge from the horrors of anarchy will be under the comparatively peaceful shelter of military despotism."[29]

Some explained this degeneration by the pervasive lack of morality and virtue, exhibited in greed, materialism, hunger for power, alienation, and dissatisfaction with one's lot in life, all the more dangerous because it accompanied expansion of the suffrage. A few blamed city life with its loss of community sense and the disappearance of honesty. The National Republicans focused on the chief villians, the Democrats. For the maver-

ick Alexander H. Everett, Jackson's policies were a system of cold-blood-
ed massacre of which a Nero or Domitian would have been proud. Martin Van Buren, with whom Bancroft had tried to ingratiate himself, was
a narrow, sordid, selfish Dutch pettifogger. The *New England Magazine*
blamed "the flatterers of the people" for contemporary ills. The Boston
Courier and many of Bancroft's acquaintances thought it was a matter of
time before the American experiment collapsed under the weight of its
own shortcomings.[30]

Bancroft's volume earned immediate welcome for its historical arguments against the gloomy forecasts. The nation received a scholarly, if
not soberly written, reminder that the past had also been out of joint,
that it had not been a smooth, harmonious development, stemming from
a long-lost golden age, but quite to the contrary, that its origins were
turbulent, unstable, full of strife and struggle. To the pessimists and the
optimists, to those who cried over lost innocence or abandoned the hope
for improvement, whether political radicals or conservatives, Bancroft
conveyed lessons of immediate applicability.[31]

John Davis's moans about the decay of public spirit had antecedents,
and the preachers who worried about novelty and experiment learned
that the quest for the new, the ideal, the hitherto untried had been the
essence of American development. Henry Ware, Jr., could find in the
volume numerous instances of how his revered forefathers departed, in
their day, from the customary ways. Charles Sumner's visions of riots
and bloodshed had also been part and parcel of the American past. Then,
too, seemingly insurmountable obstacles had been surmounted; and myr-
iads of small rebellions placed contemporary factionalism and misguided
leadership in proper perspective. The volume, laudatory as it was of the
American heritage, did not ignore the pitfalls, the failures, and the less
than creditable struggles of early days.

This feature, more than any other, accounted for the book's success,
which cut across all political lines, so that Whigs and Democrats alike
paid tribute to the author while reviewers of every stripe united in praising it. All could take heart from Bancroft's fundamental optimism, for
he showed, in incident after incident, how the American people determined national destiny. Everyone applauded Bancroft's misquoted motto
(taken from Bishop Berkeley), "westward the star of empire takes its
way," which reassured those who feared the excesses of democracy as
well as those who welcomed them. If the volume voted for anyone, it
was for the American people rather than for their political doctrines or
leaders. The still nominally National Republican historian produced a

work of lasting influence and immediate popularity precisely because he based himself on the broadest common denominator and in the course of his chapters steered clear of partisanship.

The book dwelt at length on the origins of the American colonies because, in Bancroft's interpretation, the seventeenth century commenced the evolution of a society new in the world's annals. That too no one could dispute; many Americans since John Winthrop had said as much. Bancroft showed how the character of the people shaped a new nationality; in spite of their diverse origins, the newcomers facing common challenges in the wilderness had become one people. He proved that the American rhetoric about the centrality of the people in the country's development was but a reflection of history, factually correct and legitimate. Bancroft regarded the people not as a mob to be feared, but as the repository of national virtue, the primary force behind national achievements. The past had been theirs; so would the present and the future be.

No one, in 1834, at either end of the political spectrum found this unacceptable—in theory. "The people are beginning to awake," Frederick Robinson, a local trade union leader told his Boston audience that summer. "Whom can you more safely trust," Edward Everett asked rhetorically, "than the majority of the people; who is so likely to be right, always right, and altogether right, as the collective majority of a great nation?" The Boston *Atlas,* one of the town's most conservative publications, agreed. The fact that many readers had servant problems, the editor wrote, was a welcome sign reflecting an open society and equality of opportunity. In this blessed land, none need devote their lives to drudgery. All were out to make their own way in the world and become rich. Politicians spread that message in orations, speeches, diatribes, and political harangues, glowingly when Democrats or Workingmen took the podium, more cautiously when their opponents did.[32]

How did the people shape their own future? Here Bancroft (no Michelet) hedged enough to write something quite traditional. In his narrative the people often remained in the background while the leaders took center stage. But at crucial moments they saved the day and those instances clinched the historian's argument. Thus in Virginia in 1619 the people wrested the first colonial assembly from the London Company, and in Maryland, jealous of their rights, they carried forward the torch of popular liberty. The Pilgrims instituted "popular constitutional liberty" and thereby "humanity recovered its rights." The settlers at Salem in 1629 were "the depositories of the purest truth," just as the inhabitants of Connecticut, "near to Nature," listened "to her voice and easily copied her forms." All were but "humble immigrants and yet the benefactors of humanity."[33]

Familiar elements enhanced the persuasiveness of the message and reassured its readers. As they leafed through its pages they sensed a kinship with Bancroft that made his guiding theme palatable. The vision of the past as but the sum of God's providence, which made history a form of revelation and the historian the Lord's scribe, placed him squarely in the familiar tradition of Puritan historiography. Yet he did not assert that God governed through special providences and miracles as his earliest predecessors had. Instead he stressed divine involvement through constant, general laws. Their divine Creator remained in the background and the forces of history, although ultimately linked by His plan, were understandable in purely human terms.[34]

Nonetheless God was crucial, sustaining the eternal validity of the moral law, maintaining continuity, and justifying Bancroft's message. Each and every event was the necessary component of a general scheme, linked in overall significance to what preceded and what followed it. The concept of providence assured the reader that rapid changes, seemingly unrelated events, and temporary triumphs of evil were only superficial manifestations of deeper forces. There was logic in creation and hence the consolation that, while the individual might be lost, the salvation of humanity was assured. That salvation, the progressive aspect of human development, Bancroft defined as man's growing awareness of the moral law and his increasing willingness to subjugate himself to its postulates, a conclusion appropriate for a historian raised on moral philosophy.

Since progress rested on myriad individual acts of will, Bancroft used the past to counter the "fear of a malignant destiny, by showing events as the issue of exertion and not the consequence of a blind and inexorable fatality." Faith in continuous progression did not lead to an indolent expectation of supernatural intervention but upheld a self-relying diligence to duty. Man proposed and God disposed; only proposals that paralleled the divine scheme for the nation would succeed. By implication, radical social transformations or attempts to break the laws of human development were doomed from the start.[35]

Without yet using that terminology, the *History* treated the never ending struggle between the party of the past and the party of the future as the central dynamic of human development. To comprehend contemporary manifestations, one had to perceive their earliest beginnings. The

Antinomian controversy in Massachusetts, a small incident, was a case in point. The founders of Massachusetts Bay in that dispute were clearly the party of the past bent on preserving the social order they had established. Newer arrivals, representing in Bancroft's dialectic the party of the ideal, "followed the principles of the Reformation with logical precision to their consequence," in this case, "resisting every form of despotism over the mind." While doing so, however, they ignored the unpreparedness of those around them for "so anarchical a doctrine as the paramount authority of private judgment."[36] The old and the new, that which was and that which ought to be, clashed. The reformers tried "to distinguish between abstract truth and the outward forms under which truth is conveyed, between underlying principles and changing institutions," while their opponents were satisfied with what they had achieved. The future lay with the reformers who wanted change. But time-bound social institutions reflected the state of awareness and morality at that given moment. The reformers lost, in the short run, because their proposals outdistanced the general level of comprehension.[37]

In the Antinomian dispute the people saved the commonwealth because they supported the side that represented tyranny over the mind of man. A reckless threat of the reformers, which raised the specter of English intervention, clarified the issues. What mattered most was salvation of the colony's political liberty, since Massachusetts was not yet ready for that victory of intellectual freedom over clericalism which marked its later emergence to maturity. The people supported their leaders because only expulsion of the heretics and preservation of the commonwealth's relative independence ensured a future triumph for ideal truth.[38]

The Antinomian controversy was one incident among many that illustrated Bancroft's popular message. The people as a whole were not to be feared or curbed, but trusted, for they had proved themselves wiser, more perceptive, more cautious, and more in tune with the divine plan than the few. Instinctively they perceived the evolutionary thrust and were unwilling to outrun the possible or to foster what society was not prepared to accept. Their guidance was therefore the surest barrier against excess, error, and despotism. Evolution was the attribute of the race, not of the individual, and development hinged upon the general readiness to receive and institutionalize new ideas. "The public mind," by which Bancroft meant the sum of popular opinions, was thus a conservative social and political force, at times rejecting truths, however seminal. This barrier to swifter evolution made progress slow and cumbersome, which, he implied, ought to reassure those who worried lest society rush heedlessly along in directions for which it was not prepared.

This profoundly anti-individualistic and conservative approach originated in Bancroft's native background, which no amount of German education could obliterate. He never forgot his Congregational upbringing, the years at Harvard, and the meaning of moral philosophy, all of which nurtured doubts about human creativity, autonomy, and perfectibility. "Individual conscience is often the dupe of interest and often but a more honorable name for self will." Fearing man as an individual, Bancroft wrote his history in part to reassure himself and his audience.[39]

In the next few years political experience fleshed out a democratic theory based on his vision of the people's conservatism. That theory also focused on the people, on the race, and only very rarely on the individual. And much of its backing would be historical, drawing on the network of ideas that informed Bancroft's handling of the past. The partnership of God and the people in making history, one of the distinguishing features of that network, also shaped his historical methodology.

The assumption that human development proceeded on two interrelated levels was an integral component of Bancroft's Harvard education. The temporal and particular, subsidiary to the universal and eternal, corresponded to the two worlds man inhabited—the material and mortal and the spiritual and immortal. On the upper level the divine plan, the pure version of the rules of creation, existed in perfect form. There, history unfolded in continuous, linear fashion toward an ultimate ideal state when man would live by reason alone, freely accepting the moral law. On the lower level, the laws were only partly operative, their purity blemished by human imperfection. The interplay between events at the two levels shaped the *History,* which proposed not to recount meaningless details, but to discover sequential occurrences that created a causal chain, succeeding in time.

God rules in the affairs of man, the volume proclaimed, as it sought to fathom His secret purpose. But divine will remained mysterious, rarely manifest in concrete historical illustrations. Since the ever present people were also difficult to describe, Bancroft settled for alternative ways of writing about divine intervention and the central role the people played in it. He opted for a complicated narrative structure and a multilevel description of events. The evolution of mankind proceeded along several distinct though interrelated lines, a construct that made room for the divine plan, for popular influence, and for those occasional heroes whose presence did not contradict Bancroft's fundamental anti-individualism.

The uppermost level of the divine plan, where the laws of history and creation existed in pure form, was so far removed from daily occurrences that it rarely appeared. A second plane—of universal history—allowed Bancroft to examine the worldwide significance of events. The third level placed events squarely in their local context. The explication of any cluster of historical facts involved all three—illustrations of the divine plan's general laws; their place in mankind's development; and the autonomous interpretation of the event at the time of its occurrence. This design deepened the narrative beyond chronology and emphasized collective actions and group behavior, which to Bancroft best exhibited the divine movement of intelligence and the power of the people to shape the nation's destiny.

The settlement of Plymouth, for example, was introduced against its European background. In thirty-five pages readers traversed the road from Wittenberg to Plymouth Rock, guided by the Olympian assertion that "the mysterious influence of that Power which enchains the destinies of states, overruling the decisions of sovereigns, often deduces the greatest events from the least commanding causes"—a paraphrase of Bancroft's sources, William Bradford and John Winthrop. Principles were at work, the crucial results of the Reformation, "the enfranchisement of the mind from religious despotism," leading "directly to the inquiries into the nature of civil government" and "the doctrine of liberty which sheltered their infancy in the wilderness of the newly discovered continent and within the space of two centuries have infused themselves into the life blood of every state." From the nineteenth century the reader then moved back into the sixteenth, when Henry VIII's personal needs "advanced the genius of the age," and "even though it sometimes faltered in its progress along untried paths," the demand for "the emancipation of the mind" persisted. When James I ascended the throne, "the interests of human freedom [were] . . . at issue." Only then did Bancroft introduce Robinson's congregation. The climax built up to 1620 when in the *Mayflower* cabin "humanity recovers its rights," the "birth of constitutional liberty" took place, and all at once the narrative descended to a detailed, precise, and accurate description of the first settlement.[40]

The generalizations tying the narrative into a coherent framework at times required leaps of faith that Bancroft's readers, if not later generations, willingly took. The Plymouth chapter, for example, presumed that

Luther's justification by faith alone, the signing of a political compact by a Calvinist congregation, and nineteenth-century New England democracy were all interrelated. Bancroft knew full well that something happened to transform a concept that in 1620 stressed the rights of the elect into the belief of 1834 in the rights of all. He could not provide factual proof to tie together the commonwealth founded on the basis of the rights of the visible saints and the democratic society of his own time. But he nonetheless felt comfortable with the generalization because his theory of history held that the immediate context only partly determined the meaning of an event. The seventeenth century might well have found the nineteenth-century concept of democratic society an abomination, but that was the true measure of progress—the growing willingness of the people to arrange their society in accordance with the perfect forms suggested by the divine plan.

The trading corporation that was the Massachusetts Bay Company, to use another example, acquired in 1634 a democratic form of government when a revolution instigated by the deputies "as an expression of the public mind" followed "the laws of the moral world" and expanded their share in the colonial government. True, the polity remained "a sort of theocracy"; but Bancroft had evidence that the clergy were "refused the least shadow of political authority." There was also an aristocracy, but "not of wealth"; and if the franchise was limited, it was better to restrict the right to vote to the pure than to the rich. Nonetheless Bancroft asserted that Massachusetts was "unconsciously becoming a representative democracy" when the magistrates overstepped their charter authority, and not even Cotton's opposition to "rotation in office" could stop them. The leaders of this small revolt did not know what they were doing, Bancroft explained to his readers, but the mysterious functioning of Providence determined the outcome.[41]

Virginia was another instance where "unconsciously" a representative democracy arose when the crucial factor of abundant land maintained and augmented the rights of Englishmen after the transition from corporate to royal government. A planter aristocracy based on slavery, an impure Anglican church, and deep ties to the mother country notwithstanding, the encounter between English liberties and the virgin soil created "this nursery of freemen," this "nearly independent democracy." The history of early Virginia, like that of Massachusetts, exemplified the inner logic of the past and the hidden meaning of events—their interrelatedness, multilevel significance, and place in the divine scheme. Historical knowledge was thus a form of intuitive insight and deductive reasoning about the relation of individual appearance to universal laws.[42]

Volume One concluded with a long assessment of Puritanism, the "religion struggling for the people," a chapter that summarized the implications of Bancroft's method. There had been progress from Luther to Calvin, to New England, all appearances to the contrary notwithstanding. The "outward forms which gave the sect its marked exterior" were "outside peculiarities," indicative of the seventeenth century, but not "the definitive genius of the sect itself." The mission of Puritanism was "to engraft the new institutions of popular energy upon the old European system of feudal aristocracy and popular servitude . . . the good was permanent, the outward emblems which were the sign of party were of transient duration." By separating the temporary from the eternal, the historian could interpret contradictory facts, like instances of persecution and bigotry as but "a train of mists, hovering on an autumn morning, over the channel of a fine river, that diffuses freshness and fertility wherever it wound." Puritanism "constituted not the Christian clergy but the Christian people the interpreter of the divine will. The voice of the majority was the voice of God and the issue of Puritanism was therefore popular sovereignty." By 1834 most of his readers agreed with the second part of his statement. It soon became Bancroft's mission to convince them of the first.[43]

The Massachusetts Democratic Party became the vehicle for his task. A minor organization in a major state, it consisted of several constituencies, each with its own history and program, all fluid in outlook, adaptable to opportunity, rarely distinguishable from their opponents. David Henshaw, the Democratic chieftain, was a successful entrepreneur who had expanded his interests into insurance, manufacturing, and railroads. He dominated the Customhouse or *Statesman* or the post office faction as his people were sometimes known after Jackson appointed him collector of the Port of Boston. Businessmen and lawyers, some of them social parvenus, whose success buttressed their faith in the limitless opportunities of American life, followed Henshaw, demanding a share of political power commensurate with their property. Bancroft cooperated with this group almost to the very end of his Massachusetts political career.[44]

Sincere followers of Thomas Jefferson, its members thought that Jackson would ensure national unity, the freedom of American enterprise, and the rights of the common people. Let us have no more talk about political abolitionism, anti-masonry, locofocoism or anything else but pure old-fashioned democracy—Jeffersonian, Madisonian, Jacksonian, and Van Buren democracy, they urged. Their goal was to prove their respectability on the side of freedom and reform, not as a factious minority, but as representatives of the American mainstream. National Republicans found something incongruous in the cry of wealthy and successful men for the rights of the common people, but the stance of Henshaw's followers stemmed directly from their own experience. They did not advocate economic equality or expansion of government authority, or any tampering with economic and social laws. Work, self-reliance, moral stamina, and exploitation of opportunities would alleviate discontent, a social vision not far removed from that of their opponents, and one that Bancroft, rhetoric notwithstanding, easily assimilated.[45]

Their perennial gubernatorial candidate was Judge Marcus Morton of Taunton, a man of some political insight, a Calhoun supporter, but not averse to occasional cooperation with the National Republicans. He worked with Henshaw whenever necessary, although he found the messages emanating from Boston too radical and feared that extremist factions might disrupt his loose network of supporters. For that reason also Morton spent much of his time trying to weed out former Federalists who had infiltrated the ranks.[46]

Morton's loyalty to Andrew Jackson was also uncertain. The Democracy of Massachusetts was weak, he complained, because of the leadership in Washington; monotonous electoral defeats induced him to suggest disassociation from the national organization in 1831. However, by 1834, once more a stalwart Jacksonian, he had discovered that the President now "exercises his firmness and his wisdom in protecting our constitution and our honor from the violence of domestic factions." Yet Morton persisted in quarreling over administration appointments and considered the local organization inadequately represented in Washington—too many former Federalists were getting offices in Massachusetts. Later that year he was ready once more to resign, only to change his mind and accept Samuel Lothrop—a former Federalist and now Anti-Mason—for the second spot on the Democratic ticket. Numbers had to be reckoned with and besides, he reasoned, "it is always safer to take persons of no principles than those of bad principles . . . The former may act right, the latter must act wrong." Qualms about Henshaw's banking views he kept to himself, as he lobbied for yet another deposit bank in Boston.[47]

Morton and Henshaw sought support to expand the Democratic constituency. They realized that poor soil, inferior markets, and competition with cheaper western products created pockets of unrest in the state's small farming communities. Suspicions of the urban center and hostility to corporations and to exclusive privileges also created potential Democratic votes. The Democratic Party alternative would provide artisans a means to oppose the Lawrences and Appletons, and attract the Irish as well as fishermen resentful of wealthier merchant fleets. Such discontented and increasingly angry voters deserved to be heard, because much of what they had to say was right and in line with Henshaw's Democratic doctrine, to which Morton was forced to convert.

Workingmen's organizations, which sprouted around the state, united farmers, mechanics, and artisans; while their labor contributed to the country's general well-being, they believed they suffered "oppression, poverty, and debasement." A few explained the current malaise by the lack of respect paid manual labor, and a corresponding effort by the rich to keep wages low. Others pointed to aristocratic influences, improper literature, and poor education as causes for unrest, and addressed moral issues advocating Christian values and republican simplicity. To allow all to enjoy the fruit of their labor, it was necessary to put down "the arrogance, impudence and imitation of foreign nobility," annihilate monopolies, cut budgets, and elect honest politicians.[48]

Many speakers employed a radical terminology that increased in shrillness under National Republican and later Whig attacks, for both parties evoked frightening visions of a future struggle. Frederick Robinson, in the summer of 1834, talked menacingly of the "idle living in luxury and the laborer in want and disgrace." Samuel Clesson Allen hailed the producing classes, whose wealth exploitative aristocracies skimmed away. The rich controlled the government, Theodore Sedgwick said. "The world is governed too much," Robert Rantoul complained, piously expressing the hope that with "intelligence, morality, temperance, industry and economy" the future would be brighter than the present. But the sharp language concealed a fundamental optimism that took the basic health of the society for granted and assumed that maladjustments could be set aright without major upheavals. Bancroft's facile and swift adoption of the Workingmen terminology reflected that outlook.[49]

In Northampton, Workingmen entered independent candidates in local elections. Invariably such men presented themselves as part of a popular protest movement abjuring all radical alliances. But their opponents thought otherwise. The Northampton *Courier* claimed that they were disguised Jacksonians, and disgruntled National Republicans who had in the past been rebuffed in overtures to these organizations agreed.

"Infidelity [a reference to the Workingmen] and Anti-Masonry," a former Democrat declared, "are the two horses which draw the mud cart of the [Democratic] party whenever they ride out on their political excursions." By 1833 Henshaw and Morton placed the names of some Workingmen candidates on Democratic slates.[50]

The Anti-Masonic organizations active in the state since 1828 also flirted occasionally with the Democrats. "The chains of foreign servitude," thundered Amasa Walker, "had been severed, but the grim genius of tyranny still haunts our land and stalks abroad in many a plausible and dangerous form." Masonic orders, an insidious form of aristocracy, controlled public opinion, the press, and numerous voluntary associations, he thought. Others sought to broaden their chances for a better life through politics, by advocating the secret ballot, an end to the Bank of the United States, and limiting government involvement in the economy, while relying on unhampered private initiative to promote railroads and other large enterprises. The Anti-Masons split into town and country alignments, some sympathetic to John Quincy Adams and the National Republicans, others pro-Jackson; they were difficult to control and often politically unreliable. Because of their support for Daniel Webster, Henshaw sometimes regarded them as auxiliaries of federalism and political pirates.[51]

Their Boston leader, Benjamin F. Hallett, kept his options open but after 1831 spoke against the United States Bank and the Hartford Convention party, a Democratic appellation applied to National Republicans and nascent Whigs. For a while he cooperated with David Henshaw and Charles G. Greene, editor of the Boston *Statesman,* but his party preferred to run independent candidates for the governorship, and in 1832 William Wirt was their presidential contender. "Beware of falsehoods," their organ, the Boston *Advocate,* cried, unable to swallow Henry Clay's candidacy and jealous of its independence. A year later Hallett regarded Jackson as "the scourge of his country," whose banking policy, Indian removal, and judiciary reform were Jacobinical threats, second only to Freemasonry in pernicious influence. But the Boston *Atlas* referred to Hallett's newspaper as "an anti Masonic sewer," a sign that he had not come closer to the National Republicans. When he yet again shifted ground in 1833 and argued that the cause of anti-Masonry was also the cause of liberty, Henshaw and Morton were ready to mobilize some of his supporters under the Democratic banner.[52]

This was the state of the opposition parties in 1834 when Bancroft, still nominally National Republican, reviewed his options. The Cleveland bank was doing well, and the Dwights were ready to send him on yet another expedition to the West. He purchased more stock in the Bank of Lake Erie and became a financial adviser to friends considering similar investments. His involvement in local affairs deepened; in Northampton and Springfield, he made contact with Workingmen and with Anti-Masonic groups. The family welcomed any political connections and saw nothing incongruous in such activities. Yet he hesitated to make his views known.[53]

Congressional experience, Bancroft told himself, would improve Edward Everett's books. Yet his friend's frustrations in Washington proved that only mediocrities succeeded in politics, "since the highly intelligent were always in advance of public opinion," while good politicians swam with the current. It took "time for a great truth to find its way to the crowd, and justice is not a favorite with the selfishness of parties." Bancroft wondered whether he was patient enough to wait upon the crowd.[54]

The answer was yes. On the threshold of a flourishing career as a historian, he regarded past restlessness as an asset and came to terms with his inclinations. The self-confidence engendered by recent success hastened the search for a new activity, while the ideas delineated in the *History* and the duties he envisioned for men of letters persuaded Bancroft to turn to politics on the side that seemed the worthy heir of the tradition he had described. To dispel doubts about his own suitability for a public career, he tried to explain his political interests to himself and others. The scholar who recorded the saga of the Americans was in a unique position to contribute to their redemption, Bancroft thought; and politics was a means of self-justification and of exerting influence. But even when Bancroft informed Everett that the man of letters had to be the man of the people, he said nothing about the Democratic Party— that was what Everett also thought himself to be.

As a historian Bancroft thought he knew the main lines of national development. The American experiment flourished by surmounting obstacles providence had purposely placed in its path—persecution, a virgin continent, the wilderness, clashes with European powers. The measure of progress was the extent to which society, institutions, customs, and government came increasingly into harmony with the moral law, the framework that tied together the country's evolution. Since 1830 Bancroft had maintained that the character of American institutions had yet to receive the impress which they were to bear forever, bringing to a close the experiment begun in 1606, the foundation of society on a set of eternal laws reflecting man's true dignity. In 1834 he decided to help that process along.[55]

Providence, he reasoned, had provided the present with new challenges, in the form of monopolies, aristocracies, and paper currency. These vague concepts derived from the vocabulary of the opposition groups appeared as the current obstacles on the road to the perfect society. By themselves they did not imply anything amiss with the society. Bancroft found the appeals of Workingmen, Democrats, and Anti-Masons persuasive only insofar as they accorded with his own vision of social redemption, which emphatically did not involve a rebellion against the past.

A whole summer passed as Bancroft weighed his options. In the fall events moved more swiftly. Frederick Robinson's oration that proclaimed the Workingmen to be "the pioneers in the great cause" quickened Bancroft's resolve. In September 1834 a leading Henshaw supporter, John D. Eldredge, urged Bancroft to come to the Worcester convention, a sign of Democratic interest in his availability. The Hampden County Workingmen had been observing his activities for some time, Bancroft was told. Their principles "constitute the very essence of the democracy," a Workingman wrote, adding that monopolists were but the "dynasty of modern states," the descendants of those who tried to retard colonial growth back in the seventeenth century. "You know no party but the people, whose welfare and interests alone appear to be your guiding star." By October external pressures and internal desires coalesced.[56]

Two letters in local papers announced Bancroft's political views. The first attacked the unholy alliance between wealth and political authority in the context of the banking debate. The menace of "the increasingly unequal distribution of wealth" lay in "the dishonorable manner in which it was achieved . . . [by means] of unequal aristocratic legislation." The conflict between the house of have and the house of want was due not to different capacities, but to a new aristocracy that produced little and garnered the fruits of other men's labor. There would always be a struggle between the propertied and the propertyless, but "he who will act with moderation, prefer fact to theory and remember that everything in this world is relative and not absolute, will still the violence of the contest."[57]

On the strength of this letter Bancroft filed as an independent candidate for the General Court from the Northampton area. He had not joined any political party and genuinely believed that his statement was an appeal on which men of differing persuasions could agree. Some might be offended by its shrill vocabulary, but otherwise, Bancroft reasoned, he had not said anything offensive. The preference for moderation, for stilling the contest, for fact over theory, and fundamentally for open opportunity and not artificial equality—this was an agenda perfectly palatable to individuals of different political persuasions.

The suspicious Workingmen, reading this appeal, demanded further clarification before granting him their support. A second letter followed. Bancroft now reviewed his impeccable progressive record—the Northampton oration and the Bank article for the *North American Review*—and declared that the people could not tolerate "vast associations of wealth," which threatened to convert an independent yeomanry into a dependent tenancy. He praised labor but assured the workers that wealth did not guarantee happiness—what mattered was the mode of acquisition. Misery was not God's design for mankind, but the remediable result of human institutions. At the same time he also added that "inequalities can not be narrowed, any more than the circle squared . . . The nature of man leaves every state of being imperfect and democracy must have its foibles, errors and regrets."[58]

This only confused matters further. If Ticknor and Story winced at the assault on vast associations of wealth, they too were wholeheartedly in favor of an independent yeomanry. That wealth did not guarantee happiness had been said often enough by many respectable people in Boston, who likewise hoped to alleviate misery and poverty, if not necessarily by political means. And the last sentence of the second letter, which asserted that efforts to eliminate inequality were impossible, fended off any accusation that he was a radical out to upset the social order.

He repeated the ambiguous message when he now published a speech earlier delivered to the Workingmen of Northampton drawing parallels between the decline of Rome and the current situation in the United States. The ancient republic collapsed because the "plough was in the hands of the slave," an elite ruled, the class of independent yeomen shrank, and poverty spread. "The progress of change in the condition of the laboring class" in America was slow, he thought, but the day of the people had arrived, even if in the past "the greatest number has been forgotten by the annalist, as its happiness has been neglected by the lawgiver." Bancroft, the annalist and lawgiver, would alter matters. In a republic, he asserted, "he that will execute great designs must act with an organized party" and while he had yet to outline his own design concretely, he was ready to join a party.[59]

Such pronouncements earned Benjamin Hallett's confidence. An

Anti-Masonic convention in Springfield on October 14 approved "the fearless and independent republican spirit" of the letters and endorsed their author's candidacy. When the Boston papers spread the news, messages arrived in Northampton lauding Bancroft's moral courage. "There is more democracy in your letter than appears on the surface," wrote one correspondent, revealing the general confusion created by the slippery content that each reader could explain according to his wishes. Undismayed, indeed pleased, by the options this variety of interpretations left open, Bancroft requested an affidavit from Alexander H. Everett absolving him from any guilt for that infamous sentence in the Bank article. He also made sure that the Albany Regency heard of his latest pronouncements.[60]

To get elected required some campaigning, and Bancroft tailored his message to his largely rural constituency. It did no good to talk about monopolies and aristocracies in a district where banking problems were remote from daily experience and where differences in wealth were hardly visible. Instead Bancroft stressed status, order, and sentiments of resentment, all the while disclaiming appeals to passion or demagoguery. "The small farmer passes in the world for less than he did fifty years ago," he cried whenever the opportunity presented itself, "and the mechanic is not what he once was." In the olden times they were not called "the lower classes." He thought that he thus called attention to "permanent principles" while the opposition preferred to sling mud.[61]

Joseph Buckingham, editor of the *New England Magazine,* greeted Bancroft's campaign with dismay—his young friend seemed strong in slogans and weak in particulars. The opposition papers concurred. Bancroft's "flaming electioneering documents" ignored Jackson's real abuses, while "a string of generalities" gave the impression that he abhorred opulence and loved the poor. A wealthy capitalist appealed to "jacobinical feelings which do not flourish among the intelligent yeomanry of the district." This "demagogue," said the Boston *Atlas,* "this most dissembling time server," "this most awkward and calculating politician" was out to dupe the people.[62]

Bancroft's opponents, the Whigs, wooed the same potential voters with similar arguments. They warned mechanics that they might be experimented out of their daily bread (a reference to Democratic banking measures). Artisans, styled the bones and sinew of the community, were assured that there was no natural hatred between the rich and the poor and reminded that the Democrats were a wealthy lot, that while Henshaw, Simpson, and Bancroft spoke of putting down the moneyed aristocracy, Jackson was bent on denying to the poor and the middling classes the opportunity to grow rich. All should join the revolt against this Tory President and show that "the spirit of Revolution is neither dead nor sleeping," cried the *Atlas*. That same spirit, Bancroft replied, should sway the voters in his own favor.[63]

To clinch their case, Bancroft's opponents dredged up his unstable past and charged that he was drunk with German infidelity. His career at Harvard proved that this candidate of the supposedly oppressed had benefited from the generosity of those he now attacked. An *Atlas* editorial plainly stated that only the idle "in the halls of infidelity and atheism, the dram shops and the dram cellers," who "live off the earnings of other industrious people," would vote for such a man. Scorning his learning and erudition, several "Real Workingmen" published satires complaining about Bancroft's vocabulary and apologizing for their own lack of education, while priding themselves on common sense. "You ain't so great a man as you think you are," he was told, "and we ain't such confounded fools as you think we are."[64]

Such tactics surprised Bancroft. "The community was made to believe," he wrote to Edward Everett, "that there was danger the Bible would be taken out of their hands . . . Democracy was said to be a branch of atheism . . . a perfect fever was got up." He was being tarnished by an unfair association; after all, Bancroft was running as an independent, not as a Democrat. Matters became worse when the Democratic *Morning Post*, in his defense, accused its rivals of slander. This was hardly the force of moral opinion he had lauded in the first volume of his *History*.[65]

The outcome was predictable. Bancroft lost, getting a meager total of 167 votes. Lacking a political machine, with only vague political connections and no financial support, he was insufficiently prepared for an electorate that found other arguments more persuasive. His loyalties were also suspect because of his earlier approaches to the National Republicans; and the charge of political opportunism was damaging.[66]

Surprised and hurt, he wondered, "Are the people of Boston outrageous against me? Or is all the abuse a mere tempest of electioneering?" His friends expected that this taste of campaigning would finish his political career. The Boston *Courier* urged "a return to the garden of literature from the wilderness of politics," adding the hope that "he would write no more letters to the Workingmen nor to any political cabal in the future." The Northampton *Courier* implied that he was wasting his talents, and John Davis suggested that the determination to continue the *History* should keep Bancroft at home.[67]

All miscalculated. Bancroft believed that he could write his next volume and make a political name for himself at the same time. He also made sure that Van Buren was aware of his trials. "My crime consists in refusing to calumniate the present administration," he explained to the Vice President, "and in asserting that the Whig party is making an insidious attempt to win political power through the influence of wealth and against the rights of the people . . . My effort has been an attempt to awaken the spirit of democracy among the hills of New England." One defeat could not swerve him from his chosen task. Marcus Morton and Samuel C. Allen sent encouraging notes. "It will be some years before a popular party can become powerful in the state. But it will rise and in six years it will culminate," Bancroft told Everett. In fact 1840 would witness serious Democratic defeats in the state and the nation. But in 1835 he declared himself "a radical in principle and a radical in feeling," delighted to discover that unmerited censure did "not in the least disturb my peace. I have never enjoyed greater tranquillity."[68]

VI

DEMOCRACY IN THEORY
AND PRACTICE

By CAMPAIGNING as the Workingmen's advocate in 1834, Bancroft had not abandoned hope for a place in the National Republican—Whig—organization. Only after he perceived that he would pass unnoticed in its crowded ranks did he move to the Democracy, and he constructed an elaborate defense when slanderous vituperation greeted his decision to do so. He then shaped a democratic theory of man and society, appropriate for the United States and progressive in orientation. Much of what he said was derivative, but it was also persuasive enough to alter the fortunes of the Democratic Party in Massachusetts.

From the outset Bancroft defined himself as more than a mere politician. He was teacher to the masses, the man of letters enlightening the people, the intellectual defining new tasks. Since great social changes followed from the spread of new ideas, public education in the broadest sense was the best way to reorder the state. That lofty self-definition compensated for the distasteful features of political life and put to use the skills he had sought, if unsuccessfully, to apply in the past.[1]

The young man who only a few years earlier had expressed aversion to shouting with the multitudes had changed his mind. He acquired a new vocabulary and a radical rhetoric which, he sincerely believed, posed no threat to the existing social order. But since Bancroft rarely descended to particulars or definitions, he appeared to be a greater menace than he was. Tagged as a turncoat radical, the reluctant reformer remained a conservative closer to the Whigs than his opponents realized. The occasional shrillness of his terminology did not conceal an optimism that ignored real problems and assured all of the basic health of society.

John Davis cautioned that the American government was in the business of protecting equal rights, not privileges, usurpations, and oppressions. Bancroft happily concurred. He could agree with Hubbard Winslow, a conservative Whig who railed against the radicalism totally destructive of accumulated wisdom and experience. To ask the electorate, "Will you have a government of money or a government of many?" was not radical in 1835; everyone agreed on expelling the money changers from the temple. Men of different political views feared newly or speculatively acquired wealth, and Bancroft concurred in that judgment. In days of excessive opulence, he wrote some time later, "inequalities of condition" excited envy and political feuds, to be remedied without tumult or bloodshed, through "the still small voice of public opinion."[2]

To arouse this small voice of public opinion Bancroft set out to win over to the Democracy the middling elements—the artisans, shopkeepers, journeymen, small businessmen, merchants, and prosperous farmers, all neither wealthy nor poor but all convinced that they deserved more than they had. To get rich in this society of limitless opportunities nothing more was required than elevation of the laboring classes to their rightful enjoyment of moral culture. Bancroft never defined what the elevation involved, nor did he ever propose concrete measures to attain it. But the familiar phrases touched chords well known to his audience.

Because many found these slogans palatable, the Democracy's fortunes in the Whig state improved, especially after Bancroft received a chance to exercise his considerable managerial talents. But the achievements were short-lived. The party never bridged the gaps among its various factions. In spite of Bancroft's efforts to define a common ground, splinter groups persisted in going their own way. The level of political consciousness and personal involvement was not high enough to overcome ingrained habits, and the democratization of Whiggery made further inroads on Bancroft's following. Even the election of a Democratic governor before the decade ended in the long run proved meaningless, for it reflected the ambivalences embedded in Bancroft's democratic philosophy and Democratic politics.

The independent about to turn Democrat became at once a favorite target of abuse. "You must be encased in armour," his sister Lucretia wrote, assuming that he was impervious to denunciation. "There is but one thing which prevents me from siding with you in politics," she added, "and that is the companions you are compelled to be mixed with," a common judgment of Bancroft's friends. Orestes A. Brownson, sarcastically observing the reactions to Bancroft's *History,* noted that the Whigs endured him as a historian, "but as a man he finds no mercy. He has committed the sin of democracy and in a democratic country too, and absolution he must not hope for." The *American Monthly Magazine* shied away from rumors that Bancroft was "a mentally deranged, avowed atheist," but branded one of his speeches "a sophistical, sycophantic, abusive, political harangue" that would shame the logic of a child. He was one of those "incendiaries who are endeavoring to wrap the community in midnight conflagration and to bear off the treasures from the ruins." Did he really believe, a Whig asked incredulously, that men "are angels willing to do what is right without compulsion?" He and his kind, said another, talked of classes where there were none, fostered political corruption and mobocratic rule, incited the poor against the rich, and destroyed respect for constituted authorities. The Boston *Atlas* pointed out that Bancroft and Alexander H. Everett, who also joined the Democratic Party, had recently courted three different political organizations and hoped that this unholy alliance of literature and Locofocoism would be signally defeated.[3]

Bancroft advocated precisely such an alliance when he argued that men of letters should also be men of the people. But he remained oblivious to the meaning of his actions and at the end of 1834 blithely offered to help his Whig friends, including Edward Everett and John Davis. Nothing in Whig doctrine contradicted his own views, and only when the *Atlas,* the *Courier,* and other newspapers persisted in their attacks did he develop a keener sense of his political radicalism.

When the Democratic Party acknowledged his existence, Bancroft began to present the Workingmen's argument in a more coherent, better-digested fashion, toning down some of its extremism. In that process, he borrowed ideas from the Whigs as well. The swift transfer of loyalties required mental agility and political acumen; but he never dispelled the charge of opportunism, and remained a slippery political thinker, so vague as to stand on both sides of all but the clearest political issues.

To justify himself, Bancroft tried to show that his involvement was a respectable response to Whig cries for enlightened leadership. He fully agreed with Theophilus Parsons, certainly not a radical, that it was the duty of the learned to prevent "the poisonous influence of passion and vice and of craving for unhallowed power to corrupt public opinion." Otherwise, Parsons warned, a fearful struggle would result from the cries of "the poor against the rich." Bancroft, who incautiously raised such a cry in 1834, never repeated it. According to Parsons, the masses had to learn "that favor and security to the rights of property on the one hand and to the rights of industry on the other hand are one and the same thing, and a universal good." This too Bancroft found acceptable. He differed from his Whig detractors only in the remedy prescribed. Since wealth was a fact of life, the only way to offset its possible negative impact was through the political process. The "influence of wealth must be balanced" by the "power of numbers."[4]

The man of letters was central to this precarious balancing act, Bancroft believed. The voters required guidance that only he could provide, while the people would stimulate him "into the bold pursuit of speculative truth." "The judgment of the race" would confirm conclusions formulated "on the principle of humanity and right," and arrived at by one free from the strings of wealth or other affiliations likely to hamper thought. He would "run a glorious career amidst the applause of the people," his powers renewed in the consciousness of public sympathy. All of which would more than compensate for the abuse encountered along the way.[5]

"Politics are but morals applied to public affairs," the budding intellectual informed the people, promising to have no part of demeaning partisan squabbles. "It is alone by infusing great principles into the common mind that revolutions in human society can be effected," Bancroft declared. Society could change, the human race could advance "only by moral principles diffused through the multitude." He did not elaborate what revolution he had in mind and what principles he hoped to infuse, but grubby searches for votes were not for him.[6]

Leadership called for organization—drawing up platforms, distributing patronage, winning elections—all of which involved compromises, deals, manipulations, and subterfuges as well as the reduction of complex concepts to simple, understandable terms. There were bound to be disappointments when the people were not willing to be enlightened. And because Bancroft's vision often floated away from reality to poetical musings scarcely to his purpose, he succeeded in personal terms but failed in the larger context. The philosophical democrat and the Democrat with the capital D were one and the same person. But theory couched in visionary philosophical terms diverged from practice; and in the down-to-earth skirmishes of reality, theory often dropped out of sight.

"The present age is prophetic," wrote Orestes A. Brownson. "The seers are on the watch towers gazing with serene eye upon the moral firmament, reading the aspects of the lights and shadows which alternate in the moral heavens; solving the problems." Bancroft saw himself as one of these prophets who not only stood preaching on the watchtowers but also fought below. The tragedy of the endeavor, which no amount of personal success obliterated, sprang from the unwillingness of the people to follow the self-proclaimed apostle, and from the refusal of his friends to concede the aptness of his message.[7]

The message proceeded from the seemingly incontrovertible proposition that "a spirit in man," the attribute of the race, connected the individual to God, enabling him intuitively to understand the eternal principles that guided the universe. This faculty counterbalanced man's earthly, sinful, and mortal character, gave him "the power . . . to discern good from evil, right from wrong," and accounted for "the capacity for progress."[8] This faculty also made a democratic society feasible and legitimized the electoral process. By collectively exercising their power to distinguish right from wrong, the people became the highest earthly tribunal. The common judgment—the people reasoning on particular issues—balanced out the passions and errors to which individuals were prone and yielded decisions close to the voice of Reason since "as opposite unjust passions balance each other, justice emerges." "Providence never disowns the race," Bancroft concluded, and "the spirit of God breathes through the combined intelligence of the people."[9]

Numerous instances recorded in his *History* showed that popular collective wisdom was "superior to that of the wisest individual." Their "combined moral qualities" generated a force neither violence nor bribery deflected, while even so seminal a rebel as Roger Williams erred insofar as he left the people behind and outdistanced the possible with ideas too advanced for their time. All major social changes through which mankind moved toward perfection were contingent upon popular support. Martin Luther triumphed only because a nation was behind him; George Fox succeeded when the poor folk followed; religious toleration in Maryland was not the gift of far-seeing proprietors but a popular achievement; and Puritanism was religion struggling for the people in spite of the Cotton Mathers of the moment. "Who can doubt that the people collectively exercise the appointing power more wisely than any individual?" the historian asked. "The people are less shaken than the prince," was the moral of another event; on another occasion "the uneducated population . . . formed conclusions as just as those which a century later pervaded the country." What had been the case in the documented past would extend on into the present.[10]

While few Whigs quarreled with Bancroft's historical vision, some refused to make that leap of judgment to the present. By ascribing to all men "the same rights and liberties," Bancroft's democratic theory made a mockery of God-given differences. By contrast, many Whigs wanted votes weighed, not counted, for individual standing, influence, and worth in society depended on merit and attainments, and not solely on human nature. "Love of freedom," Hubbard Winslow argued, was "a noble spirit" but unless enlightened, tempered, guided, and restrained, would "rush headlong to its own destruction." And the amount of freedom a society tolerated was directly related to each person's willingness to curb his appetites.[11]

Bancroft rarely denied these Whig propositions and regretted that he could not persuade his opponents how close his own views were to theirs. He too argued for guidance and leadership—that was one reason he had entered politics. Nor did he advocate the abrogation of all restraints. But their effectiveness, he maintained, ultimately had to come from the individual, another issue that brought him closer to his opponents, who were fond of quoting Edmund Burke on just that point. To answer challenges and assuage his own fears, Bancroft elaborated a social vision of the mechanics of a free society.

A democratic society, in his view, had "to eradicate established abuses and to bring social institutions and laws into harmony with moral right." Few contemporaries disputed the worthiness of the goal. Popular government Bancroft defined as one conducted by "the mind of the country, freely exerted and freely enlightened." That too many could live with. The decisions of such a government, he continued, were "the nearest expression of the law of God, the voice of conscience, the oracle of universal reason," because the mechanism of a free society canceled out factionalism, private interests, and class conflicts.[12] The multitude was neither "rash nor fickle." Its natural dialectic was a safer guide than the "logic of schools," since the people were "firm and tranquil," always acting in moderation because they were but "slowly impregnated with new ideas and effect no change except in harmony with the knowledge acquired." The first volume of the *History* said as much, as did the second, nearing completion; and both pointed out the absurdity of fears of oppressive majoritarian regimes. The people's government was the world's mildest and strongest for, "discarding the implements of terror, it dares to rule by moral force and has its citadel in the heart."[13]

Bancroft scoffed at the Whig charge that this theory portended the end of all social bonds; he wanted liberation from oppressive man-made

limits, not the loosening of restraints. No one had the right to do as he
pleased, and in a free society all would voluntarily wish to do only what
was good—for only through the common good could they further their
own. The definition of that good rested on the electoral process, not on
the pronouncements of self-appointed leaders. "The duty of America is
to secure the culture and happiness of the masses by their reliance on
themselves"—a worthy goal Whigs like Caleb Cushing and Robert
C. Winthrop could easily accept.[14]

George Bancroft and the Whigs did not understand each other. He
ascribed to his opponents an attachment to constitutions which, he maintained, rested government "not on anything that is in man but on parch-
ments and title deeds." That mistaken outlook denied the validity of
man's divine spark and treated liberties as products of bargains measured
by grants, "their title deeds in the records of the past . . . [their] security
in the graves of the dead." But Daniel Webster had already abandoned
that erroneous position and the Whigs knew how uncertain constitutional safeguards were. They had discarded their outmoded heritage and
had adapted to democratic times. Bancroft's counterassault was as unfair
as any from which he suffered. Ignoring fine distinctions, he stoutly
maintained that God had implanted the law of justice "in man's heart
long before a parchment was scrawled upon or a constitution devised."
Few opponents denied that interpretations of immutable laws, altered
and purified in time, demanded corresponding changes in the frames of
government.[15]

Since the Whigs often branded the Democrats infidels and blasphem-
ers, Bancroft identified his theory with practical Christianity, a favorite
Unitarian term. He pointed to the natural alliance between a doctrine
that stressed man's worth and religion that "performed its works upon
the heart" and reformed the exteriors of life by improving "moral affections." Christianity, having enfranchised the masses, was the natural ally
of democratic theory, a set of beliefs "hastening reform, yet always conservative, proclaiming absolute equality among men, yet not suddenly
abolishing the unequal institutions of society, guaranteeing absolute freedom yet invoking the inexorable restrictions of duty."[16]

Bancroft bristled when some clergymen asserted that inequality of
individual wealth was "the ordinance of providence and essential to civilization." He knew his Bible and needed no reminders that the poor
would never cease out of the land, but he disputed fatalistic assumptions
that God had meant this state of affairs to remain unchanged. God did
create distinctions, but as a stimulus to exertion and progress, encourag-

ing accountability, frugality, and industry. The outcome of the race depended on factors over which society had no control, yet it had to be open to the participation of all. This he had been taught all his life, among others by his beloved John Thornton Kirkland, that pillar of the New England establishment, who urged his wards to strive upward, to better themselves for everyone's benefit.[17]

But equal opportunity did not imply tampering with reality. Bancroft aimed not to upset the existing order, only to dignify labor, "to elevate that class into the higher regions of moral culture and enjoyment," without affecting the social and economic differentiations inherent in creation. Yet Bancroft never made clear how he would bring this about, nor did he perceive that such an elevation demanded more radical changes than he supported.[18]

The goal of elevating the laboring classes set the limits of Bancroft's reform impulse and accounted for the stress he placed on morality, spiritual growth, individual regeneration, and progress. He never developed a sense of the difficulties faced, and none of his messages described the genuine hardships of the workers. There ought not to have been any. Bancroft found enough support in reality for his fervent faith in the promise of American life to be able to ignore its other, contradictory aspects. In this abundant land, everyone could share in the national wealth. While Bancroft never asserted that the poor were happier than the rich, his message to the Workingmen in 1834 extolled the virtues of labor and came close to telling them that they were indeed more fortunate than drones who lived from the proceeds of capital. Beneath the thin veneer of the class-conflict doctrine his early letters seemed to espouse was a fundamentally optimistic view of a classless society, troubled only by easily shed foreign or unnatural accretions.

Now a Democrat, though still avid for Whig approval, committed by his understanding of history to assign the people a central role in politics, yet eager to deny opposition charges that he led a popular assault on the established order, Bancroft desperately sought an intellectual formula that would justify the route he had taken, to himself and to others. His agile mind seized on transcendentalism, then much discussed in Boston's best circles, and discovered in that movement links to familiar thinkers whom he had ignored in the past. His German education now became more relevant as ideas tucked away in the back of the mind acquired fresh significance. Never fully at ease in the world of German idealism, he did not abandon his Harvard moral philosophy and he remained forever puzzled by the excitement the Europeans generated. But since they angered his political enemies, Bancroft fell back on the Germans to assert his respectability and prove himself right.

Harriet Martineau, whom Bancroft had once met in Northampton, impressed him with her battle against materialist philosophy, which, he now realized, involved more than mere changes in terminology. Her own writings, as well as those of S. T. Coleridge and Thomas Carlyle, simplified the complexity and murkiness of the German idealists and fleshed out useful slogans that buttressed his own democratic theory. He found *Sartor Resartus* a quaint and original work and was suitably impressed with the French eclectics. All supplied him insights to substantiate his political outlook.[19]

Bancroft neither read the Germans carefully nor fully worked out the implications of their ideas. He now understood Kant as little as he earlier had Hegel. The immediate task, however, was not to construct a philosophical system but to garner arguments by which to sustain a political stance. Bancroft rather superficially adopted an idealist framework drawn by others from Kant, Jacobi, Schleiermacher, De Wette, and Herder. He thereby broadened his inherited common-sense outlook and decreased its Lockean components. He rudely mingled the common-sense philosophy acquired at Harvard from the Scottish philosophers with the intuitionalism gleaned from the German idealists. It was a measure of his misunderstanding that he identified German idealism with the Quaker inner-light doctrine, which, he also thought, was identical with the True Reason as defined by Coleridge and Carlyle. John Locke may have been America's greatest philosopher, but he was still a Whig favorite, so that Bancroft chose to stress other strains more in line with present needs.

Locke, Bancroft wrote in 1835, had erroneously sought "wisdom by consulting the outward world, confounding consciousness with reflection, and trusting solely to the senses for the material of thought." There was a connection, the historian concluded, between that bent of mind and Locke's one substantive, and disastrous, contribution to America—the constitution for the Carolinas. The pitfalls of Locke's metaphysics interested Bancroft only tangentially, but he realized what was at stake when George Ripley, Ralph W. Emerson, and Orestes A. Brownson proposed a new theory of knowledge and cognition, based on spontaneous reason and intuition. By asserting that the mind could transcend experience and make contact with truth directly, they validated his claim that ordinary people could know what was correct. Hence, innately good but also flawed, man had a right to shape his own destiny and express his inner self. Bancroft enthusiastically seized upon this murky idealism to buttress his argument for the elevation of the laboring classes, casually employing the vocabulary his new friends popularized.[20]

Friendships and acquaintances within the transcendentalist movement enhanced the impact of idealism. George Ripley, Ralph Waldo Emerson, Theodore Parker, Frederic Hedge, Nathaniel Frothingham, Bronson Alcott, and others considered themselves cultural reformers, shapers of a new American mind, and in their own way were bent on a task similar to Bancroft's. They sought, like him, to infuse new principles into a society not at all eager to receive them. His attitude toward the transcendentalists, however, was ambivalent. Emphasis on the divine spark in man, on the intuitive grasp of truth, and on transcendent ideas showed his indebtedness. But differences of character and intellect, as well as politics, kept him from becoming one of them. Idealism never entirely replaced moral philosophy. Nor did he ever break through to a self-reliant individualism like Emerson's. The vague and often unfocused musing that emanated from other members of the group confused Bancroft, who had no patience for their Olympian stand, with its occasional disdain for the common man and its contempt for American society. He prided himself on realism.[21]

Political activity forced Bancroft to deal with issues they could ignore and thus steered him in a different direction. His admiration for Emerson endured; the two maintained a cordial relationship throughout their lives, secretly aware of how far their thoughts diverged. Emerson distrusted men of Bancroft's type, made derogatory comments about politics, and remained hostile to the kinds of activities organizational involvements thrust upon Bancroft. Bancroft had made peace with the age of the common man and busily exploited its opportunities. He could not accept Emerson's orientation toward absolute principles, which called on man to assert his individuality by rebelling against history. Nor did the historian accept Emerson's view that the past was the source of institutions, thoughts, and life patterns that shackled freedom by putting barriers between the soul and reality and by blinkering the intuitive understanding of spiritual forces. Civilization, for the Concord thinker, had "the bad effects that crutches have of destroying the use of limbs they are meant to aid."[22] Nature, for him the realm of absolute knowledge, was a liberating force, while history, merely representational knowledge, dealt only with secondary causes. To understand the universe man had to become a little child in spirit, discarding the burdens of knowledge. Integrating himself in nature, he would learn the correspondence of the outward world to the inward world of thoughts and emotions. All nature was a metaphor or image of the human mind, the teachings of creation writ large.[23]

Bancroft by contrast always qualified the concept of spirituality. Even though "transcendental claptrap" crept into his rhetoric, he never lost his profoundly historical orientation.[24] The voice of God in man's soul was a powerful impulse; but history with its laws of progression always provided a material standard by which to measure each assertion of human sovereignty. Humanity could not lift itself out of history, which gave man's spiritual character the concrete forms expressed in institutions, laws, customs, society, and the state.

Nor did Bancroft accept Emerson's extreme individualism and subjectivism. The thrust of his endeavor was to persuade the electorate that the Democracy did not advocate radicalism of any sort and that a free society was immune to anarchic disrespect for law, constitutions, traditions, and authority. Emerson's view of human sovereignty, extended to politics, would have justified such fears. As a historian and politician, Bancroft concluded that the deeds not of man, but of men, moved society. The perception of the laws of nature might be intuitive but only the jostling of minds in close proximity brought forth a correct understanding, and this process occurred not in the solitude of one's study but in the political arena.

In 1835 Emerson delivered a lecture on George Fox, the founder of the Quakers. At the same time, writing the second volume of his *History,* Bancroft included an extensive discussion of the origins of the sect, which he thought would please his friend. In fact the two portraits were very different. Emerson's Fox was man freed, the "idealist seeking to accommodate the show of things to the desires of the mind," who forswore society, returned to nature, and received a practical lesson on morals. Fox, the hope not of men, but "of the race of Man," was the individual who fought a society that held "fast not to truths not to things but to usages."[25]

Many of these terms reappeared in Bancroft's second volume. But to him Fox was "the representative of humanity," the product of turbulent times when "complete enfranchisement of the mind" was the guiding mission of the age. His doctrine of the inner light foreshadowed democracy, and the Quakers were the product of the common people. Despite the danger "that liberty may be pushed to dissoluteness," the truth Fox uncovered was "a moral principle . . . tested by the attempt to reduce it to practice" as he gained adherents among the yeomanry and the illiterate mechanics. "Divine revelation," Bancroft added in an aside, was not "to be confounded with individual conscience, for the conscience of the individual follows judgment and may be warped by self love and debauched by lust." It was, instead, "the light of universal reason, the voice of Universal Conscience manifesting its own verity . . . by the experience of all men."[26]

As enfranchisement of the mind had been the mission of the seventeenth century, establishment of a political system based "on reason, reflection and the free expression of deliberate choice" was that of the nineteenth. For more than a year Bancroft hesitated. But then in the winter of 1834–1835 he took the plunge, seeking to infuse "great principles into the common mind" so that the advancing "moral and intellectual powers of the people" would fulfill the earlier promises of American life. The prophet and seer, the philosophical democrat and popular advocate, became a Democrat to guide the masses—a difficult task when the Whigs kept winning. John Davis in 1834 received a majority of twelve thousand votes over those cast for his three opponents, a Workingman, a Democrat, and an Anti-Mason. Judge Morton gained four thousand more votes than in 1833, but that reflected a general increase in the number going to the polls. Had he added all the Workingmen and Anti-Masonic votes to his total, he would still have lost.[27]

Adept at reading figures, Bancroft pondered their significance. The splinter alignments offered little hope. Benjamin Hallett in Boston commanded only a fraction of the Anti-Masons; most of his followers preferred the Whigs. Nor were the Workingmen numerous enough to promise Democratic victories. Morton, Bancroft decided, erred in claiming "that Democrats, Workingmen and democratic Anti-Masons constitute the majority party of the state." Instead, Bancroft concluded the party's fortunes would rise through the support of conservative Democrats, former Federalists, dissatisfied Whigs, intellectuals who had remained aloof from party politics, Boston businessmen, merchants, and the middling classes. The "middling interests," and former National Republicans, would augment the already visible Democratic constituency. And for that purpose Workingmen rhetoric would not do. The curious mixture of radical outbursts and fervent conservative assurances that from 1835 on shaped Bancroft's orations expressed his effort to present a viable alternative to the Whigs—in large part by preempting their arguments.[28]

The move to Springfield that paralleled this decision delighted Sarah and also expanded Bancroft's political base. The new house, furnished with the aid of the Dwights, was spacious enough for an expanding family—daughter Louisa and John Chandler, born in April 1835. Springfield was also the center of Democratic and Workingmen activity and, while still inferior to Boston in Bancroft's view, was a marked improvement over Northampton. He became friendly with the Dwight social circle, some of whose members—like George Bliss (a business partner in the years to come)—participated in the far-flung Dwight enterprises. Whigs like George Ashmun, as well as Democrats like Harvey Chapin and O. H. Warner (soundly defeated by William B. Calhoun in the congressional race a year earlier), also became acquaintances. Springfield was a cultural center of some standing, and the Bancrofts, an attractive couple with important connections, were much in demand.

Since Bancroft's party identification was but a few months old, his role as yet undefined, he was very careful in what he said and how he said it. Many still regarded him as a former Whig or at best a Jacksonian Federalist. In his newly found inoffensiveness, he became all things to all men. Leading Democrats regarded him as a possible outside force to patch up their chronic divisions. David Henshaw sensed a kindred soul—a Democrat of political sagacity, shrewdness, and tact. For Marcus Morton, Bancroft symbolized the new man the party needed. Nor did his associations upset the Dwights—friendly relations with the Democratic administration in Washington augured well for their banking interests. Even John Davis and Edward Everett maintained cordial relations despite the shift in allegiances. The Democratic Party had yet to admit officially that it had gained a new and prominent member, but Bancroft now presented himself as a Democrat who defended the people against the aristocracy. In response to Vermont Democrats who invited him to a celebration, he declared that modern Democracy began in New England.

To William H. Prescott, Bancroft seemed to be "evaporating in newspaperials," unable to ignore "the penny trumpet of fungus popularitas." Such comments were less serious than the problem of the stubborn Springfield Workingmen, who ran independent candidates and occasionally voted for Whigs. In the fall Bancroft joined the committee that drafted the address of the Massachusetts Democrats to the people. "I hope there will be no wild, thoughtless and extravagant doctrines introduced," Charles G. Greene of the *Morning Post* cautioned.[29] He need not have worried. The address Bancroft helped write, one with which Henshaw, the *Morning Post,* Morton, and Workingmen all could live, repeated the standard slogans, asserted devotion to principles, and contrasted the Democratic platform with that of the party of the aristocracy. It also asserted that "pure democracy inculcates equal rights—equal laws—equal means of education and equal means of wealth also, as incidental to other blessings." Such incidentals sounded more radical than they were, in part because Bancroft never spelled out how they were to be achieved and soon enough asserted that equal means of wealth meant open opportunity, nothing more. Marcus Morton considered the address "a textbook for the Democracy."[30]

Yet it did little to lessen the tensions among the party's constituencies or materially to affect the fall election. The Workingmen thought the Boston Customhouse party remote and refused to dismantle their local organizations. In spite of Bancroft's assurances, they doubted that he, Morton, and Henshaw honestly opposed all exclusive privileges, representing as they did an "aristocracy of the democracy." Many preferred to vote for Edward Everett rather than Marcus Morton, on the assumption that they had a better chance of fulfilling their ultimate aims with this avowed gentleman aristocrat. Nor was Bancroft more successful with the Anti-Masons. It was not enough that Morton at his behest declared his loyalty to "pure radical Democracy" and denied that he had ever owned a dollar's worth of stock in any Boston corporation.[31]

Numerous minor parties confused the fall campaign; many potential supporters were lost to Everett, the Whig candidate, to the Agrarian Party, to the Free Bridge Party and to thirteen others. The Abner Kneeland trial, still in progress, reminded everyone of Henshaw's and Dunlop's defense of this Jacksonian blasphemer; and a Boston mob almost lynched William Lloyd Garrison. The result was a foregone conclusion. Morton felt sorry to see the citizens "throw themselves under the feet of their oppressors and persecutors." He gained almost six thousand votes, but Everett still won by ten thousand.[32]

Undismayed, Bancroft pressed on—ever available for yet another oration, yet another rally, happy when in motion. Mounting correspondence and the exigencies of the *History* occupied him while at home, but he was often off to New York, Philadelphia, Washington. On a trip early in 1836 to Montpelier, Virginia, a long conversation with James Madison left Bancroft convinced that the former President was a Van Burenite. So were Benjamin F. Hallett and some Anti-Masons; and Edward Everett's call for maintenance of the status quo on slavery antagonized Whig supporters and brightened Democratic prospects for the future.

In May 1836 Edward Everett, Robert C. Winthrop, and other state officials came to Springfield to celebrate the town's second centennial. Bancroft, on excellent terms with all of them, played the host, and together with George Ashmun and George Bliss was one of the vice-presidents of the day. Laying partisan feelings aside, they joined in toasts to the town's heroes. But with the anniversary over, partisanship returned with a vengeance. Several groups planned rival celebrations for July 4, when Bancroft delivered the town oration. The Workingmen and the Whigs each conducted their own festivities and refused to join the Democrats in listening to Bancroft.

His speech that sunny afternoon, long on theory and short on proposals, mixed transcendental ideas with Workingmen rhetoric. Orestes A. Brownson had reservations about its social philosophy (too quiescent) but recognized in it the philosopher of humanity, working in the cause of civilization. Bancroft expected the merchants, the mechanics, the farmers, and the artisans to tread "the central path of duty" and vote for the Democratic Party in the contest between "physical force and moral power, a monied interest and the people . . . the treasures of wealth and the treasures of the mind . . . blind possession and living intelligence, the force of material interests and the wisdom, purity and power of the multitude." He called upon the people to rally against "the scarecrows of corrupt politicians . . . the horrible hobgoblins of the most experienced panic makers . . . the foggy exhalations from the fen of Whig despondency."[33]

Such pronouncements furthered Bancroft's nebulous role as party ideologue, arbitrator, and organizer. The speech evoked a chorus of praise from Pennsylvania politicians, from the Albany Regency, and even from Joseph Cogswell, despite some theoretical reservations. Brownson hoped that Bancroft's statement would persuade George Ripley, William Ellery Channing, and other Boston luminaries to vote for the Democracy. The one controversial note—an attack on southern nullifiers because of their contempt for northern free labor—brought a rebuke. To preserve unity for the coming presidential contest, any sectional antagonism was to be avoided. Bancroft never repeated his assault. His mother, informed by her daughter about his growing reputation, reported, "Van Burin [sic] says you are the first in Massachusetts." Approval from the party's highest quarters in Washington strengthened Bancroft's role in Massachusetts.[34]

A brewing struggle over the collectorship of the Port of Boston complicated the situation. David Henshaw chose John K. Simpson as his successor, while Democrats in the General Court preferred Abel Cushing. Other candidates also came forward, including Robert Rantoul, the conservative former Anti-Mason William Parmenter, and the Democratic Workingman Frederick Robinson. Morton promoted John Mills and rumors hinted that he wanted the job for himself. This scramble for office reflected poorly on the party, and Bancroft did his best to discourage it. Henshaw also moved to close the rifts with rhetoric. In Boston, a rapt audience heard this conservative businessman praise "the progress of free principles" and call for the election of judges. Much in line with Bancroft's theory, Henshaw also assaulted "ultra anti monopolists," agreeing that wealth was not presumptive evidence of dishonesty. Riches were "proof of industry, and frugality, and honesty; for rogues are more generally poor than honest men." He defended Abner Kneeland against the state authorities and attacked monopolies, including Harvard, that "seminary rich in the mortmain funds, rich from income thus wrung from the hand of labor, but musty in age and indolence and loitering half a century behind the progress of the Age." Bancroft the Harvard graduate agreed and rejoiced when Henshaw came out for Van Buren and hailed Morton as the Democracy's true representative—"he too, has sprung from the people." [35]

Morton, however, made reconciliation nearly impossible. While assuring Henshaw of his sincere attachment, he complained to Van Buren that "a set of men" in Boston were destroying the party, having more to gain by defeats than victories. But Van Buren refused to become involved in the local squabble. Unable to pacify the warring factions, Bancroft then urged postponement of the contest over the collectorship until after the presidential elections. [36]

Meanwhile he attended to his own campaign as the Democratic congressional candidate for the Springfield area. His Whig opponent, William B. Calhoun, had made a name for himself as Speaker of the Massachusetts House, where he presented the resolves condemning nullification. In 1834, his successful campaign for the congressional seat had emphasized his poverty and popular origin; and nothing in the intervening years had increased his wealth or lessened his appeal.

If it was difficult for Bancroft to brand Calhoun an aristocrat, the Whig press had a field day demolishing his own candidacy. The Boston *Atlas* jeered at his education and erudition, suggesting that he should deliver his speeches in Greek and Latin the better to delude the people. How could this "white kid gloves and silk stocking democrat" appeal to the poor? another newspaper asked. Would the Workingmen support a Dwight son-in-law with banking connections? And did the Anti-Masons truly want Bancroft in Congress? The answer on all fronts was no. Bancroft lost, 2,878 to 3,958, hardly an encouraging total, although he had polled four hundred more votes than the Democratic candidate in 1834.[37]

Statewide elections went slightly better, and Van Buren's national victory offset local disappointments. Furthermore, two congressional victories assured Massachusetts some Democratic representation in Washington. The party would have done better, Bancroft thought, but for Whig chicanery and champagne. That its platform may have been inadequate did not enter his mind. Having tied his future to "the party of improvement" and of social progress, as opposed as the Whigs to radicals willing to "pull down the old building about the ears of society, instead of removing it stone by stone," Bancroft considered its doctrine sufficient to the needs of the day. Democratic fortunes would improve in coming years: "it is now for the yeomanry and the mechanics to march at the head of civilization," he informed Brownson; "the day of the multitudes had dawned."[38]

Economic depression however postponed the arrival of the day of the multitudes and wiped out the Democrats' meager gains. While Bancroft celebrated the birth of his third child, George, and worried a little about Sarah's health, the panic of 1837 struck. "Mecanicks have been very much injured . . . there are so many bank failures," his mother wrote, describing the scene in Worcester, "is it possible they can keep their credit? . . . Oh George, I hope you are not among the loosers. I have some time quaik'd for you." The extensive Dwight funds tided him over financially. The political losses were harder to bear. The seer floundered, as the Whigs dredged up his rosy description of the American economy in the Springfield oration.[39]

Democratic measures, the opposition cried, had caused the collapse, diminishing the price of labor and goods and leaving as beneficiaries only "the rich capitalists retiring from business, brokers, usurers, pensioners, salary men and office holders." The metaphysical speculations of the pseudo-economist Bancroft prevented the poor from becoming rich or even acquiring a competency, while before Jackson "among the rich men of New England, nineteen out of twenty," Francis Baylies observed, "had begun without a dollar."[40]

Internally divided, the Democratic Party mounted no consistent defense. Benjamin F. Hallett blamed the Whigs, banking, and paper currency. Henshaw, Simpson, and others defended state banks, while Morton tried to hold a middle ground. Brownson, astounded by the closed factories, the growing number of unemployed, and the suffering, noted greater hatred of the rich than ever before. In May 1837 his sermon entitled *Babylon Is Falling* blamed the spirit of gain, and called for an end to the struggle between the rich and the poor "by giving to all, not equal wealth, but equal chances to wealth." Robert Rantoul railed against the few busy "fertilizing the rich man's field by the sweat of the poor man's brow," and called on the people to free themselves from the thraldom of the Bank and the proud paper bearing feudality. [41]

Perhaps the Middle Ages had not altogether ended! The suspicion intruded into the second volume of the *History*, published during the depression. Bancroft there explained how twelve colonies had freed themselves from seventeenth-century monopolies, oligarchies, and feudal classes, assuming in the process the character of a free people. The perspective, wider than that of Volume One, permitted the author to extend to other parts of the country the tribute earlier confined largely to New England.

New Englanders and southerners—"Anglo Saxons in the woods again," with "the inherited culture and intelligence of the seventeenth century" were on the verge of becoming a free people, developing a "system conforming to reason yet kindling enthusiasm, always hastening reform yet always conservative, proclaiming absolute equality among men yet not suddenly abolishing the unequal institutions of society, guaranteeing absolute freedom yet invoking the inexorable restrictions of duty." Their version of "practical Christianity," a legacy of the Reformation, exerted "its largest influence on politics." Immediate emancipation from the decaying institutions of the past was impossible. But surveying the history of the twelve colonies, Bancroft traced the simultaneous death of the old and birth of the new. The conclusion was in accord with the general theory—"the selfishness of evil defeats itself and God rules in the affairs of men." [42]

That survey recorded multiple efforts "to construct the future according to the forms of the past"—a futile maneuver, Bancroft reminded Whigs and Democrats in 1837 as they searched for ways to end the panic. Good laws were "the arrangement of men in society in their just and natural relations," and reforms could not go beyond the limits of their age, since "nations change their institutions but slowly" and conditionally. The New England towns succeeded because they were "the natural reproduction of the system which the instinct of humanity had imperfectly revealed to our Anglo Saxon ancestors," while the first constitution for the Carolinas failed—as did all reforms guided by a decrepit philosophy (materialism), outward forms (of the dying feudalism of England), and the contrivances of an intellectual (John Locke). [43]

Progress, Bancroft reminded the hotheads in his party, depended on strange alliances, even if ultimately "the fortunes of the human race are embarked in a life boat and cannot be wrecked." The disappearing monopolies of prelates, princes, and sovereigns, for instance, gave way to other forms of oppression which only time would erode. The great reformer whose idea of justification by faith kindled the democratic revolution preached obedience to tyrants. The republicanism of Calvin and the mercantile classes survived through an alliance with "the party of the past," the decaying feudal aristocracy. In such mysterious ways were the abuses of the world ameliorated, the outcome, "freedom of mind, applied to the contemplation of God . . . the end of life."[44]

"Vice and poverty could be banished by intelligent culture," but lest enthusiasts call for more, Bancroft reminded his readers that "virtue is happiness," and perfection from sin was actually more attainable in the abodes of the poor than in the palaces of the wealthy. Bancroft asked for no more than "the harmonious development of man's higher powers, with the entire subjection of the base to the noble instincts." With William Penn, he wished that "the people be neither rich nor poor, for riches bring luxury and luxury tyrants," and counseled patient faith "in the moral power of ideas [which] is constantly effecting the changes and improvements in society."[45]

Personal tragedy overshadowed the political ravages of the panic, the Democrats' confused responses, and the laudatory reviews of Volume Two. Sarah, never fully recovered from her last pregnancy, died in June 1837. In a depression such as he had not experienced for years, Bancroft left the children with the Dwights and with his sister Mary in Springfield, and sought to escape his gloom in a long journey to Montreal.[46]

Solitary rambles in the mountains, tracing the battlefield where Montgomery and Arnold fought, discovering the spot where Jacques Cartier landed, did not dispel mournful thoughts. Not even bishops and cathedrals took his mind off events in Massachusetts. Worries about the children persisted in spite of Mary's reassurances; and reports of Whig gains and Democratic losses enhanced Bancroft's unhappiness. Was he right to throw in his fortune with an uncertain political alignment that carried little weight with the electorate though blessed with divine favor? Or should he abandon politics altogether and devote himself to history? What would happen to his three motherless children? Would his all-important Dwight connections suffer by Sarah's death?[47]

Despondent, Bancroft returned to Springfield in August. The Dwights were supportive and the public awaited his further historical researches. But his party also made calls on him. Out of his private ordeal Bancroft emerged a more confirmed Democrat than before.

On July 4, 1837, in his absence, an assembly of Democrats at Bunker Hill heard speaker after speaker attack monopolies, aristocracies, the credit system, and corporations. Several weeks later Bancroft and Morton organized a standing committee, with Hallett as secretary, to rally the faithful for the coming battle. Bancroft followed Theodore Sedgwick's advice to refrain from abuse, denunciations, and violence; and the address to the party's annual convention expressed his theory of middle-of-the-road Democracy. He argued neither for leveling wealth nor for other radical changes. Pointing out that conscience was "often the dupe of interest and often but a more honorable name for self will," he insisted that society, not the individual, was the Democrats' major concern. The party still held to the theory of the harmony of interests and was unwilling to use governmental authority for improper ends. David Henshaw had explained that "the legislature exercises an undisputed right to regulate the business of individuals and to define their rights to property," but only "for the common good" and not to be expanded by "enlarged construction" for any end whatever.[48]

Moderate tactics failed to offset the difficulties of the national administration. Van Buren, unable to come up with an immediate cure for the panic, remained loyal to past Jacksonian measures and expected local organizations to do the same. "Perish commerce—perish credit," the Whigs cried, "or perish the clergy, says Abner Kneeland, and perish the whole nation, says the administration." They denounced Van Buren's subtreasury scheme as executive usurpation, which set the country on the road to "fraud, speculations, robbery and murder." Morton, tired of "being a mark to be shot at," threatened to retire, and the conservative New York Democrat William Marcy also had doubts about his party's recovery measures.[49]

Bancroft too had doubts, although he kept them to himself. A trip to Washington designed to guard the Bank of Michigan from undue government pressure confirmed his misgivings. The administration was in disarray and no one knew what to do next. Bancroft labored hard to persuade the secretary of the Treasury to grant the bank another extension, and to prevent a withdrawal of government deposits that kept it afloat. He proved "an efficient friend in court," and the success of his lobbying efforts delighted the Dwights.[50]

Back in Massachusetts Bancroft labored to counter Whig assaults, expand Democratic support, and keep his party in line—all in vain. The electorate refused to listen, and even those who only a year earlier had supported Morton switched to the Whigs. George Ripley noted that "almost to a man those who show any mark of genius or intellectual enterprise" were philosophical democrats, but none wanted to vote their conscience. A more efficient party organization, structured around county committees and conventions, was of little use. Even Bancroft's mother, Lucretia, not politically minded, read the signs of the times that November. "It is thought friend Van Burin [sic] must take care now all his own state have forsaken him—how will it affect your worldly concerns?" she asked her son.[51]

Those concerns led Bancroft to abuse the national bank, "the bulwark of the aristocracy," but say little about state banks. His statements arrayed material interests against the wisdom and power of the multitudes and equality against privilege. As local elections approached he abetted Hallett's diversionary maneuvers to revive anti-Masonic sentiments, even though that issue was then a red herring. "Masonry is taking a new form," the *Advocate* cried, "it is sheltered behind money power. Anti-Masons are also anti bank men. They oppose exclusive privileges." In the meantime Morton fended off charges that he politicized the judiciary by retaining his Supreme Court seat. When the results were in, Edward Everett triumphed five to three, Hampden County went Whig, and the losses everywhere were considerable. Once more, Bancroft concluded, Whig chicanery had clouded the judgment of the people.[52]

At the close of 1837, the unresolved battle over the collectorship added to Democratic woes. No one wanted to drop out of the race and the inability to agree upon a candidate pointed to Bancroft as the ideal compromise. Only he seemed wily enough to deal with the new issues of the coming years—slavery, the right of petition, Texas, and the extent of congressional powers. Morton, at first displeased, in December changed his mind, and Bancroft agreed, although he did not want the job. It demanded time and effort, was controversial, and called for choices he was reluctant to make. The collector was constantly in the public eye and deep in disputes over appointments, allocations, and patronage. But the new post also carried power no previous position had given him. At the end of December, Levi Woodbury officially notified him of the appointment, implying that Bancroft was to bring the bickering factions into line. By default he thus rose to the state's most important political office and became one of the leaders of the Massachusetts Democracy.[53]

The Boston Customhouse was a respectable political plum, with a sizable budget, staff, and influence. It included naval officers, surveyors, the wine and spirit keeper, numerous clerks, weighers, gaugers, measurers of salt and coal, appraisers, and inspectors. The collector earned $5,000, while he disposed of jobs that added up to $100,000 a year. In addition he advised on most state and federal appointments, distributed his dependents throughout the city, and dispensed a lucrative printing business. Bonds and securities placed with the Customhouse usually found their way to his favorite bank, once Henshaw's Commonwealth Bank, now the Merchants Bank of Boston.

The office however had limits. Important in Boston and the coastal towns, the collector could do less for communities farther inland. Internal bickerings also circumscribed his power. The Customhouse faction would not disband just because Henshaw retired; and the animosity that group aroused in other parts of the state would not soon subside. Finally, Bancroft knew that others felt as qualified as he to run the Massachusetts Democracy. They were familiar with the city and its wards, had long-standing local connections, and regarded the new Springfield arrival with suspicion.

When he took up his post Bancroft did not know in what direction to turn. But the fortuitous collapse of the Commonwealth Bank identified with Henshaw and several oldtime Customhouse associates eased his task. Funds of the Commonwealth Insurance Company, of which Henshaw had also been a director, went down the drain, as did government deposits and the assets of the Warren Association, organized to develop the South Boston flats. Whigs blamed the Democratic Party for the disaster, and in Washington Daniel Webster called for an investigation. It was a matter of sheer luck that the bank collapsed nine days before Bancroft formally assumed his post, for the failure involved not only Henshaw men, but also prominent Democrats like William Parmenter and John Mills, who became embroiled in audits, suits, and the four official investigations that followed, all to the glee of the Boston *Atlas.* But Henshaw's eclipse eliminated one source of political contention for the time being.[54]

Other conflicting claims were not so easily disposed of. Benjamin Hallett reminded Bancroft of past contributions while promising to "rally around you." He wanted the post of district attorney and more aid for the *Advocate.* The conservative William Parmenter and others urged help for the Henshaw people, while Samuel Clesson Allen argued that the future lay with the farmers and mechanics, and Morton cautioned against antagonizing local bankers. Bancroft had to please his predecessors, satisfy numerous office seekers, personal friends, and former rivals, work with

the Boston commercial community, and look out for the party's fortunes.[55]

Still unfamiliar with the city organization, he asked J. G. Harris, a
New Bedford newspaperman, to prepare a memorandum that would
help determine the standing of the various Democratic factions. He received a vituperative portrayal of Henshaw as "a shrewd and selfish
man" guided by "absolute hatred . . . an unforgiving spirit yearning for
revenge," and of the Boston *Post,* the *Advocate,* and Benjamin F. Hallett
as a motley collection of enemies. Only the reform alignment of local
workingmen's and journeymen's associations deserved attention. Bancroft wisely disregarded the advice. But he meant to show that the party
had a new boss who intended to lead as well as to pacify; in Washington
Hallett marshaled the Democratic members of Congress behind Bancroft
and committees all over the state assured him of their loyalty.[56]

To unify the party and also assert his independence, Bancroft helped
establish the *Bay State Democrat,* as an alternative to both the *Post* and the
Advocate, both too closely identified with particular factions to serve as
voices of the entire organization. He wanted a new, not necessarily more
radical, paper. Anti-Masons, Workingmen, Morton, and Amasa Walker
endorsed the step, showing the range of support Bancroft mobilized.
Greene and his friends were less pleased until it became clear that the *Bay
State Democrat* would not cut into the *Post*'s circulation. Bancroft knew
little about newspaper management but had a sense of what the public
liked to read and as an author was familiar enough with publishing to
make good appointments. A large reading room in the office, to replace
the space Henshaw had provided in the now defunct Commonwealth
Bank, became a favorite meeting place. Bancroft also extended his largess
to other journalists, among them J. B. Phinney, the Barnstable editor,
Munn of Northampton, and Daniel Henshaw, editor of the Lynn *Record.*

Sarah's death left a gap in Bancroft's life that neither politics nor
writing filled. A home was important for stability, security, and order,
and he wanted someone to supervise the prosaic details of life. The children too needed a more structured framework than their aunt and the
Dwights provided. Their father knew he had neglected them and wanted
to make amends. It came as no surprise to Bancroft's friends therefore
when he began to court the widow Elizabeth Davis Bliss, mother of two
sons and former wife of Daniel Webster's law partner. Intelligent, sensitive, and shrewd, she was worldly, witty, and mature as Sarah had not
been, more experienced and better able to cope with uncertainties. She

was also financially independent, living off a handsome legacy in comfortable lodgings in Boston's fashionable Otis Place. Bancroft considered her an ideal second mother and companion. His friends and the Dwights agreed.

The children, Louisa in particular, were less enthusiastic. She had no objection to Elizabeth but saw her father's remarriage as a betrayal. Bancroft tried persuasion—Louisa, John, and George were never to forget their mother who was in heaven, but they also needed an earthly guide and Elizabeth would play that role. But the children remained hostile, and initial altercations with their stepbrothers William and Alexander boded ill for the future. Elizabeth, more sensitive and patient, tried to reassure him—the children's feelings were natural and ought to run their course. Given time they would come to their senses. They did not, and Bancroft, who treasured family ties and who in later years spent money and time looking after his own brothers and sisters, faced three discontented offspring who caused many problems and would not forgive him for his neglect.[57]

In May the engagement became public and a private ceremony during the summer sealed the union. Bancroft sold his house in Springfield and moved into Elizabeth's place, bringing the three children with him.

The duties of the collectorship proved less burdensome than he had feared. Work on Volume Three progressed while several articles and reviews kept his name before the public, as did yet another battle with a magazine editor. Bancroft corresponded with out-of-state politicians, entertained visiting dignitaries, and relished his new status. Levi Woodbury consulted him about affairs in New Hampshire, while Silas Wright provided information about New York. From Frank Blair came inside news about Washington, and Pennsylvania politicians, among them Henry Gilpin, solicitor of the Treasury, became lifelong friends. They valued his opinions, which was flattering, and also enhanced local stature.

As collector, Bancroft proved an excellent administrator. He oversaw the accounts and made sure that the Customhouse was milked of fewer funds than in the past, handled appointments judiciously, and tried to lessen antagonisms in the ranks. He saw to it that cashiers kept their hands out of the till; and he aided Henshaw's efforts to settle his Customhouse account (a process that dragged on till 1841). Bancroft also steered an even course among the contending parties to the suits arising out of the Warren Association fiasco, a by-product of the Commonwealth Bank's collapse, and in an act of political sagacity appointed the Whig Rufus Choate counsel for the United States government in one of them. If there were more officeholders like Bancroft, the secretary of the Treasury said, "there would be no need to send out circulars and lose sleep over the public interest."[58]

The political front was less manageable. City and country divisions remained, Boston Democrats grumbled, and the case of the United States versus the Commonwealth Bank, dragging through the courts, provided the Whigs with further campaign material. Party unity also suffered when Bancroft sought to get back at the untrustworthy Morton by spreading the rumor that one of the judge's supporters was involved in the financial disaster. "I fear that the revolution you hoped and toiled for is yet distant," Henry Gilpin wrote in the summer of 1838.[59]

For the sake of that revolution Bancroft carefully planned the tactics of the next electoral campaign. Theodore Sedgwick became Morton's running mate, a sop to the liberal faction, while Robert Rantoul and other dissidents stayed in line. Benjamin Hallett thought of combining the *Advocate* and the *Morning Post,* with Bancroft's blessings. And the local organization cautiously avoided issues such as the right of petition and slavery that would ultimately drain its strength. Such efforts had limited success. The Whig counterattack blasted "certain metaphysical and mystical dogmas borrowed apparently from the most violent Jacobins of the French revolution," and charged that party radicals "proposed to reconstruct the order of society." Campaign slander also portrayed Bancroft as antagonistic to property and claimed that his party was "remorseless and unappeasable [in its] . . . hatred of the mercantile classes." These persuasive, though untrue, accusations defeated the Democrats, although by a smaller margin than a year earlier—the party had 44 percent of the vote. Bancroft's political strategy seemed to work.[60]

The praise for his political sagacity did not ease Bancroft's life; his financial problems were just beginning. At the end of 1838 the Bank of Lake Erie in Cleveland, in which he had a large investment, faltered; it paid no dividends and had difficulty collecting its debts. The Bank of Michigan, another Dwight venture, also needed help, and on a trip to Washington after the elections Bancroft persuaded the secretary of the Treasury to grant that bank yet another extension. Determined to set his finances in order, Bancroft also tried to recoup other investments—in an insurance company and in western properties bought with money received from the Dwights. A secret letter to Van Buren transmitted by the solicitor of the Treasury and extensive contacts in the capital helped. The banks of Lake Erie and of Michigan held their own.[61]

A government suit instituted against the Bank of Michigan in 1839 proved that Bancroft's arrangements were temporary. Since $30,000 of his own money was involved, he did not stint on effort at defense. The frightened Dwights once more called upon his services, which included a long memorandum to the secretary of the Treasury, requesting some "liberality." "These banks are sore thornes in my side," Woodbury complained, after being swamped with Bancroft's messages, "and give us an infinite deal of trouble and reproach and anxiety beyond what most persons can conceive."[62]

Bancroft shared that anxiety, for the Merchants Bank of Boston, in which he had large interests and where he kept Customhouse funds, was also in trouble, and Woodbury threatened to withdraw government deposits. Frantic letters to Washington had their intended effect. The last thing the Democracy of Massachusetts needed was a repetition of the Commonwealth debacle. "I hope your banks will prove strong and faithful to their trust," the secretary of the Treasury cautioned, promising all possible indulgence. The Merchants survived, and the Michigan institution received another government deposit.[63]

Luck (or providence, as Bancroft would have called it) was on the Democratic side. Governor Everett's annual message to the legislature counted as one of the Whig accomplishments the law designed "to dry up as far as possible the acknowledged sources of poverty" by limiting the sale of alcohol to quantities of no less than fifteen gallons. Democrats of all stripes, and many Whigs besides, thought the measure discriminated against the poor, another example of an aristocracy usurping the people's rights. "I can not detect by what conjuration or necromancy our grave and reverend legislators," thundered Hallett, "have arrived at the grand discovery in voluntary morals, that the Imp of the bottle is to be found only in the gill cup and the angel of temperance in a fifteen gallon jug." All factions united against this design to restrain the appetites of the laboring classes while leaving free the indulgence of the rich.[64]

Whig leaders understood the folly too late to do anything about it. Edward Everett forecast that the election would depend on "10,000 good, lazy Whigs who will stay home on the eleventh of November one on his farm and one at his merchandize and allow the battle to go against us." Daniel Henshaw reported encouraging developments from Lynn— "The Democrats are waking up here"—and news from other parts of the state was equally hopeful. For weeks after the eleventh of November the results were uncertain because of the closeness of the tally, but in the end Morton won.[65]

Congratulations poured into the collector's office from all over the country. "The Davids of Democracy," wrote Senator Niles from nearby Connecticut, "with their sling—a free press, have smitten the Goliaths of the Phillistines (the Federalists) and scattered their hosts . . . [causing] the rout and overthrow of their modern Babylon." Levi Woodbury exulted that "it is mind, mind, mind, truth, truth, truth which have conquered." Even Springfield gave the Democrats a majority—"such long faces as our opponents wear are a curiosity," an enthusiastic Democrat reported. There was no doubting Bancroft's achievement. He had given a major Whig state a Democratic governor.[66]

But this one victory did not portend a political revolution. Massachusetts remained Whig. A lackluster campaign had kept people at home, giving the advantage to the interested minority. Whig preemption of Democratic slogans presented another challenge. To become more like the opposition had been the thrust of Bancroft's strategy. But as the Whigs democratized, blurring the distinctions between the two parties, middle-of-the-road voters had little cause to switch to the Democracy. And finally, under Bancroft's leadership, the party in Massachusetts ignored the increasingly ominous implications of the slavery controversy, perhaps the most serious long-term error of his career.

Throughout the 1830s Bancroft touched only briefly on the subject. His second letter to the Workingman (October 1834) had called for an end to slavery in the District of Columbia and for suppression of the slave trade. "Slaves are capital, the slave holder is a capitalist. Free Labor will be the first to demand the abolition of slavery; capital will be the last to concede it." This was his last public statement on the issue; occasional innocuous references in the *History* offended no one, and the volumes were as popular in the South as in the North. A brief reference in 1836 extolling free over slave labor was not repeated, and further attempts to draw him out on the question failed.[67] He did not reply when Angelina Grimké objected that his account confirmed the southern belief that it was a divine institution. Nor in subsequent editions of the *History* did he revise the judgment that blamed bondage on British greed and implied difficulty in assimilating a black race in a white society. He did not accept Joshua Leavitt's invitation to attend the National Anti-Slavery Convention in Albany, in July 1839, and when Carl Follen wanted him to subscribe to an antislavery quarterly Bancroft demurred. All along, he ignored this politically divisive issue. The divine scheme of things would resolve it too.[68]

On the other hand, Bancroft responded to a request from Tennessee for "a good strong letter" to reassure the South that the North was determined "to stand by their original articles of the national compact," by proving that neither he nor the Massachusetts Democracy was in any sense abolitionist. When his sister Jane moved to Louisiana, Bancroft advised her not to buy any slaves on the grounds that they were a risky investment. But Jane disregarded his advice, and upon her death (by which time her husband was in a Massachusetts insane asylum) the slaves became part of her children's trust. Bancroft had the Louisiana lawyer sell them as soon as possible, giving no thought to manumission; the orphans needed money, and if a crisis of conscience was involved there was not a shred of evidence for it.[69]

Bancroft ignored the unrest, passions, and divisions slavery occasioned, and while others spoke out he remained silent. Probably he agreed with Edward Everett and leading Whigs that the abolitionists were a social menace; and as 1839 drew to a close other matters were uppermost in his mind. Morton's governorship promised the Democracy a chance to implement its program, a problem for Bancroft, who had all along confined his pronouncements to glittering generalities, almost never descending to particulars. The party ideologue and organizer, having elevated Morton to the State House, now had to become the manipulator of the legislature and reduce ideas to practice.

VII

✣

THE POPULAR WILL

A CONTEMPORARY compared George Bancroft to a Japanese lacquer composed of layers applied over a period of time. In the 1840s the man of letters, the party chieftain, the scholar, the clergyman, and the pedagogue coalesced into a coherent whole. Intercourse with the great, fame, and influence laid on a varnish of manners, enhancing a taste for admiration and pleasure. The great historian and radical politician became a celebrity prized in elegant salons and around elaborate dinner tables. Bancroft's sardonic humor attracted the friendship of William H. Prescott, who detested politics, of Edward Everett, a Whig of sorts, and of Joseph Buckingham of the *Courier,* as well as of Charles Sumner and a host of transcendentalists, lawyers, businessmen, and bankers. Otis Place became one of the usual stops of distinguished visitors, among them Charles Dickens, Marshal Bertrand (Napoleon's friend in exile), and Von Raumer, the German explorer. When Harvard granted Bancroft an honorary LL.D. in 1843 he knew he had arrived.[1]

Bancroft the party leader was the man of action, decisive, sharp, and swift, who could produce a document on demand and cut his losses when necessary, the manipulator who glided smoothly from one faction to another. His well-developed capacity for rationalization and the ability to disregard unpleasant truths and to alter principles when necessary were useful in a changing political climate in which worn-out Democratic slogans held less appeal than in the past.

The political executive was also a scholar, clergyman, and pedagogue. "Think not party spirit rules my days," he informed a friend; "I follow virtue, where she shines I praise." Virtue lay in scholarship, pursued relentlessly—Volume Two, published in 1837, was followed by

Volume Three, which appeared in 1840, carrying the narrative of colonial history to 1700. The demands of the subject widened Bancroft's researches into European archives, where well-paid agents copied documents for future use. Friends abroad ransacked private collections and negotiated for books and manuscripts. Numerous individuals, in the United States and elsewhere, badgered for information, shared their findings, disputed his interpretations, and praised his work.[2]

The clergyman and pedagogue blended with the scholar and politician. Bancroft rarely missed a chance to preach his democratic theory even when arguing for votes rather than morality. But then the two were one and the same in his mind, a vote for the party was a vote for God, Christianity, and a just society. Speaking earnestly and passionately, the still youthful-looking, thin, and bespectacled Bancroft preached politics as he had once preached from the Bible. The failed pedagogue, who had tired of Round Hill's schoolboys, reveled in the much larger arena now open to him.

His message subtly changed its scope. New issues, ignored or shoved aside in earlier days, posed new questions and called for altered strategies. Five years of political involvement brought awareness that Massachusetts would not soon move to revolution; instead a growing conservatism signaled the end of Bancroft's reform enthusiasm. He gradually dissociated himself from earlier allies when the effort to maintain a united party proved futile. While others reeled in disappointment when the populace proved fickle in the log-cabin and cider campaign of 1840, Bancroft retained his aplomb. His efforts to track down, indeed anticipate, the popular will seemed sometimes little different from expediency. But his faith in the moral power of the Democracy remained unshaken; local failures only inspired the certainty that the party would succeed in a wider context, and that would ameliorate the fortunes of the state organization.

The tide turned in 1844 when national politics offered a way out. The political man of letters who rationalized every setback as but a temporary obstacle on the road to victory persuaded himself that he had little to do in Massachusetts. The fact that the state persisted in preferring Whig to Democratic candidates did not matter. In Washington, closer to the helm of power, he would steer reform sentiment in a direction continental in scope. Territorial expansion, redeeming the entire nation, would carry Massachusetts along.

Morton's election in 1839 excited the Democrats, who now had the opportunity to translate principles into legislation. "Measures are neces-

sary to carry out principles, and men are necessary to carry out measures," Brownson informed Bancroft, exulting that for once the party had
power. Van Buren expressed his "intense interest and all prevailing solicitude," indicating the widespread attention success aroused. For Bancroft, Morton's victory, despite its narrow margin, marked the state's
reconciliation "to the principles of popular rights . . . the homage of the
commonwealth to the truth . . . the offering of the state on the altar of
patriotism . . . the throbbing of the mighty heart of the people sending
the beautiful life blood of freedom through its whole body politic." But
Senator Niles warned him that "you have been so long under the bondage and the despotism of a purse proud oligarchy . . . so long accustomed
to the fetters of federalism that you will not know what use to make of
liberty."[3]

The next few months proved that Niles's warning had a point. However, not a purse-proud oligarchy but their own shortcomings circumscribed the Democrats' use of liberty. Bancroft never overcame the
handicaps of nebulous perceptions formed in opposition. Having called
for the elevation of the laboring classes, he did not know what to do
about it. Massachusetts had emerged in 1839 "from the darkness of federalism"; surely the "feast of reason and flow of soul" would follow, on
the road to redemption. Such ringing sentences, hedged by prudent qualifications, suggested few concrete measures.[4]

Bancroft joined the Democratic chorus in praise of the new era about
to commence. In the opening lecture to the Bay State Association, the
preacher and educator traced the progress of those eternal principles that
a Democratic governor in a Whig state would institutionalize. "Our
aim—perfect political equality, entire freedom of the mind," the *Bay
State Democrat* proclaimed. The object of the new legislation was "true
happiness," not the accumulation of wealth, "that real happiness which
is only won through moral action, not that sensual gratification mis-
called happiness which is begotten by the potency of Gold." Having
vanquished the enemy, "the mammon spirit," the people would prefer
virtue to vice and live "the true life, which is that of doing good," and in
which higher wages and shorter working hours did not matter. Therefore, in advocating free competition, Bancroft did not wish "to equalize
property, but the facilities for acquiring it," since the danger stemmed
not from unequal acquisition but from unjust use of property. Democracy "was a principle which recognizes mind as superior to matter, and
moral and mental power over that of wealth and physical force." When
pressed for particulars, the *Bay State Democrat* outlined the agenda—an

independent treasury, curtailment of state expenditures, and loyalty to the spirit animating the Pilgrims in the cabin of the *Mayflower*.[5]

The euphoria evaporated when it became clear that a Whig lieutenant governor and a largely Whig legislature would limit Morton's capacity to redeem the state. Since Bancroft had never seriously considered what the steps to redemption were, foreseeable difficulties spared him the need to translate theory into practice. Nonetheless, with his help, Morton prepared a message that outlined a program of sorts. For the sake of "the elevation of the depressed," the Democracy, "in harmony with pure religion" and expressing "the collective will of the people," was about to perfect the social order by universal male suffrage, an end to partial legislation, support for the independent treasury plan, and opposition to charters of incorporation and privately financed internal improvements. The new governor also wished to limit paper currency, end state financing of railroads and excessive government expenditures, ease debtors' laws, and revise the militia system and the criminal code. Nathanael Greene, David Henshaw, Benjamin F. Hallett, Levi Woodbury, and William Marcy, representing various factions, found this proper Democratic dogma. The small minority, like Brownson, who had doubts were easily ignored.[6]

The Whigs, assuming correctly that Morton's narrow margin proved that the people were unpersuaded by Bancroft's message, stifled most of the governor's proposals. The poll tax qualification for voting remained, tax reform proposals were buried, as were efforts to change the lot of debtors and reduce the number of capital crimes. In the fiscal realm the Democrats were more successful; they cut expenditures and the deficit, reduced credit to railroads, and eliminated some salaries. In 1841, for the first time in years, the state's treasury would show a small surplus.[7]

Bancroft was only tangentially involved in getting these measures passed, for the approaching presidential contest absorbed his attention. In December 1839 the Whigs nominated William H. Harrison, with the Virginia Democrat John Tyler as his running mate. In May 1840 Martin Van Buren became the Democratic standard-bearer, a choice Bancroft approved, but for the second spot he followed Jackson's lead in favor of the Tennessean James K. Polk. Richard H. Johnson, however, was nominated for the vice-presidency, in spite of his irregular private life and drinking habits, which, Bancroft thought, were sure to cost the party votes in Massachusetts.[8]

More damaging were the new Whig campaign methods. The opposition formed clubs that blurred its platform and stressed personalities rather than issues. Networks of workers coordinated activities and scheduled speakers, circulated material and turned out audiences. Caleb Cushing and Richard Hildreth wrote short biographies of the Whig nominee, while local Workingmen argued that Van Buren had been a disaster to the laboring people. A pamphlet entitled *The Contrast* compared the plain, simple, humble, folksy Harrison to the effete, dandified, devious, and aristocratic Democratic contender. In terms that people presumably could understand, the Whigs in Massachusetts presented a well-articulated alternative to the Democrats, while popular activities clouded their program.[9]

Bancroft and his fellow workers were slow to realize the import of tactics by which Whiggery democratized itself. As the Whigs got off their stilts, took the people by the hand, and carried popular banners along with them, news from nearby states showed that the strategy worked. In Connecticut the Whig state convention—a "noisy and sense-less pageant," according to an envious Democrat—branded Bancroft an anti-Christian, while Democratic newspapers in New Hampshire were unable to fend off Whig raids on their own contents. As for Massachu-setts, Alexander H. Everett was sure that the Democracy was "going backward into the puddle of Peter Parleyism," dangerously quiescent and resting on its oars.[10]

In Natick, for instance, Henry Wilson, the village shoemaker, chal-lenged local Democrats to debates and harped on Van Buren's economic disasters. Once ridiculed as "that Natick cobbler," Wilson exploited his working-class background to refute the charge that he was an aristocrat. "Van Buren an enemy to the laboring man," Wilson repeated in over sixty towns. Democratic measures robbed the workers of employment and good wages, dampening the spirit of enterprise and retarding the elevation of the laboring classes. In the Springfield area William B. Cal-houn ran a similar campaign, denying that Harrison was a radical aboli-tionist while also asserting his own antislavery stand.[11]

Rubbish, deceit, and lies, countered Bancroft. "My bosom swells with indignation . . . I stand amazed at the desperate recklessness of am-bition . . . I feel a summons to go out among the people and to denounce the fallacies of these appeals." He called on the worker to reflect, to use the gift of reason, to see through these falsehoods, to pause "and his own mind will whisper to him full replies to the artful appeals of [those] who, pretending to advance his interest are, in reality, the advocates of the maxims of the aristocracy." The subject of slavery he did not mention.[12]

While Bancroft preached, the Whigs put on shows. Democracy "is spreading dismay over the ranks of the mummers," one hopeful noted, but the people thought otherwise. In Springfield a log cabin raised on a wagon drawn by six horses paraded through the streets beneath a Harrison arch, much to everyone's delight. Bands from neighboring communities helped citizens sing Harrison ditties, and revolutionary soldiers appeared, the American eagle floating in the air, while symbolic Democratic arches lay in ruins. The Hampden *Post,* under the editorship of E. D. Beach, tried to rally the Springfield Democrats, in spite of the stuffed roosters, toasts, and drinking booths. These instances of "intoxicating revelries or empty noise" ensured that the people would see through the sham, Bancroft consoled himself.[13]

On July 4 Bancroft encountered Daniel Webster in the town of Barre. Later the Democrats would charge that Webster failed to live up to his reputation and that the food ran out too soon. Although the newspapers gave conflicting partisan accounts, Webster carried the day, helped by the Fitzwilliam Artillery, by a parade, and by Harrison banners and emblems, as well as his own reputation. A mere six hundred listeners turned out for Bancroft, compared to the five thousand who crowded to hear the Lion of the Age. "In the contest of freedom there may be momentary reverses," Bancroft shouted as he tried to make himself heard over the din, "but the issue is always safe." No one, he told those still willing to listen, "could subvert the laws of the moral world."[14]

Instead of seeking a new approach, Bancroft fished out old speeches, dusted off tired slogans, and tried belatedly to improve the machinery. Contemptuous of the opposition, he could not conceive that its tactics would succeed. Since the Whig methods were but "the credit system of electioneering as we have seen it for the last five or six years in money dealings," he felt no need to offer more in response than a rehash of his morality exhortations. "Years ago the democracy of Massachusetts published its faith," he said, "and from that faith it will never swerve. We repeat—to assert the rights of labor is the mission of the age."[15]

In the overall disaster the one cheerful note was the unheard-of party unity. One of Hallett's co-workers on the old *Advocate* became editor of the *Bay State Democrat,* which changed from a weekly to a daily. Newspapers sprouted all over the state to advance the party's message, their life as short as the campaign. Bancroft lectured about the mission of the Democracy to audiences in Dedham, Newbury, Boston, and elsewhere. He presented the *Mayflower* story, the early days of Plymouth, the fortunes of the Pilgrims, and other incidents of the state's history as proof that the laws of the moral world had been entrusted to the keeping of the yeomanry (or the mechanics, or the artisans, or the fishermen, depending on the location of his address). Just as the "loco focos of the 17th century" relied on their faith, so the workingmen of 1840 could withstand the chicanery of the opposition. The conservative Puritans had triumphed in their effort to preserve a doctrine coeval with creation; their latter-day descendants could do no less. God did not forsake the Pilgrims, nor would he abandon the Democrats; "His providence is ever watchful over the cause of reform, of freedom, of the power of the people."[16]

While Bancroft was placing his trust in the divine plan, Orestes A. Brownson was losing his. An article in the *Boston Quarterly Review*, the Democrats' intellectual mouthpiece, lent substance to the wildest Whig charges, much to Bancroft's chagrin. Brownson foresaw an imminent crisis in the relations of wealth and labor and argued that traditional remedies could never improve the lot of slavelike workingmen. Land ownership was no longer a viable solution, nor did the church have the answers, for priests were in collusion with the masters. Only an end of the wage system and the abolition of the hereditary descent of property could elevate the laboring classes, and that would require "a war the like of which the world as yet has never witnessed." According to the Whig press, the article revealed the intellectual origins of Van Burenism, traceable to Tom Paine, Fanny Wright, and Robert Dale Owen.[17]

Bancroft privately regarded Brownson as a deluded fanatic and political innocent, and considered the Whigs' logic fallacious. The article should not have been published, he told his friend. Conscience mattered but party fortunes came first, and the Democratic program was the best present circumstances could accommodate. Righteous zeal, such as Brownson's, might pull the house down upon all. In response the *Bay State Democrat*, which had only recently lauded the *Review* as faithful expositor of Democratic principles, suggested that the editor was a misguided visionary, and Bancroft dissociated the party from its former ally. The *Boston Quarterly Review*, he implied, was a Whig paper in disguise, "never recognized as a Democratic organ." Brownson's own statement—"there is no party for which we can vote"—showed how far he had strayed. The Democracy of Massachusetts, Bancroft concluded, was no more responsible for Brownson's notions than the Whigs were for Mormonism.[18]

Tactical considerations apart, Bancroft's theory excluded Brownson's analysis. The identification of wage labor with slavery was unacceptable, for the worker was a free man. Brownson's charge that social mobility was a chimera challenged Bancroft's vision of an open society sustained by the nation's wealth. The existing order, Bancroft always maintained, could be reformed without violent upheaval. To call for economic as well as social equality meant an alteration of property relationships and a violation of the God-given order, neither one a possibility. Instead, Bancroft followed the party line; when Van Buren declared in favor of a ten-hour day, Morton cautiously plodded along. A mild Democratic appeal to the mechanics of Charlestown declared "each laborer is a freeman" but advocated neither trade unions nor collective bargaining. So innocuous were the Democratic appeals that Whig newspapers reprinted them and agreed. Traditional attacks on the aristocracy, Hartford Federalists, bank schemers, and Whig oppressors left audiences unmoved, while "down with Martin Van Ruin" was an effective slogan.[19]

"You are falling into the rear—fast," Prescott warned. Too late Bancroft realized that Whig hard cider produced Democratic hangovers. "The sword of Truth will conquer," an Ohio Democrat tried to console him, without giving a definite date. And meanwhile the campaign strained Bancroft's friendships and family relations. Edward Everett, blaming his former student for the abuse heaped upon him by the Democrats, requested a return of his letters and for a while severed connections. John Davis, Whig gubernatorial candidate, was chagrined to have his brother-in-law a party to the charge that raising the tariff had taxed the poor. The *Post* declared that Davis, this arch-Federalist, gave three cheers in the streets of Worcester at the news that the British had sacked Washington. Furthermore, Davis was called a hypocrite who speculated in lands and bonds for his own enrichment. The fact that his Democratic brother-in-law was a full party to the same land and banking speculations remained unknown.[20]

In October Bancroft still lashed out at gloomy forecasts. The election was "a struggle of the concentrated power of the business classes of the world against the freedom and happiness of the whole people." To doubt "the issue would be to admit into our hearts a little of that distrust of the people for which our opponents are entitled to a monopoly." But ever fewer Democrats expected the people to see through Whig chicanery and "triumph over frauds as in past times they have triumphed over the monied interest."[21]

They did not, and the extent of the Whig triumph raised disturbing questions for a Democratic theoretician. The Harrison steamroller cast doubt on the nature of the popular will and intelligence, that supposed reflection of divine reason. Was vox populi vox dei when it voted for

Tippecanoe and Tyler too? Why the preference for privilege and wealth, for aristocracy and Federalism? Could one trust the people to govern themselves effectively if coons, arches, parades, and cider swayed them more easily than appeals to their self-reliant judgments?

Bancroft evaded these challenges with facile optimism. While Brownson rejected the Democracy and Morton wailed about the cause-less defeat, Bancroft, by now an experienced politician, knew that one battle did not mean the loss of the war. Armed with a versatile theory of politics, he distinguished between subversion of the popular will (Harrison's victory) and its complete demise (a cosmological impossibility). The voters would come to their senses, he was sure, persuaded by Van Buren's new slogan—the people's "sober second thought" would make up for the initial slip.[22] Indeed, the preacher-pedagogue rationalized Harrison's triumph into a component of the divine plan, designed to foster vigilance and exertion. One setback did not curtail the reign of the general laws that swayed the moral world. Since the future belonged to Democracy, the momentary triumph "of the selfish passions of a party" was "as evanescent as the material interests involved in the transient conflict." History would take care of itself, and Bancroft was sure it would be on the Democratic side.[23]

Meanwhile he was about to lose his position in the Boston Custom-house. Ironically, though, this believer in the Jacksonian principle of rotation in office refused to apply it to himself, and determined to hold on as long as possible. There was no certainty the Whigs would pro-scribe him, a friend counseled, and Morton suggested that, by remaining at his post, Bancroft would consolidate his power base. In January Ban-croft traveled to Washington only to learn that the Whigs also believed in a thorough change of the guard. "The proscribers of proscription will . . . disgrace themselves once more," Bancroft sadly concluded. On March 8, 1841, he sent in his resignation.[24]

He thereby lost $5,000 of his income—not a major financial setback, but a diminution of revenues which he keenly felt. By 1841 he was well off, but his expenses were increasing; there was a family with six chil-dren to maintain—including little Susan Jackson, born in 1839—a way of life that imposed its own demands, and a passion for writing that also drained his resources. The cost of the *History* in spite of appearances exceeded its returns, although Bancroft hoped that a new contract with Little, Brown for an abridged school version would be profitable. The Bank of Michigan brought approximately $2,000 a year and other specu-lations—in western lands and New York and western banks—helped. But Bancroft wanted more. The death of his father-in-law promised a further infusion of capital, for the will entitled the Bancroft children to some $70,000 at their maturity.[25]

On the assumption that this money was rightfully his and also that his earlier services warranted a handsome retainer, Bancroft requested a loan, demanding in addition payment for aid rendered to the Dwight firms and the income from his children's trust for their and his own benefit. He also asked the Bank of Michigan for a $3,000 fee. The Dwights refused and a long-drawn-out, acrimonious public dispute followed. The new Whig administration in Washington reduced Bancroft's utility, and the Dwights made it clear that he had been living on their generosity for years. The trustees of Dwight's estate saw no reason to help him with money that was not his and for purposes of which they did not approve. Of the proceeds from the children's trust, they agreed to forward $700 a year, as opposed to the $1,500 he demanded. Angry when thwarted, Bancroft accused them of profiting from his exertions and of giving him bad financial advice. Arbitration finally awarded Bancroft $1,200 annually for the next five years, but failed to settle other issues.[26]

His financial situation worsened when hard times forced the Bank of Michigan to lower its dividends drastically. In desperation Bancroft tried to sell some of his western lands but found no buyers. When the Bank of Monroe and the Bank of Buffalo also faltered, Bancroft's judgment gave way. He accused the Michigan trustees of conspiring with the Dwights to ensure his fiscal ruin and charged Sarah's family with pocketing a retainer that was rightfully his. "We live in a land of law and healthy opinion," one Dwight coldly informed him, implying that Bancroft respected neither. In response Bancroft spread the rumor that the Dwights had been great stock manipulators and published figures and private correspondence to prove it. He also offered to sell his Bank of Michigan stock—valued at about $35,000—to the Dwights, but they refused to buy.[27]

Mutual recriminations led to the *Bancroft* v. *Dwight* case, which brought little credit to either side but provided further proof for Bancroft's political enemies, who for years had charged him with being greedy, self-serving, and unprincipled. Levi Woodbury penned a detailed memorandum to bolster Bancroft's case, and lawyers analyzed Bancroft's voluminous documentation—they alone benefited from his rapacity. The court ruled against him. The Dwights, the judges decided, owed him nothing, and he had to pay half the expenses of a case which brought him grief and ill will.[28]

The Dwights had "been willing to avail" themselves of "time, . . .

labor and the accidental influence of [his] position to secure great pecuniary benefit," Bancroft bitterly complained, "and without defraying even ... expenses." Abusive letters brought the expected response—Henry considered him beneath contempt and cut short all communications, while Edmund, answering for the entire family, accused Bancroft of lacking a moral sense. Further correspondence would be returned unread.[29]

The political world, Alexander H. Everett noted, was a vast bowling alley where Dame Fortune set up and knocked down statesmen for her own pastime. For Bancroft 1841 was one of Fortune's fickle years. Morton, discouraged, pleaded for guidance—"you are my only advisor" and "I wish you to tell me what to do," he wrote to Bancroft. A mid-March Democratic gathering revealed temporary unity among the factions in the face of the past year's losses, but the *Bay State Democrat* floundered. And the Liberty Party, the first political antislavery movement, was a force to be reckoned with. When the Suffolk Democratic committee nominated Bancroft to run for the state senate, he declined. The year was not a total loss, however, for the Liberty challenge harmed the Whigs as much as the Democrats.[30]

As head of the state committee, Bancroft confined the 1842 party platform to the standard agenda, ignoring the thorny issues of slavery and territorial expansion. The convention renominated Morton for the governorship, supported the independent treasury, and attacked despotic congressional power and aristocratic legislation. It also appealed for "a national domain for public happiness," a call so vague no one could argue against it. Van Buren identified the Massachusetts Democracy with Bancroft, but defections continued as some members edged toward the Whigs and the protective tariff and others moved into antislavery activities.[31]

The major enemy in 1842 was still the Whig Party. Bancroft's followers attacked Davis and branded his supporters the coon party in an effort to recall the people to their senses. Meetings all over the state acquainted voters with candidates and issues, and Bancroft traveled extensively to deliver Democratic messages. "I shall go into this campaign like wildfire into a cane brake," Rantoul promised; "in union there is strength," the Worcester County committee declared; "the battle goes on bravely ... we shall render a good account of ourselves," Morton was sure. A Faneuil Hall mass meeting on election eve brought out an array of talent. Confident that nothing was left undone, Bancroft was certain of a Democratic sweep.[32]

He was overoptimistic. On November 14, 1842, Morton led by fifteen hundred votes in the three-way race. The Liberty Party showed some strength, and since it would not patch up its differences with the Whigs, Morton carried the election in the legislature. He was once more governor, given the chance, Bancroft exulted, of proving that the Democrats were competent to run the government.[33]

Hard campaigning and the Dwight fight took their toll on Bancroft that winter. Almost ill with exhaustion, he left Massachusetts for a trip to restore his health, to further his historical research, and to increase his income through lectures. In December he spoke to the Mercantile Library in Philadelphia, meanwhile gaining a closer understanding of Pennsylvania politics. He visited numerous battle sites and collected anecdotes from survivors to flesh out the *History,* also meeting local celebrities, including Lucretia Mott, who had long aroused his curiosity. While he disapproved of her abolitionism and had little use for women's rights, Bancroft was pleasantly surprised that she seemed a lady. Her heart was in the right place, Bancroft would have said, always maintaining that woman's feelings were superior to man's. Their brain, however, was something else. "It is time that the rights of women were asserted, not in the spirit of Wolstonecraft, but in the spirit of Christianity."[34]

A venture into the South was also illuminating. Everywhere Bancroft met a cordial reception. In Annapolis, Maryland, a lecture on "The Spirit of the Age" brought out a respectful audience, while an afternoon with the governor, a sensible man, with the right views on slavery and favorable to Van Buren, was encouraging. "The mass is in harmony with our northern preference," Bancroft concluded, as true in Baltimore and Annapolis as in Philadelphia and Connecticut.[35]

A meeting with Charles Carroll of Carrollton was particularly fascinating. The huge estate, in the heart of Maryland, covered twelve square miles, and included two hundred slaves. The Catholic owner was gracious and well mannered, his wife graceful and dignified. The planters were aristocrats, Bancroft thought, but more benign, charitable, and humane than their northern counterparts, and treated their bondsmen well. In return Bancroft assured his hosts that the Democratic Party would in no way undermine their unfortunate human property.

The journey lasted almost four weeks and netted $400. Pleased with such evidence of his own popularity and confirmed in his belief that the party stood to regain the White House, Bancroft was back home by January 1843, and deeply involved in his party's second shining hour, the institutionalization of the people's moral welfare.

Morton's inaugural address sounded much like that of three years earlier. But whereas in 1839 Whig legislative hegemony defeated most of his proposals, there was now a possibility that Democrats might control the legislature if they took some disputed seats. The governor called for alteration of the tax system to transfer the burden from real to personal property and thus alleviate the load on the farmers and the poor. He also demanded a reduction of the poll tax, a constitutional amendment limiting the legislature's power to borrow money, a change in the balloting method, and abolition of capital punishment. The predictable Whig responses (Bancroft thought they were out to dupe the people) also pointed to the governor's silence about slavery, the fugitive slave law, and the power of southern Democrats in the party.[36]

Bancroft, fresh from a tour of the South, found this part of the Whig assault incomprehensible. That slavery was a moral evil he acknowledged, as did most of his opponents. But neither he nor they could suggest anything to mitigate it for the time being. As a politician he saw no practical alternatives; and as a historian he believed in the operation of providential forces impervious to human intervention. The black man in his vision was white in potential, rather than biologically inferior, but degraded by bondage that made him "naturally vicious"—all obstacles that only time would solve. Appalled at the potential explosiveness of the problem, he thought that "fury and violence," even for a morally justifiable cause, were doomed to failure.[37]

He had explained it all in the *History,* which blamed the introduction of slavery on English greed but also noted the profits reaped by Americans. Parliament, swayed by material interests, fastened upon unwilling colonies the dubious benefits of "a trade which bore the gigantic character of a crime." English rapacity also thwarted efforts to suppress both the trade and slavery. Bancroft thus conveniently accepted the standard rationalization of commentators since the eighteenth century. Nor was he more original in his readings of the southern slave codes, which, by protecting the landed aristocrats, created a society dependent on the institution and compounded the difficulty of assimilation. The tragedy, Bancroft felt, lay in color—blackness differentiated between slave and master, and neither education nor skills nor legal status could influence the prejudice associated with the color of darkness. "The Negroe whom the benevolence of the master enfranchised was not absorbed into the mass of the population. His color adhered to him, the indelible mark of his specie."[38]

Those who remembered his 1834 assault on slavery would charge

Bancroft "with occasional spasmodic efforts to shake off [his] quasi abolitionism," but for him, emancipation had "to flow from internal activity, developed by universal culture; rather than through exterior philanthropy." Permanent reform could only be "the sudden plucking of a fruit when it slowly ripened." Generations had to learn to live with difficulties they were powerless to solve in the belief that ultimately providential guidance would accomplish what they could not do on their own. Bancroft therefore had little sympathy for misguided visionaries, for the "reckless violence of men of desperate audacity," out of touch with the process of social change, "who would employ terror as a means to ride on the whirlwind of civil war." Every period in history had "a moment when the tendencies to reform . . . assume a thousand visionary, strange and fantastic shapes." Wise men waited them out.[39]

Nor did he sympathize with those who tried to impede that process, as the Whigs seemed to in the spring of 1843. Since the election results were close and the House almost evenly balanced, contested seats forced Bancroft, Hallett, and Rantoul to work overtime to prove the case of deserving Democrats. The intense battle over the choice of presiding officers caused even some party members to balk, and one Democrat from Worcester County resigned his seat rather than submit to the browbeating of "those few adventurers who can discover no other fruits in a democratic triumph than money in their pockets." Bancroft did not propose to profit directly from his position, but he intended to exercise his power. In the end he prevailed by default—the Liberty Party members refused to compromise their purity through an alliance with the Whigs and gave the Democrats working control of the legislature.[40]

The governor, however, frittered away the fruits of victory. Unwilling to submit to Bancroft's dictates, he sapped the strength of the fragile organization. Morton as always begged for advice, but balked at a suggestion that he patch up his relations with Henshaw and interpreted the proposal that he retain Secretary of State Bigelow as a plot to install a spy in the State House. Endless feuds erupted over the staffing of the state central committee, over the choice of Frederick Robinson as president of the senate, and over Hallett's designation to the Governor's Council. Sadly Bancroft concluded that he still had some influence only in the Boston Lyceum—no one objected to his reelection as vice-president.[41]

The approaching presidential contest exacerbated the legislative difficulties. The aspirations of rival hopefuls played havoc with the party and encouraged defections. Harrison's death a month after the inauguration brought John Tyler, a Democrat, into the White House, reviving dormant factions. The new President's weakness and ambition opened the field in the race for the Democratic nomination in 1844. In Massachusetts Lewis Cass, Levi Woodbury, and John Calhoun lined up supporters, and national figures invaded the state with some regularity, seeking Bancroft's approval.[42]

The shambles they left behind destroyed the unity necessary to enact Morton's program in the legislature and in effect undermined the control Bancroft exercised over the ranks. "The party collar has been fitted so very close that in spots it is wearing thin," the Whigs jeered, as conservatives refused to join radicals in ending state loans to railroads, in new regulations for corporations, in property reassessment, and in a general reapportionment plan. The salaries of several judges were reduced, state expenditures were lowered, and a number of offices were abolished. But Bancroft's optimism notwithstanding, Massachusetts was as far from revolution as ever.[43]

Bancroft at first thought the presidential contenders attracted "two or three dissenters," a small group of malcontents. He decided to act, however, when reports from various towns indicated the growing importance of the Tyler and Calhoun forces. Morton tried to undermine their influence by dredging up *The Chronical of David,* and recounting Henshaw's involvement with the Commonwealth Bank. This maneuver backfired by reviving memories of an unsavory chapter in the Democracy's history. Furthermore, Tyler was President, and could and did exercise his authority in favor of his supporters. In Springfield a Democratic meeting chose his men for the state convention; and Robert Rantoul, once Bancroft's ally, now "a mere supple tool" of the President, became collector of the Port of Boston. After a visit to Boston to inaugurate the Bunker Hill monument, President Tyler nominated David Henshaw to be secretary of the navy. Rival factions published their own newspapers, confusing the issues and the voters, and exposing Democratic fissures.[44]

Bancroft, still known as a Van Buren supporter, and still unable to explain what was happening, had to counter those forces. Everything was going to "the hands of men with but one distinguishing quality—corruption," he reported to the former President. How else could one interpret Robert Tyler's proposition that Morton run as a vice-presidential candidate on his father's ticket? Pro-Calhoun messages flooded Maine and Connecticut, and Cass and Woodbury also fished in Bancroft's pond. "The summer has been a period of more intrigue in politics than I remember ever to have known," Bancroft decided. "You have no idea of the corruption which has been attempted here," he told Van Buren, "odious, disgusting and injurious to the party."[45]

But former allies continued to move into new orbits. The entire Essex district was no longer safe, and Whigs had an easy time beating Democrats with murky allegiances. "Never had a party a better opening than we have in Massachusetts," Bancroft lamented, "if all would but profit by our position. But they will not."[46] Local Democratic meetings were more disruptive than ever, playing into the hands of the opposition. Occasionally, even when local offices went to the Democrats, the elected candidate was an anti–Van Burenite, infuriating the regulars and revealing Bancroft's political weakness. The machinery he had laboriously constructed now fell to pieces. The flimsy structure, held together by external pressures, promises of rewards, common enemies, and a dash of principle, disintegrated. On the question of choice of a presidential candidate he kept the options open; but the façade of union collapsed. And he could explain the outcome only by corruption—the evil desire of men for offices and rewards.

These trials made 1843 Bancroft's most difficult political year. The state may have been on the verge of conversion to his democratic theory, but if the leadership was so weak as to yield to outside temptations, what could be expected of the electorate? "I blush to think what associates I have had in politics," Bancroft wailed, charging that party members seemed bent on ensuring Morton's defeat. The serious opponents were not the Whigs, but Democrats eager to commit political suicide.[47]

In preparation for the state convention, expected to commit its twelve delegates to a candidate at the Democratic National Convention, Bancroft and Morton spread the rumor that Calhoun's election would yield Whig officeholders. Both considered the South Carolinian Van Buren's most serious rival. Those who did not care about patronage were reminded of the former Vice President's stand on the Rhode Island suffrage issue and his slavery views. Some members from Boston, Salem, and Charlestown nevertheless declared for Calhoun, while others, like John Mills and E. D. Beach of Springfield, supported Van Buren. Only Bancroft's willingness to compromise and offer concessions in return for restraint and votes prevented a deadlock. Eleven of the twelve delegates scheduled to go to Baltimore were committed to Van Buren, but the resolutions that followed were, as Bancroft admitted, "exceedingly temperate [in] tone," which boded ill for the Van Buren wing.[48]

For the time being, Bancroft's commitment held firm. He agreed when New York Governor William Marcy suggested that he write a campaign biography of the former President—stressing humble origins, self-propelled rise to power, intimacy with the people, and work for the good of humanity—and quickly produced the required number of pages. Dry in detail, lacking flair, his "contribution to the cause" had little merit and was never published during the campaign. When Van Buren, years later, requested a copy for his files, Bancroft denied that he had one.[49]

But as the weeks passed, that commitment faded. Aware that "the current of democratic opinion is rather in favor of annexation," he privately supported Tyler's proposal for admission of the Republic of Texas to the Union, and informed Van Buren about the Texas fever in Massachusetts. The eagerness of manufacturers, cotton spinners, and fishing fleet owners for opportunities in new markets would outweigh opposition charges that the Democracy was truckling to slave power. Van Buren's nomination, Bancroft implied, hinged on a positive statement, which would also steal Whig thunder.[50]

Many Democrats, once fearful of a war with Mexico, had changed their minds—Bancroft among them. Yet Van Buren declared the immediate annexation of Texas a dangerous gamble and preferred an amicable adjustment of all claims. The party's southern wing then openly rebelled and even some northern Democrats looked for another candidate. By April 1844 Bancroft too was sure that Van Buren's renomination would cost the Democracy the presidency. Morton counseled loyalty, but pessimistic reports from Washington noted the erosion of the former President's strength.[51]

To be true to itself, Silas Wright wrote, the party had to stand by Van Buren. "Defeat rather than disgrace" should be the cry of the Democracy. But the number willing to take up the banner on Van Buren's behalf dwindled, and Bancroft envisioned troubles on the local level with another Whig administration in Washington. When Wright reported that the situation was shockingly bad, Bancroft agreed, but for different reasons. He gradually dissociated himself from Van Buren despite numerous letters approving the former President's principled stand.[52]

On the way to the Democratic convention in Baltimore, Bancroft stopped in Lindenwald, Van Buren's country home. As always he was captivated by his host's personality and character, his modesty, humility, and charm. But the further Bancroft got from Lindenwald the clearer became the need for a drastic change in Democratic strategy and leadership. By the time he reached Washington, the cards were all on the table—Virginia opposed the former President and the gossip was all against him. Meetings with Wright, Benton, and Allen revealed that Van Buren had some friends left, but their efforts were falling short.[53]

Two-thirds of the delegates' votes at the convention were necessary for nomination. That rule, Bancroft realized, could save the party and himself some embarrassment, by showing the Van Buren forces the futility of supporting the former President, and giving them a graceful exit so that someone else could carry the day. An effort to prevent the adoption of the two-thirds rule would split the party, Bancroft advised Van Buren. "I do not so much fear cabals against the proper nomination, as I do that they may make that nomination of no value," he reported. Such cryptic statements amounted to recognition that Van Buren's political career was for the time being finished. Rantoul suggested that another northerner get the nomination. Bancroft was less particular; he had nothing against a southerner.[54]

That southerner was James K. Polk, a possible party unifier, a candidate the Van Burenites might support if for no other reason than to eliminate some of their more detested foes. When the eleventh hour subterfuge to replace Van Buren with Silas Wright failed, Bancroft assumed that only Polk would do. Several other politicians, from Pennsylvania, reached the same conclusion. Bancroft's delegation joined those from sixteen other states in voting for the two-thirds rule and thus effectively eliminated Van Buren's candidacy. In the actual balloting, Massachusetts scattered its votes among Van Buren, Cass, and the Pennsylvanian James Buchanan. That night Bancroft, with Gideon K. Pillow and Benjamin F. Butler, moved among the delegations trying to swing votes to the Tennessean. "It flashed upon my mind," Bancroft later wrote to Polk, "that it would be alone safe to rally on you," forgetting to add that this project had probably been prepared days in advance. Morton went along, as did representatives from New Hampshire, Tennessee, Alabama, and Mississippi, but pacifying the New Yorkers proved tedious, and Bancroft never really succeeded in regaining their confidence. Yet when he went to bed he knew that the choice had been made. Another long day of balloting brought the rest of the party around. George Dallas became the vice-presidential candidate and the convention approved a platform. Almost as gratifying to Bancroft as Polk's nomination was the call by a Pennsylvanian, "three cheers for the Historian of the United States."[55]

The loyalty to a man he would soon defend as a southerner with northern principles seemed at the time and later the shrewd step of a political manipulator who luckily sensed which way the wind blew. It was more than that. Bancroft had all along been embarrassed by some of the more radical factions to which his fortunes in the past had been tied. Since 1840, also, experience showed that Van Burenite slogans were losing their relevance. In Massachusetts the Democrats floundered, and Morton's electoral failures were glaring. Polk might cure the chronic factionalism of the Democracy by galvanizing the popular enthusiasm of the country with the issues of territorial expansion.

Territorial expansion would replace the anachronistic problems of aristocracy, monopoly, and corporations in the party's vocabulary. Bancroft had been willing to abandon those terms for some time, and had criticized the "fanatical exaggeration of abstract principles" that fostered "collisions with established interests." Never at ease with his own early class-warfare visions, Bancroft had long hedged his pronouncements and sounded more like an enlightened Whig than a radical Democrat. "Who denies that the heart of many is deceitful and desperately wicked," the former clergyman asked, and as a historian he repeated the judgment "desperately wicked is the heart of man." Confident that he followed where history led, Bancroft concluded that "the greatest principles in which the peculiar glory of our country must rest" were veering in new directions. That "love of order . . . and spirit of conservatism" which he praised in others informed his own mind too, as that "ocean of experiment" on which he had embarked as a young man dried up. By 1844 he sounded much like William Ellery Channing, whom he admired for his "faith in moral power to renovate the race. Not the organized union of men, not temperance societies, not abolition societies, not conventions but MORAL POWER." And that moral power was about to receive an international focus.[56]

"Nothing appears more self determined than the volition of each individual and nothing is more certain than that the providence of God overrules them for the good," the third volume of the *History* declared. The will of man was "free in its individuality [but] in the aggregate subordinate to general laws." By 1844 those laws pointed away from traditional conflicts; the people needed additional territory to work out the implications of their victory. Now that democracy was a fact of life, the future of the Union and the safety of the free society, Bancroft decided, required new lands; and the attractiveness of annexation brought him to Polk, who would infuse the old Democratic agenda with badly needed fresh blood.[57]

When he returned to Boston after the convention Bancroft knew that his stand required explanation, for the initial surprise of some local

Democrats gave way to disgust and dismay. Amasa Walker presented strong antislavery resolves at the Worcester meeting, only to be shouted down. He, like others, was being driven out of a party accused of belying its principles. But still others, like David Henshaw, saw great opportunities in the annexation of Texas. Unity meetings, held all over the state at Bancroft's instigation, proved useful, in part to combat the suggestions that Democratic abolitionists should vote for Henry Clay, the Whig contender. A grand clambake in Swampscott, a large procession in Lynn, and a mass meeting in Cabotville applied against the Whigs some of the lessons of the 1840 campaign. For two hours Bancroft tried to rouse enthusiasm for Polk at a mass meeting in Faneuil Hall, largely by concentrating attention on the candidate's Democratic credentials; and Hampden County delegates refuted charges that the Democracy truckled to southern slave owners, at Bancroft's behest. A speech in Concord expanded on the Texas issue, and, when reprinted in a Tennessee newspaper, delighted the future President. Later, Bancroft traveled to New Hampshire and other neighboring states for the cause and began a short Polk biography.[58]

At the same time he pondered the best way to bring himself to the nominee's notice. After a month of agonizing over the choice of words, he penned a masterful letter with just the right combination of shrewdness, flattery, and fortitude. He reminded Polk of Massachusetts's early support and his own zeal to get him the vice-presidential slot in 1840, implying that the failure to get that nomination contributed to the party's defeat. Nowhere did Bancroft mention his loyalty to Van Buren. Instead he stressed his pivotal role in Polk's success and said not a word about rewards.[59]

Activities on behalf of the national organization meshed with Bancroft's own political endeavors that fall. Reconciled to a predictable defeat, unwilling to join the Polk bandwagon, Morton proposed that Bancroft be the Democratic gubernatorial candidate. The latter was not pleased by the suggestion, but he accepted and offered to make his ailing friend Charles Sumner aide-de-camp in the unlikely event of a victory. He knew that his chances of winning were small, but a spirited battle against the Whig nominee George N. Briggs might aid Polk and further his own credentials with the new party leader.[60]

In accepting the nomination, Bancroft declared it "the manifest purpose of Providence that the light of Democratic freedom should be bourne from our fires to the domain beyond the Rocky Mountains." He attacked his opponent's party for overtaxing the middle classes, subsidizing railroads, catering to corporations, and adhering to an "absurd . . . two sided policy about Texas." Local and national issues became indistinguishable; the aim of the Democracy remained advancement of moral reform, which as of 1844 demanded expansion of the American heritage to Oregon and Texas. The slavery aspect of the controversy was irrelevant, Bancroft added. Annexation might even alleviate the burden of bondage, since slaves, preferring the warmer climate of central America, would have a greater chance of escaping into an area with less racial prejudice. This too was part of the Democracy's effort "to elevate and bless humanity."[61]

Briggs's stand on expansionism was ambivalent—he followed Clay's lead as much as Bancroft did Polk's. But for the Democratic contender the benefit of territorial expansion outweighed all drawbacks. If one of the classical threats to republicanism was excessive wealth and luxury, anything that promised to widen property ownership and thus diminish the influence of plutocratic elites was welcome. This the annexation of Texas promised to do.

Next to territorial expansion, affairs in nearby Rhode Island dominated the local campaign, focusing attention on the thorny questions of popular sovereignty and the right of revolution. A seventeenth-century charter, with severe property restrictions on suffrage that denied the vote to a majority of Rhode Island's inhabitants, produced a rebellion by the reform faction led by Thomas Dorr, elected governor under a new constitution. In 1844 Dorr was tried for high treason and sentenced to life imprisonment. The activities of his followers had been a side issue in Massachusetts politics for several years; and Bancroft could not ignore the challenge of his Whig opponents, who charged that Massachusetts Democrats openly aided the subversion of the legally constituted government in a neighboring state.[62]

The Briggs charge stemmed in part from the fact that leading Massachusetts Democrats made no secret of their sympathies. Alexander H. Everett, Marcus Morton, and Benjamin F. Hallett, among others, endorsed the Dorrite constitution and argued that the suffrage party proved the viability of popular sovereignty. Judge Story, speaking for the opposition, described them as abandoned men, who were party to an illegal effort to overthrow the government of Rhode Island. In September 1844 Morton traveled to Providence to attend a mass meeting that called for Dorr's release. Bancroft, unable to participate, sent a letter expressing disgust with the conduct of the authorities.[63]

In theory he agreed with the Dorrites that the majority had a right to alter or form constitutions, binding the minority to its decision—a doctrine that Briggs branded dangerous and subversive. But Bancroft also advocated the use of legally established procedures, which excluded the forcible overthrow of existing abuses. He was not that far apart from his Whig opponent, but Dorrism lent itself to passionate demagoguery and Briggs tried to make the most of it. "Dorrism is one of the rankest and most loathsome ulcers that ever festered upon the fair face of a state and locofocoism has grasped it as buzzards grasp the Providential feast of shipwrecks and storms," a Whig newspaper declared. When local Democrats began a fund to defray the legal expenses arising out of the rebellion, Whig fury reached a new pitch.[64]

Their outrage put Bancroft in an embarrassing position. How could he appear as a moderate, even conservative candidate while defending a rebel against an established order? Cornered, he scrambled out of an untenable situation by ignoring theoretical niceties and taking a humanitarian stance. When in doubt, be understanding and declare a plague on both houses, he suggested. Without endorsing the actions of either Dorr or his opponents, Bancroft declared both sides at fault. Much could be said against a popular uprising that disturbed the social order. On the other hand, Dorr's punishment outweighed his transgressions and deserved Christian leniency.[65]

Bancroft could not have argued otherwise. Like Edward Everett, George N. Briggs, and Judge Joseph Story, he believed that constituted authorities had the duty to safeguard society from civil war. Popular sovereignty inhered in the people not as an unorganized mass, but as a corporate entity acting through established forms of law—good Whig dogma which Bancroft never disputed. At the same time many Democrats and some Whigs thought, as he did, that Dorr's treatment was inexcusably harsh. In fact the enthusiasm generated by Bancroft's letter was so pervasive that it seemed to him as if "but a very few people in Boston . . . have savage natures enough to wish to persecute the Rhode Island Rebel."[66]

The uses of history also became a political issue. The Whigs, having argued that American history was an antidote to a rebellious, restless, and future-oriented present, went to great lengths to distinguish between a revolution against England and a rebellion against domestic institutions. On those grounds alone Bancroft would have been safe. But his reading of the past returned to haunt him when the Whigs discovered sections in Volume Two of the *History* that praised the very Rhode Island charter in dispute in 1844. They quoted liberally, delighted to have a locofoco authority for denouncing the rebels who had subverted a legitimate government that even a radical Democrat found praiseworthy.[67]

Since defeat in the state was certain, Bancroft, while still collecting materials for his *History*, devoted more time to national campaigning than to his own race. In September he was in New York, delivering orations, patching up fences with the Regency, and garnering votes for Polk. Martin Van Buren, notified of his presence, extended a warm invitation to Lindenwald, all past disagreements forgotten. The state was crucial for a Democratic victory, but Senator Thomas H. Benton's anti-Texas agitation and the New York *Evening Post*'s attacks on the Tyler-Calhoun annexation treaty were helping the Whigs.

In response, Bancroft applied his researches to political ends, all the while enjoying the wide publicity and the number of reporters who followed him everywhere. At the New York State Agricultural Fair, before friendly local dignitaries and a responsive audience, he expounded on the significance of the agriculture interests. He traced their heritage to Robert Livingston, John Jay, and DeWitt Clinton, all toilers in the same cause. Their occupation, the farmers heard, was near to heaven, their outlook just and enlightened, their political persuasion clearly Democratic. Nothing less could be expected from tillers of the earth who in their spare time read Milton and Shakespeare. All this was "horrid loco-foco doctrine wrapped in sugar," Bancroft joked, as he repeated a similar message to the Sons of Tammany in New York City.[68]

Back in Boston in October Bancroft encouraged the formation of Young Hickory clubs and the raising of hickory poles that dotted the landscape in many communities. Atop the poles, banners proclaimed his name to the electorate. "The old coon is groaning," the Democratic press reported, as it praised the gubernatorial candidate for his intellect and principles, and for remaining impervious to the influence of his own naturally aristocratic environment. A Cambridgeport celebration ended with a parade through Otis Square, torches held high; Bancroft graciously spoke to the crowd from his home balcony, to the annoyance of sleeping Whig neighbors.[69]

The November results were only slightly less exhilarating. "The Whigs have saved the state but lost the Union," the *Bay State Democrat* proclaimed, blaming Bancroft's defeat on the Irish, the blacks, abolitionist Whigs, Catholic influences, and corporate pressures, all of which prevented the people from expressing their true interests and made them vote for Briggs. Splinter groups undoubtedly drained Democratic strength, but even had their votes been added to his total, Bancroft would still have lost. But this loss mattered little; Polk's victory more than compensated for his own defeat.[70]

VIII

MANIFEST DESTINY

THE PARTY LEADER was about to become a bureaucrat; and more consequential problems replaced local bickerings as reform yielded to expansionism. The transition was partly political; by supporting Polk, Bancroft shifted loyalties in a move that required explanation and justification. In addition, a Washington appointment revealed new perspectives on a wider world and with them the pitfalls of conducting foreign policy in a democratic society.

The move from Boston to Washington also reflected Bancroft's disenchantment with his previous occupations. The Massachusetts Democracy was disintegrating; it had never been a really united force, guided by long-range programs or conceptions. The motley collection of factions, allegiances, and leaders held together by sentiment and vague promises finally wore away Bancroft's sense of responsibility.

The Washington bureaucracy proved equally obdurate. The reformer who failed to revolutionize Massachusetts hoped at first to succeed more readily in running a professional service, only to discover that the forces of habit and the demands of the moment frustrated his design. The realization that even a small bureaucracy had set ways of action, not amenable to rational persuasion, soured Bancroft's governmental career.

But the next eighteen months also witnessed the beginnings of territorial expansion, which, Bancroft argued, would restore the promises of American life. There were, however, deep differences about the definition of those promises. The controversy aroused by Polk's foreign policies, of which Bancroft became an enthusiastic and loyal supporter, left him in the long run more cautious and less optimistic than ever before.

197

Once again, a democratic society seemed bent on frustrating the very steps necessary for its survival, and opinion makers as well as leading politicians obstinately refused to see the light. Bancroft's services to a Democratic administration, the culmination of his politically active years, revealed how divisive his God-given truths really were.

By the end of 1844 Bancroft had come as far in Massachusetts politics as he could go. Another governorship race was likely to bring the same results, and eight years had exposed the impossibility of Bancroft's task; while Morton still felt that "you and I shall continue to have a perfectly good understanding of each other's views," privately he found his ally intolerable, a feeling several other local Democrats shared. A meeting at Bancroft's home to decide the party's future left everyone dissatisfied. "Geographical jealousies" and Whig strength, Bancroft concluded, would keep the Democracy of Massachusetts always a small, marginal force.[1]

The cooling reform ardor stirred a restlessness which sought new outlets. A minor slap at Harvard charging the college with elitism and sectarianism produced another round of reciprocal slanders and the realization that the institution, unreconstructable in the past, remained impervious to Democrat-religiously orthodox assaults in 1845. Boston, so exciting when compared to Springfield, lost its attractiveness; it had become stifling, boring, and provincial. In search of different challenges, Bancroft seized the opportunity to get out and never regretted his choice.[2]

The only question was whether a European appointment was preferable to a stint in Washington. The former seemed almost a necessity— Bancroft's contracts with Little, Brown set definite datelines for the completion of the *History* volumes, and the materials necessary for their writing were still largely in European archives. But Massachusetts was not up for a diplomatic appointment, Bancroft learned, as he followed rumors about Polk's possible choices. One bit of news made him secretary of the Treasury, another the future director of the Smithsonian Institution, and yet another the holder of an unspecified cabinet post. Meanwhile there were accounts from the collectorship still to settle. Determined to be available and without any strings attached, he chafed at the "terrible tomorrow, this more terrible next week" which met his requests for a closing. The Treasury Department claimed that he still owed $2,000 which he refused to pay, having proven to his own satisfaction that he had taken care of all bills.[3]

No one knew what the President-elect would decide, and Bancroft in Boston struggled with the uncertainties. Letting people know how close his relations with Polk were opened him to requests for favors, while speculation on the effect of his troubles with the Albany Regency complicated matters even more. A letter to Polk languished on the President-elect's desk for almost a month. Only at the end of January 1845 did Bancroft get his eagerly awaited summons to Washington.[4]

He arrived in the capital a few days later, protesting that he had never expressed any desire for office, that all his letters were designed to make the President "not to think of me." Bancroft tried to cover all grounds, assuring the New Yorkers that his actions in Baltimore were wholly disinterested, while reminding the President-elect's friends of past services. Various cabinet lists, he discovered, floated around Washington— Benjamin F. Hallett had seen one without Bancroft's name on it. To add to Bancroft's difficulties, Morton exploited his absence from Boston for some Democratic housecleaning, exposing the former collector's powerlessness to protect allies.[5]

"Time will unfold all things," Bancroft informed his wife, "among the rest whether you are to mope in Otis Place or reign in Washington or freeze your nose in some German Lapland." While Polk kept his own counsel, Bancroft called on John Calhoun, enjoyed a visit with Senator Thomas Hart Benton, and heard John Frémont describe the beauties of Oregon. "If anybody asks," he told Elizabeth, "say I shall possibly go as envoy to Japan." At the end of the month, Bancroft's desire and Polk's needs meshed. Harassed by office seekers and party conflicts, the President-elect searched for compromise figures and a chance reference in a letter from Van Buren reminded him of Bancroft. "Things are arranged entirely to my personal satisfaction," Bancroft rationalized, which was not quite true since he would have preferred a European appointment. On March 5, his reward for services rendered at Baltimore became public—George Bancroft, historian and Democrat, was the new secretary of the navy.[6]

The announcement placed him in the middle of an inevitable quarrel between the President and outraged Van Burenites, a quarrel Bancroft was powerless to resolve. Van Buren was creating problems by rejecting the inevitable, Bancroft thought, as the struggle over appointments exposed Democratic factionalism. The new secretary of war was William Marcy (a conservative Democrat and anathema to the Regency), while James Buchanan became secretary of state, a post the former President thought should have gone to Silas Wright. In a blistering letter to Bancroft, Van Buren complained that he had not "a particle of real bona fide influence ... an evil which neither civil words nor the disposition of patronage can repair and which, under the circumstances, nothing can justify." Bancroft never answered, for what was there to say? Van Buren's stand on Texas relinquished party control to others, and the future was theirs even if no one yet suspected the consequences.[7]

The appointment also affected Bancroft's ties to the Massachusetts Democracy. After his return from Washington, as a matter of form, he consulted Morton on patronage but bluntly added that the organization could not be rebuilt by reading people out of the party. "Conciliation will heal the breaches," he hoped, assuming that the Morton and Hallett feud would cease. It is not clear what the judge stood to gain; perhaps by disposing of Hallett he hoped further to undermine Bancroft's power base. Faced with the choice of supporting Hallett or Morton, Bancroft chose the former, who all along had created fewer problems. The former Anti-Mason, according to Bancroft, was a good Democrat and "a political friend." In a final cut that almost broke the relationship between the former collector and the former governor, Bancroft suggested that Morton's mind was clouded by "the vapours that rise from factions bickering for office."[8]

Glad to distance himself from these suicidal impulses, Bancroft left Elizabeth to take care of the moving arrangements and returned to Washington. He was present at the inauguration and warmly endorsed the President's new agenda for the nation—annexation of Texas, a strengthened Union, clear title to Oregon, and extension of the blessings of self-government to the Pacific. After a two-day round of celebrations, the secretary of the navy informed his wife that he would soon "lay his laurels, no, not that, his trident at her feet."[9]

But the appointment required Senate confirmation, where Bancroft's arguments that the annexation of Texas would lessen the political influence of slavery occasioned misgivings. When the Whig Senator Archer of Virginia decided to look into the matter, Bancroft took the temporary setback calmly but privately expressed chagrin. His past did not make him an abolitionist, he repeated. Polk, anxious to resolve the Texas matter and get his cabinet in order, mobilized friendly senators, and Allen of Ohio as well as John A. Dix of New York spoke on the candidate's behalf. On March 10, 1845, the appointment passed.

Reactions were mixed. "He is said to be an unfrocked Parson," Thomas Corwin of Ohio thought, "having graduated in the spiritual mysteries of Unitarianism first and closed with the propagation of universal salvation." Others assumed that reputed acquaintance with the abstract philosophies of Kant, Spinoza, and Schelling made the new secretary ignorant of the science of halyards, gunwales, and mainmasts. To Prescott, Bancroft was dissipating his talents, while Theodore Parker hoped that he would aid emancipation and represent "truth, justice and integrity in the cabinet." The Boston *Times* found it proper for the historian of the United States who explained the bearing of Texas on America's political and social interests to take an active role in shaping future policy. That "edge on [Bancroft's] . . . mind," which could "cut through the difficulties of active life and deftly divide truth from error in speculation" augured well for the navy, according to the New York *World*. Mrs. Bancroft agreed, and her opinion counted more than others.[10]

In spite of Elizabeth's eagerness to follow her husband, she remained in Boston for several months, completing arrangements for their move and fretting about the health of their "transcendental baby," as Susan Jackson was called. Polk had ordered all his cabinet officers to reside in the capital, and much as Bancroft wanted to help her he had to stay in Washington. While he was busy getting an expensive landau—dark maroon color—and furnishing an appropriate place for his family, Elizabeth worried about Susan's deteriorating condition, since the child seemed to grow thinner and paler by the day. Her worsening health twice delayed the family's departure. Toward the end of October she seemed to be recovering and they set out for Washington. Suzie reached Philadelphia with her mother and died a few days later.[11]

"Your lovely, now sainted child [is] gone," Bancroft was informed. He consoled himself by remembering his father's admonitions about the transitory nature of life and the meaning of eternity. Also "being of angelic purity, darling Suzie entered heaven without the evils of the mortal state." But Aaron Bancroft had possessed an ardent faith and fervent piety, while his son wrestled with his own sorrow much as he had before, by burying himself in work.[12]

Elizabeth joined him in Washington, while John and George remained in Roxbury at John Weisse's Family School, from which a stream of reports informed their father about their shortcomings. John was irascible, quarrelsome, lazy, and uncontrollable, while George stammered and had difficulty reading. Their rooms were always a mess; both refused to brush their teeth (bringing Bancroft expensive dental bills in future years); and their behavior alternated between excessive playfulness and shyness. "No one can do well without great and persevering efforts," he told the children, to little effect. The Dwight allowance paid for their escapades and for extra lessons, but in spite of help their English compositions remained poor and they did badly in other subjects as well. Bancroft was particularly upset about their inability to write. Sons unable to complete their sentences disappointed a man who prided himself on his style.[13]

Nor was Louisa easier to handle. Always closer to the Dwights than to her father, she disliked her stepmother and whenever possible stayed in Springfield. For a while Bancroft considered leaving her there, but upon reflection changed his mind. Louisa followed him to Washington, where life in a young ladies' boarding school was not to her liking. Elizabeth's sons, at least, did tolerably well at Harvard. William, on the verge of graduation, did not know what to do with himself and begged for advice. More amenable to reason than John and George, he was apprenticed to a Greenfield judge before entering law school.[14]

The children's unhappy state reflected years of neglect by their father. While he obviously cared for them, his tolerance and patience were limited; Bancroft lectured and preached and told them of his expectations, which they felt unable to fulfill. Left in the indulgent care of others, George and John also lacked what their father had in abundance—discipline and perseverance. Letters from Washington, however stern, were no substitute for parental supervision. And the more Bancroft threatened, the more recalcitrant the boys became. A stern schoolmaster helped. By the end of their stay at Roxbury the structured environment caused some improvement, which encouraged Bancroft to counsel their teacher to push them even harder. High demands would channel their exertions into a proper course.[15]

Much as he would have liked to, Bancroft was unable to shake off other problems left behind in Boston. During his first months in office Massachusetts politics took up more time than naval affairs. Communities, full of knots and cabals in the past, remained pockets of discontent, while former Governor Morton thought that "the surest way of building up the party is strict adherence to principles," by which he meant his own. Frederick Robinson, hoping to be the new collector of the port, branded Rantoul a schismatic Tylerite and implied that Morton lacked rank-and-file confidence. Charles G. Greene pressed for Hallett's appointment as district attorney, condemning Morton's manipulations. Parmenter seconded Greene's judgment, but John A. Bolles wanted the post for himself. Hallett denied that he was a soldier of fortune and an abolitionist, while Pliny Merrick, another Anti-Mason, also demanded rewards.[16]

Against Bancroft's better judgment, Polk decided to appoint Morton rather than Robinson to the collector's post. The judge seized this moment to assert his control over the party, and in a way that only worsened matters. Well before receiving congressional approval, the former governor began to read people out of the Democracy, augmenting Bancroft's already voluminous mail. Pro- and anti-Morton letters also reached the senators who would pass on the nomination, making a mockery of Bancroft's oft-expressed sentiments about harmonious Democracies.[17]

The Boston Navy Agency, under his jurisdiction, proved another trouble spot. The agency collected funds and in the past Bancroft had seen to their deposit with his favorite bank—the Merchants of Boston. Isaac H. Wright, a Tyler appointee, in his capacity as navy agent transferred the money to a rival institution and defended himself in the Washington *Globe*. The angry Merchants' Bank directors asked for help, and in response Bancroft ordered the return of the deposits. Wright refused and only the threat of dismissal forced him to yield.[18]

In the Charlestown Navy Yard Morton and Greene supporters exchanged mutual recriminations. By the summer of 1845, some Customhouse officials went over Morton's head and complained directly to the secretary of the Treasury. Hallett, whose appointment as district attorney Morton blocked, joined Robert Rantoul in enlisting southern antiabolitionist sentiment to delay Senate approval of the former governor's appointment. Morton blamed Bancroft, who in turn charged the judge with favoring Van Burenites. More and more the secretary of the navy relied on conservative Massachusetts Democrats for advice; his break with Morton was almost complete.[19]

William Parmenter became Bancroft's liaison man and tactics toughened. The Springfield convention in September 1845, dominated by Polk men, nominated Isaac Davis for the governorship. Morton's flirtations with abolitionist Democrats proved strong enough to override a Bancroft-sponsored antiabolitionist petition, but in Salem anti-Morton resolutions passed in October. The disastrous outcome of the November elections showed the results of the infighting.

For more than eight months Bancroft tried to run the party from the capital. By December 1845 he knew he had failed. Warnings that a Massachusetts Democracy tainted with abolitionism would prevent Congress from confirming Morton in the collectorship went unheeded, while some Democrats accused Bancroft of neglecting their needs. "My interest in the Democracy of Massachusetts will never be chilled but by the hand of death," he responded. Privately Bancroft's patience wore thin. "It is a grief to me that I have not been able to do more for Massachusetts," he concluded, washing his hands entirely of local party affairs.[20]

Meanwhile, Bancroft turned his attention to the navy. Determined to economize, streamline operations, clean up the department, and introduce a degree of professionalism, he thought that he could shape a small bureau more easily than an amorphous local party organization. After slightly more than a year in office he could look back with satisfaction on a series of efforts that pointed the way to the future. If not all of them bore immediate results, at least they set precedents for other secretaries of the navy.

Political and administrative talents enabled Bancroft to devise programs, assess situations, balance wishes against possibilities, and persevere in the face of opposition. The experience acquired in Massachusetts helped him address problems in a politic manner. Never pushing past the limits of his influence, Bancroft dealt ably with recalcitrant congressmen, manipulated House committees, persuaded and cajoled, much as he had once done on behalf of the Dwight banking interests, only now it was for the national security.

The new secretary of the navy entered a department prepared for his views. His predecessors had often declared themselves in favor of a more efficient operation and had called for greater cost-consciousness and an end to waste and extravagance. The abolition of the Board of Navy Commissioners, once responsible for managerial duties, also eased Bancroft's task by relieving him of the difficulties of dealing with an entrenched organization. Instead of the board, Bancroft faced five bureau chiefs, most of them professional officers who knew their duties. If they at first regarded him with suspicion, he quieted their doubts by persuading them that he had the best interests of the department in mind. Furthermore, the patriotic fever aroused by territorial expansion offset the traditional preference for a small fleet and the common Democratic hostility to peacetime armaments. Several attacks of war nerves, prior to the Mexican War, underscored the navy's unpreparedness, justified some of Bancroft's criticisms, and created greater congressional receptivity for his proposals.

Bancroft did not believe a larger navy was in the country's best interest. In spite of its shortcomings, the service fulfilled its peacetime functions and war would require no great changes. The transportation of troops and equipment, occasional blockades, and a few naval battles—for these a reshaping of existing forces would suffice. In cases of dire emergency and short of war with England (in which case the American navy would be at great disadvantage anyway), subsidies to convert private shipping for military needs would be enough. A powerful and aggressive navy was not necessary since the United States did not seek an empire and required only force adequate to back up its legitimate claims under the Monroe Doctrine.

Subordinates in the department supported the effort to balance reforms with a navy of traditional size. Lieutenant Matthew F. Maury, one of his aides, and several others realized that bad management and sloppy legislation had to give way to several proposals Bancroft endorsed—better rank and pay for officers, improved education and training possibilities, a more scientific approach, greater professionalism, and less politics. Maury's advice helped the secretary shape policy. Together they exploited war needs, which enabled them to implement suggestions that in time of peace would have met abuse. That they failed to accomplish more was due to Bancroft's short tenure. His acquaintance with operations also remained spotty, but he kept alive a series of proposals that would one day alter the character of the service.

Bancroft's first task was to satisfy office seekers from all corners of the nation, a duty most Washington politicians found burdensome, as did he. Never entirely a believer in Marcy's dictum that to the victor belonged the spoils, he tried to steer an even course, but soon floundered on the shores of factionalism, general incompetence, and Whig hostility. Determined to reform, economize, and retrench, Bancroft fired some unworthy Whigs for the sake of worthy Democrats, displeasing many, satisfying few. Patronage rarely conciliated contending factions and often placed Bancroft in the middle of the crossfire.

It was easy to respond to the pleadings of a mother on behalf of her son, or the lady begging a job for a cousin, but when William Cullen Bryant sent in several lists of candidates for the New York port and customhouses, Bancroft was unable to decide whom to appoint. "What on earth is the explanation of the president's extraordinary delay in his action on the removals and appointments in this city?" John O'Sullivan asked, after the administration had been in office only two months. Bancroft consulted James Buchanan and Henry Gilpin about Pennsylvania and several Rhode Islanders about Providence, but some felt left out and complained accordingly. Others, instead of asking questions, threatened vengeance against the administration if the foot dragging did not stop.[21]

A few hirings and firings, done in the name of reform, earned the secretary of the navy criticism in hostile newspapers. The Baltimore *Patriot* charged that hatred of Tyler governed this bookish gentleman who knew nothing about the sea yet dismissed devoted workers because they were Whigs. Others accused him of playing politics with national security, of dabbling in issues that were none of his business, and of prolonging courts-martial when he disagreed with the verdict or to benefit politically loyal lawyers. The Whigs also claimed that Democratic contractors lined their pockets with government funds. Personally honest and always scrupulous about accounts, Bancroft by 1845 had developed enough immunity to take such accusations in stride.[22]

With efficiency the goal, he streamlined the flow of data, gathering useful geographical and statistical information. Several navy yards ceased for a while to be income producers for traders and contractors when their commandants had to submit monthly statements of contingent expenses, while Bancroft personally supervised the appointment of officers. On his orders a board of captains simplified and unified regulations. A technical evaluation for admittance to the engineer corps assured competence, and other examinations helped decide on the promotion of all line officers.[23]

Reduce expenditures, cut duplications, dispose of superintendents where engineers could do the job, and provide better training methods, the secretary suggested in his annual report to Congress in December 1845. He also recommended an end to the seniority-based promotion system (an un-American principle, he thought) and the retirement of unfit captains. Of thirty-one masters at full pay, Bancroft wrote, only three or four could navigate a ship, an untenable state of affairs if the country was to defend its borders. Furthermore, in a free society, competition best determined eligibility and might raise the sons of common citizens to the navy's higher management levels. This was "the democratic law," one favorably disposed writer commented.[24]

The call for the abolition of seniority ran into formidable opposition, resurrecting the arguments for experience as against innovation. The charge that advancement "due to seniority alone, irrespective of capacity for duty," placed "personal interests before the public good" infuriated those who used the navy for sinecures. "All the brave and generous minded officers," said one Whig, were loud in their condemnation because Bancroft deprived them of the navy's most experienced personnel. Meanwhile Bancroft made clear how wasteful seniority really was. His review of the Marine Corps showed that out of thirteen captains only one was at sea, and of fifty lieutenants thirty-three were on land, living off government salaries and never going near the water. Nor were the pursers made happier when the secretary proposed to fire some for corruption, inefficiency, and doctored accounts.[25]

Bancroft could accomplish little as long as the idea of promoting younger officers seemed a trick to advance Democratic worthies by retiring older commanders at half pay. He proposed to use Jacobin principles, his critics contended, politicizing the navy. "Abject sycophancy and toadyism" would be the result. Several senior naval officers sought his removal from office, while hostile newspapers accused him of benefiting personally from his post—clerks paid with government funds were reputed to spend their time working on his *History*. For some time to come, seniority as a principle of naval promotion remained in force.[26]

Bancroft's one permanent accomplishment was the founding of the naval academy in Annapolis. Previous agitation for an institution similar to the army's at West Point had invariably foundered in the House. Bancroft realized the importance of such an academy and determined to do something about it, although most officers still deemed book learning incompatible with the actual duties of seamen, while several congressmen thought that mathematics and navigation sciences taught aboard ship were good enough. But the advent of steamships called for more thorough training, to be acquired at a professional center, with a clear program of studies concentrating on the sciences but not neglecting broader humanistic studies. Such an institution would produce competent midshipmen and gentlemen.

In theory no one in mid–nineteenth-century America opposed the combination. But the experience of his predecessors showed Bancroft that an appeal to Congress for more funds would be useless, nor did he want to force yet another unpopular measure down the navy's throat. In order to win approval, Bancroft requested the board of officers convened at the Philadelphia Naval Asylum (where some midshipmen received their training) to report on the advisability of a new school. The board's approval implied that the navy, and not only its controversial secretary, would stand behind the effort. In search of a good Democrat to aid him, Bancroft asked John L. O'Sullivan to head the new academy. O'Sullivan declined, but the board agreed with Bancroft, recommended Fort Severn as a site, and outlined a plan by which the graduates would be integrated into the navy after passing entrance examinations and a course of studies parallel to that at West Point.[27]

Bancroft incorporated the board's suggestions into his own proposal. By exploiting existing legislation and taking appropriations from other programs, he bypassed Congress and had enough money for the academy's modest beginnings. He drew upon available instructors to teach courses stressing morality and discipline, making midshipmen "as distinguished for culture as they have been for gallant conduct." The former Harvard instructor and pedagogue of Round HIll knew enough about schools to limit his goals, and if Bancroft was somewhat vague about what naval training involved, he understood that what was available would not do.[28]

A general order, with Secretary of War Marcy's consent, transferred Fort Severn from the army to the Navy Department. A navy man with solid credentials was appointed superintendent, while the midshipmen who were to be his wards remained subject to the needs of the service, satisfying critics who feared that an academy would deprive the navy of manpower. In spite of the general opinion that "you could no more educate sailors in a shore college than you could teach ducks to swim in a garret," Bancroft recruited the first group of students through the abolition of shore duty, and hoped for the best.[29]

On Friday, October 10, 1845, officers, instructors, and midshipmen gathered in the makeshift quarters to hear the superintendent's first address. An official letter from the secretary dwelled on the future rather than the primitive present and asked the students to disregard initial discomforts and inconveniences, a small price for rehabilitating the service and abandoning traditional and largely political staffing. Such makeshift beginnings—"a noble . . . democratic seed" in the words of the Brooklyn *Eagle*—provided the foundation upon which future secretaries could build.[30]

Foreign policy soon absorbed most of Bancroft's attention. Profoundly affected by the vehemence of the opposition to President Polk's conduct of international relations, Bancroft reacted much as he had always done when faced with real challenges—by taking refuge in irrelevancies. In stressing the long-range historical outlook in light of which immediate passions and the mistaken concerns of transitory mortals were unimportant, Bancroft salved his conscience and justified his political position. Unable to come to terms with the administration's critics, he defended himself with glittering generalities, completely inadequate for the moment.

In so doing, he was only becoming more honest with himself and others. The cautious, restrained, and faintly conservative tone evident in the past became more pronounced. Bancroft in 1845 denigrated impatient visionaries who wanted utopias here and now. "The appeal from the unjust legislation of today must be made quietly, earnestly and perse-

veringly to the more enlightened reason of tomorrow." This message
was not a dramatic departure from his previous statements, it had only
become explicit. "In a popular government, injustice is neither to be
established by force nor to be resisted by force," Bancroft declared,
showing how far he had come from those heady days when he deemed
assertion of the rights of labor the mission of the age.[31]

Territorial expansion now replaced the rights of labor as the focal
purpose of the age. Bancroft, explicating the meaning of annexation
while shaping its course, did so with the same fervor with which he had
formerly defended the Democracy. Even the slogans were similar, although their scope was greater. Having argued once that the elevation of
the working classes would cure all social maladjustments (never bother-
ing to say how), Bancroft in 1845 made territorial growth the panacea
for most of the nation's problems.

Several ideas defined the framework of Bancroft's rationalization.
The American heritage had in the recent past not developed as it should
have—democratic in its politics, egalitarian in social terms, and open in
economic opportunities. The West, Bancroft now said, had the answer
to these difficulties, and providentially was about to give the nation a
second chance. The influence of the newly acquired territories was crucial and would redound on the older states by furthering desirable
changes where local reform had failed. More land would alleviate hardships caused by an expanding economy. Productive outlets for commercial growth would drain off excess riches and diminish the danger of
envy, greed and political unrest. An end to the influence of rapacious
manufacturers, to low wages, to periodic recessions, and to the overex-
tension of capital would be among the other by-products, also vindicating the immutable laws of a free economy.

Even more important than the economic benefits of annexation were
its social implications. "Taking possession of the wilderness" would
mark the birth of a new man, replaying the drama of the first settlement
of the New World, repeating an earlier historical pattern. A whole new
race, shaped by an encounter with a virgin soil, would be led "of necessity" back to "first principles" which had been neglected since the early
nineteenth century. Free from "the bonds of hereditary establishment,"
the born-again American would trust only his conscience and native
judgment, valuing right more than usage and shaking off the irrelevant
burdens that saddled an overly civilized society. The Anglo-Saxon would
be in the woods again, as he had been in the seventeenth century, but
ironically this time he was to discard some American rather than European
irrelevancies. The revival of old values would arrest the republic's back-

sliding, disposing of the pessimists who bemoaned the loss of a golden past and frustrating the dangerous visionary schemes of extravagant reformers.[32]

The historian who stressed the beneficial impact of the American heritage on the nation's future acknowledged, although not explicitly, that the past had failed to solve present problems. The United States, as it was, could not overcome the pernicious influences of monopolies and aristocracies, but the new lands would make them unimportant. To seize that providentially given second chance demanded an abandonment of old slogans and support for a fresh agenda. Annexation was to be the focal point of the national effort cutting across party lines, submerging other issues, and making the Jacksonian heritage national rather than merely Democratic. The past was thus absorbed into the present.[33]

To formulate that agenda and to outline its components became Bancroft's self-appointed task when Polk asked him to be his main spokesman on the occasion of Andrew Jackson's death. Standing on the east portico of the Capitol, speaking gravely, sometimes haltingly, in a high-pitched tone that some of his listeners did not like, Bancroft delivered the main commemorative address in August 1845, outlining the intellectual justification of the new administration. Inadvertently the speaker also revealed how much he had changed during a decade of political involvement.[34]

The eulogy was sparse in detail and broad in conception—less an ode to bygone days than a prophecy of future greatness. The death of Jackson marked the end of an era, the passage of that "age of creative power," the nation's formative period. By linking Jackson with Washington, Jefferson, and Adams, Bancroft endowed the dead President's administration with the hallowed mantle of a sacrosanct past to which battles and scars were irrelevant. Jackson was praised for placing American laws on squarely American foundations and freeing the nation from such European vestiges as the tariff ("restrictive privileges") and the Bank ("the thraldom of monopolies"). But aristocratic legislation, a stock Democratic phrase since 1834, the struggle between the house of have and the house of want, and the vision of a society out of gear were never mentioned. The speaker implied that the past of which those slogans had once formed an integral part was a closed book. The nation could start anew. Its second chance had come.[35]

The continental destiny of the republic demanded a new frame of reference, and Bancroft's democratic theory shifted accordingly. Of the old persuasion there remained the faith in the people, in progress, and in freedom and equality. Jackson was praised for trying "to ensure the fruits of their industry to the workers." But the transcendental terminology, which was never really Bancroft's, had vanished. Terms such as the spirit in man, the soul of the people, the higher vision of the masses, yielded to a more concrete evaluation of motivations and historical forces. "The people can discern right and will make their way to a knowledge of right," he said in 1845, which was different from his earlier statement that "the common judgment . . . is the highest authority on earth, the nearest possible approach to an infallible decision." Bancroft by then had enough experience with popular fallibility to be more cautious.[36]

Instead of floating away on the wings of Democratic propaganda, Bancroft outlined the promises of territorial growth—in no less lofty tones. Conquering the wilderness, he assured his listeners, involved the transformation of nature and the Americanization of immigrants, "those children of sorrow on whom the old world frowns" and those sources of domestic discord whom some would have preferred had gone elsewhere. The virgin land yielding to plowshares guaranteed that "theirs shall be the soil, theirs the beautiful farms which they teach to be productive," making a new race out of the refuse of European societies and a lush but wild scenery into civilized domains. What was true for the newcomers would be even more so for Americans willing to build new homes in the West.[37]

Nature would succeed where past generations had failed, just as the "collective man," and not the individual alone, would lay the foundations of the new society. Hence the celebration of Jackson as "the unlettered man of the west, the nursling of the wilds, the farmer of the Hermitage, little versed in books, unconnected by science with the traditions of the past." The fact that the new territories lacked a history, Bancroft suggested, freed them from the dead weight of outmoded institutions and customs. The "natural dialectics" of wilderness life, the freedom from the "bonds of hereditary or established custom," were bound to affect the fortunes of the entire nation. The West, having learned from experience, would not repeat the mistakes of the East.[38]

For the West was but the latest addition to that moral force which defined national strength, and also its geographic scope. Jackson's body, Bancroft declared, had "its fit resting place in the great valley of the Mississippi, his spirit rests upon a whole territory, it hovers over the vales of Oregon and guards in advance the frontier of the Del Norte."[39]

By the time the dead President's spirit was summoned to bless the administration's foreign policy, Polk had taken steps to see to its fulfillment. Years later Bancroft revealed the details of a private meeting after the inauguration, when he said the President outlined his goals for the next four years: settlement of the Oregon question, acquisition of California and a large district on the coast, reduction of the tariff to a revenue level, and reestablishment of the independent treasury system. By the time Bancroft saw fit to tell his story, Polk's star was very much on the decline, and the historian may have wished to emphasize the President's success and his own share in it. Living into a generation which saw a direct connection between the Mexican and the Civil wars, Bancroft took pains to separate the two. He always remained proud of his own contribution to the tumultuous events that expanded the country's borders in the nation's best interest.

The credit for advancing those interests Bancroft ascribed entirely to Polk. The more he watched decisions made in the capital, the greater became Bancroft's respect for the tight-lipped, hardworking President, who knew what he wanted, was certain that his course was correct, and had enough determination to follow through. To the end, Bancroft judged Polk "one of the very foremost of our public men, and one of the very best and most honest and most successful presidents the country ever had." Prudent, farsighted, bold, and undeviating from democratic principles, Young Hickory deserved the mantle of Washington.[40]

Bancroft, an eastern and cosmopolitan Democrat, somewhat an Anglophobe, was as well informed on European affairs as other cabinet members, perhaps more so, all of which made him a valuable aide to the President. But the naiveté with which he surveyed the domestic scene also affected his world outlook—Bancroft never really appreciated the complexities of international intercourse or showed much understanding for the opponent's viewpoint. The great enemy of the United States in the nineteenth century was England, and since much of the President's foreign policy was designed to thwart British encroachments upon American interests, Bancroft was rarely out of accord with Polk's proposals to the cabinet. Perseverance, patience, occasional bluster, and frequent shows of strength—these were the methods by which the administration and Bancroft proposed to teach John Bull lessons he would never forget.

The Baltimore Democratic platform proclaimed a clear and unquestionable claim to the 54° 40' parallel as the boundary of Oregon, a good statement of the party line which England placidly ignored. Polk's inaugural statement was less extreme but enough to provoke a furor on both sides of the Atlantic. Bancroft wholeheartedly supported the assertion of the conflict in terms of American hegemony over the New World. "Our title to the country of the Oregon is clear and unquestionable," the

President said, which did not necessarily mean all of Oregon, but gave the British a clear indication of where the administration stood. The secretary of the navy did not believe that war would be needed to settle the matter and was willing to compromise, but he did not doubt that English jealousy of American advances where its navy was powerless to halt the march of Providence caused the ensuing stalemate.[41]

When the cabinet met in mid-July 1845 to draft its formal proposals to England, Bancroft supported Polk's compromise offer, which suggested that the United States would agree to the division of the Oregon country at the 49th parallel, giving England free ports on Vancouver Island south of the 49° line. When this offer was summarily rejected, the President adopted a tougher stance and demanded that the next communication should once more assert the United States' claim to the whole of Oregon. That to Bancroft was a proper response to these English cat-and-mouse games, but he was also cautious, and in the dispute between Buchanan and Polk over the question of continuing the negotiations he sided with the secretary of state and against the President, who was willing to break them off.[42]

Antipathy to England was conditioned by Bancroft's historical research, Democratic politics, and anti-Whig battles. While Bancroft could be as eloquent as Daniel Webster on the subject of positive English contributions to America, ultimately, of course, the United States perfected them all. And in his political exhortations the Tory and English Whig constitutional views were standard straw men to be toppled. In the nineteenth century, he thought, England still remained a jealous former mother country, ever ready to clip American wings. Luckily she was impotent to do real harm—military conflict was unthinkable; warlike British responses were so much hot air. Bancroft agreed when Polk suggested to his cabinet that the United States had to pursue a correct policy, regardless of English threats. He also found persuasive Polk's argument that if war was necessary, better now than later.[43]

All the while, the administration faced a deteriorating situation in the Southwest. The House resolution on the annexation of Texas the previous winter in effect had committed the United States to the defense of the Rio Grande boundary, which Mexico regarded as an act of robbery. Bancroft concurred when the new cabinet decided to let the annexation agreement, arrived at by the previous administration, remain in force. Nor did he object when *The Union,* apparently speaking for Polk, implied that California too would be part of the bargain.

Already in April 1845 Bancroft commanded Robert F. Stockton to proceed to the Mexican coast, and later in the summer the secretary of the navy strengthened the squadron in the Gulf. At the same time he was telling his friends in Washington and Boston that the administration had no intention of provoking an incident that would lead to an attack upon an adjacent state. His own instructions to the American forces were designed to prevent just such a possibility. Relations with Mexico were officially cordial, and the United States would do nothing to upset them. Even the order of June 15, 1845, which Bancroft, in the absence of the secretary of war, issued to Zachary Taylor, to move into the western frontier of Texas was viewed by Polk and the cabinet as a purely preventive measure. In the communiqué to Commodore David Conner on July 11 that same year Bancroft made clear that "while the annexation of Texas extends our boundary to the Del Norte, the president reserves the vindication of our boundary if possible, to methods of peace."[44]

Taylor's forty thousand men were emphatically not to be an army of conquest, as far as Bancroft was concerned. Polk, in a private letter, said as much, as did Marcy in another dispatch to Taylor at the end of July. And the news emanating from Mexico that summer indicated that war might be avoided. Nonetheless a small crisis of nerves followed the information from the Prussian ambassador to Washington, Baron Gerolt, that a Mexican force intended to cross the Rio Grande and attack Taylor. New instructions specified that such a crossing would constitute an act of war, in which case Taylor was to attack Matamoras, while secret orders told Commodore David Conner to blockade the Gulf coast and then attack Ulua. At the same time letters from Bancroft's commercial friends confirmed his expectation that Mexico really wanted peace and would be willing to negotiate on the issue of Texas and its boundary.[45]

California meanwhile was very much on his mind, and at a mid-September cabinet meeting Bancroft voted with Polk to authorize John Slidell's mission to Mexico. The envoy's shopping list was to include Upper California and New Mexico. Should war break out, however, Bancroft had already in June instructed Commodore John D. Sloat to seize San Francisco and other ports. But he repeatedly stressed the need to avoid provocations—Sloat was to proceed according to directives only "in the event of a declaration of war on the part of Mexico against the United States." On October 17, 1845, the order to Sloat was repeated.[46]

Bancroft's precise plans for California were unclear. Perhaps with the President he hoped for a vote by the local inhabitants to join the Union. Apparently to further that goal, Bancroft, with Senator Thomas H. Benton's help, aided John Charles Frémont's third expedition across the

Rockies to the Great Basin and California—that is, into Mexican territory, believing, as did other influential Americans, that unless the United States acted decisively, Great Britain would seize the area. When on November 6 the Navy Department received a dispatch from Conner stating that Mexico was willing to negotiate, Bancroft was sure that Polk's territorial aims would be settled amicably.

That also remained his view in December when he ordered Sloat to move north from Mazatlán, to maintain contacts with the American consul in California, and to supply arms to settlers in the Willamette Valley. In February 1846 Polk informed the cabinet of yet another way out of the Mexican morass (through the good offices of Santa Ana) and suggested that Slidell take stronger measures to pressure the Mexican government, and Bancroft concurred. He believed that European efforts to impose a monarchy upon her would drive Mexico into American arms, since "the public mind," if not the politicians, was "temperate and unwavering" in its desire for a peaceful resolution of the dispute. While a little war might be good for the United States—"it would increase our self reliance"—he would not complain if it did not come.[47]

For that reason Bancroft remained slightly more cautious than the President, objecting that a request for public defense funds might provoke hostilities. At whatever cost the United States should not appear the aggressor. At the same time, Bancroft informed Louis McLane, the American ambassador to Great Britain, that the nation had sufficient forces massed along the border and the coast of Mexico to repel an attack. As of the end of March 1846, he was sure that the prospects for peace were better than ever before.[48]

By April the President was losing patience and on April 25 the cabinet was told that "only a bold and firm course towards Mexico" would end this protracted stalemate. Polk, certain that conciliatory moves had failed, asked for a declaration of war. By then even Bancroft admitted that "Mexican affairs are a little awkward," especially since dispatches from Taylor reported Mexican reinforcements. On May 9 the whole cabinet, Bancroft excepted, agreed on a war message. He kept urging the administration to wait, but accepted Polk's decision and went to his office to collect the documents that would accompany the message.[49]

While he was still at work news arrived that the Mexicans had crossed the Rio Grande and had ambushed an American force. American blood had been shed on American soil, on the east bank of the river which, in dispute or not, was American soil for him. The war message of May 11, 1846, summarized the administration view—the United States had been reasonable and peace-loving, Mexico belligerent. Congress was to authorize the creation of an armed force to frighten the enemy into submission. Bancroft had no doubt that the war would be quickly won and that the criticism it might engender would subside. The vociferous, self-righteous opposition that had marked every previous national conflict would have no effect.

What would the country fight for? The question dominated a stormy cabinet meeting on the evening of May 13, when the President and his secretary of state submitted conflicting proposals. Buchanan urged the government to disavow any intention to dismember Mexico, and was willing to assure the world that desire neither for California nor for New Mexico defined the American policy. Polk, dismissing Buchanan's fears and apparently ready to battle France, England, and Mexico at the same time if need be, demanded that Mexico pay certain American financial claims; and since she obviously had no funds to do so, territorial adjustments in California and other parts of Mexico would do as well. In this dispute Bancroft, once again, found himself on the President's side. Had he acquiesced in Buchanan's proposal, the year and a half of diplomatic maneuvers and failed negotiations would have all been in vain. "We have got into a little war," Bancroft exulted as he set about establishing communications, providing supplies, and exploiting his ties with Boston's commercial community for the navy's benefit.[50]

Part of his effort was designed to seize California. The secretary of the navy ordered David Conner to blockade the Gulf coast, conquer Tampico, and encourage secession in the coastal Mexican states. John D. Sloat in the Pacific was to seize Monterey, Mazatlán, and possibly Guyamas. By the end of June 1846, with Sloat on the way, California was declared an independent republic. Sloat arrived at Monterey on July 2, where a detachment of marines five days later raised the American flag. On the following day Captain John B. Montgomery took possession of the posts on San Francisco Bay, while later in the month Stockton, with the cooperation of Frémont, seized Southern California. In mid-August, American forces entered Los Angeles. Many of these moves had taken place without Bancroft's knowledge, others went counter to explicit instructions, but the result, by whatever means, was the same—California was in American hands and Mexico had to accept the fait accompli.

This was as far as Bancroft's involvement in the Mexican War went. If in the summer of 1846 he had been asked whether anything had gone wrong with the President's policies, Bancroft's reply would have been a resounding no. Those policies involved a set of measured responses to various pressures and factors, emphatically neither a blunder nor a con-

spiracy. Mistakes were caused by misinformation, lack of detailed knowledge, faulty communications—not by poor judgment. The Rio Grande
boundary, New Mexico, and California were bound to come into the
orbit of American influence. Mexico, corrupt, unstable, poor, and inefficient, was unworthy of its possessions and ought to have ceded them
peacefully. Certainly Polk had done everything possible to settle the
dispute without arms. But Mexico refused, the war followed, and territorial gains were the proper outcome.

All would have been well except for the growing opposition to the
President's policies, that swelling chorus of discontent which more than
anything else brought about Bancroft's disillusionment with the political
process. He neither understood nor appreciated the emotions and passions involved. It was all so clear and simple to him. Why not to everyone else?

At the admission of Texas, Bancroft's friend and fellow historian
Prescott had commented, "I had rather she had thrown herself to the
devil where indeed, it is probable most of her population at some time or
other will go." George Sumner, Charles's brother, another acquaintance,
thought that "Texas we have gulped whole, it is hard enough for some
of us to digest it at all." For brother-in-law John Davis, Polk was "obliged to bow down and worship the juggernaut of slavery and embrace
Calhoun's solecism that slavery alone can make us free. The annexation
of Texas nails it to our back with all its sins and crimes." Davis was
certain that "the moral sense of the public will revolt at piracy and
robbery whether by highwaymen and brigands or by statesmen—especially if we plunder to give new strength and power to slavery." Springfield in 1846 elected political rival William B. Calhoun state senator on
an antiwar platform, while Theodore Parker called every volunteer "to
this wicked war a stripe on the nation's back."[51]

Bancroft expected such judgments, unwelcome though they were,
but the controversy also gained him some unexpected allies. The people
who had been besmirching Bancroft for years vigorously assaulted Robert C. Winthrop, who voted for war supplies. And when the Boston
Atlas spoke of the war in terms not far different from those of the Boston
Post, Bancroft knew something had changed. To be on the same side of
an issue with Abbott Lawrence, Nathan Appleton, Edmund Dwight, and
Samuel A. Eliot was encouraging, but to be told by a southerner, as
Bancroft was, that "you will not regret your advocacy of Southern
rights" was a painful reminder of how confused the issues were.[52]

Manifest destiny played havoc with politics, contrary to Bancroft's
expectations. The debate over the territorial aims of the war revolved

around slavery, despite his repeated denials that the issues were related. Splits in the Democratic ranks paralleled those among the Whigs; some of Bancroft's former co-workers assumed an antiadministration position. In the Senate a filibuster led by John Davis killed a request for an appropriation to negotiate a treaty with Mexico, infuriating Polk and the secretary of the navy. That money, in Bancroft's judgment, would have shortened the war and gained California and the rest of the desired territory. Abstract, erroneous principles and political vindictiveness were undermining the chances for a peace based on thorough assertion of American rights "with unanimity and dignity." Critics, denouncing the government as a violator of international law and of the Constitution, deepened divisions at home and impelled enemies to "unreasonable and impossible demands."[53]

Knowing of Bancroft's cordial relations with former president John Quincy Adams, Polk once suggested that the now congressman come to a White House dinner. Adams, huffing and puffing, told the secretary of the navy that he would not accept the invitation, recalling that he had successfully resisted Andrew Jackson's effort to lure him into sharing a meal. For the leader of the antislavery forces in the House to dine with the President would have been hypocritical. Polk remained unperturbed. "It was a matter of no consequence whether [Adams] . . . was invited to dinner or not."[54]

This little incident was emblematic of others exposing the divisions the war created. Yet Bancroft could not comprehend why civilized individuals were unable to mingle socially just because they held different political opinions. In spite of abuse, disagreements, and differing persuasions, they were supposed to share certain values that transcended their private views. Polite intercourse had been the hallmark of most Boston dinners, if not of the Boston press. But by 1846 it appeared that slavery views penetrated even the previously immune private spheres. Perplexed and dismayed, Bancroft continued to hope that the war, once over, would repair the divisions which that summer seemed bent on its prolongation. But the long congressional ordeal, the difficulty of conducting a distant war with faulty communications, and the uncertainty of the political conflicts deflated Bancroft's initial enthusiasm. That some Whigs proved obdurate and obstructive came as no surprise, but the inability of prominent Democrats to see broader issues disturbed the usually sanguine secretary of the navy. They damaged their own political future and the whole course of American development.

He dated the disintegration of the Democratic Party to those hectic times when friends and allies dropped away from the administration. A note of caution crept into his usually ebullient pronouncements. At stake was the Union. The new territories, redeemed rather than conquered, would dissolve the traditional North-South division and replace it with a new alignment of Northeast and West, thus supplying the union with "a foundation that can not be moved."[55]

Until early June of 1846 neither Polk nor Bancroft knew where the national boundaries would be. Then the trader Samuel Hooper pleaded with the secretary of the navy to seize the California coast south to the thirty-second parallel, taking in all the good harbors down to San Diego. Bancroft's response was swift: "if Mexico makes peace this month," he wrote, "the Rio Del Norte and the parallel of 35 may do as a boundary. After that 32, which will include San Diego." In mid-July he sent orders to Sloat to seize that town as soon as San Francisco and Monterey were secure. In taking possession, Sloat was to "endeavor to establish the supremacy of the American flag without any strife with the people of California"—an example of redemption, as opposed to conquest.[56]

Luckily, European diplomats in Washington maintained standards of civility in spite of the city's shabbiness and their own frequently derogatory opinions of the country. Dinners at the French, Prussian, and English embassies were amusing, elegant, and occasionally the source of important news. At such gatherings Bancroft practiced his European languages while forming valuable contacts. Selling the Mexican War to foreign diplomats was no hardship, for in spite of raised eyebrows, most of them acquiesced in American expansion, and if they did not, lacked power to do anything about it. They could understand the polished, educated, and knowledgeable cabinet officer, with his gentlemanly ways, gracious wife, proper manners, and European connections. Rarely did he allow his own enthusiasms to go beyond good taste, and he subjected few diplomats to the outright propaganda that infused his political statements.[57]

Such diversions did not make up for the hardships of officeholding. After eighteen months in the capital, Bancroft decided that he had had enough of being secretary of the navy. The academy at Annapolis was functioning, but his seniority proposals were floundering and promotion by merit would have to wait. The constant stream of letters made writing difficult and, with the military course set, Bancroft doubted that he had much to contribute to the disheartening debate on war aims. By the summer of 1846 he wanted a respite and looked for it in a wider world beyond Washington.

Diplomacy

IX

THE COURT OF ST. JAMES'S

THROUGH the spring of 1846 the local newspapers reported on Bancroft's unhappiness in Washington while he reminded Polk of the promise of an ambassadorial post. One account had him shivering in the swamps of St. Petersburg, while another assumed he would become the new ambassador to France. Bancroft's choice was England—for its prestige and importance, for the advancement of his scholarly pursuits, and also because of his rivalry with Edward Everett, who had held the position under Harrison. When John Calhoun and Martin Van Buren turned down the President's offer, Bancroft gratefully accepted the appointment. It had always been his lot in life to get plums others had turned down, but London was so attractive, he felt no qualms about it.[1]

The eagerness with which he clutched at this chance to leave the United States reflected his growing disgust with politics. In June 1846 a coalition of dissident Democrats, Whigs, and abolitionists elected John P. Hale senator from normally Democratic New Hampshire. In Massachusetts antislavery sentiment in the rank and file boded no good for the organization, and Morton blamed Bancroft for the revival of factionalism. A fact-finding trip Bancroft undertook for the President revealed that party leaders in Kinderhook, Albany, and New York City ascribed the party's decline to the administration.[2]

Bancroft, of course, thought himself above squabbles and narrowmindedness, although his own appointment reflected Polk's partisanship and generated some misgivings. The new ambassador assured a correspondent that "public feeling" was not so bitter toward him as it sometimes seemed, and that he hoped to be not the Democratic but the American representative at the Court of St. James's. Meanwhile he solicited letters of approval from the business, scholarly, and political communities to show the breadth of his support.[3]

So pleased was he to get out of Washington that an exultant note to Secretary of War Marcy "was written as if he was well charged with exhilarating gas." Bancroft swiftly prepared for departure and carefully laid the ground for his London arrival. Letters of introduction from Edward Everett and others would assure a welcome from those who knew the historian of the United States by his controversial reputation, while Elizabeth collected addresses and advice that would make settling in a foreign capital easier. Bancroft knew he was expected to subsidize the embassy out of his own pocket and, unlike one of his predecessors (Edward Everett) and his successor (Abbott Lawrence), he did not have a fortune to rely on. Samuel Hooper agreed to take care of his still sizable debts to Boston banks and mercantile firms and the well-nigh worthless Michigan lands. But financial problems paled in the face of what was coming. Polk extended his blessings, and in October Bancroft embarked for England with his wife and Louisa, leaving behind his two sons, whose school reports again became unsatisfactory. He then severed his ties with the city of Boston, to which he would return but rarely in the future.[4]

In a stormy crossing on the *Great Western,* Elizabeth spent her time praying for terra firma while her husband read Tacitus. His first port of call was Liverpool, where he exercised his charms on local dignitaries who urged a change in the tariff laws. "They hung upon me as an oracle to hear how much corn the valley of the Mississippi can produce," Bancroft wrote to Polk, proving English dependence upon American foodstuffs. The journey to London and the reception at Long's Hotel were pleasant in their marked contrast to the days when an impoverished student wandered the city streets alone. Bancroft found a competent staff, a legation in relative order, and no pressing business. He quickly established a permanent residence at 90 Eaton Square, not far off New Bond Street, presented his credentials to Lord Palmerston, and immersed himself in a round of social duties.[5]

Such pleasant beginnings diluted some of Bancroft's Anglophobia. He could not however escape reverberations from the faraway home front. Reminders of how controversial manifest destiny had become arrived in the first messages from across the Atlantic, reporting the disastrous elections in Massachusetts, where the Democratic gubernatorial candidate got only half the votes Bancroft had received in 1844. Newspapers, regularly sent to the legation, reported difficulties about which he could do nothing and for which he did not feel any responsibility. The same polarity marked the rest of his European stay—the pleasantness of English life and disquieting news from the United States.[6]

Bancroft proved an able minister, closely following the secretary of state's instructions, rarely quarreling with his own government, and on the whole very successful with the locals. With few exceptions his duties did not differ radically from those performed in Washington and Boston; explicating the ways of God to men was transformed into justifying United States government policies to the English. Mollifying public opinion and defending the American position drew upon capacities and arguments employed in the past in another setting. Bancroft also had time to write numerous lengthy reports on other European countries, which, though widely read in Washington, exerted little influence on Polk. Interesting and detailed though they were, the limited scope of the administration's policies made them irrelevant.[7]

Those reports, however, revealed a good deal about Bancroft. The application of familiar methods and judgmental categories to the Old World produced results as controversial as in the past. The theoretical democrat, who had failed to revolutionize Massachusetts and hoped to hasten American progress through expansion, perceived multiple signs of similar democratic developments in Europe, and with equally unfocused vision. In the end, it scarcely mattered that his prophecies proved illusory, that the reports were inaccurate, or that he mistook gossip for substance; Bancroft's predictions always assumed that current events were only incidental in the long run.

A new postal convention and more favorable trade arrangements, among his substantive achievements, were the results of his capacity to act in the local political world—tactics good for the Boston Customhouse and the Navy Department proved useful when applied to the British Parliament and Her Majesty's Cabinet. Throughout his stay, Bancroft remained loyal to his promise to Buchanan that he would conduct himself with circumspection and lay aside his well-known prejudices, and his charming social graces went a long way toward helping him to accomplish his objectives. For a man who frequently maintained that human nature was the same everywhere and under all circumstances, this came as no surprise.

The anticipated English hostility toward the United States that Bancroft often stressed at Polk's cabinet meetings did not extend to the minister plenipotentiary. Invitations to breakfasts, receptions, literary events, country weekends, and official functions showered upon the Bancrofts. Lord and Lady Palmerston, Sir George Gray, the Prussian minister Chevalier Bunsen (whom Bancroft had met twenty years earlier in Rome) were among the early callers. Bancroft also gained entrée to the Travellers Club and the London Atheneum, a privilege but rarely extended to Americans. Such flattery, however deceiving, went a long way to quiet his suspicions. At glittering dinners in Holland House in Kensington, Lord Morpeth and the son of the Archbishop of York provided exciting conversation, while Macaulay and the sister of Lord Clarendon were guests of honor. The Earl of Auckland, head of the Admiralty, was curious to learn the views of the former United States secretary of the navy, and the Marquis of Lansdowne inquired about his historical opinions. Lady Byron proved a good conversationalist and the poet Samuel Rogers was full of amusing anecdotes. There were several invitations to Windsor—the Prince of Saxe-Weimar escorted the Queen to dinner, while Bancroft chaperoned the Duchess of Kent, his fluent German helpful on the occasion. Lord John Russell proved less of an ogre than Bancroft had expected, and a meeting with Lady Charlotte Lindsay, the only surviving child of Lord North, was a reminder of the past.

Elizabeth, as much overwhelmed by this stylish world as her democratic husband, thought they were the greatest diners-out in London. "One soon gets used to all things," she sighed, enjoying every opportunity to take precedence, in right of her country, over marchionesses and titled ladies. "We have everything to make us happy here," she informed her sons, and Bancroft concurred, believing that there was nothing incongruous or hypocritical in the way he adjusted to this hierarchical society, with its strict protocol and antidemocratic sentiments. After all, he knew full well that this was a waning world, while he stood for the forces on the ascendance; meanwhile he would enjoy that decadent world.[8]

Movement in exalted circles required the right equipment. Gone were the days of republican simplicity espoused by John Adams and other early American ministers in Europe. Bancroft readily accepted Lord Palmerston's helpful suggestion that plain dress would not do for Victoria. Bancroft purchased an embroidered suit, chapeau, and sword and drove about in a maroon-colored coach with silver moldings and American arms on the panel. He arrayed his lackeys in blue and red liveries and on court days decked himself out in blue-plush breeches, white silk stockings, and buckled shoes. The days when Everett's yellow coach and drab flunkeys aroused a howl of protest in the Democratic press were over.

Life became "more like a drama than reality," a display in polished drawing rooms of aristocratic manners in resplendent dress. To see the distinguished men of England was like observing the pictures and statues of Rome, Elizabeth thought; country weekends resembled staged productions on a vast scale, with their formal procedures, set speeches, and protocol. Court receptions reminded Bancroft of a well-orchestrated show, unreal but fascinating. Elizabeth, introduced to the Queen, performed her motions with proper dignity; but the Queen said nothing, only smiled, playing her part. The upper classes put on a splendid performance, in which the American representative and his wife were willing actors.[9]

There was more to London than the court circles. Bancroft attended more relaxed intimate gatherings with people not normally encountered in the houses of the great aristocrats. Mrs. Otis back in Boston got away with mixed crowds; in London few dared, and the opportunity to move in a variety of cliques gave the Bancrofts an edge over some of their hosts. At a dinner at William Macready's, intelligentsia gossiped and argued while Carlyle carried on about everything under the sun and Charles Babbage conversed on mathematics and the state of the English press. At Sir Roderick Murchison's, scientists discoursed on their discoveries. While the *History* was not a best-seller in England (Bancroft had problems with his publisher about the appearance of the volumes in England at all), the work was well enough known to open other doors. The Bancrofts participated in meetings of scientific societies, attended lectures, and were delighted to go to museums on days when they were ordinarily closed to the public.[10]

The couple moved with comparative ease in both the worlds of government and its attendant political and social groups and in the circles gathered around men of knowledge. Elizabeth proved adept at drawing out the juiciest pieces of gossip, often for the benefit of American visitors, such as Ralph Waldo Emerson. But the separation between the various social circles confirmed Bancroft's theoretical prejudices about the iniquities of hierarchical societies. Yet he reveled in his status and out of self-esteem forgave his hosts some of their practices. That self-esteem, bruised at home by political opponents, was reinforced in London by lavish attention from people who had no use for his theories whatsoever.

The names of the high and mighty, of dukes, princes, and members of Parliament soon studded the legation's guest books and the letters home. The attractive mixture of wealth, power, and intelligence, the simple manners and the unaristocratic demeanor of the English peers, impressed the Bancrofts, who nodded sagely when one visitor informed them that it took time to make people, like cathedrals. Americans seemed crude and primitive by comparison with this cultivated and polished society. No one in Boston could match its taste and resources or meet the standards of the London luminaries.

But that was not the whole story. Later American intellectuals frequently found their host countries a great improvement over the United States. Bancroft however had no illusions about England, and his political attitudes precluded sympathetic insight into its problems. The contrast he found between English and American society sharpened his critical faculties. His facile assimilation into London high life denoted no loss of democratic sensibility. It was a pity, he realized, that his own society boasted no parallels for achievement based on secure social position. But he also knew that it allowed men like himself to rise in the world and that his charming English hosts were a dying breed. Closely examined, Elizabeth informed Sarah Polk, the British upper crust was not really superior to its American counterparts. "We need not be ashamed of ourselves . . . our best portions of society can bear a comparison with theirs." Her husband was an example—the poor son of a Worcester clergyman about to dine undazzled with Victoria. Bancroft never forgot who he was, and bristled when English acquaintants, though not snobs, sometimes exhibited less likable traits. On a visit to Abbotsford, Walter Scott's home, Bancroft was not surprised at the sneers of the grandee who showed him around. Such people "cannot bear to have a poet and a man of letters make a place for himself in the landed aristocracy."[11]

A few, not really significant, English achievements were enviable. Their hotels were better—the Adelphi in Liverpool, as quiet as a private house, attended to its guests properly. Local trains were superior; the Bancrofts always traveled first class—almost like being in a private carriage, Elizabeth thought. No American matched an English aristocrat in the number of servants, costly plate, glittering liveries and footmen. And Boston could use their little teas—"no supper, no expense, nothing but society," and so enjoyable.[12]

Elizabeth also conceded certain advantages to Englishwomen, who talked more about "general" subjects, ignored domestic duties, never sewed, and knew how to carry off a very social life and were therein superior to the Boston blues. Miss Murray, the Queen's maid of honor and one of Elizabeth's warm friends, was connected with half the noble families of England, granddaughter of the Duchess of Athol and a descendant of Scott's Countess of Derby; yet she was independent in her thinking and spoke freely on all subjects.

To the Bancrofts America nevertheless remained better in everything that mattered—cleaner, newer, and more sober, not as picturesque as the English countryside, but more self-reliant and less hypocritical. The English nobility had more jewelry and lace than any American Elizabeth knew, but that was by inheritance and produced an overdressed society, tiresome glitter and pomp, and a life basically boring. "Upon the whole, I love my own country better than ever," she maintained, and George echoed her judgment. "The same round of ceremonies, forms and society" year after year was enough to weary anyone. "For us it is a new study and invaluable for a short time, but I could not bear it for life," she concluded.[13]

Bancroft pointed out that English aristocrats, born to lead, had no need to put on airs, while their American counterparts, upstarts all, were less secure, more haughty and presumptuous. But the English upper classes exacted heavy social costs—their paternalism, for example, fostered the gratitude but also the apathy of peasants. On one occasion Bancroft observed an elderly couple receive a watch as their reward for having reared six children after burying seven, all without parish aid. Such perseverance deserved recognition, but it branded habits of subserviency to the aristocracy into the national character.[14]

Subserviency, which pervaded all walks of life, destroyed self-reliance. Young girls clung too closely to their mothers; no spirited American would long submit to parental domination. There was no English equivalent of the New England culture and good sense, no sturdy and independent yeomanry, no politically conscious mechanics. A hierarchical society with a strong oligarchy and downtrodden lower orders—this was the condition of England. People without political training, a parliament selected largely on the basis of landownership, a press restrained by a stamp tax, and tenantry dependent on landlords accounted for national stagnation.

Other American pilgrims to England shared Bancroft's misgivings. Even the most favorably disposed found some of their hosts shallow or dishonest. Those who made the trip in the 1840s—like Edward Everett, Daniel Webster, and Ralph Waldo Emerson—were impressed by the advances in science and industry, but wondered whether they were worth the cost. Bancroft's observations, tinged with his democratic theories, were very much like those of his Whig friends, who, though pursuing a different political line, shared many of its components.

To improve their lot, the people needed political authority, but also training and experience not available under the existing system. Change depended on a class, rare in England, that loved freedom more than bread. Occasional crumbs from the aristocracy forestalled meaningful concessions while the Poor Laws kept the masses in a state of perpetual dependence. Chartism asked for what in Pennsylvania were matters of course, yet the English, "content to obey patrician councils," had "neither the intelligence nor the daring to make themselves felt."[15]

The complacency with which Bancroft evaluated his own culture and social order disappeared when he faced a different and largely hostile terrain. His often perceptive insights into English society, revealing sensitivity never exercised at home, grew out of the support that the condition of England, as he saw it, provided for his own theories. Everything Bancroft saw from London confirmed his American beliefs in hard work, social mobility, and material acquisition.

More immediately, Bancroft's analysis reflected his public role as spokesman for the Polk administration. Since hostile public opinion hampered his efforts to present the American version of the Mexican War, Bancroft's interpretation reacted to English responses to United States foreign policy. The more hostile those responses became, the more he fleshed out the failures of the society from which they stemmed. He repaid some of his hosts in kind—if they articulated doubts about the benefits of republican, egalitarian, and democratic orders, Bancroft countered by pointing out the shortcomings of the alternatives.

The villain of the Mexican War, according to official English sources, was the United States. The London *Times* had charged that "the head of the American government has, with as much deliberation as he is capable of, plunged his country into this most flagitious war." A hostile British press and the two political parties shared those sentiments and argued that the conflict was an act of aggression by a strong neighbor against a weak state to spread slavery. Frequent sneering references to America's immoral position, her rapacity, greed, and warmongering, were so at odds with Bancroft's own version that he became even more critical and sensitive.[16]

Pessimistic and contradictory reports from the United States hardened Bancroft's defensive posture. "The war is becoming increasingly popular throughout the country," Buchanan wrote in December 1846, "and should the Mexican government refuse to treat . . . it will arouse a spirit among our people which will be difficult to control." But Marcus Morton informed Bancroft about the slavery debate's ruinous impact on the Democracy, and by February 1847 even Buchanan took account of the growing controversy.[17]

Behind the English reaction to the Mexican War, Bancroft concluded, was fear lest the American precedent democratize Great Britain. The Tory Lord Mahon, whom Bancroft frequently met and whose scholarship he admired, as well as more liberal writers, politicians, and scholars such as Richard Monckton Milnes, Emerson's reviewer, revealed in their ambivalent attitude toward the United States unfounded prejudices. Thomas Carlyle, whom Bancroft also befriended, went further than either Mahon or Milnes in disdain for the dignity of labor, a phrase dear to the American envoy. From Henry Hart Milman, Dean of St. Paul's and historian of Christianity, Bancroft learned about the aristocratic concern for democracy's instability and its incapacity to withstand popular pressures. Like Macaulay, whom Bancroft considered the most erudite man he had ever met, Milman preferred a society ruled by an educated class and devoted to the preservation of property and order. Not only Tories, but good Whigs, repelled by American swagger, coarse manners, and lack of culture, pointed out the republic's shortcomings—shallow partisanship, mediocre leaders, and popular vices.[18]

Bancroft could do little to disabuse his hosts, but he consoled himself with the thought that such judgments were irrelevant to events at home. Proud as they were, the English would learn that "America means to go on her own way . . . Europe, though it may gaze with envy, must give up the thought of swaying her destiny." The English "do not love us" Bancroft reported to Washington, "but they are compelled to respect us," which was even better. Everyone, he thought, realized that California had to belong to the United States, and events were outdistancing Palmerston's belief that "John Bull is everything and that international law, treaties and interests of all sorts must yield to British pretensions." "We can do without England better than England can do without us," Bancroft concluded. John Bull would have to swallow the Mexican War whole, like it or not.[19]

When Lord Ashburton told the American ambassador, "You are the lords of Mexico," Bancroft knew he was right. Even Lord Palmerston had to interpret the war's outcome as proof of Anglo-Saxon superiority over the Latin race. Newspapers still vented their spleen, but it was "becoming a fashion, rather," Bancroft informed Polk, "to expect the absorption of all of Mexico." At first Bancroft was unsure whether this was desirable, but upon reflection he decided that the United States should acquire as much territory as possible, regardless of misgivings at home or abroad.[20]

The misgivings abroad were comprehensible, but not, Bancroft thought, the storm at home over the administration's war aims. The Whig "cry of no more territory" was absurd, and badly timed, coming at a moment when many Europeans hoped to see Mexico regenerated through American influence. This "war of civilization" and "the valor of our soldiers in Mexico has raised our character throughout Europe," he told Polk. Bancroft jokingly suggested to Prescott that the time for writing a second conquest of Mexico had not yet arrived, but he had no doubt that the utter humiliation of Mexico would prove to the world in general, and to the English in particular, the strength, health, and stability of American society.[21]

To these spectacular achievements Bancroft hoped to add two entirely of his making—a new postal convention with England and the abrogation of the British navigation acts. America's democratic principles demanded an equitable mail arrangement and an end to the old mercantile system. The proposed changes would also demonstrate the President's capacity to deal with issues other than Mexico. Having participated in the Oregon negotiations, Bancroft was ready to deal John Bull another lesson in open Democratic diplomacy.

The demand for a new postal convention arose out of the unfair charges Americans paid on letters to Europe that passed through English ports. The British post office charged the same postage on letters carried on American vessels, at American expense, as if they had been carried on British craft at British expense. Bancroft asked for fair treatment that would not discriminate in favor of either side and hoped through firmness to persuade the British to give up their monopoly. Lord Clanricade, with whom he negotiated, proved, however, unbending, and when discussions dragged on intermittently through the summer of 1847, Bancroft threatened to abrogate all existing conventions. To show the English that monopolies were no longer in good standing, he also threatened to prohibit the passage of the Canadian mail through United States ports.[22]

Abrogation of the navigation laws was a much more complicated problem that involved not only conflicting English interests but also American uncertainty about the benefits. Bancroft, who thought he knew the needs of the mercantile community as well as the merchants, was sure that free trade could only be beneficial. The Americans could easily compete with the British, and opening the West Indies trade to their ships would be a signal Polk achievement, advantageous to the United States.

To assist him in bringing the British to their senses, Bancroft enlisted all the help he could. He urged the President to give as much publicity as possible to these negotiations in order to prove that the administration was not bogged down in Mexico but was also advancing other great national interests. Nor did the historian of the American Revolution underestimate his own potential contribution in compelling the former mother country to abandon an antiquated trade system and thus bring to fruition the principles of 1776. Friendly businessmen were asked for their views, while favorable articles in United States newspapers informed public opinion. In London Bancroft solicited the aid of members of Parliament and government officials, exploiting every opportunity to press his case.[23]

The ensuing delays and complications, Bancroft implied, were due to England's appalling social conditions, frightening overpopulation, and the terrible state of the working classes, which made the ruling classes intransigent. "The employer must either employ six to do the work of three" or "support three in total idleness as paupers." The lack of hope for the poor distressed the democrat, "their youth . . . dreamy and indolent, their prospects of old age horrible." Finances were disordered, business stagnant, and by the fall of 1847 everything was "ominous of a serious struggle." Under such circumstances, the navigation acts and the postal convention were not the government's major concerns.[24]

Ireland was, and Bancroft avidly followed the challenge posed by English misrule and exploitation. Only radical concessions, he thought, at the expense of the Anglo-Irish church and the absentee landlords, could alleviate the appalling conditions there, but centuries of mistakes and cruelty made all solutions inadequate. A vast number of parasitic bureaucrats distributed charity, which made the Irish dependent on public aid; indifferent to their own welfare, they lacked self-reliance and imposed a terrible vengeance for having "been burdened with pensions to the English aristocracy."[25]

Bancroft's evaluations reflected his own prejudices and glossed over some conflicting facts. At the end of 1846 and into the spring of 1847, the British government employed almost three-quarters of a million Irishmen, helped to support another three million, and kept alive at least one million people who would otherwise have perished. None of this information found its way into Bancroft's dispatches. Nor did he report that the authorities did all this in the face of an opposition which liked to believe in a Nature carrying out her work, however cruel. In his effort to present the English in the worst possible light, Bancroft also failed to mention that such great Irish landowners as Lansdowne and Palmerston plowed back some of the profits of their estates to improve the lot of the tenants.

These conflicting details, the basis for a more balanced assessment, merely complicated what Bancroft considered the classic case against English rule. The sincere if faltering efforts of his hosts were less important than the parallels between the Irish and American situations. Bancroft's *History* frequently compared the state of the colonies and of Ireland; and having read Benjamin Franklin's warning, Bancroft thought that the colonists would be in the same state had it not been for their timely revolution. Almost with glee Bancroft forwarded American funds for Irish relief to Dublin, demonstrating how lucky the Americans were to have escaped centuries of British oppression.[26]

Some Americans, however, tried to help their relatives more directly. A few tangled with British law and found themselves in jail, which transformed a theoretical issue into a diplomatic problem. On Buchanan's instructions, Bancroft tried to impress the British with the American definition of naturalization—United States citizenship absolved the immigrant from old country obligations. British law held that only an act of Parliament divested a subject of allegiance; not legal quibbles, but illegal activities landed Americans in Irish jails.[27]

The Irish-American detainees, charged with treason and sedition, appealed to their families and to politicians back home for help. Congress and the Democratic press made much of their plight, while deriding the doctrine of perpetual allegiance. Bancroft favored quiet diplomacy and was more successful through private pressures than through statements that branded British actions "thoroughly arbitrary . . . and utterly despotic." On the question of naturalization, he got nowhere.[28]

Time not spent on freedom fighters, postal conventions, and navigation negotiations Bancroft devoted to family, finances, and historical research. The "little monkeys" in Roxbury, chafing under the stern mastership of John Weisse, felt abandoned, lonely, and miserable, their anguish stoked by enthusiastic letters from Louisa about the excitements of London. As long as their school reports were bad, Bancroft decided, they would remain where they were. He could afford to do so, for the Dwights regularly remitted child-support payments, part of which Bancroft used to pay off his own debts. Unable to convince their father how sad their situation was, the boys complained of inadequate instruction. Bancroft's sister Lucretia echoed their pleas, describing the school's savage regulations, strict regimen, and poor teaching. When George, Jr., decided to become a farmer, Bancroft realized that something had to be done before the damage was irreversible.[29]

In the fall of 1847, the boys came to England and stayed with their father for a while. But Bancroft, always impatient when the children were around, soon found convenient places for them—a school in Vevey for John and George, and one near Geneva for Louisa. They would learn proper manners, French, and German, and improve their characters in preparation for suitable careers. Their stepbrother Alexander, who wanted a year off from Harvard to dabble in history, poetry, and the classics, was told that was "not tasking the mind enough . . . and all too vague." Such pursuits were "but solace and incidental employment," not a preparation for life. Similar advice to John and George left them unpersuaded; the letters to London from Switzerland were as sad as those sent earlier from America. But, out of sight, the children ceased to complicate their parents' activities in the metropolis.[30]

Improved finances, ably managed by Samuel Hooper in Boston, permitted Bancroft to live well in London. Land in Ohio, disposed of for $5,000, offset some debts, while income from stocks, from the Dwights, and from Little, Brown, as well as profits from the sale of insurance policies and of shares in the Monroe Bank, contributed to a style appropriate for the American ambassador.[31]

Successful financial ventures also augmented Bancroft's historical activity. Whenever possible he stole time from official duties to burrow in the archives, employing copyists, negotiating for the purchase of private papers. He spared no expense when it came to acquiring yet another set of documents. Chevalier Bunsen secured him access to Prussian collections, and other connections opened state papers offices all over the Continent. "I prefer history to the drawing rooms," Bancroft explained, even though "to plough a little deeper furrow in . . . manuscripts" was time-consuming. Secretary of the legation John Broadhead, a historian in his own right, also helped, as did Ben. Perley Poore in Paris. Most people responded favorably to Bancroft's requests. The one exception was the Duke of Buckingham, the owner of the Grenville papers, who was offended at the use to which Macaulay had earlier put those documents, and even Bancroft's extensive contacts failed to change his mind.[32]

Observing history in the making was almost as exciting as rummaging through the archives. Bancroft followed with great interest and exaggerated hope the revolutions of 1847 and 1848, the pivotal events of his European stay. This eruption of the reform impulse, as he called it, seemed to justify his prophecies. Washington received glowing accounts, filled with extravagant predictions, that glossed over conflicting facts and details. The overwhelming moral certainty that he was right, that he voiced the judgment of divine approval, that he came from among a people the rest of the world was destined to follow, obscured the American ambassador's vision. Vastly overoptimistic when assessing the chances of the liberal movements, he was right only in the long run. The man of letters yielded to wish fulfillment and even insincerity; entertaining great liberating ideas and knowing, theoretically, what the alternatives to existing social and political arrangements could be, he searched for every available evidence that their time had come—reality notwithstanding.

In Paris during the winter and spring of 1847 Bancroft saw the early signs of upheaval. The masses hated the king, he noted, and the high bourgeoisie could not prop up a tottering throne because "the moral power and physical strength of the disfranchised" was too great. Yet Louis Philippe rejected the slightest political concession, telling Bancroft that the moral and material advancement of the people ought to be enough. On the other hand, the opposition was anarchical; to the American, his fellow historians Adolphe Thiers and François Guizot seemed neither republican nor democratic, nor champions of popular liberty. And Louis Blanc, somewhat more congenial because he had the interests of labor at heart, also lacked the right answers.[33]

Bancroft gleaned this information, transmitted to the State Department, in Parisian salons, where he also heard that the fear of republicanism, radicalism, and Jacobinism was widespread enough to maintain the law-and-order party in power. He disagreed with Victor Cousin, who thought the moneyed classes ruled France, and approved of the ministry program which seemed similar to what the Democrats tried to do in Massachusetts—assure middle-class interest in reform through fear that intransigence would strengthen the extremists. As 1848 began Bancroft hopefully disregarded warnings and trusted the people, who, he thought, were beginning "to reason calmly." France seemed like "the hollow of a wave" which the king and his ministers hoped would stand still.[34]

This idealization of "the people" and sympathy for the political and intellectual leaders with whom he associated in Paris reflected Bancroft's bifurcated vision. Those leaders were, he sensed, kindred souls, men like himself—belonging to a select group and yet committed to mobilizing the masses, to uplifting their society, to reform. To be sure, Bancroft did not know the details of their conflicting programs, just as the French remained to him an abstract concept, even more mythical than the American people. But all problems faded in the face of a dogma.

On January 12 a revolution began in Sicily and spread to Naples, where the king, under duress, granted a constitution. On February 24, the Parisians deposed Louis Philippe, and on March 13 an uprising in Vienna exiled Metternich. March 18 saw a revolution in Berlin and March 24, one in Madrid. On April 10, the Chartists held a mass demonstration in London, and in November the Romans rebelled against papal government.

The initial response in the United States was favorable. Richard Rush, the ambassador to France, was the first to recognize the French Republic, with Polk's and Buchanan's approval. Senator Allen of Ohio introduced a resolution congratulating the French people, while John P. Hale of New Hampshire tried to thank France for emancipating slaves in her colonies. Public meeting, parades, newspaper articles, and political rallies expressed the general enthusiasm. Bancroft, reading about the reverberations in London, was certain that the United States was revolutionizing the world by its example.[35]

But, as Charles Sumner noted, the chorus of approval was not universal. The Boston commercial classes worried about their property, blamed the revolution in France on socialists and communists, and feared the effects of unrest on their own already turbulent society. News about national workshops and the nationalization of the railways increased the misgivings. Southerners were hostile to French antislavery decrees, and to Calhoun the revolutions proved that Europe had not advanced beyond Dorrism. Webster concluded that the new French government, composed of poets, writers, and dreamers, was worse than none at all. Ticknor too was skeptical about a working-class revolution in a country where people had little practical wisdom, and predicted a general conflagration and military despotism. Many Americans shared his doubts.[36]

Bancroft at first was sure that the time was right; historical developments had progressed enough to spell the doom of monarchs. "Nations in the nineteenth century," Bancroft commented, "have learned that they were not made to be the slaves of a dynasty." With some glee he chuckled at the hushed conversations in London where some of his hosts feared for their safety. As uncertainty led to the cancellation of one social event after another, the English revealed their "deep repugnance to republican institutions," preferring anarchy in France to a healthy and stable republic. The entire diplomatic corps was in a fix, except for Bancroft; the Old World was passing through a reorganization that the New, he thanked his lucky stars, did not need.[37]

While the English dreaded progress, reform, and democracy, the Europeans were about to create governments patterned on the American example. The Germans, the Italians, the Swiss, and the French were overthrowing aristocracies and groping toward universal suffrage, trying to establish their own more perfect union. The New World had shown Europe the possibility of casting off feudalism and enthroning the middle classes, and Jacksonian democracy was about to engulf the world. The moral forces for good were on the march, and Bancroft's sympathies reached out to people whose history he knew but vaguely, but who had real grievances and lived in deeply flawed societies. These upheavals stemmed from uncaring, irresponsible, and oppressive political systems about to be liberalized, hopefully on the American model.

"The high aristocracy dread the future," Bancroft exulted, thinking perhaps of the fears once generated by his own political activities. Riots in Glasgow, Edinburgh, Manchester, and London were portents of improvement, and the reaction of his English hosts out of tune with historical progress. While the nobility sank into gloom, he was one of the few at court "to speak, think . . . with hope, with subdued exaltation, with trust" in the future. "There will not be a crown left in Europe in twenty years, except in Russia," Bancroft prophesied, even if, sad to tell, England would hold out longer than the rest.[38]

For a while Bancroft's hopes focused on central Europe. "If it were not for the princes . . . Germany would tomorrow establish a federal union like the United States. Every day awakens the people more to the stupidity of the princes . . . The people are coming into their own." Their nation was "trying to rise from its deathbed and renew its life by adopting the spirit of the American institutions," Bancroft informed Polk, since federalism was "the essential condition in the progress of civilization and national development . . . Through Germany the example of the United States will spread to the Slavonic races." When in May 1849 the Roman forces under Garibaldi and Mazzini fell before the French army, they too were fighting for American principles.[39]

An Englishman who once heard a Bancroftian political oration asked his companion whether the American historian believed all he said. The same question could be asked about Bancroft's interpretation of European events during these two years. He did, and in the face of overwhelming contradictions. As a politician and a historian he knew that reform efforts were risky where centuries of inertia created traditionalist, conservative societies. Even in a more open and flexible environment—like the United States—his own attempt to change institutions was a long and thankless task. He had often enough complained of how slowly the public mind assimilated novelties, while also taking comfort in its conservatism, a set of concepts which lay at the heart of Bancroft's democratic theory and Democratic politics. But always that other side to his persuasion assumed that under certain circumstances sheer acts of will could overcome the dead weight of the past.

This seemed to happen in the spring of 1848. What would never have succeeded in the United States, and what Bancroft would have denounced as visionary and speculative, could occur in a different context. France, Germany, Italy, and Switzerland, their history, governments, society notwithstanding, were on the verge of institutionalizing a just order. This selective perception, on the part of a thinker-politician who always advocated, in a realistic fashion, only the implementation of the possible under given circumstances, showed Bancroft's neglect of what the objective situation was. Favorably predisposed to what was going on, Bancroft indulged in expectations. To have done otherwise would have been tantamount to an alliance with his English aristocratic hosts and their fears. Under the divine plan and with God's will, nations moved forward regardless of obstacles.

Nor did Bancroft doubt that intimate connection between the American experiment and the upheavals on the Continent, although he never made clear exactly what the link was. The silent propagandizing of the New World, Bancroft said, made noisy by the reverberations of the successfully concluded Mexican War, was evident in all European liberal movements. He was cautious enough to admit that each nation shaped its institutions in line with its heritage and that the American example could have no European counterpart, but the very success of a democratic and republican society in the New World disproved reactionary apprehensions. The Old World was about to yield to the overwhelming popular demand for freedom.[40]

That demand, and not idealists or fanatics, overthrew the French monarchy and guaranteed the acceptance of republicanism. The assembly about to be elected in the spring of 1848 in Paris would be moderate and free of passions, ensuring the security of property and order. No one

Bancroft met advocated confiscation or drastic wealth redistribution. All was peaceful. Liberty had "calmed passions" and club meetings were more orderly than American ward assemblies. The republic in France "will be under the safeguard of the organized people, and not at the mercy of a mob." This was but another example of "the Old World . . . shaking off its chains and emancipating and enthroning the masses."[41]

Bancroft was cautious not to predict what form the French republic would take. "A constitution should be the representation of the national character," he reasoned. "To translate ours into French is not enough." One did not have to be a conservative like George Ticknor to believe in evolutionary development. Pleased to be an explicator of the American governmental system to the French, Bancroft relied on Lamartine to find forms suitable to the national character. No one could read the future and the situation might change, but everything confirmed the belief "in the rule of the people." Nothing but "universal suffrage can give to freedom the security which it needs in planning legislation suited to the advancement of the race."[42]

Bancroft stayed in Europe long enough to see all his predictions proved wrong. In the summer of 1848 the French provisional government, in which he had placed so much hope, collapsed, and pressure from conservatives suppressed the national workshops. The unemployed were drafted into the army or sent to work in the provinces. Barricades went up and Lamartine resigned. In four days of street fighting in Paris ten thousand people died. At the end of the year Louis Napoleon Bonaparte was elected president of the republic. In the spring and summer of 1849 Bancroft was back in Paris, confronting a grave crisis, beaten liberals, and a disorganized assembly. "All parties are in the wrong," he concluded, "everybody is in the wrong." Common sense disappeared, "impatience triumphs over reason."[43]

When all else failed, there was, as always, the refuge of prophecy. "France can not escape being a republic," even if for the time being the forces of reaction triumphed. What mattered was not the lack of accomplishments, but the underlying higher purpose. "Who can read the future?" Bancroft asked, after trying and failing to read it correctly. "I have all along believed that matters would grow more and more confused," which was not what he had said six months earlier. The spring of nations had come to a crashing halt.[44]

So, it seemed, had the Jacksonian spring back home. "When you come back," Bancroft was told, "you will find great changes in political relations and associations," an understatement the magnitude of which he soon realized. Antislavery sentiment split the New York Democracy into Barnburners and Hunkers; in Massachusetts rural voters joined with the antislavery forces; and noisy debates over the Wilmot Proviso polarized opinions. At the Worcester convention in 1847 former Democrat and Anti-Mason Amasa Walker called on the party to fight the further spread of bondage, only to be shouted down and his resolution rejected 367 to 1. But several county conventions adopted Walker's suggestion. A year later when the new Free Soil Party convention met in Worcester, many rank-and-file Democrats were on hand. Some of the leaders Bancroft had worked with were prominent in the third-party movement, including Morton, Walker, and John Mills. The Democracy the American ambassador to England had helped construct had split apart in his absence.[45]

When the Democrats gathered in Baltimore on May 15, 1848, Polk had renounced a second term and Lewis Cass led the presidential race. Some Massachusetts Democrats balked, remembering his maneuvers four years earlier, but when his nomination became certain, they joined the majority. The platform, read by Benjamin F. Hallett, affirmed traditional Democratic positions, condemning abolition and efforts to induce Congress to interfere with slavery. Cass argued that only the territories should decide the future of their institutions. His Whig opponent, General Zachary Taylor, hero of the Mexican War, followed Harrison's example eight years earlier and said nothing. Most people expected him to win.

Political chaos in Europe thus had its counterpart in the fierce presidential contest in the United States. Samuel Hooper reported that the Democratic Boston *Post* denounced Van Buren and Morton with the vigor once confined to the Whig *Atlas.* "What a revolution" the Free Soil issue caused, wrote Bancroft's sister, who disapproved of John Davis's loyalty to Taylor and planned to vote for the Free Soiler, Van Buren. Her brother, "as cautious as an old rat at the sight of tempting bait," thought that support for the regular Democracy was the best alternative. As for the Free Soilers, spoilers, a "geographical party," sectional rather than national in its appeal—"how [could] a party organization comprising Whigs of every hue, men who were loudest in denouncing Mr. Van Buren eight years ago," end slavery?[46]

Cass was a tolerable choice in light of shifting allegiances. He, at least, was the candidate of union, and the Democratic plank on slavery adequate. Only an appeal to "the collective judgment of the nation," a decision arrived at by "the whole country . . . nurtured by the reason of the whole people" would have everlasting validity. Those with qualms about slavery, like the quixotic Charles Sumner, should act with an organization which had a chance to do something about it. Van Buren should have remained in the Democracy rather than become a tool of the Whigs.[47]

The real cause of national disarray, in Bancroft's view, was prosperity, not slavery. Bondage would disappear under providential guidance, while the people had to learn to live with wealth and abundance. The Mexican War, designed to toughen the national fiber, brought the United States untold riches; instead of assimilating them in socially productive ways, people were being led astray by an issue that for the time being had no solution. And the country seemed to disintegrate under the weight of indolence, laziness, lack of self-reliance, and mistaken notions. To reverse this trend Cass had to win, as Bancroft thought he would.[48]

In November Cass lost, while Van Buren failed to gain a single electoral vote. "Here in Massachusetts," Charles Sumner concluded, "the old Democratic party is not merely defeated but . . . irretrievably broken." Bancroft disagreed, for he thought that Van Buren's inexplicable treachery, not anything inherently lacking in the party, led to the defeat. Bancroft did not know that southern Democrats also deserted Cass, and that those who hoped for a Democratic victory in 1852 would have to win the southerners back to the fold, as well as the 45 percent of the Free Soil supporters who came from his own political organization.[49]

Bancroft's negotiations with the English government over the postal and navigation treaties presented more immediate problems. His tenure in office would soon end; but in the meantime the new administration would surely extend the support needed to complete arrangements with the British. A change of government did not imply discontinuity in national policy, and what was good for the United States under Polk would continue to be so under Taylor. At the end of November 1848, the post office treaty took final form and the prospects for abrogation of the navigation acts looked good. Talks with members of Parliament and with government ministers convinced Bancroft that the English were finally willing to open up the West Indian trade in return for a share of American coastwise commerce. Two years of patient lobbying were about to bear fruit, and Buchanan expressed his appreciation. "Commerce and navigation," the outgoing secretary of state wrote, "relieved from the fetters which have so long restrained them, would bound forward with invigorated energy. Mutual benefits and blessings would thus be conferred." Bancroft agreed and thought he had won Palmerston's approval.[50]

But Buchanan also predicted a Whig housecleaning, increasing Bancroft's uncertainty. Not knowing what to do, he pleaded for guidance. "Shall I resign? Shall I wait?" he asked. Buchanan at first vacillated, then, together with Polk, told Bancroft to carry on, whereupon he decided to remain in England until his negotiations were completed. "The executive of course, can change its agents if it will," but the Whigs would surely not be selfish enough to dismiss him at this delicate moment when, as the president of the Board of Trade implied, the United States was about to gain the East India trade, as well as that of the West Indies.[51]

The negotiations having come to a crucial point, Bancroft made sure that favorable articles about his accomplishments appeared in the American and English press. The end of the colonial system was at hand in the abrogation of commercial regulations that still treated the New World as a colonial possession. Confident of success, Bancroft in March 1849 forgot about his own uncertain status.[52]

The New England shipowners and many Whigs had different ideas. A resolution in the Senate introduced by Daniel Webster charged that Bancroft had exceeded his authority and damaged local interests through his concessions. The Whig press took up the cry, infuriating the minister. No, he did not exceed his authority, Bancroft protested, and no, he did not desire to embarrass the new administration. Hard work done "in the most disinterested manner and with the singleness of purpose" was going down the drain thanks to Webster's unprovoked attack and the shortsightedness of New Englanders. "Shame that party spirit should defraud me of the just meed due," Bancroft complained, just when the House of Lords was to pass his bill. While Whigs and Tories in London congratulated him on the successful conclusion of his efforts, political enemies back home were bent on his destruction. The Taylor administration, Bancroft concluded, did not know the meaning of honesty and sought only to humiliate him, forcing him to reveal the more sordid aspects of American politics to his hosts. "The terror of protectionists," he informed Lord Grenville, "springs from the fears that this liberal measure here will give us, who in America share the principles of commercial freedom, enough influence to arrest any retrograde movement."[53]

In a bitter and disappointed mood Bancroft prepared for his return to the United States. Louisa was ordered back to England as soon as possible, and John was recalled from Vevey. But George, whose aunt felt that he ought "to grow up American in character and habit . . . to belong to the new world," remained in a Swiss boarding school for another year.

Bancroft now ordered his finances, asking John Davis to deal with the Dwights over the dissolution of the Michigan Bond and Mortgage company. "They dislike me," Bancroft wrote of his former in-laws, and "I wish to have as little to do with them as possible." He preferred even a sizable loss in investment to further direct negotiations. At the same time he instructed Samuel Hooper in Boston to turn his own and Elizabeth's financial assets into safe and easily convertible bonds. "I have been battered so often," Bancroft felt, that "I am modest in my expectations." There would be no more speculation if he could help it.[54]

At the end of May the bill ending the restrictive mercantile system passed the House of Lords and, in Bancroft's words, "the old colonial system has [received] its death blow." Abbott Lawrence, his successor, had delayed his crossing to wind up business affairs. But Bancroft decided not to wait. A round of dinners and celebrations followed. Oxford granted him the degree of Doctor of Civil Letters, Honoris Causa, which "the radical and heretic" vastly enjoyed. In September he sailed for the United States, to find, upon arrival, a farewell letter from Lord Palmerston. It only confirmed what Bancroft had said all along—for manners, style, and sensitivity, the English aristocrats were far superior to the small-minded American Whigs.[55]

X

THE SCHOLAR AS GENTLEMAN
AND CITIZEN

THE BANCROFTS returned in 1849 to a country in crisis, one precipitated by the Mexican War, in the conduct of which the former ambassador was proud to have shared. But he was tired of controversy and determined to conclude his *History*—a retired, scholarly existence seemed preferable to the spotlight of politics. Bancroft chose a new place of residence, acquired a new circle of friends, and immersed himself in the past. But personal problems and national difficulties left an unmistakable imprint upon his work. Try as he would, he could not shut the world out.

Volumes Four to Seven now took shape, based on the voluminous records he had acquired from European archives. No one mounted a serious scholarly challenge to either their premises or their messages. Bancroft's quasi-monopoly was so strong that others could only chip away at the edges, without damaging the monument. But he always prided himself on being a philosophic historian, who elicited a broader meaning from the amassed details and applied his conclusions to the present. This he proceeded to do in the 1850s; what changed was the relevance of those conclusions to contemporary problems.

During the decade, issues earlier glossed over returned to haunt him, his party, and the nation. The misapprehensions, shallow impressions, and miscalculations, part of the general climate of the day, were especially significant for a man who had staked his reputation on the assumption that the tragedy now actually unfolding could never take place. When Bancroft belatedly joined the effort to save the Union, he tried to salvage the foundation on which he had long stood, politically and intellectually. It was a testament to his mental agility that he succeeded.

When Bancroft left Boston, that town of solid men, in 1845, he knew he would never return, and the years abroad only reinforced his decision. In retrospect Massachusetts seemed oppressive and narrow-minded, the scene of many a triumph but also of ultimate failure. While literary reputation and political success saved him from social ostracism, he had tired of the struggle against any conformity other than that he himself defined.[1]

Ironically, he was as Bostonian as George Ticknor, Edward Everett, Andrews Norton, or Samuel A. Eliot, and upheld the same conventional standards of manners, gentility, politeness, courtesy, and good breeding. But he would not concede the values others placed on lineage, connections, or wealth, attributes associated with Episcopalians and Whigs but not with Democrats, and sometimes not with Unitarians. While Bancroft felt himself equal in all respects to his former friends and had developed enough self-confidence to slough off derogatory treatment, in some respects the boy from Worcester had not lost his awe of the powers that ruled the town.

By 1847 Bancroft thought that Ticknor resembled Robespierre—both were "incapable of respecting abilities superior to their own," which was one way of dealing with cold-shoulder treatment. While he would have agreed with his former friend that "in a society where public opinion governs, unsound opinions must be rebuked," Bancroft believed that he was the better qualified to define the unsoundness of opinion.[2]

Loss of his power base in Massachusetts further alienated the socially insecure man of letters and of action. Former allies had joined the Free Soilers and would soon enter the Republican ranks, both moves of which Bancroft disapproved but which he was not prepared to combat. Whigs like Caleb Cushing now ran the Democracy, proof of how far matters had deteriorated. And in any case action was no longer the answer to his needs. Too many pitfalls faced the thinker as doer. For the time being Bancroft reverted to a role he had alternately praised and denigrated earlier—that of the seer, gazing at the stars. In this case the stars were the American past and the seer was a historian.

Bancroft chose New York City as his residence and announced that his political life was over. Some who had known him in the past thought he was only biding his time. But Bancroft assured Charles Sumner that politics would have to wait at least six years until he finished the *History*. When the Democrats won the White House in 1852, Prescott cautioned Bancroft against a return to Washington: "Life is fleeting though art be long." Bancroft agreed and immersed himself in scholarship.[3]

The New York to which the Bancrofts came in 1849 was a bustling, expanding metropolis, half civilized, half barbarian, partially settled, but still largely rural. More than 500,000 people lived in lower Manhattan, spilling over into Brooklyn and New Jersey. The streets, alternating between mud and dust according to the season, yielded more than 160,000 loads of manure a year. Ragpickers prowled about, bags slung over their shoulder, iron rod in hand, scavenging for junk and competing for food with roaming pigs and cattle. Children still accosted passersby, offering to clean the streets in front of the houses, "please give me a penny sir . . . sweep, sweep, sweep." The fire alarm tower at Tenth Street went up in flames, but the city no longer suffered from conflagrations which had plagued it in the past. The cholera epidemic that had ravaged New York and that worried Elizabeth was petering out, to the delight of Bancroft, who was more fatalistic about such things. New fashions were the talk of the day, and the National Academy of Design opened in a renovated stable.[4]

Merchants, bankers, and lawyers dominated a city that had established its commercial preeminence; and its impressive cosmopolitan character, varied population, overseas contacts, and vigorous temper offset its unfinished appearance. New York had old families, art patrons, literary figures, artistic events, music, and theater and was free of Boston's crusty ways. In this environment, Bancroft could pursue his interests and become a social figure of consequence, the great historian and diplomat, free from the incessant demands of politics and yet a man whose opinion would be listened to.

"A traveler who leaves New York sees no day so happy as the day of his return," Bancroft soon told the New-York Historical Society, where his activities overshadowed his former tenuous connections with the Massachusetts Historical Society. Friendships were more hearty, "honorable action" applauded, the varied and exciting atmosphere of the city a stimulant to scholarship. If he sometimes grumbled that New York was also "the encampment of dollar hunters with few scholars," he never regretted his choice.[5]

The comfortable home at 17 West 21 Street accommodated all his needs. Of the children, only Louisa lived with her parents, since John was at Harvard and the Bliss boys in Boston, while George, Jr., had stayed behind in Vevey. The building's third floor became a library, housing a mass of manuscripts and books, which freed Bancroft from dependence on other collections. Here he worked from early morning till the afternoon, devoting the later hours to horseback riding and the evenings to reading, friends, social events, and civic obligations. A proper lady's maid, butler, and cook helped manage the residence.[6]

For a change of seasons Bancroft also purchased a large lot in Newport, promptly selling part of it at a handsome profit which financed an acceptable if small house. Elizabeth liked the seashore and after years at Nahant and other places delighted in her own summer home. Bancroft supervised the gardeners and corresponded with nurseries and friends on the subject of roses and fruit trees. But he relished those summers much less than Elizabeth did and whenever possible stayed in New York. The next eighteen years were the most productive of his career. Between 1834 and 1850 only three volumes of the *History* had appeared; six more followed by 1867.[7]

Though he often stole away from social engagements to peruse the books of his hosts, neither he nor Elizabeth intended to become recluses. Agreeable, witty, and a sprightly conversationalist, Bancroft was much in demand as a guest. Philip Hone ignored locofoco loyalties and invited him to meet General Winfield Scott and August Belmont. At Blatchford's Bancroft enjoyed the company of wealthy New Yorkers, and at David B. Fearing's James W. Otis, J. G. Pierson, and the Brown brothers from Philadelphia exchanged news from the wider world. At dinners in the home of William B. Astor, Bancroft encountered Joseph Cogswell, Horace Greeley, and George Templeton Strong. In honor of William Marcy the guests gorged on an elaborate meal, served on gold plate, with plenty of expensive wines. When Samuel Ruggles celebrated his sixtieth birthday, Bancroft attended, along with three former New York governors, an explorer of the North Pole, and Francis Lieber. At Delmonico's, Fernando Wood played host to Washington Irving, Commodore Matthew Galbraith Perry, and Bancroft's former political hero, Martin Van Buren. The Strongs too held brilliant soirees where George and Elizabeth mingled with politicians, artists, journalists, and clergymen.[8]

Bancroft's intellectual eminence also attracted foreign diplomats and travelers. When Richard Cobden, the radical member of Parliament, came to the city, to be dined to death, as he thought, Bancroft guided him through local society, admiring the Englishman's conversational powers. Bancroft also took William Thackeray on a tour of the town which a friend of the Englishman described as one unbroken indigestion. Bancroft thrived—at fifty he was still youthful-looking, energetic, and active. Never having been sick a day in his life, he was at the height of his powers.[9]

In England the Bancrofts had developed a taste for music and a passion for opera, and in New York were caught up in the rage for Verdi and Donizetti. They also appreciated Bellini and Mendelssohn, Mozart's *Don Giovanni,* and Meyerbeer, and wondered whether Beethoven's symphonies were superior to Mozart's. Bancroft listened grimly to the first presentation of Wagner's *Tannhäuser,* unsure of his opinions, but consoled himself with lager beer and cakes sold during intermission. The mania for Jenny Lind swept the Bancrofts along, charmed alike by the singer's voice, generosity, and intuitive understanding of public relations.

They devoted other evenings to literature and poetry. At Anne Charlotte Lynch's on Saturday nights, William Cullen Bryant, FitzGreen Halleck, Catherine Sedgwick, and Bayard Taylor held forth. Political disagreements and religious differences did not prevent Bancroft from renewing his friendship with George Ripley, now a writer for the *Tribune.* In bad financial shape, with a wife immersed in Catholic activities, with many shattered dreams behind him, Ripley gratefully accepted the Bancrofts' help and hospitality. Both enjoyed the foibles of their adopted city. In one of his jibes Ripley had a Philistine ask, "Can you tell me what Mr. Bancroft meant by his oration?" "Certainly," was the reply, "he meant to astonish the natives. He succeeds very well, nothing astonishes a New Yorker so much as a general idea."[10]

All his life Bancroft relished gossip and New York rarely lacked subjects. Rumors made the rounds that Eliza Winthrop had broken her engagement to George William Curtis on the grounds of uncongeniality. Bancroft, who knew Curtis well, could not understand Eliza's motives. Daniel Sickles, suspecting that his pretty young wife paid undue attention to Philip Barton Key, shot the young man. Bancroft, remembering Sickles's disreputable political career, sympathized with the wife. In this world women were more often than not the victims of unscrupulous men, and the very dutiful and traditional husband tried to help.[11]

Always a voracious reader, Bancroft avidly followed scholarly developments. Gracious and generous in praise, he felt no rivalry with others and corresponded extensively, soliciting information, providing help, evaluating manuscripts, and disputing facts. Other men of letters were brothers in a common enterprise; the success of one furthered all. Bancroft, conscious of being a member of a community, attended meetings, spoke on historical topics, and encouraged others. He hailed each volume of Washington Irving's biography of the first American President with a kind note, but also followed up on less well-established authors, in the belief that more information would further the truth. Prescott's *History of*

Philip II elicited similar approval, and in spite of the differences between them, Bancroft cultivated his friendship with Emerson, whose apolitical stand and controversial opinions did not weaken their cordial ties.[12]

Occasionally Bancroft lent his name, if not his purse, to worthy civic causes. He served on a board to advise commissioners debating the fate of what eventually became Central Park in New York. He was a charter member of the American Society for the Prevention of Cruelty to Animals. More aware than most of the importance of detailed, correct factual data, he supported and served as president of the American Geographical and Statistical Society. To advance professional education, he helped the New York Academy of Music, although with a smaller donation than the trustees expected. Always cautious about money, he never considered himself wealthy.[13]

The still undissolved Michigan Bond and Mortgage Company brought $4,000 a year. Little, Brown augmented his income, on the average by about $3,000 annually, while the Dwights also contributed. Sales of the Michigan lands brought extra cash, much of it invested in stocks, steamships, and railroads. But there were also losses—such as the $5,000 invested in the New York and California Steamship Company, which disappeared in the company's bankruptcy. Since he always relied on outside advice and on tips from friends, Bancroft blamed such debacles on others, excusing himself as a retired scholar from understanding the ups and downs of the economy.[14]

"My income is sufficient for all the demands put upon it," Bancroft reported, satisfying "unostentatious and simple habits," allowing him to live comfortably and to write—out of a sense of duty, the desire for approval, and love of employment. At the age of fifty-four he had reached his goal; the gentleman of letters did not have to work for a living, even if his habits were far from simple. He served only good French wines with dinner, his shirts and gloves came from Paris, his hats from a favorite Boston firm, and copies of paintings (Correggio and Titian) from Italy. The income also paid for books and copyists in European archives.[15]

Occasional shocks disturbed this easygoing life. Bancroft remained close to his two remaining sisters and assisted them financially. When Lucretia's wealthy husband, Welcome Farnum, lost his fortune, she knew her brother would help out; and when John Davis died in 1854, leaving Eliza distraught with grief, Bancroft did all he could to alleviate her sorrow. Brother Tom, unable to work, led a hand-to-mouth existence, boarding with families. Bancroft sent a monthly check to cover his expenses. In 1850 Bancroft's remaining daughter, Louisa, died. Her last letter to her father, written from her beloved Springfield, where the Dwights always seemed kinder than her own family, was full of the joys of life and of a planned trip to the Catskills. Her death was a blow, and harder to take than earlier sorrows.[16]

His sons were no consolation. John's college career floundered and George, who returned to the United States in 1852 to become a Harvard freshman, did even worse. In a few months George quarreled with the faculty and acquired fast friends; endless begging notes infuriated his father, whose response antagonized the boy even more. Parental helplessness had turned to anger when John complained that he was not sure what he wanted to do with his life; but at least he was not a troublemaker like his brother. Since no material change could be expected, George was asked to leave the college and move to a country residence where, freed from the temptations of Boston, he would devote himself to studies.[17]

Bitter, George paid his father back with determination, anger, and cunning. "You trample on my affections," Bancroft wrote, as he castigated his younger son, providing just the guidance the touchy George did not want. John tried to pacify both sides—telling Bancroft that George did not really mean what he said, while advising his brother to be more diplomatic. But Bancroft interpreted his sons' behavior as a desire to do nothing and waste money and found their rebelliousness intolerable. When John implied that the daily drudgery of most men was not for him and that he wanted to become a great painter, Bancroft bluntly said no.[18]

George of his own free will, as he stressed, decided meanwhile to move to Lunenburg and stay with the Reverend William Babcock. But Lunenburg proved monotonous, the books boring, and the reverend too pious. Disgusted with his son's letters, Bancroft cut off all relations, which George promptly interpreted as yet another instance of his father's indifference. Pathetic appeals and threats left Bancroft unmoved— and hopeful that country living, exercise, and lack of opportunity to waste money would teach George to husband his resources. At least John proved amenable to reason; having graduated from Harvard, he agreed to study law.[19]

In a climactic act of rebellion, George set fire to his room, certain, as he blithely informed his father, that this "fire will be productive of good results for me." It was an accident, according to the Reverend Babcock, although George preferred to give the impression that it was a deliberate act of will by one imprisoned in the country while the family, according to the newspapers, enjoyed their friends' yachts in Newport. The $100 in damages Bancroft paid did not help, though Babcock prayed for the "spiritual baptism" that would redeem George from childish anger and make him realize that he would stay where he was until he passed his Harvard examinations. In January 1855 George was back in Cambridge.[20]

By then John, sick of the law, decided to study music. When Bancroft would have none of it, John, bored, frustrated, and all the time longing for "the dolce far niente" of Newport, agreed to work for the Dwights. The arrangement at first pleased his father, who commiserated with William H. Prescott, whose businessman son had just lost $20,000 in a bad investment. A year later, however, John squandered the better part of $17,000 of his mother's inheritance in a California speculation. Bancroft could do nothing except hope that John had learned a lesson. There was also some consolation in the thought that George, Jr., was too young to get his hands on any Dwight money.[21]

While John went off to Surinam for a vacation (leaving behind unpaid debts), George graduated from Harvard and categorically refused to study law. He pondered an offer from the Dwights and thought of joining a New York shipping firm. He knew nothing about the business, but the commissions were very attractive. When the thought led to no jobs, he spent his time in New York doing nothing.[22]

Neither boy ever understood why their father, the philosopher intellectual, set so much store by money. Nor did they comprehend Bancroft's grief at their dissipation, purposelessness, and contempt for work. John and George were so different from what he had been like at their age that Bancroft did not know how to deal with them. They in turn resented his hectoring and preaching. John blamed him for all his problems—having done what his father wanted him to do, he failed—while George implied that his father was not the only show in town. In 1857 John, determined to become an artist, bluntly stated that he would not "shackle . . . [himself] to time, place or profession" and followed George, Jr., on a trip to Europe.[23]

Bancroft never had any faith in John's talents (rightly so, as it turned out) but assumed that such an excursion might be beneficial in other ways. More ready to forgive the diplomatic John than the resentful George, Bancroft opened his purse and rationalized away John's waywardness as due to lack of a steady occupation. Meanwhile George demanded more money (which his brother received without having to write pathetic letters) because he wanted to enter the wine and liquor trade in Malaga, Spain. "Although you have a very meager opinion of me," George wrote to Bancroft, the venture had possibilities.[24]

To sell brandy, Bancroft replied, was worse than being a painter. Not only did George know nothing about this disreputable business, he was degrading the family and would surely lose all his funds to sharpers. The money was already gone, George replied; he had pledged the funds before their receipt. "A fool and his money are soon parted" was the withering response. Threatening to change his will, Bancroft also delayed the transfer of the Dwight share of George's inheritance. A friend's consolation—that all fathers were doomed to disappointment and had to do their duty while hoping for the best—did not help. George had come of age and a portion of Sarah's inheritance was legally his.[25]

While John, who had also been to Spain, made his way north, with generous allowances and letters of introduction, George, Jr., now in Madrid, bided his time. In the absence of letters, Bancroft suspected that something was afoot and requested the help of the American embassy. The uncharacteristic silence, he was informed, was due to a new disaster—George had married the twenty-two-year-old Mrs. Mora, mother of one child, who had wed a rascally Spanish Catholic priest in England at the age of fifteen but now was free to find a new husband, since her first marriage was declared invalid in Spain. The couple decided to move to France, where, however, their union required parental consent. This George requested of his father, adding that his wife was pregnant, and that they needed money for a farm, for which they would also welcome a few American trees. The former Mrs. Mora, now Mrs. Bancroft, George stressed, was the perfect wife for him.[26]

"I am delighted with the laws of France" was Bancroft's response. He utterly forbade the marriage and was on the verge of renouncing his son altogether. But his hopes of having the union invalidated proved vain. George was legally married and determined to stay that way. Already expecting one child, he looked forward to having a large family, which required support. His father cut off all correspondence for the time being, but found himself transferring ever greater portions of the Dwight inheritance to France.[27]

He was also subsidizing the unhappy John, who, after studying art in Germany for two years, still did not know what to do with himself. An unhappy love affair with the landlord's daughter in Düsseldorf landed John in the street with all of his possessions, after a lecture about the improprieties of proposing without means of support. Crushed and desperate, and still bent on marrying his beloved Marie, John moved to Paris in June 1860. With some relief Bancroft read a letter from John's prospective father-in-law, informing him that the German family wanted to hear no more of their unfortunate American lodger.[28]

Louisa's death, the boys' problems, and his sisters' difficulties aged the hardworking historian as the passing years had not. He had arrived at the twilight of his life, Bancroft thought, not knowing that more than three decades remained to him. The urgency with which he met his obligations and an increasingly religious bent reflected fear of the end. In the past he had been a casual churchgoer, maintaining pews in Boston and New York for appearance's sake. But intimations of mortality resurrected the dormant theologian, and for a while led Bancroft into spiritualism.

Tennyson's *In Memoriam,* published in the year of Louisa's death, wrestled with the relationship between religion and science and suggested a kindred spirit; but Bancroft chose a different path. Having long ago decided that all was to the good, he rejected Tennyson's gloomy broodings in favor of Charles Lyell's certainty about the workings of a creative intelligence in nature's wonders. Tennyson suggested that a veil prevented man from penetrating divine secrets and forced him to reason on immortality and love in the light of science. Bancroft's response was an unequivocal affirmation of God as a benevolent, caring providence. Tennyson should have accepted Carlyle's dictum that in the final analysis intuitive beliefs revealed more than scientific evidence. *In Memoriam* expressed "grief . . . without hope . . . without faith . . . without love."[29]

The theme cropped up again in an oration on the progress of mankind delivered before the New-York Historical Society in 1854. The speech was less a statement of democratic dogma than a hymn to God, "the fountain of all goodness, the inspirer of true affection, the source of all intelligence," the guarantor of progress. Those who thought otherwise subverted the hope that, in the face of discord and difficulties, the people and the nation were safe. Down went the positivists with their limited conception of knowledge, bound beneath the yoke of their senses. Atheists were materialists, usurpers, negators of life and liberty. The true believer always sought to bring "his own will into harmony with divine will. Piety studies the law, obeys the law and through perfect obedience becomes perfectly free."[30]

George Templeton Strong, listening to Bancroft's speech, thought it all "unitarianism savage and furious," which it was not. A careless reference to "the truth of a triune God" also brought a query from a Massachusetts clergyman—had the son abandoned his father's faith? Not so, was the reply; these beliefs rested on the authority of God, supported by inward witness, those "clear revelations which millions might see and feel," trusting "in the ever continuing union of God with man." Aaron Bancroft's faith lived, though the terminology had changed.[31]

Mingled with these theological gropings was an interest in spiritualism. The seances with turning tables, mysterious hat tricks, and rappings fascinated Bancroft; while a group of visitors held hands, a leader translated the raps into an alphabet, words were recorded, enunciations discovered, names appeared. Bancroft attended the appearances of the Fox sisters and joined George Ripley and William Cullen Bryant for a private session with them at the home of a friend. Margaretta Fox's capacity to anticipate or penetrate unspoken thoughts so impressed Bancroft that he eagerly seized the chance to see her again at Horace Greeley's. And he was not surprised to learn from Joseph Cogswell that a ghost haunted the Astor library. The rationalist in Bancroft doubted the veracity of the spiritualists, yet the believer in him could not dismiss the possibility that ways existed to pierce Tennyson's veil.[32]

Every age, he assumed, advanced in its grasp of the divine truth, even to the point when the material and spiritual realms one day would coalesce, as the spiritualists suggested. There was nothing heretical in spiritualism; on the contrary, it was a healthy antidote to materialism, skepticism, and atheism, a confirmation of the reciprocal relationship between God and humanity. The existence of a spiritual world was as certain as the existence of extraterrestial life; it was only a matter of time before communications with other planets were established. Bancroft was not alone in his belief; thirteen thousand people signed a petition presented by Senator James Shields of Illinois, requesting congressional funds to study the possibility. One observer suggested that the Senate Foreign Relations Committee was the appropriate body to consider the matter.[33]

For several years the gentleman scholar remained aloof from politics. Bancroft declined to participate in a local rally of the Friends of Hungary and turned down an invitation to a Democratic celebration. He gave no publicity to privately held opinions, refused to endorse candidates for office, and very rarely exploited former political ties for his own or anybody else's benefit. The man of letters no longer insisted on being also the man of action, but instead withdrew into his study and produced volume after volume. But the volumes, written at a time of crisis, were not as immune to outside influences as he liked to think.[34]

Favorable reviews had long praised the *History* as a guide for the present and had informed the author that his readers structured their opinions in the light of what he told them about their antecedents. Royalties certainly proved that the *History* sold, while references to "Mr. Bancroft" in sermons, tracts, political orations, and scholarly papers revealed its influence. The extent of that influence was uncertain and Bancroft could never be sure to what use others would put his work. But he had always argued that it had a use and in the past had insinuated contemporary allusions into the narrative to guide the reader's thought along proper channels. His self-imposed exile from current affairs did not put an end to this practice. For a time his messages were confined to conclusions intelligent readers could draw from his text. Only when the national crisis deepened after 1854 did he become again the activist intellectual who advised politicians and influenced public opinion, through letters, newspaper articles, and orations, as well as through the *History*.

Between 1850 and 1852, while Bancroft wrote his fourth and fifth volumes, the nation weathered a serious political storm. A convention of southerners in Nashville openly threatened secession, while northern abolitionism gained strength. The debates over the fate of the territories produced a compromise that admitted California as a free state, organized the remaining areas without reference to the Wilmot Proviso, strengthened the Fugitive Slave Law, and referred all unresolved questions to the judiciary. On none of these momentous questions did Bancroft publicly express an opinion. The intellectual who once thought he had all the answers remained silent except insofar as he spoke through his interpretation of the past. To southerners who argued that their way of life was more important than the Union and to northerners who believed that the Union was worthless if slavery survived, he demonstrated in Volumes Four and Five (1852) that everyone had a stake in maintaining the Union.

The narrative dealt ostensibly with the overthrow of the European colonial system (1748–1763), which formed the first epoch of the American Revolution, followed by the second epoch, America's estrangement from England (1763–1774). The idea of the free individual was about to be modified by "the creative energy" of "collective reason." Those years defined the nation's revolutionary heritage, one very much on the political agenda in 1852. Bancroft's pride in the revolution's "radical character," tempered by the stress on its "benign tranquility" and utterly conservative cast thus contained a message to fire-eaters north and south.[35]

The revolution, Bancroft wrote, developed "from the intelligence that had been slowly ripening in the mind of cultivated humanity"; it aimed "at the advancement of the principle of everlasting peace and brotherhood," its radical "plebeian democracy" reflecting "God [who] never showed more visibly his gracious providence and love." The rebellious colonies were "living plants, whose inward energies obey the Divine idea without effort or consciousness of will." Their political edifices determined the federal Union, "the noblest work of human intellect," which eliminated "every motive to its destruction, by insuring to each successive generation the right to better its constitution, according to the increasing intelligence of the living people." The Union, "founded on reason," would "last as long as the empire of love and reason."[36]

Behind these poetical musings was an interpretation that almost separated revolutionary events from the participants and ascribed success to causes other than human volition. By utilizing the multilayered narrative construct, Bancroft brilliantly fulfilled his historical function while endowing successive events with an ahistorical significance. The validity of the latter did not impair the integrity of his scholarly task—by being relegated to the higher sphere of significance, it did not impinge upon the account of day-to-day happenings. But the implications were inescapable—man proposed but God disposed; and it was a delusion to assume that momentous occurrences like the War for Independence and the creation of republican societies depended solely on human choices. "The eternal flow of existence" carried events forward, "principles informing the public mind, gaining mastery over events, following each other as they are bidden and ruling without a pause" were the real movers. The outcome reflected "the influence of time . . . moulded by the creative forces of reason, sentiment and nature."[37]

Reason, sentiment, and nature would also resolve contemporary dilemmas, although Bancroft offered no blueprint. The stress on continuity, on the immortality and unity of the human race, and on the interdependence of historical periods buttressed this conservative and fatalistic outlook. These concepts also supported the belief that change by definition depended on society's readiness to progress, which was what he had said all along. "We are the children and the heirs of the past with which as with the future we are indissolubly linked together," Volume Four proclaimed. The radical attempts of northern abolitionists and southern disunionists to break those links in the name of their ill-conceived plans were doomed to failure.[38]

This was the historian's message to the extremists. Institutions, like all mortal creations, were bound to change and in time disappear; they were "step[s] in the ladder by which humanity ascends towards the perfecting of its nature." But laws, customs, and ways of life could neither

be destroyed before their time nor replaced instantaneously by more perfect creations. The rise to a higher state of being followed stages which
could neither be skipped nor thwarted, a comforting conception which
promised change, but at a snail's pace.[39]

Ultimately, everything hinged on "the increasing intelligence of the
living people." And whatever happened, the *History* proved, was fruitful
only insofar as it coincided with ideas—or principles, as Bancroft liked to
call them. Those too advanced were inconsequential because confined to
a minority out of step with the majority. "Principles grow into life by
informing the public mind and in their maturity gain mastery over
events," a process that could be neither hastened nor hampered. Social
change had its own logic, that of the divine plan, evident in America's
greatest contribution to humanity—"to substitute for hereditary privilege the natural equality of man." "God never showed more visibly his
gracious providence and love" than in the process of transforming "fee-
ble settlements in the wilderness" into "the new empire of democracy."
The abolitionists would have their way when the time was ripe, while
the southerners would in the end lose their chattels because slavery too
was destined to extinction under providential guidance.[40]

On the subject of bondage Bancroft said little in Volumes Four and
Five. But his emphasis on the unity of the human race implied a measure
of humanity for blacks. "The world was instructed that all men are of
one blood, that for all there is but one divine nature and but one moral
law." The natural equality of men, which the Revolution asserted,
would one day be translated into the social equality of all. Since that time
had not yet come, Bancroft was willing to wait. Others, to his great
sorrow, were not.[41]

The eagerness of some to hurry the process along, to shatter and
destroy in the name of futurity, raised the specter of anarchy, which
affected many of Bancroft's contemporaries who shared a frightening
vision—that of a society out of gear, lacking cohesion, going in all directions, questioning traditional values and institutions, without proper substitutes. Some observers traced such problems, which they considered
endemic in a democratic society, to excessive individualism, while others
blamed crowded cities, loosening restraints, mad philosophies, and a general breakdown of morals.

These responses to incomprehensible social developments left Bancroft unmoved. He had been witness to such forebodings since the
1820s, and had successfully interpreted the concept of individualism in
line with his general conservative theory. The principle of individuality,

meaning that "the separate man" grew "aware of the inhering right to the unfettered culture and enjoyment of his whole moral and intellectual being," did not spell the end of organized society, although an exaggerated individualism was undoubtedly one of the vices of the age. Occasionally Bancroft paid tribute to Emerson's self-reliant man and argued that here indeed was the hero of modern history. But individualism, Bancroft was fond of saying, was validated by general needs. The "faculties of each individual mind are limited in their development," he reminded his readers, only "the reason of the whole strives for perfection."[42]

To assure himself that current antisocial tendencies were but manifestations of an inner stability, Bancroft fell back on his original vision of American democracy. The "idea of the freedom of the individual" was indeed a revolutionary concept, but still inferior to "the creative but long latent energy that resides in the collective reason." Not the individual, but the people triumphed in the *History;* while the New World did "assure self direction of the individual mind," the focus was on the "harmonious exercise of collective reason of the state." Individualism embedded in the social and political institutions asserted itself only in the natural equality of men, not in elevating the self above society. Whatever effect they could have, individual responses were meaningful only when, paradoxically, their individualist content disappeared. After a long and dramatic narrative of various American reactions to the Stamp Act, Bancroft concluded by saying that "opinion was echoed from mind to mind," differing according to conditions and circumstances—what mattered was that "every hue [was but] an emanation from the same fires." Not individual responses but the general sentiment of resistance counted.[43]

Lest present-day disturbances be legitimized through comparisons with the equally rousing disorders of the past, Bancroft also distinguished between the unrest of the 1850s and eighteenth-century riots. The latter, he emphasized, were orderly and popular, expressing general sentiments, not the vision of a few who claimed the sanction of a higher law. The divine plan justified rough responses to British measures and even occasional excesses, but not William H. Seward's higher law doctrine, or the personal liberty laws in northern states, or abolitionist attempts to spirit slaves to freedom, or other efforts to hurry history forward.

Between 1852 and 1854 Bancroft completed the sixth volume of the *History,* which concluded the narrative of the causes of the Revolution.

"The knell of the ages of servitude and inequality was rung; those of equality and brotherhood were to dawn." From the hindsight of 1854, what happened between 1766 and 1774 had to happen, for "events in their course . . . follow laws that are much older than Andes or Ararat, that are as old as those which upheaved the mountains." What appeared "irrational confusion" was but "the web woven by light, liberty and life." At the moment of conflict no one could foretell the outcome; only later would the wise exclaim, "Lo God is here and we knew it not."[44]

The day would indeed come when "man will dwell with man as with his brother, when political institutions will rest on the basis of equality and freedom," but this result would flow from "internal activity, developed by universal culture," and not in response to "exterior philanthropy." Reform was contingent on "inward germs"; generations had passed before eighteenth-century Americans were ready for independence and self-government. And the world was still full of nations "in a state of unripeness," whose "inward law" was insufficiently clear. By contrast, the freedoms of nineteenth-century Americans incorporated a level of social tolerance inconceivable one hundred years earlier. Yet since "the materials of which society is composed partake of imperfection," to "extirpate all that is imperfect would lead to the destruction of society itself."[45]

This elaborate network of ideas justifying the status quo clouded Bancroft's vision of the coming upheaval. By 1852 others in his circle realized that old parties were disintegrating, that slavery had created new sectional alignments, and that the political rules had changed. They pointed to the shrillness of the debate, to the fact that the sections no longer responded on the basis of shared values, and to the level of violence that seemed to reach new heights. Bancroft's interpretation of past experience and his present-day social analysis assumed that everything was only a matter of patience and time.[46]

Theodore Parker, like Bancroft, believed in the progressive unfolding of the divine laws in history, independent of man's will. "The moral actual of the human race," he preached in 1854, "is constantly rising higher and higher." Bancroft's *History* documented that proposition, as well as the preacher's assertion that "without reverence for the Higher Law of God everything will be ruled by interests of violence. The Church will collapse into nothing. The state will go down to ruin." The historian indeed proved that New England was, in Parker's words, "a monument to the memory of those men who trusted God's Higher Law."[47] The two parted company over the inferences. For Bancroft

1854 was not, like 1776 or 1620, a revolutionary moment. There was no excuse for irresponsible and unscrupulous agitators to whip up mob frenzy, and those who tried to wipe out century-old institutions verged on criminality. The higher law, for Parker a divine sanction for action, remained for Bancroft synonymous with the perpetual law of nature—a mechanism built into the universe and operating of itself. Out of sympathy with those who actively tried to mold the actual to the ideal world, although recognizing their usefulness, Bancroft opted for "reform." In his scheme of cosmic development, the higher-law advocates canceled out blind resistance to any change; the future lay with the middle forces—reconciling extremes, carrying history forward.[48]

Several extensive trips in 1854 and later in the decade seemed to validate his judgment. He had seen very little of the nation he so often glorified. Eager for an audience, Bancroft now seized the chance to speak and meet people in various parts of the country beyond the eastern seacoast. Travels to St. Louis and the Falls of St. Anthony in 1854 were followed a year later by a trip for a celebration of the Battle of King's Mountain in Yorkville, where a stirring oration explained the success of the revolutionary generation by its capacity to forget sectional differences. Excursions to Florida, Ohio, Illinois, Kentucky, Georgia, and Maryland took him slightly off the beaten track, and also quieted growing fears.

Everywhere he found signs of the West's importance to the Union as the counterforce to northern and southern sectionalism. Growing towns were monuments to manifest destiny; fertile soil, thriving commerce, schools, and transportation networks were emblems of civilization. And exciting statistics—300 houses built in Davenport, Iowa, in 1854, 1,500 wagons passing through Peoria, Illinois, in one month, 12,000 immigrants crossing to Chicago in one week—substantiated Bancroft's hopes.[49]

In the South, gracious and well-managed plantations occupied a contented population. Bancroft judged his hosts leniently, noting the effects of slavery but emphasizing other facets of their lives. He traced their immense wealth to hard work and ability, not to human property, and thought that northern abolitionists, while not exactly wrong, were wide of the mark. The saddest aspect of the situation was the barrier slavery placed in the path of white mechanics, artisans, and farmers. Yet in Richmond, Savannah, Columbia, and Raleigh, Bancroft met only sensible, moderate men, neither fire-eaters nor oppressors whose Christian character had been eaten away by slaveholding.[50]

These excursions provided evidence that the vision of two great sections drifting apart was inaccurate, and Bancroft informed his Newport and New York friends that their gloom was unjustified. Southerners who talked of a balance of power were defensive rather than aggressive; and western settlement in any case tilted the balance in favor of freedom. As late as 1858, after another foray into Georgia and South Carolina, Bancroft was sure that "the love of union [is] as strong at the South as at the North, Charleston is thoroughly national, the tone of feeling very strong against mischief makers."[51]

But superficial impressions and optimism could not indefinitely wish the crisis away. When, late in the day, its magnitude became clear to him, Bancroft looked to traditional politics for solutions. He argued that the Democracy was still the faithful expositor of the general will, and after 1854 the only alternative to social and political as well as moral upheaval. Earlier in life, he had stressed the divinely implanted constraints of conscience as curbs on antisocial passions. After 1854, the blatant inadequacy of those transcendental musings forced Bancroft to emphasize the positive role of institutions, social bonds, parties, law, and the Constitution as counterweights to rampant individualism and the exaggerated reliance on an inward sense. Change would come in practical ways only through the Democratic Party, not through violent efforts to overthrow the past.

Without abandoning his self-imposed isolation, he supported the Democratic candidate for the presidency in 1852. Flattered by references to his literary merits, practical wisdom, prudence, and community standing, Bancroft agreed to write a short campaign document comparing the history of the two major parties. The victory of Franklin Pierce, a New Hampshire man of southern sympathies, was a hopeful sign.[52]

In retrospect, the national slide toward war began in March of 1853, when the new administration, which included several of Bancroft's political friends, faced the need to organize the territories west of the Iowa and the Missouri lines. In January 1854 Senator Stephen A. Douglas of Illinois introduced a Nebraska bill, built around his version of popular sovereignty—the people of each region would themselves determine whether to admit or exclude slavery. This proposal Bancroft thought was in perfect accord with a fundamental American assumption—that the Union rested on a Constitution which empowered the territorial legislatures to rule in all domestic concerns. Douglas's bill would free the nation for more important tasks than dealing with such insoluble problems as bondage. Having already assumed that the West would unify the country and fulfill manifest destiny, Bancroft regarded Douglas as the new Jackson who would save the party and the nation.

Douglas, like Bancroft, would gladly have buried the slavery controversy. Neither man had any special sympathy for the blacks, and both acquiesced in the existence of bondage for the foreseeable future. Pacific railroads and the prosperity of America's heartland were the shared components of a nationalistic vision. The fury that greeted the Nebraska bill did not make Bancroft more cautious; instead he clutched at Douglas's next expedient, repeal of the Missouri Compromise and the division of the area into two territories—Kansas for slaveholders from Missouri, and Nebraska free. When Pierce's administration proved unequal to the peacemaking task Bancroft prescribed "adversity and a return to first principles in their unadulterated purity" to cure the nation's ills.[53]

By January 1856 Kansas suffered from two governments, sporadic bloodshed, and enough violence to become the symbol of national conflict. The New England Immigrant Aid Society directed abolitionist settlers into the territory, while southerners from Missouri crossed the state line to vote. Pierce's powerlessness, bitter debates in the Senate, Sumner's Bleeding Kansas speech, the murderous assault of Congressman Brooks on the Massachusetts senator, the sack of Lawrence, and John Brown's murders along Pottawatomie Creek were symptoms of a crisis that Bancroft laid squarely at the door of a debauched Democratic Party. Northern subservience, he began to think in 1856, matched southern arrogance; a "bastard race" controlled the Democracy—too many Whigs and too many pseudo-Democrats. "This cruel attempt to conquer Kansas into slavery is the worst thing ever projected in our history," Bancroft fumed.[54]

"Wise statesmanship" would make Kansas free "in the manner that will least disturb tranquility," but Bancroft did not bother with the details. Angry and frustrated (for much that was happening belied his predictions), his reaction lacked substance. This was what the party of the ideal, with its talk of higher law and individualism, led to—battling private armies, anarchy, and the rejection of authority in the name of conscience. "Society, before it can be constituted aright, must turn its eye upon itself, observe the laws of its own existence and arrive at the consciousness of its capacities and relations," he had been saying since 1854. Instead violence, "desperate audacity," and a willingness "to employ terror as a measure to ride the whirl wind of a civil war" ruled.[55]

Bancroft breathed a sigh of relief in November 1856 when the Democratic standard-bearer, James Buchanan, won the presidential race. The

former ambassador had had disagreements with the pompous and flatu-
lent former secretary of state whom he had more recently accused of
violating the Compromise of 1820. But Buchanan at least was steeped in
the party's tradition. Victory, Bancroft thought, gave Buchanan the authority to enforce constitutional government in the territories. "There is
no such logic as the logic of the people," Bancroft wrote to Secretary of
State–designate William Marcy, calling for the exclusion of all "who
have shown reckless partiality." Their replacements had to be men "who
really love liberty and right and true law and just order." Should
Buchanan truckle to the "ultra Southern party, he is ruined now and
hereafter." The President was to bring Kansas "into the union as a free
state, and with the general acquiescence of the South."[56]

The historian's hopes evaporated when Buchanan's prosouthern sympathies became clear; everything the President did and said seemed to
Bancroft a monumental mistake. Which was not to say that General
Frémont, whom Bancroft knew but did not trust, would have been a
better choice. Meanwhile the antislavery agitation continued and fugitive slave cases kept the issues before the public. Only the Supreme
Court remained, a last resort to bring the nation to its senses by a proper
judgment on the constitutional aspect of the debate.

Roger B. Taney's Dred Scott decision, which protected slavery in the
territories, struck Bancroft as objectionable on several grounds, not the
least of which was that it did nothing to relieve the President from the
burden of political decisions. Ironically though, historical insights Bancroft shared buttressed the Supreme Court's argument and compounded
the historian's quandary. The American Revolution was not an offspring
of fanaticism, the chief justice declared, or of theories spun by political
dreamers, but an effort to maintain traditional usages. The Declaration of
Independence, he continued, was an expression of national conservatism,
just as Bancroft had said. But Bancroft disagreed when Taney also declared that Jefferson excluded the Negro from the assertion that all men
were created equal. Even more upsetting was the blow at popular sovereignty. It was not really in the South's interest, Bancroft moaned, to
"limit the full power of the states over the status of the colored man."
Taney was encouraging a latitudinarian interpretation of the Constitution, warranting "almost any interference with the relation of labor."
Finally the Supreme Court was also wrong for not showing mercy to a
weaker race. The Fugitive Slave Law had to be obeyed and a master, to
recover his runaway property, was right in seeking legal redress, but a
free black from Pennsylvania, kidnapped and sold into slavery in Texas,
also deserved protection.[57]

Meanwhile Bancroft sighed for an Old Hickory or a Polk as if the southern threats of 1857 echoed those of the old nullifiers of the 1830s. But the party of Andrew Jackson was gone; instead the Democratic organization, Bancroft concluded, had lost its soul to nefarious aristocrats, who held Buchanan's administration under their thumb, with the help of turncoat Whigs. "I remain of the old states right's school," he declared in 1857, but that bore no relation to what the concept had become in the hands of disunionists north and south.[58]

To counteract these profoundly illegitimate and immoral influences Bancroft tried to bolster the authority of Stephen A. Douglas. "Stand by your Nebraska bill in its plain signification," he advised the Illinois senator, "do not allow it to become in hands of timid or unprincipled men an imposture and a sham." Only Douglas could rescue the party from "the most corrupt set of political opponents ever encountered." That man "of firmness and truly national views, comprehensive and impartial," would prevent the South from cramming slavery down the throats of Kansas. Black Republicans and southern nullifiers "wished to usurp the inalienable rights of the people"; the country had to stand by the Little Giant.[59]

Chosen to preside over a grand meeting of the New York Democracy to support the Illinois senator, Bancroft gladly accepted the honor. "I have not attended a political meeting for many years," he wrote, but this was not the time to sit back. "Keep the ball rolling" came the word from Washington; "arouse the country on the great issue of self government and all will end well." Even John Chandler Bancroft in Europe read with approval about his father's principled stand on Kansas. But the proposed rally aroused little enthusiasm, in part because merchants assumed that a quick end to the Kansas problem on Buchanan's terms would free the administration to deal with more urgent economic matters. Aware of their attitude, Bancroft addressed himself to their self-interest by suggesting that neither businesses, trusts, corporations, nor property was safe when the principle of popular approval was violated. Corrupt schemers, assembled in an illegally constituted convention, might some day "assume the absolute right to change the fundamental law of the country without reference to the people." But this appeal carried little weight; only one prominent businessman signed Bancroft's petition, while a counterpetition gained the support of August Belmont and others.[60]

In August 1858 Kansas voters rejected the proposal that Kansas attain statehood and accept slavery, thus laying the issue to rest. On a trip to Charleston and Augusta a few weeks earlier, Bancroft found everyone in favor of this temporary solution, and when the news came he, too, quieted down. Perhaps talk of an irrepressible conflict was, after all, nothing but Republican propaganda.[61]

When not busy with his activities on Douglas's behalf, Bancroft wrote the next installment of the *History*. The seventh volume (1858) was another affirmation of faith in the people. They, and not their representatives, acted on the basis of "the laws of being" and "the decrees of eternity" that determined "the change that divine wisdom ordained." Their will attracted the elements of the nation to a center and shaped its Constitution. The Union, Bancroft reminded his readers, "came from the whole people" and expressed "a community of its thought and will," liberating itself from the past by "the unfolding of its own internal nature." Implicitly he asked whether that community of thought and will still existed in 1858.[62]

The volume also stressed "those voices from the south" that, despite their heritage, joined the national struggle. Even the planters, loving civil rights more than ease, set their interests aside. When Bancroft described the effects of Lexington and Concord, it was not just literary convention that caused him to declare, "with one impulse the colonies sprung to arms, with one spirit they pledged themselves to each other . . . with one heart the continent cried 'Liberty or Death.'" He had evidence enough to know that the generalization was untrue, but he felt justified in making it because in the end the common spirit rather than differences decided the outcome.[63]

There were few signs of one spirit and one heart in 1858, however. Clutching at straws, Bancroft even encouraged William H. Seward's attack on Buchanan. The Whig, Free Soiler, black Republican, and abolitionist who castigated a Democratic President and described the struggle as one between aristocracy and democracy seemed moderate in the light of growing secession sentiment in the South. This was not the time to be influenced by antecedents. Bancroft also offered to help Douglas plan an address upon the right of the people to govern themselves without federal interference by supplying parallels in the controversy between the colonies and the mother country. Since the eighteenth century, Americans, whether as colonials or free citizens, always claimed the right to legislate "in respect to their internal polity, slavery included."[64]

Three years earlier Bancroft had argued that the next president should come from the South; by 1859 such speculations had proven illusory. Where were "the conservative, calm, national and union loving men?" a Kentuckian asked. Everywhere, Bancroft replied, if they could only make themselves heard above the racket of divisive minorities. Ban croft's sister was sure that if the North yielded to the South on the choice of a Speaker of the House, the country was lost. Here Bancroft disagreed; one loss, after all, did not spell a complete rout. 'I have not seen your name in the newspapers as one of the union savers," said a Boston friend. To this Bancroft had no answer, conceding that the southerner was right who wrote, "Events march on and no man can stay them."[65]

It had for decades been Bancroft's cardinal political tenet that the Democracy was in line with that march of events; in 1860 not even the candidacy of his old mentor Edward Everett was attractive enough to dissolve Bancroft's political loyalty. While he watched with horror the behavior of the southerners at the Charleston convention, all his hopes centered on Douglas. Bancroft was relieved at the outpouring of popular sentiment when the New York Democrats met at Cooper Union in May to demonstrate the state's support for the Illinois senator. Anything was better than the possibility of black Republicans, the first sectional party, in control of the central government. And when Douglas broke all rules to campaign through the Atlantic states, Bancroft was one of his hosts. Having shut his eyes to much that had happened since 1854, he voted for the Little Giant, believing that the westerner had a chance and the nation with him. With the results in, he said, "I have anxieties about the union and suffer more than ever before. But I still hope."[66]

XI

❦

THE FURNACE OF AFFLICTION

THE INSTALLMENT of the *History* that covered events between July 1776 and 1778 appeared shortly before the presidential election of 1860, and explained, indirectly, why so late in the day Bancroft indulged in hopes for peace and union. Every society, he reminded his readers, balanced the demand for organic unity against individual rights: "all governments contain the two opposite tendencies, and were either attraction or repulsion, central power or individuality to disappear civil order would be crushed and dissolved." With the party of the past and the party of the future always at war, "the fanatics of conservatism" happily offset "the enthusiasts of ideal freedom," lest society "perish in chaotic confusion or stagnant calm." The former were the southern slaveholders, the latter the abolitionists; neither could be victorious. Were either to gain total control, that would be the beginning of the end, and Bancroft was certain that the demise of the American republic was emphatically not part of the divine plan.[1]

That winter he provided, if indirectly, other answers to present questions. He dismissed southern justifications for secession with the argument that the union of the people antedated the Revolution. When James Otis argued against the writs of assistance, when Christopher Gadsden cautioned "there ought to be no New England man, no New Yorker, known on the continent but all of us Americans," they refuted the southern secessionists of 1860. Loyalty to a national democracy antedated the ratification of the Constitution, and that perpetual contract, derived from the people as a whole, was an outcome of the common revolutionary struggle and older than the separate states. In short, the southern insistence on a limited voluntary compact lacked historical legitimacy.[2]

Nor did history justify southern rejection of Jeffersonian values in favor of a closed society based on slavery and white superiority. The concept of a free society was a national heritage, as Volumes One through Seven stated. To argue otherwise meant support for an outdated vision, contradicted by the divine plan. "The problems of politics cannot be solved without passing behind transient forms to efficient causes," Bancroft sagely noted. The former, involving society, laws, and institutions, were amenable to change. But the desire of southerners to safeguard their peculiar property and their drift toward a closed society, with its disregard for "the unvarying conditions, principles, and inherent wants of men," were insufficient to undermine a free society or wipe out the nation's heritage.[3]

The Union could not fall apart. The Declaration of Independence proclaimed the birth of one people. The Americans were one nation. And those in the north who used the Declaration as a banner under which to wipe out slavery were as wrong as their opponents. The Declaration of Independence, Bancroft asserted, was not the sanction for a revolution—not in 1776, and certainly not in 1860.

Its preamble, so hotly debated in 1860, remained for Bancroft a statement of ideals and goals, not the higher law of the Union. In 1776, the people who approved Jefferson's draft "had grown weary of atrophied institutions . . . and hoped to fathom the mystery of the public life." Their spirit "yearned for a nearer converse with the eternal rules of right as the generative principles of social peace." All of which did not lead them to propose the establishment, forthwith, of the perfect society. They knew their own limitations and did not demand either complete equality or the immediate liberation of the slaves. The preamble was thus not a prescriptive dictum to which society had to conform, for reality, in 1776 as in 1860, belied the concepts expressed. Someday humans would fully assert their natural equality, but wise statesmen did not attempt the impossible. They decided "every question as it presents itself on the side of freedom" and brought "the actual state nearer and nearer to the best possible state." In the meantime Bancroft hoped "to preserve a strong and sufficient, though narrow isthmus that might stand between conflicting floods." He remained convinced that society by degrees would work itself clear of the difficulties of that year. After November 1860 Bancroft realized that Lincoln's election brought the crisis to a head.

What he did not know was its magnitude, duration, and cost.[4]

Secession came as a profound shock. Only a few months earlier, Bancroft discounted the possibility, having concluded that "the voices of discontent among us are but the evanescent vapors of a man's breath. . . . Our little domestic strife is no more than a momentary disturbance on the surface, easily settled among ourselves. . . . The love of union has wound its cords indissolubly around the whole American people." The winter of 1860–1861 proved otherwise. The disunionists were in the saddle, and even moderate southerners, many on cordial terms with Bancroft, held a conception of union that the North could not accept.[5]

By February 1861 no concession to slave power was likely to receive wide support and Bancroft watched the defeat of all compromises with grim satisfaction. He knew then that nothing short of southern disavowal of secession and acknowledgment of the perpetuity of the Union would have meant a total northern surrender. "The boundless and indefinite desires of the South," with its "wild cravings of excited passions," were intolerable. The South's appeal to the right of revolution asserted "the doctrine of individualism," which threatened to dissolve the nation "into atoms as lifeless and unconnected as the particles of sound." This was what he had been warning against for several decades; when it came to pass, he did not know how to respond.[6]

The tension, uncertainty, and chaos of the new year seemed to belie everything for which Bancroft and his *History* stood. William was sure that his stepfather was about to lose his occupation: "nobody will want to read the history of the formation of a government by our forefathers which we have let fall into pieces." In a conversation with the British journalist William H. Russell, Bancroft appeared confused, full of abstract philosophical speculations, but also sure "that the republic, though in danger, was the most stable and beneficial government in the world." However, he told the astonished visitor, "it had no power to coerce the people of the South or to save itself from the danger." Several days later Bancroft expressed similar opinions at a dinner with Horatio Seymour and Samuel Tilden.[7]

How reliable was Bancroft's rosy view of the past, John Chandler asked, in light of such a horrendous predicament? Lucretia, who welcomed the split, implied that her brother had not foreseen the possibility of secession because of his doctrinaire faith in progress. "What is to become of the experiment of self government?" a friend wondered. "Are we to fall victim to mobs and mass meetings or can the people be brought back to reliance upon their constitution and forms of government?" For once Bancroft, the man of ready answers and eternal optimism, remained silent, appalled, and terrified.[8]

When the boom of guns ended the suspense, he felt enormous relief and thought in retrospect that the popular awakening after Fort Sumter was "the sublimest spectacle . . . [he] ever knew." The people were about to save the nation. Overnight, Bancroft became a convert to vigorous prosecution of the war. All thorny ponderings became irrelevant when volunteers responded to Lincoln's call for troops in numbers that taxed available facilities. James Buchanan, who only two months earlier thought that nothing could be done, Wendell Phillips, who had urged that nothing be done, and Horace Greeley, who had suggested that the South depart in peace, all shared the experience. This "uprising of the irresistible spirit of the people in behalf of law and order and liberty" settled the matter and vindicated Bancroft's lifelong faith. "The north is the country and will make good the rights and the Constitution of the country."[9]

The "people" were those who lived and thrived by "self imposed labor," educated, frugal, teeming with "ideas and fertile in plans of enterprise," eager for wealth, "less for ostentation than for developing the resources of the country," family men, lovers of peace. Farmers, mechanics, lumbermen, students, and workers, "the sons of pious ancestry, with a clear perception of duty, unclouded faith and fixed resolve to succeed," interpreted the firing on Fort Sumter as a personal blow, and being the "constituent part of this republic" chose to defend their dignity. Instinctively they realized (Bancroft thought) that the war was a God-given trial of their willingness to fight for liberty. They were the ultimate national salvation.[10]

Bancroft was not alone in being swept along by popular enthusiasm. The aristocratic George Ticknor commented that "the heather is on fire. I never knew what popular excitement could be. . . . Indeed here at the North, at least, there never was anything like it." Like Edward Everett, he credited salvation of the Union to the people's mighty will; and that also diminished Emerson's contempt for the masses. Walt Whitman, whom Bancroft read, knew that mass democracy best expressed the divinity of human nature. The popular uprising vindicated the historian's most cherished beliefs—in the wisdom of the "collective man," in the inherent self-destruction of evil, and in the providence of God. That uprising would also, once and for all, take care of individualism, an outcome of more consequence than the fate of slavery.[11]

In response the man of letters once again turned activist—if the peo-

ple marched, it would be unseemly to lag behind. Nor was this the time
for historical research. On April 6, 1861, Bancroft, along with A. T.
Stewart, August Belmont, William H. Appleton, and other leading New
Yorkers, signed a call asking all to abandon past party affiliations and
rally together. Three days later he participated in a mass meeting in
Union Square. With Thurlow Weed, Henry Bellows, and Henry Wilson, he reviewed the parade when the Massachusetts troops arrived on
their way to Washington.

On other occasions, called upon to speak, Bancroft used these opportunities to untangle transient forms from efficient causes, and explain
why the war came, salvaging along the way the conclusions of his writings and the rationale of his political career. The thorny problems of
slavery and of political balances in the Union, he would declare, were
but surface manifestations of fundamental forces, which made the war a
God-given crisis for higher ends. Seemingly the result of human bungling, it was in fact the outcome of hidden forces moving in mysterious
ways. Everything that happened in history happened because it had to;
the historian had but to explain the necessity.

Bancroft's interpretation, common enough in 1861, traced the war to
a conspiracy. A demoralized southern plantation system, so the theory
went, created a lazy, parasitical aristocracy that debased poor whites and
fostered mob violence, political dishonesty, and treason. The Confederate leaders, bamboozling their people, embarked on a revolution effected, everywhere but in South Carolina, by a minority. They failed to
realize, however, that the North would fight, and that their departure
from the Union portended an internal war within the South, between
the rich, interested in a controllable number of high-priced slaves, and
the poor, in quest of cheap hands, willing to reopen the slave trade and
inundate the region with blacks. Northern determination, an unstable
social order at home, and lack of material resources would bring the
conspirators to their knees, and soon.[12]

With few variations, Bancroft never abandoned this explanatory
model, which, however deficient, fitted in with his outlook. The war
was the work of a deluded clique; and the rest of society and the republican form of government were free of guilt. The anomaly of slavery in a
free society led to a conflict that would demonstrate the durability of
American institutions as well as his own democratic theory. Bancroft did
not explain why the southern planters could impose their will with im-
punity on the people, nor did he elucidate what happened to the national
tradition in the South. He was interested neither in the legal nor the

constitutional challenges posed; by glossing over inconvenient problems, this interpretation left his cherished beliefs intact.

As the conflict lengthened Bancroft fleshed out the details of his thesis by showing how the plotters hatched their scheme. The Revolution had left the slave oligarchy in possession of its property, perpetuating a "spurious feudalism" that survived the cleansing fires of the war for independence. Jefferson's generation was the last to grapple with the issue realistically. Then the idea that bondage should cease died and a new aristocracy rose to prove slavery a positive good. Having formed a political party founded on slavery "under the guise of a zeal for the rights of the states" in 1840, these aristocrats allied themselves with the Whigs. In 1848 Van Buren was their dupe ("we judge him not but the consequences were sad"), all of which weakened the Democratic Party, the major defense against their design. When the Compromise of 1850 aligned the slaveholders with the northern magnates, burying the Whig Party, the second bulwark disappeared.[13]

Then came the Dred Scott decision, the product of "a depraved judiciary," written by "a man profoundly immoral," who treated "the people of the United States as a shrew to be tamed by an open scorn for the facts of history." While the Court and the President sacrificed national interests for slavery, the conspirators turned Kansas into a battleground, and by 1860 determined to elect a hostile president in order to unite the South behind them. With the Democratic Party in the hands of traitors, and "with an administration hardly more suited than for a summer's wear" in office, the plotters moved "to fire the passion of the Southern portion of the people." They became the aggressors on the morning of April 12, 1861, and fought for a new government with slavery as its cornerstone.[14]

This expanded version of the conspiracy thesis left a few points untouched. It did not explain why these terrible deviations from the national tradition could occur. Nor did it touch on Bancroft's own involvement in affairs that contributed to the war's outbreak, such as the Mexican War and territorial expansion. Bancroft held neither Polk nor the true Democratic Party nor manifest destiny responsible for problems only civil strife could ultimately settle. Van Buren was at fault for undermining the organization, but the Jacksonian heritage from which Taney and Buchanan descended was somehow divorced from the events of the 1850s.

As to the future, Bancroft in early 1861 was certain that, after a sharp initial struggle, the Confederacy would collapse. While the headlines urged everyone on to Richmond, no alternative was conceivable. Members of the Century Association, other friends, and numerous editorials agreed—the war would be short and the traitors would soon beg for mercy. The South lacked the wealth, manpower, and resources for a prolonged struggle. It was only a matter of time before the southern people, true heirs to the Union, would rise against the usurpers and restore the rebellious states to their rightful place. As for slavery, Bancroft was cautious. In the short run no "perfect Jerusalem" could be built since "the palingenesis from an intolerable wrong can not be hoped for without suffering." This meant that "slavery will remain but will cease to reign." Eventually freedom "will gradually but surely develop itself in its light and purity," but meanwhile the condition of half a million "semi barbarous . . . semi civilized" slaves, "unfit for the political franchise of citizens," would not change. The only substantive outcome would be the destruction of an oligarchy that conspired to impose bondage on the entire country.[15]

The obstacle to the speedy realization of these limited goals was the "black republican" administration in Washington. Lincoln's "monstrous political imbecility," his "criminal dilatoriness," and the lack of an honest political party and capable leaders unnecessarily prolonged the struggle. Therefore unionist sentiments North and South had to be encouraged at all cost, as an antidote to governmental failure. Bancroft supported two clergymen from North Carolina on a fund-raising mission. They represented, he thought, strong unionist sentiments in the South, important enough to call to Lincoln's attention.[16]

The Civil War, Bancroft also informed the President, was "the instrument of Divine providence to root out social slavery," increase the number of free states, and liberate the southern people from bondage. Apparently God meant the war to achieve what no political compromise had. But this call for eradication of social slavery was quite out of character. More characteristic was the suggestion that it be done on the cheap. The people on their way to Richmond had to remain "in favor of rigid economy in the public expenditures." The federal government was not to exploit this divine instrument for social revolution by expanding its own powers or purse.[17]

The distance between the ideal and the real thus remained uppermost in Bancroft's mind and with it recognition that the call for the eradication of social slavery countenanced a revolution he was unwilling to support. Political unity and national sovereignty took precedence over future needs. And neither the federal government nor state authorities could legitimately claim the powers to meet them.

In mid-December 1861 Bancroft traveled to Washington and with a government pass visited the camps, chatted with the soldiers, and met people whose families the conflict divided. Some of John's classmates were in the Corps of Engineers, very critical of their superiors. Sadly he concluded that laxity, incompetence, ignorance, and pettiness reigned. In the capital Mary Lincoln presented the historian with a meager bunch of flowers—"a fair counterpart of Mr. Lincoln's brains," Bancroft snapped. Meetings with government officials and cabinet members revealed that the country "under incompetent hands is going fast to ruin," and an interview with Lincoln deepened Bancroft's gloom. George B. McClellan (a deep thinker, he thought) left a more favorable impression. At a dinner with Samuel Hooper, Charles Sumner alternately defended and attacked the administration, an indication of the confused state of affairs. Secretary of State William H. Seward was "dirty, rusty, vulgar and low," his fatalism yet another symbol of national disarray.[18]

Only when the war moved into its second year did Bancroft conclude that the eradication of slavery ought to be one of its goals. The shift from his earlier stress on conspiratorial causes to emphasis on the divine origin of the conflict made him willing to justify steps not otherwise countenanced. "The country is bleeding," Seward was told, "as if an artery had been touched. Relief must come soon," in the form of an increase in the number of freedmen. This was the message of Bancroft's February 1862 address to the citizens of New York, which defined the war as punishment and as the opportunity to purge national guilt.[19]

Compromise "from feverishness and impatience" was inappropriate to days of terrible retributive justice, a purifying bloodletting for the sin of slavery. Most people, Bancroft thundered, supported the war effort, and he praised the city's poor for their "disinterested resignation." Their power would "not fail to crush the conspiracy." The war was also a class struggle, not in the old sense of the house of have battling the house of want, but of the free against those who denied them the opportunity to prove their worth. The soldiers of the North fought against "the rich . . . opulent men who count labor as their capital," the "enemy of our national life," who sought to reduce the people to serfdom.[20]

Not everyone in the audience found this use of history persuasive. At an official banquet after the speech Bancroft raised a toast to the memory of Washington and his opposition to slavery. Congressman James Brooks offered the second toast, to the real Washington, and the astonished historian heard himself castigated for doing that of which he had just accused Taney—that is, of falsifying the record for political ends. Traditionally the Common Council ordered speeches printed and extended a vote of thanks to the orator, but alderman Henry Genet led an opposition which claimed that Bancroft "belied the sentiments of the common council and the people of the city of New York," scuttling the move. A few days later the *Caucasian,* a prosouthern paper, added to the charges of falsification by quoting more extensively from the document Bancroft had used to show that Washington, far from being an early abolitionist, had opposed Quaker aid to escaping slaves. Only Republicans defended the historian, an uncomfortable situation for a longtime Democrat.[21]

Evidence of a more favorable reception consoled the historian. "Your words breathe and burn and advance and invade and conquer," wrote a young relative from the field. The end of the rebellion was in sight, Bancroft assured another supporter, and with it the end of luxury, dissipation, and extravagance, of all sources of moral degradation. The preacher whose sermons years before dwelled on the furnace of affliction now repeated the same theme on a national scale; good would come from the purification by fire.[22]

Euphoric pronouncements subsided a few weeks later when popular enthusiasm gave way to acceptance, resignation, and finally the rumblings of discontent. With an incompetent government, a handful of irresponsible generals, and defeat after defeat, the North might falter. The failure of the Union armies, disappointments with McClellan, and the divisions at home brought awareness that the war would not end soon. Bancroft shared with other Americans in 1862 a gloomy sense of hopelessness. "We are drifting in currents and the currents know the way," Emerson wrote. This was "a war of instincts," which he trusted more than the guidance of statesmen. But Bancroft lacked faith in instincts—uncontrollable and destructive, like the passions that had caused the struggle in the first place. Conversations at his clubs and at dinners and the tidings of the daily press heightened his misgivings. The country was about to miss the God-given opportunity to set its house in order.[23]

Slowly and painfully these considerations led Bancroft to argue more forcefully for emancipation, as the only measure to offset the government's "dilly dally policy." He neither suggested a workable policy nor gave wide publicity to his views, which he confined to private letters to Washington. Since the country yearned for decisive action and the army was in good shape, surely "the acquisition of Virginia and Tennessee must end the matter." With Grant's capture of Fort Henry and the southern retreat from Shiloh, Bancroft was certain that the Union ought, "constitutionally, this winter," to make the District of Columbia free "as an advertisement . . . that this is really and essentially a government of the free." But his hope vanished when McClellan's move on Richmond collapsed, when Pope suffered a beating at Second Bull Run, and when Lee moved into Maryland.[24]

Meanwhile the family felt the cost of the war. Alexander "Sandy" Bliss, quartermaster general, was relatively safe, but young Wilder Dwight, in the thick of fighting, was wounded in battle. Elizabeth fretted and worried about sons of friends in the front lines and almost collapsed at the news that young Dwight was dead. Whatever misgivings Bancroft still harbored about his first wife's family disappeared when he heard that Wilder's brother Charles took his place. John continued to be a problem—back in the United States and ashamed to stay at home, he searched for a commission, except that none seemed suitable for an art student.[25]

George meanwhile lived on a farm in France, his family contacts reduced to pleading, mawkish, or angry letters, begging for money and approval, neither of which he got. "I have no father, no home, no country," George wrote, after Bancroft cut him out of his will and demanded that he change his name. In an effort at reconciliation George brought his family to America, hoping that sight of the grandchildren would mollify his father, but Bancroft refused to see them. This was just the kind of extravagance his youngest son would indulge in, he thought, wasting money and expecting others to pick up the tab. Go back to France, was the message. "I wish not to have my old age clouded by your misconduct and complaints. . . . You can waste your property, you shall not waste mine. I am sick of hearing of the unpleasant consequences of your connections. You have been no son to me." "With a heart not full of bitterness but of sorrow, ulcerated yet healing, I turn to my father," George responded, expecting that Bancroft would not allow him to default on his debts and live in pinched circumstances. "You have no faith in me." "What have you got against me?" other letters asked. Could Bancroft procure him a consulship? No, was the frosty reply.[26]

As the war dragged on, Bancroft bemoaned southern strength and northern defeatism. He fretted about those "angry collisions of opinion . . . on the subject of the negro and a madness in favor of slavery." A pro-Union article in the French *Journal des Débats* which counted Edward Everett and Bancroft in the antislavery party was correct only in the sense that they were staunch Union men throughout. Both would have been willing to settle the war in March 1862 by restoring the rebellious states to their antebellum status. In the confusion of the carnage Bancroft conveniently shelved earlier calls for emancipation.[27]

By the summer he changed his mind once more. "In revolution half way measures always fail"; and since the South was bent on revolution, "the boldest measures are the safest," he informed Salmon P. Chase. The Union would survive only through abolition, which would free northern industry from unfair southern competition, crush the rebellion, and vindicate the administration. The old states' rights historian had taken a bold step forward; the war required unprecedented measures and the use of all powers necessary to save the federal framework.[28]

Sandy Bliss, serving with George McClellan, provided information on the possible services blacks could render. "Opinion is fast spreading that the negroes must be available in the service," Bancroft concluded. "Are you at Washington aware of how fast and how far public opinion has traveled on the subject," he wired Seward; "the people are nearly unanimous now." In fact they were far from unanimous, but Bancroft, persuaded that they were, assumed that the time for debate was over.[29]

In October 1862 Bancroft declined to run for Congress because he had no desire to be in Washington. But he used his response to the invitation to preach on anti-Union sentiments in the North, since nothing infuriated him quite as much as Copperhead treachery. "We are advised to manifest at the polls our consent to a disruption of the country," he thundered. "We are asked to vote that the war has no object, that we fight only to retreat with shame if we are victorious." Peace Democrats usurped the party's name, they were "the most embittered haters of Democracy," an oligarchy which "by the very necessity of its nature, seeks to extinguish the Democratic principles." Their followers were digging the Union's grave and blighting the hope of the world. A Copperhead victory would prolong the struggle for generations.[30]

The Emancipation Proclamation met a mixed reception among Bancroft's friends. Some regarded it as a mistaken admission of weakness, others considered it useless. Horatio Seymour, now governor of New York, declared it a barrier to restoration of the Union, while other acquaintances thought it would only bolster the Confederates by showing that the federal government was in abolitionist hands. But Bancroft regarded emancipation as proper, although he kept his views largely to himself. Only toward the end of the war did he explain that the proclamation hastened the movement of regeneration. When Lincoln "wrote liberty on the banners of the armies," his greatest contribution to the nation's history, the slavocracy lost its last bulwark of defense.[31]

In January 1863 most people did not see it this way. "On politics I have no heart to write at present," Bancroft informed John Bigelow. A northern victory required the aid of blacks, but "we have not the virtue enough to be willing to give the black man a chance." In New York appeals to racial animosities, making "the most unblushing avowals of warring against the war" strengthened proslavery forces. Only "when the resoluteness of the South teaches the North to have some decent respect for the black man" would the war end. The North would win, but "we have got to do so much in the way of improvement before we deserve to do so." God indeed moved in mysterious ways, but His ways were righteous altogether.[32]

To aid His ways, Bancroft immersed himself in public activities. In the Loyal League of the Union, he joined Alexander T. Stewart, Henry W. Bellows, Francis Lieber, and John Dix in an effort to rally the city against the Peace Democrats. Vigorous propaganda countered the defeat at Fredericksburg, the carnage of Antietam, the Democratic efforts to subvert the war, and rumors that even the West would defect. Like George Templeton Strong, Bancroft wanted to prove that the struggle was being fought not only by rabble-rousing politicians but also by "the intelligent, cultivated and gentlemanly classes." The proper antidote to Copperhead associations was a gathering of intellectuals, writers, editors, and merchants, Democrats and Republicans.[33]

Yet propaganda could not overcome economic hardship, inflation, and the demand for higher wages. Strikes and demonstrations baffled a man accustomed to alliance with the Workingmen of the past. Bancroft did not know what to make of this discontent. Long a believer that the United States was the best poor man's country and author of numerous statements on the dignity of labor, he watched this unwelcome manifestation of a social revolution uneasily. Unaware that many of the poor lived permanently on the edge of destitution, he assumed that patriotic appeals could compensate for low wages, depreciated currency, lack of prospects, and hunger.

At the Loyal League of the Union, Bancroft brushed aside social dislocation, political differences, and labor extremism by vindicating the power of the people and looking forward to national regeneration. He extended his message to southern freemen trained in the school of povery and "now compelled by tyrannical power to fight for results that are in direct conflict with their own chances for advancement and happiness." Civil wars had always been "in God's providence . . . a means of rescuing men from bondage." When "bitterness will pass away," future generations, North and South, would reap the benefit of strengthened national bonds and dampened individualism.[34]

There had not been suffering enough to atone for departures from the national mission, Bancroft concluded in June 1863 as he and his wife packed their bags for their annual summer stay in Newport. The furnace of affliction had not yet done its task, he assumed, as they settled into their comfortable cottage on the seashore, amidst cool breezes and congenial company. Bands played at the Ocean House Hotel and he took pleasant rides in the countryside. The southerners were absent, but August Belmont and other New Yorkers were much in evidence. The garden was a constant joy and the Newport summer a perfect respite.

Not for long. The newspapers reported draft riots in New York, with 105 dead (contemporary rumors put the toll at 1,155). Aid to the South, two simultaneous civil wars, a weakened Union army, a society out of gear—these thoughts flashed through Bancroft's mind, as he pondered this latest evidence of anarchy. Antiwar sentiments, cheers for Jefferson Davis, threats to hang Horace Greeley, a spirit of utter lawlessness were the extreme manifestations of the individualism he feared. Bancroft always associated mobs with proud aristocracies, tools to tread on popular sensibilities. "Rabbledom and rebeldom" were in cahoots, George Templeton Strong decided, and for once Bancroft agreed with a man he never really liked, one who always considered him a pompous prig.[35]

Political divisions also penetrated the Century Association, whose founder and past president, Gulian Crommelin Verplanck, was a Copperhead. Bancroft led the opposition. Many members viewed him as "an erudite ass," and considered Verplanck, in spite of his politics, a socially acceptable and dignified member. Nevertheless, despite his "foibles and snobbishness," Bancroft became the new president by a vote of 110 to 61. "So a club for the promotion of social enjoyment and literary and artistic taste abjures its original intentions and places upon its pedestal the image of Lincoln on Bancroft," one member commented.[36]

The small victory was a portent of better things to come. In 1864, the tide of war finally turned. On a trip to Washington, Bancroft discovered the government in better shape. Letters from his niece and sister in California confirmed hopes about the future of the West in the Union, its wealth, opportunities, and social significance. John's engagement to Louisa Denny, a Massachusetts girl, also lifted Bancroft's spirit, for his son seemed ready to settle down, even if he persisted in dabbling with colors and had no steady means of support. In June Bancroft delightedly helped organize a mass celebration to honor Ulysses S. Grant, and for the first time since 1861 breathed a sigh of relief.[37]

In the approaching presidential election Bancroft edged into unfamiliar political territory. George B. McClellan was the Democratic standard-bearer. His platform tried to capitalize on war weariness, on Lincoln's arbitrary use of executive authority, on antiblack animosities, as well as the protective tariff, railroad subsidies, and the national banking system. On economic issues Bancroft was still a traditional Democrat, but those connected with the war moved him closer to the Republicans. In private he argued that everyone should vote for Lincoln. However, his name was absent from the list of prominent New York Democrats who publicly supported Lincoln and Johnson, although he made sure that the administration knew of his support.[38]

McClellan's loss and the capture of the New York governorship by a Republican pleased Bancroft, who hoped to purge the Democratic Party of traitors. The election of Andrew Johnson as Vice President was also a favorable omen. When Johnson solicited historical support for a constitutional amendment to ban slavery Bancroft eagerly replied, noting "you were in some sense my representative."[39]

In the dawn hours of reconstruction, Bancroft thought innovative measures were the most conservative. His new message, "free from fanaticism," was "PUNISH SLAVERY, SPARE THE SLAVEHOLDER," certainly less extensive than Charles Sumner's plans. A constitutional amendment would quiet the South and remove the causes of the rebellion. With slavery punished, "we can cherish the former slaveholder" in accord with "the resistless movement of ideas in the history of man." "No one can turn back and stay the march of Providence." An end of slavery was to accompany a guarantee of the civil rights of property and person for the blacks, with the franchise following when they became "educated and manifestly capable of exercising their right with discretion." It would then be safe to entrust "the guardianship of established rights to law" and "the movements of reform to the spirit of the people." When congressional Radicals rejected Lincoln's plan for the reconstruction of Louisiana, Bancroft did not share the elation of Sumner, who insisted on black suffrage as the foundation of the new southern state governments and instead supported the Union League Club's four peace terms—no armistice, no validation of rebel debt, no slavery, and no division of the country.[40]

On April 9, 1865, came Lee's surrender at Appomattox, and on April 13 Lincoln's assassination. Several weeks later in New York City 160,000 people escorted the President's body along Broadway to the railway depot, as daily life came to a halt. The National Hook and Ladder Company bore a sign that caught Bancroft's attention—"the assassin's stroke but makes the fraternal bonds the stronger"—and he made it the central theme of his own speech later that afternoon.[41]

"Heaven has willed that the United States shall live" and by its "quiet and unobtrusive example" answer questions that had plagued mankind for centuries. The war was a preordained and bloody rite by which the people passed "into a new form of being." In 1861 both sides were "compelled to bear forward the change which becomes more an obedience to the law of universal nature than submission to the arbitrament of man." By the "overruling laws of the moral world," the selfishness of evil defeated itself. Abraham Lincoln's martyrdom bound the Union "more closely and firmly than ever." The nation needed an imperishable grief to touch its innermost feelings and the dead President became a symbol of all the endured sacrifices. "The grave that received the remains of Lincoln received the costly sacrifices of the Union." His "martyrdom will plead forever for the union of the states and the freedom of man."[42]

The view of the President softened with the years. While leaving the ultimate assessment to posterity, Bancroft then and later portrayed Lincoln as the creation of the people and of the free soil of Illinois. He "lived the life of the American people, walked in its light, reasoned with its reason, thought with its power of thought," resembling "a child in a dark night, on a rugged way [who] catches hold of the hand of its father for guidance and support." Deficient in executive ability and imagination, inclined to contemplation rather than action, prone to bad appointments and lacking eloquence, Lincoln recognized himself for what he was, "had faith in the intuition of the people," and read it with rare sagacity.[43]

The elevation of Andrew Johnson to the presidency appeared as yet another divinely ordained opportunity to rectify past shortcomings. The Union Square oration ended with a call for support for the new chief executive as "the most conspicuous representative of the industrial classes." This man of the people, Bancroft declared in terms usually reserved for dead presidents, was the child of poverty and toil, deriving his "political education in statesmanship from the school of the people," a son of the South who "would consummate the vindication of the Union." To further that consummation Bancroft brought himself to Johnson's attention as a spokesman for old-time Democrats ready to guide the administration on a middle course of "clemency and moderation."[44]

That middle course, Johnson agreed, alone could restore the Union.

Like Bancroft, he blamed the war on a vast conspiracy, blasted aristocrats for duping innocent southerners, and proclaimed that the Constitution should guide reconstruction. When Johnson reiterated the old states' rights theory, Bancroft approved. To bring the South back not through military rule but by the vote of the people was good Democratic dogma. Johnson in short was what the true southerner had always been for Bancroft and would become again—a staunch unionist, a worshiper of Andrew Jackson, and a Democrat.[45]

With relief Bancroft resumed his old political affiliation. With slavery destroyed, "the Democracy will be borne into power on the wings of their sound principles of finance." Further correspondence between the two convinced Johnson that he had found a new ally, and in October a series of letters and telegrams summoned Bancroft to Washington, where he spread assurances that public opinion supported presidential reconstruction.[46]

Late in November the President drafted his first congressional address with Bancroft's help. "No pains have been spared to express your ideas with exactness," the historian noted, relishing the proximity to power. Among those ideas were recognition of the provisional governments in Confederate states and acceptance of the results of the 1865 elections. These highly controversial positions, to Republican opponents, absolved the South from any war guilt, promised that area increased power in Congress, damaged the status of the freedman, and worked entirely to the Democrats' benefit. The message was brilliant in the ambiguity of its defense of Johnson's position. The Bancroftian introduction with its gratitude to God in the name of the people, its call for popular support and reliance on the Constitution, gave the impression of frankness. Then the President rejected black suffrage for the South and called for a civilian rather than a military restoration process. The states whose powers had been "so long in abeyance" would be reinstated in the federal government as soon as Congress decided on the elections, returns, and qualifications of its members.[47]

The favorable response encouraged Johnson and Bancroft to assume that they were on the right track. Moderates were persuaded that the President was ready to work with Congress and repudiate the Radicals, while the latter thought they could win Johnson over to their views. The outcome pleased Bancroft. "In less than 20 days radical opposition" would disintegrate, he informed the President that December.[48]

Pleased, Johnson turned to Bancroft for the government's official Lincoln memorial address, an assignment others had refused. The cau-

tious Bancroft spent January 1866 polishing his address, for by then
Black Codes enacted by southern legislatures had infuriated Radicals, the
Joint Congressional Committee on Reconstruction tried to remain moderate, and the administration engaged in open warfare with its opponents. Finally on a gray February afternoon before packed galleries, the
historian rose to speak, and for two and a half hours delivered his final
judgment on the war, repeating much that he had said since the assassination.[49]

As for the present and the future, Bancroft opted for the Johnsonian
theory of reconstruction. The pro- and antislavery parties were dead, and
the country enjoyed "a new moral unity as the land of free labor," with
the southern states back in the fold "as the original, necessary, and insep-
arable members of the Union." The speaker implied that Lincoln's reconstruction policy would have been similar to that of his successor,
since both emphasized leniency, clemency, and tolerance, guarantees of
citizenship for blacks, and the right to vote for those able to meet specific
qualifications. Johnson was in effect merely institutionalizing the goals
for which the war had been fought.[50]

The most controversial part of the eulogy dealt with foreign affairs
during the war. Recognizing that his words might grate on their ears,
Bancroft had forewarned the European diplomats. Ever the preacher, he
gave them a sermon that roused furor on both sides of the Atlantic. Self-
righteous and absolutely certain of his judgments, Bancroft took the
English, French, and Austrian governments to task for prosouthern
views, and ended with a long comparison between the assassinated President and Lord Palmerston, who had died six months earlier. The darling
of the British aristocracy had wasted his life and would soon be forgotten, while Lincoln would live in the memory of the ages.[51]

The reaction to the various components of the speech varied with the
listener. Lord Russell deserved all he got, noted Gideon Welles, and
Senator Orville H. Browning judged the oration very able; but the Radical Charles Sumner was doubtful about Bancroft's grasp of reality. The
audience was also partisan. When Bancroft mentioned Lincoln the Radicals applauded; when he referred to the current President, the friends of
Johnson showed their satisfaction. Less pleased were the citizens of Baltimore, who raised a furor because Bancroft implied that Lincoln had to
cross their town by night for fear of assassination. The diplomats were
loudest in their complaints. Lord Bruce, the British ambassador, lodged a
protest with the State Department, as did the French and Austrian representatives.[52]

Before long, accounts appeared in the British press and spread to the

Continent. A scathing article in the London *Times* referred to "Mr. Bancroft, the author of a history of the United States which is easier to talk about than read," who "screamed out venomous passages in a high and broken voice," accompanied by "wild gestures and distorted countenance." Other newspapers portrayed the historian as an old rowdy, while the *Anglo-American Times* carried a letter from an irate citizen ashamed of his countryman's "disgraceful invective." But at least one British radical found the speech superb and a German translation met with approval. In remote St. Petersburg, it delighted the Russian court.[53]

The dust had not settled when Johnson's vetoes made Bancroft one of the targets of the President's critics. Early in 1866 the President vetoed bills to expand the life and functions of the Freedmen's Bureau and to guarantee minimal civil rights to all citizens. Sustained by Congress on the Freedmen's Bureau but overridden on the Civil Rights Act, Johnson declared war on the Radical Republicans. Charles Sumner wasted no time telling Bancroft what he thought of the "ignorant, pig headed and perverse" Chief Executive who had abandoned the blacks as well as the pro-Union southern whites. How could Bancroft, the Democrat, reconcile the disfranchisement of 285,000 voters with the idea of representative government? The veto message had reprehensible passages, Bancroft suavely responded, but the Radicals were pushing too far. Citizenship after all did not imply the right to vote, only the right to equal protection.[54]

Publicly Bancroft said nothing and concentrated on the finishing touches to the ninth volume of the *History*, which appeared later in the summer, just when the President was trying to create a new political alignment, castigating Radical Republicans for subverting the Constitution. Written in the shadow of the war and dealing with another war, this installment concerned events that at first sight seemed a deviation from the pattern of national development. But since everything that happened had to happen, under the divine plan, the Articles of Confederation, like the Civil War, had a message relevant for readers in 1866.

The focus of the volume was regeneration, the theme also of countless political and scholarly orations since 1864. The newly independent states between 1776 and 1781 reconstructed their societies and government, the historian said, and in so doing, ignored speculative theories, metaphysics, philosophical distinctions, and lesser irrelevancies, following instead forces that "grew naturally out of [their] tradition." The carriers of that tradition were the American people, moderate, self-controlled, and respectful of property, the exact counterpart of their 1866 descendants. Unlike the abolitionists of the 1850s, or the Radicals of the 1860s, the earlier generation recognized that higher laws were subordinate to "the law of the land and the decrees of human tribunals" and developed their national life in line with what was realizable. The volume, Bancroft's "tribute to the union" and his "plea for it on historical grounds which can not be shaken," urged policymakers to shape their views in accordance with "the inward law" of the nation.[55]

Realism, the *History* proclaimed, was the hallmark of the generation of 1776. The people then knew that "water will not rise higher than its foundation," that "elections will give a representation of the people as they are," and that republican institutions did not "change the nature of man or quell the fierceness of selfish passions." Those who fought for independence revealed their wise conservatism by rejecting the schemes of self-appointed visionaries who presumed to know better than the rest what justice and equality mean. Guided by "the general principles derived from the nature of man and eternal reason," they thought it impossible "to introduce by decree the reign of absolute right. Traditions of the inexorable past, the bequests of former generations, offer barriers which can be overcome by time and prudence," and not by governmental fiat. Since "the public mind is of slow growth," the nation was spared a headlong rush into the unknown, and the Articles of Confederation were a necessary intermediary before the breakthrough to new forms.[56]

The early Confederation was the product of "the principle of resistance to power," a loose and faulty arrangement but one understandable in light of the common battle against the overbearing mother country. In one sense the Articles embodied American individualism in its anarchic guise, a strand of great significance but really foreign to the mainstream of national evolution. In the end the people preferred "continuity and gradual reform" as opposed to "an instantaneous complete and thoroughly radical revolution," and after 1785 learned to bear restraint and authority, going "forward in their natural development," overcoming the extreme manifestations of "self asserting individuality."[57]

The implication for the generation of 1866 was clear. Untried experiments were bound to fail if they did not take into account the country's tradition and history. A nation dedicated to limited government, which for years existed half slave, half free, and which assumed that all states were equal, could not accept anything expanding federal power, disfranchising some whites, and enfranchising most blacks. Reconstruction could only succeed by dealing with the South in ways to which the region could accommodate; and that implied acquiescence in the subordinate status of the blacks, acceptance of white superiority, and even the good chance of turning the region into a Democratic Party bastion.

The bulk of Volume Nine covered the near disastrous military campaigns of the years 1776–1778, in which not all the generals or politicians were heroes. Bancroft's portraits of Israel Putnam, Charles Lee, Horatio Gates, Philip Schuyler, Nathanael Greene, and John Sullivan showed their warts; and ambitions, jealousies, and suspicions among the civil leaders matched the ineptitude of the military. Unfortunately for the author, many of his Revolutionary characters had living grandsons determined to rescue their ancestors from a historian they despised.

At its appearance the volume received the usual accolades; some found the style a barrier to accuracy and the *New York Times* suggested that Bancroft would have profited from a five-year drill on a first-class newspaper. But such carpings were few. The *History* by 1866 had become a national institution and to quibble over its writing was almost unpatriotic, even though scholarly developments before long would overshadow the epic.

More immediate, although without visible impact, were assaults originating from the *Historical Magazine* and the *Southern Review*. "Bully Dawson" (as Bancroft referred to the editor of the *Magazine*) accused the historian of reading the past in light of the present and of falsifying the record in pursuit of an American nationality where none in fact existed. He charged Bancroft with doctoring evidence to prove that a self-sacrificing folk, led by divinely inspired politicians, created a new nation. The true American revolution, said the *Historical Magazine,* was the work of a selfish officeholding class that filled the vacuum left after the flight of the loyalists. That group controlled the new state assemblies, wrote the state constitutions, never subscribed to democratic sentiments, and would not have recognized itself in a narrative written by "a proponent of centralization and consolidation" who allowed "a fertile imagination . . . or a partisan bias" to shape his work.[58]

Bancroft's long and public record of opposing centralization and consolidation prompted the silence with which he met this review. That he did not reply to Dawson's other charges was more serious, although not surprising. To engage in open acrimony with an insignificant editor was undignified, and would have given the critic recognition he did not deserve. More important, Bancroft could say little to counter the *Historical Magazine*'s diatribes, since none of them appeared relevant—Bancroft honestly did not feel that he was prejudiced, or that he falsified, or that he pushed a pet theory. He firmly believed that to do otherwise was sacrilegious—the historian who allowed his passions to seep into the narrative falsified nature and denied providence.[59]

Substantively the *Southern Review* closely followed Henry Dawson's arguments, although from a different viewpoint. Bancroft, who never had "a character for veracity," knew "the savor of many fleshpots," and he was guided by a cloud that was "either a whale or a weasel, according as the taste may run at court when he invites us to look at it." He wrote to "pander to Northern vanity and passion" with "an inconsistency, recklessness, bad faith and virulence" to be expected from one of his political persuasion. The men of 1776 were in fact "as far as the antipodes from him and his truculent Jacobinism and the frothy trivialities which he ascribes to them," since neither union, nor nationality, the reviewer thought, were motives for the revolution. Lashing out at his New England and anti-elitist biases, the review also recalled Bancroft's campaigns on behalf of Polk and the annexation of Texas and his anti-abolitionist position. The historian had once been a good Democrat and a champion of state sovereignty, but had sold his soul to the Republicans and wrote history to fit their platform. Bancroft could also ignore the *Southern Review*'s defense of a lost cause.[60]

The irate grandsons however did not confine their remarks to private correspondence or obscure publications. Intent on rescuing their ancestors from what they regarded as unscrupulous falsifications, they gave full publicity to their grievance, published their letters (and Bancroft's) in pamphlet form and, using extensive social and political connections, enlisted the support of national organs of opinion.

The grandfathers' problems differed, and the issues Bancroft considered in his evaluations varied from case to case. As a result each grandson raised a different banner. But a secure social lineage and highly conservative politics led them all to denigrate Bancroft's Democratic leanings and blame "unscrupulous partisanship" for his low opinion of their forebears. When the historian accused Colonel Timothy Pickering, the American Revolutionary statesman, of cowardice, for example, a descendant, Samuel Swett, was sure that the charge really reflected hostility to the Federalists. Such attacks hit home and required response.[61]

The most acrimonious debate concerned Joseph Reed, the Revolutionary president of the Pennsylvania Assembly, who, Bancroft decided, was a coward, a traitor, a loyalist, and a recipient of British bribes. When a bitter correspondence with Reed's descendant, William B. Reed, became public and local newspapers took sides, Bancroft answered in a lengthy pamphlet. Historians, he wrote, usually ignored petty weaknesses which "neither portray the times nor illustrate events," since the individual, regardless of his personal qualities, mattered little in the face of the grand scheme of events. But since the present Reed undertook "the impossible task of rolling his grandfather's reputation up hill into the position of a leading patriot," and dredged up what Bancroft chose to ignore, the historian replied with a full account of the case.[62]

Hostile critics swiftly pointed out that Bancroft's negative views were influenced by Joseph Reed's contempt for the New England Revolutionary militia and by William B. Reed's southern sympathies during the Civil War. The historian stood accused of visiting the sins of the grandson on the hapless grandfather, resorting for evidence to do so "to the very sewers of post revolutionary partisan falsehood and rancor."[63]

William B. Reed refused to let the matter rest. A rejoinder tried to rescue the American past from the stifling embrace of New England historians. In reply, several Philadelphians took Bancroft's side and accused Reed of being "a truffle dog . . . an expert in the art of the exhumation of the dead," a maniac guided by malice, "a desperate, double dealing, dethroned, disappointed, despised politician." Such exchanges attracted the attention of the Philadelphia press, and the *Southern Review* transformed Reed into yet another victim of northern duplicity, while the *Historical Magazine* proved to its own satisfaction that the case against him was "unworthy of the veriest pettifogger."[64]

While the Reed battle dragged on, one of Philip Schuyler's descendants decided that an unflattering portrait of the general rested on gossip, rumors, and misinformation. Bancroft's initial velvety response proved futile; a pamphlet set forth the Schuyler family defense, which charged that the historian lacked "the qualities of the heart" as well as a sense of honor. Most insulting was the implication that Prescott, Motley, and Irving were better historians. Next George Washington Greene came to the rescue of Nathanael Greene, blamed for the loss of Fort Washington. Then Timothy C. Amory did the same for General John Sullivan, and called Bancroft an "unreasonably prejudiced" popularity seeker, who succeeded in degenerate times when sensationalism allowed the mean-minded to besmirch the reputation of those no longer alive to defend themselves. Bancroft was guilty of plagiarism, sycophancy, toadyism, and dishonesty, "a politician of the dirtiest Democratic school," interested in spoils, not in principles, and totally ignorant of military science.[65]

Such sensitivity was foreseeable, Bancroft thought. Americans lived in a new society, ignorant of historical criticism and so insecure as to forget that individuals, "even the best of them, compared to the people are but as drops that glisten for a moment in the light, before they fall into the mighty and undecaying ocean." If one accepted the grandsons' views, America "will have produced a greater number of incomparable generals and faultless statesmen than all the world besides." The charge that he belittled everyone else to build up the stature of General Washington was a mean trick, since the Father of His Country did tower over his contemporaries. Nevertheless it was disagreeable to discover how much sympathy the grandsons received in *Harper's,* the *Atlantic Monthly,* and other magazines. "It is high time to kill these dwarfs with one stroke," a friend counseled. But "ghostly complaints" fell on willing ears.[66]

Most unsettling were the social undertones of the debate. The grandsons were all "from the best society," John Bigelow noted. To take from them their grandfathers was like taking titles from the English nobility or slaves from the planters. Bancroft had abandoned a controversial political career and tried to rest on his laurels in New York's polite society; renewed reminders of his lowly origins were gratuitous insults; and that was precisely what the Amorys, Schuylers, and others did when they pointed to the historian as a social parvenu who tried to climb by besmirching their grandfathers' reputations.[67]

In revising the volume, Bancroft later altered some of his judgments, but to no appreciable degree. Succeeding historians checking his data also discovered that, perhaps inadvertently, he had made selective use of evidence, and his quotation marks were not to be trusted. The criticism seemed irrelevant in 1867. Bancroft, the destroyer of myths, angrily ignored the intrusion of personal questions into subjects of which only History (and thus he as historian) was the ultimate judge. True, Washington Irving treated the campaigns of 1775–1777 in greater detail, and yet with more finesse, and Daniel Webster thought highly of Philip Schuyler. But everyone knew what Webster's character amounted to. And whether or not the historian was a gentleman mattered not at all where "great and general principles" and not "personal vituperation and asperities" were in question. Sales for Volume Nine were high and adverse publicity did not hurt royalties.[68]

Bancroft had passed unscathed through the Civil War, that furnace of affliction. Buoyed up by a pliable theory of the past, he explained away the unexpected events of a decade without injury either to his philosophy of politics or to his self-esteem. But attacks upon his scholarly competence touched him to the quick. Again he felt the need for a change; and opportunely, at that moment Andrew Johnson rewarded him for past service.

XII

❦

BISMARCK'S BERLIN

THE NEW ASSIGNMENT took Bancroft to Prussia, the largest German state, where Otto von Bismarck's supporters viewed other parliamentary forms with contempt, had little use for the principle of popular sovereignty so dear to Bancroft, and regarded amateur politicians as inefficient nuisances. The jurist Rudolf von Gneist, about to become one of Bancroft's close acquaintances, articulated the prevailing temper by arguing that sovereignty of the people was the prelude to executive tyranny. "The institutions of a people are always a reflection of its heart and intelligence," Bancroft often said. Had he remained true to this precept he would have spared himself great embarrassment. A careful witness would have hedged his lavish praises when confronted with the reality shaped by Prussian history.[1]

Always an accommodating optimist, Bancroft by now could interpret everything in a favorable light, which in the present case tallied closely with official Prussian pronouncements. Facile adoption of the government line denoted an abandonment of critical faculties unworthy of a man who prided himself on the sharpness of his insights. He was not alone among American men of letters in cheering for the Prussians in the 1870s—John Lothrop Motley, James Russell Lowell, John Bigelow, and other usually astute observers echoed much of what he said. Even the experienced Carl Schurz imagined that a liberal breeze blew across his native land.

In February 1867 Bancroft rejected an appointment to his old post as Boston's collector of the port. "The law makes residence in Boston a condition of tenure and I am not willing to transfer my home to that city even if the office were agreeable to me." Johnson next suggested the Austrian embassy, but Bancroft was unwilling to displace John Lothrop Motley, the current American representative. Nor did he consider the French appointment desirable. In April a visit to Washington for the christening of Elizabeth's grandson enabled him to make clear why Berlin would be a suitable choice. When Johnson made his decision public by the middle of May Bancroft was elated. "It is the only office in your gift which I would accept with satisfaction," he told the President, "and in so doing I hope to be able to promote the interests and the honour of the government."[2]

The years had not obliterated Bancroft's curiosity about the land of his early education and a flourishing correspondence with German intellectuals kept him abreast of scholarly developments. After 1848 he followed developments in central Europe with great interest and told German immigrants to the United States that "it is your brothers and your kindred who are to take the only worthy vengeance for what your revolutionary forefathers suffered from the petty princes of a now falling empire by inciting and teaching its immortal people to construct a free and united Germany." Count Helmuth von Moltke, who, Bancroft assumed, was hard at work on precisely this task, received a copy of Volume Nine of the *History*.[3]

Bancroft's epic (about to be translated into German) and his politics both promised a warm welcome in the scholarly community. Several delighted German liberals expected the new ambassador to be "a strong and influential supporter of the unification and liberty of [the German] nation." Bancroft did not intend to disappoint them; "I look to the advancement of mankind through the liberal tendencies and culture of Germany," he informed a friend.[4]

The next two months passed in preparations for departure and in a round of pleasant farewell parties. Bancroft rented the Newport home and installed George Ripley in the New York house to take care of his library and manuscripts. An ample salary and a contingent fund promised a comfortable existence. Since Bancroft did not intend to appear a pauper in the Prussian court, he was willing to add whatever was necessary from his own pocket. The Senate confirmed the appointment; and in the middle of July the Bancrofts boarded the *Allemania,* bound for Europe, to be joined later by Sandy and his family.

At the secretary of state's urging, Bancroft stopped first in Madrid to confer about the possibility of transferring two small islands off the coast of Puerto Rico to the United States, for use as a naval station. John P. Hale, the former Free Soiler, was the American ambassador to Spain, and his attitude augured ill for Bancroft's task. Resentful of outside interference, Hale vented some of his disappointment on the visitor, who promptly reported to Washington that Hale mismanaged his duties and that the legation was in shambles. Bancroft traveled around for several weeks, long enough to find the people superstitious, the queen lewd, her successors bastards, and a strong clerical caste frustrating progress. Nothing would induce Spain to part with any possession, and the mission petered out. A paper on possible United States commercial relations with Portugal was the only substantive result of the trip.[5]

A rest in Paris broke the journey north, with time to renew old friendships and survey the political scene. The controversial Lincoln oration did not affect Bancroft's acquaintanceships; notwithstanding tensions over Mexico, he thought everyone well disposed toward the United States. The American ambassador, John A. Dix, proved inhospitable and for no apparent reason refused the customary civilities for a visiting dignitary. The two had known each other since the Civil War, and perhaps Dix was jealous of Bancroft's connections in the French capital. A series of small altercations strained their relations, and later they would embarrass the State Department by fighting out the Franco-Prussian War between them.[6]

More emotionally taxing was the encounter with estranged son George, who brought his three children to Paris to meet their grandfather. George III, aged nine, Sarah, five, and Suzanne, three, all well behaved, decently dressed, and very much in awe of the parent to whom their father looked for help, softened Bancroft's heart. He allowed Elizabeth to treat the children to gifts and sweets but still held George's marriage invalid and rejected his son's offer to come to Berlin for yet another reconciliation session. He also refused to give financial assistance.[7]

This sad encounter was a further reminder of his parental shortcomings. He did not blame himself for George's difficulties. But since relations with John were also once more strained, something must have gone wrong with the boys' upbringing. John lacked a steady occupation, but refused Bancroft's offer of a secretaryship in the Berlin legation. He did not want to be near a father still intolerant of a painting career, who counseled, "produce pictures or give up the appearance of trying to produce what you know you can not." When informed that John was joining an investment firm, Bancroft did not hesitate to point out his son's limitations and opposed the venture, recalling the fate of Samuel A. Eliot, the wealthy friend of Bancroft's youth who entered a most respectable banking house in Boston and went bankrupt. As usual, fatherly predictions proved correct. John lost another sizable sum, forcing Bancroft to provide a subsidy even though a review of his own resources showed "no very brilliant results for a laborious life for nearly fifty years."[8]

Both sons were hapless and dependent, but Bancroft was always more indulgent toward the older. The generosity toward John never extended to George, who took to reading law books to prove that his father had no right to frown on his marriage. He also offered to change his name to spare the family any association and proposed to sue the Dwights for having given him fraudulent stocks. Meanwhile the barn on his farm had fallen down, his wife was the victim of pickpockets, and the children needed clothing. The acrimony between father and son continued.[9]

Glad to leave behind insoluble family problems, the Bancrofts arrived in Berlin in the summer of 1867 to a reception which in warmth and splendor outdistanced that of their London days. From the official German viewpoint Bancroft was a distinct improvement over his two predecessors, who interpreted Bismarck's efforts to strengthen the Prussian monarchy as a danger to European stability. Bancroft's well-known sympathies augured a different frame of mind, and soon after his arrival dispatches to Washington stressed every sign of Prussian goodwill to the United States as well as its beneficial effects for Europe.[10]

The uncritical admiration that distorted Bancroft's vision and endeared him to his hosts stemmed from his belief that the government of Prince Bismarck was triumphing over forces of which the American envoy disapproved. The Germany he remembered from his youth was not all it could have been, intellectually and politically, and Bancroft's ambivalence about romanticism and its American transcendentalist counterpart matched his impatience with a disunited nation unable to live up to its potential. The *History* paid tribute to Martin Luther and the Reformation, that dawn of the modern temper. But the evolutionary course had triumphed in the United States, not in Germany, a prostrate giant, lacking the will and the leaders to tap its resources. Political failures had their counterpart in the inability of men of letters to fulfill their duties. Bancroft well remembered the isolation, impracticality, and visionary theories of some of his early professors. In Berlin that fall of 1867, he witnessed a brand-new spirit with delight. From the king and queen down through the major political and military figures, the leading professors, conservatives and liberals, a new attitude emanated, of practicality, cool judgment, realism, and above all an appreciation for the uses of power. Without articulating it quite so bluntly, Bancroft was enamored of German *realpolitik*.

Settled into comfortable quarters on Regenten Strasse overlooking the famous Berlin zoo, the ambassador quickly became a fixture in local society. The Bancrofts entertained princes, dukes, ambassadors, leading politicians, cabinet ministers, and the intellectual luminaries. Through Bismarck Bancroft met the German political and military command, including von Moltke and Albrecht von Roon. Gossip at glittering dinners provided information about European developments, an acquaintance with the banker Bleichröder was a wedge into the world of high finance, and soirees at the houses of other ambassadors revealed much about their countries.[11]

Wednesday evenings Bancroft devoted to the meetings of a learned society, its dinners followed by the presentation of scholarly papers. At his home Karl Lepsius and Gneist mingled with Prince Chlodwig Hohenlohe, von Philipsborn from the Foreign Office, and Ernst Bunsen, son of the former Prussian ambassador to Britain. The Winckelman Association of Artists invited him to their gatherings, while the number of honorary degrees and learned societies of which Bancroft became a member increased. Some people became warm friends, as did the pathologist and radical politician Rudolf Virchow, August Wilhelm von Hofman, the professor of chemistry, Herman von Sibyl, Ranke, and Georg Heinrich Pertz. This was the company Bancroft craved—learned, occasionally radical in intellect as in politics, active, and socially responsible. "I believe my circle is wider than that of any one in Berlin," he noted, proud to be on equal terms with its members.[12]

Most flattering to his self-esteem was the attention and approval of local historians. Compared to them, the Prescotts, Irvings, and Motleys were gifted amateurs, their praise welcome but, given its limited background, of less weight. No one in the United States could match the stature of Theodor Mommsen or the achievements of Leopold von Ranke. The latter was even more impressive than Thomas Babington Macaulay, except when he told Bancroft that the *History* was the best work written from a democratic point of view. This implied subjectivity as opposed to objectivity ("as they say here"), and Bancroft thought the charge was unfounded. The democratic strain in his work, he decided, was inherent in the subject, and not his own invention. In return, Bancroft had reservations about Ranke's unwillingness to play the role of universal judge. He fully agreed that every period was equally near to God, Ranke's equivalent of regarding every epoch as part of the divine plan. But such a conception did not preclude judgments on men and events in light of the cosmic significance of their actions. In Bancroft's opinion, every man had a right to be judged from his own point of view; that being fairly done, the historian had a right to bring him up to the tribunal of universal truth and right.[13]

Berlin was also famous for its opera, ballet, theater, and music. New York and London paled in comparison. Well-bred ladies played the piano and almost every girl sang; performances by Franz Liszt and Clara Schumann were social events; and the opera presented *Faust* and *The Magic Flute,* Bancroft's favorites. A passing but impressive meeting with Richard and Cosima Wagner expanded horizons. Bancroft approved of Wagner's faith in the moral objective of musical drama but not of his private life—Cosima was the runaway wife of another man, although there were extenuating circumstances (Bancroft thought Hans von Bülow vain, vulgar, and disgusting).[14]

Bancroft also found time for old friends and extended a cordial reception to Americans who passed through Berlin, among them the Ripleys, Henry Smith of the Union Theological Seminary, Christian E. Detmold (the German-American engineer), Clara Barton, William H. Seward, McClellan, Philip Sheridan, and Clover and Henry Adams. Carl Schurz, concerned lest his role in the 1848 revolution be held against him, called on the ambassador's influence to assure a peaceful stay. Part of the legation's work consisted of reassuring worried parents that American students in German universities were safe, and countless requests for information, legal advice, and financial data kept Bancroft's secretaries busy. Aware of the power of the press, he also tried to accommodate requests of journalists, occasionally exploiting them for his own purposes. Unfortunately too many Americans wanted to be presented at court, and Bancroft sought the privilege only for those of stature. He never understood why people found such ceremonies attractive—"we republicans should not press ourselves upon courts when we are not invited." When several he turned down enlisted the services of the British ambassador, a minor incident followed, in part because Bancroft and Lord Augustus Loftus disliked each other.[15]

Relations between Prussia and the United States presented few challenges, although naturalization and citizenship issues continued to crop up, as they had in the past. Bancroft spent the better part of his first year in Berlin negotiating new agreements, drawing on his good relations with the foreign and interior ministries. Prussia's military law required service from all the king's subjects, even after prolonged absence from the country; American citizens of German descent who evaded their duty faced stiff penalties when they returned. Past efforts to reach a settlement had floundered; the military establishment vetoed any compromise, laughing off threats of a strong American response. Bancroft chose to work through civilian agencies, enlisting the aid of government officials with the argument that a settlement was in the best interest of all.

He built his case on the right of free emigration for those who wanted to become United States citizens, supporting the traditional American right of expatriation. At the same time he also tried to dispel Prussian objections, by denying that any German would stay in America merely to avoid military service. The United States had no sympathy for people who thus shirked their responsibilities. By showing understanding for Prussia's military needs and often publicly praising the egalitarian character of its army, he won over other potential foes. To ensure appropriate wording that would close all foreseeable loopholes, Bancroft consulted prominent German jurists and kept in touch with the German-American community in the United States.[16]

Bismarck's aid proved crucial. The future chancellor personally guaranteed the king's assent and extricated the document from beneath a mountain of red tape under which the departments of war and the interior threatened to bury it. In the settlement, the North German Confederation recognized that five years of uninterrupted stay in the United States legitimized United States naturalization. In return, the treaty conceded that a naturalized immigrant who renewed his residence in North Germany and remained there for more than two years without express intent of returning to the United States was held to have renounced his American citizenship. Jubilantly Bancroft reported to Secretary of State Seward that everyone had taken "a large and liberal view of the case," traceable "to the hereditary disposition of this government, unaltered since the days of the Great Frederick and Franklin, to cherish the best relations with the United States." Pleased with his success, Bancroft swiftly proceeded to negotiate similar agreements with other German principalities.[17]

He ought not to have hurried. Problems immediately made the self-congratulatory messages premature. Since he initially claimed credit for success, he also reaped all the blame his deals engendered. Thorny issues of implementation and interpretation exposed him to the charge that in the zeal to maintain the goodwill of his hosts, he had bargained away basic American rights.

Was the two years' clause enforceable only in cases of express intention? In an open letter to the *Frankfurter Zeitung* on April 28, 1868, Bancroft admitted this to be the case. Was he empowered to negotiate such an agreement? The *New York Times* thought not. While *Leslie's Magazine* and *Putnam's* praised his efforts, the *Tribune* and *Harper's Weekly* bewailed the agreement's vagueness, and the *Irish Citizen* openly referred to the document as "this booby Bancroft treaty." The United States, the *Citizen* added, was acknowledging the right of the Prussian king to restrict the movement of his subjects by conceding that he could regulate migration from his country. Others charged Bancroft with bartering away American liberties, and partiality to the German royalists. One critic seized upon the vote of three Polish members in the Reichstag who opposed the agreement—"they know best what it is to see one piece after another of liberty taken away from a people till at last nothing, save the sad remembrance of it, remained." Still others accused him also of violating a principle he had earlier tried to impose on the British— namely, once a United States citizen, always a United States citizen.[18]

German-Americans in Würzburg claimed that they were deprived of the liberty to reside as American citizens, wherever and for how long they pleased. "The treaty reads one way and is liable to be interpreted another by the North German Confederation, when it may please them," they asserted. Others spread rumors that Bancroft inserted the clause deliberately to prevent Jews who made their fortune in America from returning to Germany without fulfilling their obligations to either government, implying anti-Semitism where, on the whole, there was none. What more could be expected from an ambassador so "dizzied by the incense at a foreign court and awed by the presence of a diplomatic genius" that he stumbled "over a republican principle"?[19]

Bancroft replied that the objectionable clause was a necessary safeguard against frauds; a naturalized American, owing military duty to the Prussian government, was unworthy of protection if he returned for more than two years without declaring his intention. He also began his own propaganda war, enlisting the services of friends to persuade the Senate to ratify the agreement, while approval by the German press, by United States government figures, and by grateful citizens helped.[20]

The fate of the treaties became entangled in domestic politics—terribly bitter, Bancroft noted in the spring of 1868; he was glad to be "so far away from the tossing waves." Andrew Johnson's impeachment trial was under way, and Ulysses S. Grant was the likely Republican contender in the coming presidential contest. Late in May, the Republican National Union Convention denounced the European doctrine of inalienable citizenship, while vindicating the rights of naturalized citizens at home and abroad. The plank aimed to attract the Irish-American vote, but it was also a veiled slap at the arrangements with the Prussian government.[21]

Bancroft's uneasiness grew in July when the Democrats nominated Horatio Seymour on a platform that included a similar naturalization plank. Although Charles Sumner pushed the treaty through the Senate later that month, the predictions concerning the elections disturbed Bancroft. If, as the *Nation* and other newspapers proclaimed, the Republican Grant was to be the next president, no ambassador could count on retaining his position; and Bancroft was now as reluctant to leave Berlin as he had been to leave London two decades earlier.

"Events should be taken as fortune de guerre." But resignation was not in his character. He tried to guide fortune in a favorable direction by establishing new, non-Democratic, non-Johnsonian credentials and stretching the facts to claim that he had been a Grant supporter since 1862. The Republican candidate represented peace and moderation and would move the nation to ever higher levels of achievement—thus Bancroft now expressed himself to Grant's friends. On inauguration day a dinner in Berlin honored the new President, with the help of German hosts willing to aid Bancroft in ingratiating himself with the new administration. The German ambassador Baron Gerolt exerted himself in Washington on Bancroft's behalf. For a while the appointment seemed secure.[22]

But the controversies about the naturalization treaties kept alive rumors of a replacement, though Bancroft proclaimed Grant Lincoln's true successor and lauded the new secretary of state, Hamilton Fish. After more than a year of uncertainty, Bancroft decided to resign. The bitter letters to Washington met a mixed reception, for some members of the administration believed that he had outlived his usefulness and wanted him removed. The New York *World* urged Grant to stop this "trivial and flighty literary flibbertigibbet" from "driveling in Berlin." Despite charges that Bancroft was only trying to get richer and Grant to get more German votes, the President chose to pacify his representative, urged Congress to raise his salary, and went to some length to endorse Bancroft's pro-German views. Reassuring newspaper reports about the increase of pro-American sentiment in Prussia laid to rest thoughts of resignation.[23]

Bancroft never regretted the decision that made him an enthusiastic if uncritical witness of historic events. The meager results of the 1848 revolutions and the trials of the Civil War had done nothing to dampen either his penchant for prophetic pronouncements or his capacity to see only what he wished. Just as once he had prophesied the speedy Americanization of Europe and the triumph of the people over their past, so twenty years later Bancroft found evidence of the progress of liberalism and freedom in developments that to many contemporaries were the victories of autocracy and dictatorship.

Prince Bismarck, ever controversial, fascinated Bancroft. Those who regarded Germany as militaristic and aggressive saw the man about to become the first imperial chancellor as a wily politician willing to shed blood for a Prussian-dominated union—the ultimate incarnation of tyranny, the Junker par excellence, the new Caesar of the Hohenzollerns. When he took the unusual step of calling soon after Bancroft's arrival, and a few weeks later escorted him to the palace for the presentation of credentials, the great democrat no longer saw him as the ogre of Europe. An unusual friendship developed. The ambassador came to know the prince better than any other American, except John Lothrop Motley, who had been Bismarck's friend since their Göttingen student days.[24]

For Bancroft, Bismarck was the German George Washington, endowing his people with a new life, wrestling with the problem of how to forge a united nation out of numerous different principalities. Germany faced challenges the United States surmounted after 1789, and Bismarck's mission was to secure individual freedom by achieving a proper balance between centralization and federalism. By consolidating the North German Confederation under Prussian hegemony, Bismarck accomplished what the Revolution and the Civil War had done for Americans. He was the "great figure of the hour," the "pilot in tempest who is great on great occasions," an instrument of Providence. A man of iron will, with the stubborn resolve of Martin Luther, he also believed in liberty. Nothing less than the foundation "of modern civilization" was involved in his actions. Present at the opening of the first Imperial Diet under the new constitution of the Confederation in November 1870, Bancroft felt that Bismarck helped to fulfill hopes a thousand years in the making.[25]

Since Bancroft made no secret of his sentiments, Bismarck responded with innumerable acts of kindness and consideration; the two frequently rode together in the Tiergarten, and met at official and unofficial gatherings. The Prussian autocrat came to like this fervent democrat, who was also the perfectly mannered courtier and shared his respect for historically developed stable institutions. Appreciation of good cigars and wine helped, as did a dry sense of humor that enabled Bancroft to shrug off what seemed to contradict his vision. Soon Berlin buzzed with rumors about the special treatment accorded to the American representative, much to the displeasure of the French and English envoys.[26]

To Bismarck Bancroft remained "the ideal American ambassador," with just the right kind of "cultured repose." His portrait would hang on the wall of Bismarck's country estate, next to that of Grant and several other Americans. Never dull or self-righteous, he could discourse persuasively on the grand scope of human evolution of which Moses, the Christian Revelation, and the Reformation were stages. When Bancroft declared that "ancient and modern Caesarian powers, by the clerical and dynastic exploitation of the people," used all means of obstruction to hinder the inevitable, Bismarck agreed since Bancroft obviously had the French in mind. So favorably disposed an American ambassador was a gem, and to keep him in office Bismarck interceded through Motley and Baron Gerolt. Bancroft was grateful and neither then nor later ever revised his own estimate of the prince.[27]

The unification of Germany was one of those "inevitable" developments that depended on the right man in power at the right time. Bancroft watched with fascination how Bismarck hastened its coming, advancing the country "in power, prosperity, liberty and unity" through the 1867 Union, which was completely "in harmony with natural laws" and "thoroughly the concurrent act of government and people." Bismarck informed the historian that only one who understood the Prussian past could formulate such proper views. Even more welcome were Bancroft's evaluations of Bismarck's steps after 1870.[28]

A grave constitutional struggle achieved a precarious balance between liberal and conservative forces, between parliament and monarchy, between North and South Germany, and between a determined prime minister and recalcitrant representatives of local states. The resulting governing structure did not by any stretch of the imagination resemble the American federal system, nor was it liberal. But Bancroft consoled himself that unity for the time being was more important. Only a strong state could make way for an open, free society, the result of "universal education, military conscription and suffrage." After 1868, Bancroft, certain that "the forces of liberty were rising," condemned dissenters as men "sleeping in a bark which though they resolve not to move, is always moving onwards and taking them along."[29]

But the bark moved slowly, hampered by age-old problems, human shortsightedness, selfish interests, and political divisions. From Rudolf Virchow, Theodor Mommsen, and others Bancroft learned about the

Progressive Party's plans and became aware that the National Liberal Party, supported by upper-middle-class merchants, industrialists, and academicians, had its own blueprint for Germany's future greatness. Other major stumbling blocks were so numerous that only a strong centralized state could reconcile their demands. The Democrat who all his life worried about the increasing power of the federal government in the United States conceded that in Germany only a strong monarchy would override particularism, religious divergences, ancient prejudices, and entrenched princely authorities.

Bancroft would not be the last American man of letters to travel in a country different from his own and endow its society with features few others saw. Nor was he the first to lose his critical faculties in the process. In Prussian society and government he saw great potentials of liberalism and democracy. The unbalanced, idealistic portrayal which filled out dispatches to Washington, the tendency to mix up the real with the hoped for, the rejection of evidence in favor of broader views, were symptomatic of an effort to make sense of the strange world around him. There was also something comforting and attractive about Bismarck— strong and clear in his goals, he appeared to have comprehensive (rather than piecemeal) solutions, seeming never to bargain, compromise, or sell out, as run-of-the-mill politicians did. When the prince eventually applied force to achieve those aims, Bancroft's enthusiasm was almost boundless.

The historian was certain that the American example influenced Bismarck. Prussia's history proved parliamentary government impractical in 1868, but the legislature, the ambassador was sure, received sufficient authority to influence policy. "This wonderful result has a special interest for America," he informed the State Department, "because it has sprung from the application of the principles which guided the framers of the Constitution of our United States. The constitution of North Germany corresponds in so many things with ours that it must have been formed after the closest study of our system." At a dinner he asked Bismarck whether this was so, to which the latter replied, "a little of everything." But Bancroft never spelled out what the parallels were, for in fact the new parliament was far weaker than the United States Congress, the tripartite division of power did not exist, and the predominance of Prussia and the monarchical element were distinctive. True, as Bancroft pointed out, no offices were reserved for the aristocracy and no upper house dominated by the nobility could veto legislation originated by the government, yet these adjustments hardly showed the relevance of the American Constitution.[30]

Whenever necessary Bancroft defended the German Confederation, whose opponents fought under the banner of immorality against the laws of nature. An Austrian or French assault on Prussia would be a revolution that would "convulse the world" and show "hostility to the human race . . . opening the way to incalculable disasters." Fortunately "the good will and consent" of every power in Europe were really behind Bismarck. Until late in the day Bancroft did not expect an armed struggle. "No one can foretell into what relations the uncertain policy of other powers may drift." The French were fickle, as everyone knew, but no one in Prussia was predisposed to war, he thought at the end of 1868.[31]

In the event of a conflict, Bancroft determined to place the United States on history's right side. In November 1867 he suggested that Johnson's annual message affirm Germany's right to revamp its political arrangements without foreign interference. Should the French intervene, the resulting war would hurt United States interests. By 1870 Bancroft was certain that "were German emigration from the ports of Bremen and Hamburg alone to be interrupted, it would occasion a loss of that which nourishes the life blood of the people." In Berlin Bancroft also implied that, in case of a conflict, the United States would not hesitate in its choice. And he used all the resources at his disposal to tilt United States foreign policy in that direction, including notices to other American diplomats in Europe, warning them of the consequences should they express different views.[32]

John A. Dix in Paris did and thereby incurred Bancroft's wrath. Dix was as pro-French as Bancroft was pro-Prussian but, more immediately (and like his colleague in Vienna, John Jay), resented directives from Berlin which did not reflect official policy. Dix complained to the secretary of state. A long and heated reply from Bancroft implied that Dix encouraged the French along a course damaging to his country with "assurances as erroneous as they are unauthorized that the United States would look on as indifferent spectators during the ruin of their prosperity and the violation of their principles without warning, remonstrance or sympathy." Privately Bancroft spoke of Dix's "malevolent imputations" and neglect of truth. Without a shred of dignity, Dix lent himself to exploitation by a foreign government. This man, intoxicated with his position, one of the worst diplomats the United States had ever had, was but a "purveyor of poor gossip."[33]

This ill-tempered exchange received much attention in Washington, not all of it favorable to the American ambassador in Berlin. "The weakness of a driveler and the impertinence of a pedagogue" was Gideon

Welles's reaction. Senator Orville H. Browning also judged Bancroft's replies "in bad temper and acrimonious . . . not justified even if it be admitted that Dix was in the wrong." The ambassador to France was censured for his indiscretions, but the feud also gave rise to anti-Bancroft articles in the American press, stoked also by yet another Bancroftian reference to the Prussian military system as "a happy reproduction of the American" one.[34]

In spite of his pride at being part of Berlin's inner circle, Bancroft was unaware of the approaching crucial test of Bismarck's plans, and until the last hour remained oblivious to the complicated story of the Hohenzollern candidacy for the Spanish throne that sparked the Franco-Prussian War. When its details became public, Bancroft unhesitatingly opted for the official German explanation—the French were exploiting an internal Spanish matter to provoke a conflict. "Germany leaves Spain to choose her own government and regulate her own affairs," he informed the State Department, while "for one hundred and sixty years France has steadily endeavored to subordinate Spanish interests and policy to her own." In July 1870 Bancroft still discounted the possibility of bloodshed—"we have been very war like of late," he wrote, "but the thing seems to blow over with a good deal of bluster." Two weeks later, when the war came, Bancroft was jubilant. Prussia would teach France a long-overdue lesson.[35]

The immediate result was more business for the Berlin legation. American travelers required attention, lest they be isolated in potential war zones. Violations of the naturalization treaties increased appeals for embassy intercession. Bancroft had to secure the release of American merchants arrested as French spies and help American sailors stranded on German ships. His connections gained passes to the front for visitors and correspondents eager to see the war at first hand; and he expected the Prussian high command to find time to entertain American generals. Newspapermen received special treatment—in the coming war of words Bancroft hoped to have them on his side.[36]

In addition he had to look after his own family. His niece was traveling in Europe with her family, accompanied by Lucretia, and worried about the safety of her sickly husband and child. George, Jr., was also concerned, not so much about his security as about his financial situation. To prove how desperate his lot had become, he provided Bancroft with newspaper clippings detailing the financial mismanagements of the Dwight family. For once Bancroft was convinced, since about $30,000 of George's money was involved in the debacle. As to the effect of the current war, Bancroft assured his relatives that there was nothing to worry about. Considering the "unheard of wantonness" of the French and the perfect military preparedness of the Prussians, the outcome was clear.[37]

Bancroft's interpretation of the war was simple. Following the official Prussian line he put the entire guilt on the shoulders of the adventure-seeking French emperor and his Catholic, ultramontane country, resentful of the vigorous northern Protestant nation, ready to do everything to prevent German unity. Much like President Grant and John Lothrop Motley, Bancroft saw the war as a conflict between a personal aggressive empire and a national democracy consolidating a Reich. "Evil and good" were meeting on the battlefield, and the victories were all "on the side of civilization and freedom." "A people in arms crushes the degenerate hosts of despotism," he wrote.[38]

The United States had but one choice: to remain on God's side. Long dispatches to Washington aimed to ease official neutrality and persuade the State Department to take a pro-German stand. Bancroft marshaled moral, economic, social, as well as political arguments to buttress his case. He stressed the importance of keeping open the shipping lines to Germany, for the sake of the mail, the immigrants, and commercial intercourse. He urged Fish to make anti-French pronouncements that might help the Republicans in the fall elections. The United States could never be partial to a French war of conquest while Prussia defended "the best interests of civilization, of civil and religious liberty and of popular freedom." The "wounded self love of the French people" legitimized Germany's compensatory claims, which made the annexation of Strasbourg and of Alsace a reflection of "German patriotic national feeling." Bancroft hoped that the United States government would therefore express its displeasure at "a declaration of war so injurious to commerce and without a cause," and take measures "in some way to mark strongly a sympathy for the Germans."[39]

The answers from Washington were disheartening. Bancroft's nephew, John Chandler Bancroft Davis, speaking for the State Department, tried to restrain his uncle. Opinions at home were divided, he noted, and the United States had more pressing diplomatic issues on the agenda—the Cuban insurrection, the Santo Domingo treaty, the *Alabama* claims against Great Britain. There was a veiled warning in references to John Lothrop Motley, about to be recalled from his diplomatic post for contravening Grant's express wishes. Undaunted, Bancroft continued to send streams of advice, much of it ignored.

The proclamation of the French Republic was a potential crack in Bancroft's complete moral exoneration of Prussia. But he was proud to note that he could not be fooled into thinking that the French had really changed. Since they were still immoral, illiterate and ill trained for self-government, their proclamations were worthless. He advised against recognizing the new regime and warned Elihu Washburne, the new American ambassador in Paris, that caution, moderation, and above all suspicion were the proper frame of mind for the hour. Bancroft bristled when Hamilton Fish suggested that he influence Bismarck in the direction of peace and leniency. Germany would ask only what was hers by right. The interests of the United States were on the side of a favorable German settlement which nothing should impede, certainly not self-serving French requests for mediation, or private initiatives amounting to meddling.[40]

Humanitarian and charitable initiatives were another matter and Bancroft fully cooperated with the American representative in Paris. Since much of that aid would help Prussian nationals stranded in France, it would bring credit to the United States government without openly violating American neutrality. More difficult to handle was the more embarrassing problem of the sale of surplus American arms to the French. Luckily, Bismarck was tolerant; Americans were, he suggested, a mercantile people, in the business of making money; and it was cheaper to capture those arms on the Loire than buy them in Washington. American dealers, Fish reminded Bancroft, could not be expected "to shut up shop whenever Lew Nap and Bill Hohenzollern take off their coats and go to fisticuffs to settle which is the better man or whether their boundary should be on this or that side of the goosepond."[41]

Frustrated at the unresponsiveness of the State Department, Bancroft rarely missed a chance to make his private views known. In September 1870 Göttingen celebrated the fiftieth anniversary of his graduation and among the numerous congratulatory letters was a note from Bismarck. Bancroft's response—an effusive letter which charged the prince with the task of renovating Europe—found its way into the German press, was translated for English newspapers, appeared in the London *Times,* and thence made its way into France, whereupon the Paris newspapers vented their anger. Victor Hugo took up his pen on behalf of a French nation, "raped by the Prussians," and compared Bancroft to a dwarf whose venom could not alter the fact that he was still a dwarf.[42]

With the war over, Bancroft felt released from the unwelcome obligation to maintain American neutrality, and concentrated on making the

German peace terms palatable to the United States. At first it seemed as if the glee with which the French defeat was greeted at home promised to ease his task. But Hamilton Fish, for one, regarded Germany's territorial claims as unjust and the source of future troubles. The proclamation of the French Republic had also brought France fresh American support. Bancroft was sorry to note a new mood of pity for Prussia's enemy and a desire for leniency toward the vanquished power. News from other American ambassadors in Europe confirmed a growing fear of German aggrandizement, further complicating his task.

When the peace talks began, Bancroft learned that the United States would not support a settlement dismembering France. But he believed that the State Department did not speak for the administration. Grant, who leaned toward his ambassador's views, assumed that France had entered the war without provocation and deserved no sympathy. In an effort to reverse Hamilton Fish's opinions, Bancroft sent back dispatch after dispatch pointing out the commonality of American and German interests, and the benefits to the United States of a peace that left Germany the most powerful and freest nation in Europe. Articles in the New York *Tribune* drew on sources in the American embassy in Berlin to prove that Alsace and Lorraine were receiving, if unwillingly, the right of self-determination, and that Germany was restoring natural boundaries altered in the past by aggression. As proof of Gallic rapacity, Bancroft passed on the story that the French envoy to Berlin had offered Bismarck a deal before the war—consent to German unification in return for French annexation of Belgium and Luxembourg.[43]

In Washington Baron Gerolt, a friend of many years but, as Bancroft sadly noted, "not the wisest of mankind" even in better days, ineptly represented the Prussian cause. An old and querulous troublemaker, he pestered the State Department with endless complaints and presented his government's case in the worst possible light, much to Bancroft's displeasure. Gerolt's bitter accusations—about clandestine arms sales to the French, about French violations of American neutrality—and his own underhanded maneuvers all antagonized the secretary of state. Fish passed on the news of Gerolt's shortcomings to Berlin, and in October 1870 Bancroft submitted a formal complaint to the foreign ministry that led to Gerolt's removal.[44]

A major outcome of the war was the formation of a united Germany, a topic on which Bancroft waxed ecstatic. When the upsurge of popular demand drowned out particularist and localist sentiments and swept the

South German states into the empire, he pointed out that no coercion was needed to extend the federal framework and to crown William I as German emperor. "We Protestants by our good doctrine of the direct communion of the individual with the divine have made personal government with the strong hand impossible except as a transient dictatorship." The German union terminated the usurped sovereignty of all the petty states that hired out their subjects to George III to fight the American colonies. When Motley called "great Germany . . . the mother of us all . . . sure to become a free and magnificent commonwealth, under whatever political name it is first to be baptised," Bancroft agreed. The new empire moved "with dignity, and grandeur and tendency to popular freedom."[45]

The credulity and unrestrained admiration Bancroft lavished on Bismarck's political achievements revealed the blinding combination of moralistic myopia and a large dose of ignorance. Proximity to events did not produce knowledge, and insights derived form polished conversations in drawing rooms became substitutes for evidence. Committed to the support of Prussia, Bancroft embarked on a strangely pragmatic and relativist course which he would hardly have sustained back home. Honest enough with himself to suggest that his own favorite universal standards were inapplicable in this case, Bancroft nonetheless tempered his judgments conveniently to suit selective perceptions. Naturally he traced the seemingly liberal character of the Prussian diet to the American example, without however fleshing out the connection. And "its inflexible determination to enforce the supremacy of the state over all its citizens" also met with Bancroft's approval; it was all very democratic. "Our Congress does not more completely represent the people than the Prussian diet represents the people of Prussia." Except for "the artificially constituted upper houses," everything proved that the "freedom and the welfare of the people is not a dream" but a reality. Even the new press regulations were a marked improvement.[46]

Chief among the obstacles to liberalization were the nefarious activities of the Catholic Church. On this issue Bancroft's pro-German, anti-French, and anti-Catholic proclivities coalesced. He noted "the concentrated unity and activity of the clerical party," a band of conspirators "ever more closely welded together," headed by a pope whose will was absolute. Nothing less than "war on superstition and servitude of the mind in all its forms," was needed, since Catholic tyranny was "too terrible to be favoured or forgiven." He could hardly restrain his outrage and moral indignation.[47]

Evidence of conspiracy was easy to find. The same people in France and Germany who supported the Church had once hoped for a Confederate victory; the Archbishop of Posen who spoke out against the Prussian government set himself above the law of the state and expressed the "usurping disposition of the Vatican priesthood." That crew, bent on perpetuating clericalism and religious intolerance, destroyed independent thought, impaired mental vigor, undermined reason, fostered idleness, sensualism, and materialism, and poisoned the true faith. Bismarck's assault on the Catholic Church was therefore a war of the sons of light on the forces of darkness, and to destroy these conspirators was "the perfect triumph achieved in the contest for the rights of reason."[48]

The political implications of Catholicism were even worse. To Bancroft the 1870 declaration of papal infallibility was a reversion to medieval claims of Church superiority. Catholicism hindered political progress since ultramontane loyalties stifled patriotism. The Church revived aristocratic pretensions just as they were about to disappear because its bishops were noblemen at odds with modernity. Unless stopped, they would enter the field of politics everywhere, not sparing even the United States in the effort to thrust the western world back into the darkness of the Middle Ages.[49]

The background of these tirades was the Prussian effort to undermine clerical power in the new Reich. In July 1871 Bismarck abolished the Catholic section of the Prussian Ministry of Ecclesiastical Affairs and Education. The Pulpit Law of December 1871 threatened priests with imprisonment for remarks derogatory to the government, and required a secular education as a qualification for the priesthood. "With logical impartiality," Bancroft commented, "the bill applied the principles of equality to all places and all persons in regard to public utterances and political subjects." He also credited popular will with forcing the minister of public worship to dissolve the Jesuit houses. The May 1873 laws that subjected all church administrative matters to the government were not a denial of freedom of conscience but an expression of the state's right to defend itself "against all attacks under the veil of religion." It never occurred to Bancroft that the *Kulturkampf* might violate democratic principles. In Germany the state had to impose political and cultural freedom from above, by uprooting institutions hoary with tradition.[50]

The debris left behind by such upheavals did not concern Bancroft; it was after all the garbage pile of history to which the Catholic Church was consigned. For a man who only very rarely in the past gave any indication of anti-Catholicism, such opinions were clearly newly acquired in Berlin. He never challenged the arguments of Bismarck's opponents but rationalized repression and coercion as necessary, legitimate, and beneficial means to a liberal end. For the sake of eradicating obstacles, Bancroft willingly condoned what would have aroused howls of protest in the United States, protests he might quite possibly have led.

Several diplomatic issues, in abeyance because of the war, now absorbed the American envoy's attention. In Geneva, his nephew John Chandler Bancroft Davis was a member of a team led by Charles Francis Adams settling the *Alabama* claims arising out of the damage done to American ships by England during the Civil War. Bancroft, not directly involved in their work, kept informed, answered occasional questions, and helped draft the American case. The initial immodest American demand called on England to pay the whole cost of the war after Gettysburg, with 7 percent interest. Indignantly the British government rejected these indirect claims and threatened to withdraw from the negotiations. In Berlin Bismarck assured Bancroft that England would not carry out its warning.[51]

Hamilton Fish next proposed that the United States give up its indirect claims in return for abandonment of Britain's San Juan claim. That problem, a relic of the old Oregon boundary dispute, revolved around the question of which of two channels—the Rosario, nearer to the mainland, or the Haro, closer to Vancouver Island—was the demarcation line with Canada. Bancroft set out to prove the validity of the American assertion that the Haro line was the one agreed upon by the negotiators in 1846. When a joint commission submitted the issue to the Prussian emperor as arbitrator, Bancroft, as the last surviving member of Polk's cabinet familiar with the dispute, handled the American claim. He devoted the better part of 1871 to ransacking old maps, rereading his correspondence, and gathering information from his own files in New York, from the State Department, and from other sources. He also studied the history of the Hudson's Bay Company and of the British presence in the area. He remembered, and could prove, that while ambassador to England he had reminded Lord Palmerston that the boundary line passed through the middle of the Haro channel. Those comments in 1871 acquired new significance, suggesting that this indeed had been the understanding of the American negotiators when they signed the Oregon treaty. The assistance of the Prussian secretary of state and the cooperation of other German officials and prominent jurists persuaded Bancroft that the final judgment was certain to be in his favor.

The cartographic evidence presented was highly problematic and in the end proved inconclusive, but the geographic arguments, the historical accounts, and the diplomatic correspondence he cited more than made up for the weaker links in the American brief. Bancroft was sure of the persuasiveness of the American case when some Germans suggested that "when brother Jonathan emigrated to America John Bull let him take the larger share of common sense with him." The German emperor submitted all the relevant papers to three experts, a geographer, a councillor, and a judge, who returned their conclusions in September 1872. The majority report sustained the American claim.[52]

Delighted at this outcome, Bancroft took full credit for the result, while the furious British assumed that Bismarck had manipulated the settlement in favor of the United States and that Bancroft had done "his best to hugger-mugger the lawyers while employed in framing their report." Anti-German sentiment in England matched the anti-English feelings in Berlin, where many remembered Great Britain's sale of arms to the French and her hostility to Prussian unification. Bancroft's shrewdness and connections undermined a major initiative of English diplomacy and the gratitude of American officials compensated for the sour comments in the English press.[53]

In Geneva, meanwhile, the *Alabama* arbitration proceedings moved ahead with Bancroft abetting his nephew's defense of the American claims. Bancroft saw to it that a German version of those claims appeared in Leipzig and that Prussian newspapers carried favorable reports. As a result, when John Chandler Bancroft Davis arrived in Berlin, Chancellor Bismarck informed him of Prussia's support. In September the tribunal held England responsible for the damage done by three of the ships and ordered payment of a large indemnity.

By contrast with such important affairs, routine duties seemed dull, and by the winter of 1872 Bancroft's zest was gone. The Odd Fellows Club needed an introduction to Germany, which he provided; the Music Corps of the Grenadier Regiment, off on an American tour, received suitable references. Bancroft did his best to cultivate interest in American finances among bankers, sure that the way the United States balanced annual expenditures was another cause for the fast Americanizing of Europe. The State Department wanted Bismarck's help to end Jewish persecution in Moldavia and Walachia, but Bancroft considered the influence of Jews an unwelcome feature in German life and his protest on their behalf was perfunctory. Hamilton Fish also wished new problems with the naturalization treaties settled, all requiring numerous letters and protracted negotiations.[54]

"It is hard for me to live away from my own country, for even public

service is a sort of exile," Bancroft decided. Elizabeth's health deteriorated, and for much of the year an indefinable malady kept her away
from the capital—on the Riviera, in Switzerland, or in Italy, while Bancroft stayed in Berlin alone. Her absence was a painful reminder of human fragility, and while his own health was still excellent, he too was
conscious of growing old. Gloom descended on the usually sprightly
ambassador at the news that Louisa, John's wife and mother of his two
children, had died after a sudden illness. Very much in despair, and short
of funds, John mourned, while Bancroft offered condolences, helped
financially, grieved with his son, and tried to bear this additional burden.[55]

Life in Berlin became even less attractive when Sandy's wife, Eleanor,
fell ill with tuberculosis. Spas and medical help, goat's milk and mountain air were of little avail; the young mother of two children struggled
in vain for her existence. With some satisfaction Bancroft noted in his
diary those special days when no physician visited the house. Eleanor
died at the age of thirty-two, while Elizabeth's health worsened. Charac-
teristically Bancroft found consolation in the way in which his daughter-
in-law faced the end. Eleanor's "resignation," Bancroft wrote, "was as
sublime as it is sad, the piety and strength of character was above all
praise."[56]

Visitors to Berlin in the winter of 1872–1873 found the American
ambassador tired, careworn, and haggard. Seeking a change of atmosphere and recognizing that this was their last chance for an extended
Old World trip, the Bancrofts undertook a lengthy journey to the Near
East, facilitated by cordial consular receptions and comfortable travel
arrangements. A month in Italy was followed by several weeks in
Greece, where they met the king and queen. Strenuous but exhilarating
walks around the Acropolis and the battlefield of Marathon evoked
memories of poems learned in boyhood days and left the bittersweet taste
usual among Victorian tourists. Bancroft also enjoyed an archaeological
excavation and proudly uncovered a Persian arrow. Shrewd bargaining
sessions with local merchants, the triumphant purchase of gold coins,
added to the pleasure of freedom from irksome duties, from the incessant
demands and the eternal complaints of visiting Americans.

From Greece the couple moved to Constantinople, where they met
Sultan Abdul Aziz and the patriarch of the Greek Orthodox Church.
The splendors and servility of Eastern hospitality delighted Bancroft.
Drinking coffee from a diamond-studded cup, listening to the sultan's
compliments, the American democrat shed his prejudice against the Ori-
ental despot. In Egypt the Bancrofts met the khedive and also Ralph

Waldo Emerson, traveling with his daughter Ellen. Emerson was particularly grateful, for Bancroft, upon hearing that Emerson's Concord house had burned down, sent him $1,000 for repairs. The obligatory trip up the Nile, in a comfortable houseboat with excellent amenities on board, offered Bancroft an opportunity to practice his laboriously acquired Arabic, which he had not used since Göttingen.[57]

On the way back to Berlin the Bancrofts stopped in Italy for an audience with the pope, the thing to do, and the American was curious to lay his eyes on the ogre whom he had charged with attempting to reverse the progress of the world. Meetings with Italian officials confirmed old suspicions about the machinations of the Catholic Church and gave Bancroft further justification for his hostility toward the Jesuits. In January 1873, back in Berlin, Bancroft once again was rescuing Americans from German jails, dealing with immigration agents, with German sailors sailing under the American flag, and with local worthies who wanted to exile undesirable characters to the United States.[58]

In the spring of 1874 Bancroft decided he had been absent from the United States too long. For seven years he had served dutifully and he thought conscientiously. Nothing pressing remained on the agenda, except honorable retirement. Drawn once again by incomplete historical projects, Bancroft sent his resignation to Washington, where Grant and Secretary of State Fish chose John Chandler Bancroft Davis to be his successor.

The last weeks in Berlin were among the busiest of Bancroft's stay. Endless callers came to say good-bye and there was a long list of dinners and receptions. Bismarck and Moltke were genuinely sorry to see him go, and the emperor, in an unusual gesture, commissioned Bancroft's portrait as a farewell gift. The Royal Academy arranged a great reception, and the universities of Munich, Berlin, and Heidelberg sent a parting message signed by over one hundred scholars. "Your name," one member wrote, "is now the intellectual possession of everyone among us." Dorner, Rudolf von Gneist, Theodor Mommsen, and Virchow added their farewell greetings, and German newspapers published complimentary articles about the departing ambassador.[59]

The way back to the United States took the Bancrofts through Paris, for another meeting with the hapless George. The softhearted Elizabeth brought gifts for his children, but Bancroft remained unmoved by yet more tearful pleas. A few days later the Bancrofts departed for London, for encounters with old acquaintances like Thomas Carlyle, William Gladstone, and James Anthony Froude, and new ones such as Edward

Freeman and George Eliot. In July they embarked for America, along with 132 crates, including a Bechstein grand piano, a carriage, and thirty cases of wine. The once poor Worcester charity scholar was coming home determined to live as a gentleman should.

The History

XIII

❦

REFLECTIONS ON THE PAST
AND PRESENT

SEVENTEEN YEARS remained to Bancroft's life after his return to the United States. Fascinated with the future, uncomfortable with present reality, he continued his work and never forgot the past. Always a voracious reader, he found time for recent publications—as relevant to his concerns as John Bach MacMaster's new volumes or as controversial as Henry George's *Progress and Poverty*. Nor did his correspondence slacken, or his fighting spirit—on certain issues he could be as inflexible as always. Almost until the end he enjoyed birthday parties and greetings, moved in society with customary grace and wit, and relished the honors. If the hours devoted to writing and research grew shorter and productivity diminished, his capacity for adjustments remained strong and he found other compensations.

He had outlasted most of his contemporaries and faced a new world. Rambling pleas for stability and certitude reflected growing gaps between wishful thinking and reality. In the face of an incomprehensible present, Bancroft clutched at the unchangeable past in order to make sense of the scenes around him. He still talked of historical laws and assumed that all proceeded as ordered, but found it increasingly difficult to see the operations of providence. The bold certitudes—that the laws were indeed visible—gave way to a quieter faith in their existence.

Discerning readers found him less persuasive than before and critics, blind to the connections between his grand ideas and historical facts, charged that his dogmatic, lofty abstractions did not sustain the narrative. The gulf between theory and reality, they implied, was also evident in his long-standing membership in a party "less advanced in liberal sentiments and less wedded to reform than its opponents." Those critics identified the Whigs and the Republicans, rather than the Democrats, as the torchbearers of national progress. The accusation that he shared responsibility for "the scheming and conscienceless administration of Polk in its outrages upon Mexico and reason" was a reminder that while new issues consumed public attention, the old ones were not forgotten. Bancroft spent his last years trying to set the historical record straight.[1]

Present demands however set their own priorities. To live well into the Gilded Age called for reconsiderations of dogma. Once trust in providence was enough. That trust persisted. But corruption, depravity, faulty government, and wrongheaded legislation weakened its concomitant—faith in the people. Seeking an alternative on which to anchor the national order, Bancroft grasped at the Constitution. Erroneously labeled the great radical all his life, he died the conservative he had been all along, sounding very much like his earliest political allies—the National Republicans of the late 1820s.

The piano, carriage, wine, and crates went to Washington rather than New York for, while still in Berlin, the Bancrofts had decided on a change of residence. They wanted a dignified existence, surrounded by "a circle of friends who are devoted to the culture of truth, think with the freedom of men gifted with reason and patient or even fond of differences of opinion"; and they were more likely to find them in the nation's capital than elsewhere. There, too, Bancroft's position as elder statesman, great historian, and seasoned diplomat would ensure a warm reception. John C. B. Davis purchased for him a handsome residence on H Street, refurbished the apartments, and provided sufficient shelf space to accommodate the great library.[2]

After 1874 the couple divided their time between Washington and the somewhat more rustic cottage in Newport, with its magnificent rose garden. In the fall and winter they relished the international atmosphere of the capital, with its intersecting social circles, the older respectable families as well as those whose wealth was new and dependent on politics. Henry Adams once thought that "Washington stood outside the social pale. No Bostonian had ever gone there," but Bancroft had ceased to consider himself a Bostonian. Washington provided the environment he sought. In the summer, life in a seaside resort compensated for the growing difficulties of travel.[3]

A lengthening list of honors solidified Bancroft's self-esteem. He had long lost count of the societies of which he was a member, but regarded each new token as further proof of hard-earned status. The German emperor conferred upon him the civil Order of Merit; and the Brazilian emperor Don Pedro wished to award him a title (which Bancroft declined). A ship was called the *George Bancroft,* while literary and professional organizations all over the country adopted his name. Chicago and Brooklyn were among the places that boasted a Bancroft Historical Society, in homage to a refined Christian gentleman. Letters from various parts of the country announced the birth of namesakes, little George Bancrofts. His own activities became matters of public curiosity; poems in the newspapers marked his varied occupations. When Robert Louis Stevenson traveled in 1879 to California, Bancroft's *History,* the key explaining the meaning of the country, took up the most space in his meager luggage.[4]

The historian frequently provided books to enrich the Bancroft Literary Association of the town of Bancroft, Iowa. The first recipient of the Aaron and Lucretia Bancroft Scholarship was doing well at Amherst, another testimony to his generosity. And a $10,000 donation in memory of John T. Kirkland enriched the Harvard endowment. Bancroft supported an early Beautify America campaign and aided a Tennessee hotel owner who wanted an appropriate name for his establishment. The black chapter of the Odd Fellows at Newport appealed for a donation, and Bancroft responded. He had less patience with crank and begging letters. Sarah Chandler wanted help with the publication of her book *Sin and Its Benefits;* she never received a reply. Isaac Hughes, eager to send the historian special drinking water, since he was "anxious to have the benefit of [Bancroft's] . . . labor to the last hour," got no response either. Bancroft resented this forthright reminder of his own mortality and was never a believer in quack medication.[5]

Numerous visitors were also evidence of celebrity status. Herman, the butler and valet, who came over from Germany in 1874, presided over dinners and discreetly advised guests on the wines. The Bancrofts always set a handsome table, beautifully decorated with flowers. Expensive china and Tiffany silver added to the splendor, belying Elizabeth's proclaimed preference for simplicity. The fare was a subject of great concern, with some fish and meat imported from New York. Strictly observed decorum nevertheless left the atmosphere relaxed and informal, for Bancroft was not a snob like Henry Adams, whom he liked. Nor did he ever lose interest in people, whether servants or high government officials. They were not equal but of equal interest to him. Hence Bancroft's attention to the problems of his wife's maid, as well as his interest in the occupants of the White House.

Rutherford Hayes, once a student at the Harvard Law School, re-

membered Bancroft's stump oratory and rumors about his private meanness, but also recalled the historian as an interesting speaker. Hayes accepted Bancroft's invitations, sharing the table with judges of the
Supreme Court, senators, and State Department officials. It was a reflection of Bancroft's considerable social skills; Hayes well knew that his
host regarded the outcome of the 1876 election as a violation of the
popular will that robbed Samuel Tilden of the presidency. Even the
critical Henry Adams and his caustic wife found the time well spent.
Cordial relations with the White House continued under Cleveland,
Garfield, and Arthur, who once told a journalist that Presidents were
permitted to dine in the houses of a very select company—at those of
cabinet officers, justices of the Supreme Court, the Vice President, and
Mr. George Bancroft. Later the New York *World* quoted Bancroft to
prove that the Baptists were more committed than other Protestants to
the Reformation—all that with the intention of drawing the Catholic
Irish away from President Arthur, who had antecedents in that sect. But
Bancroft had long ceased to be responsible for the uses of his *History,*
Arthur did not take offense.[6]

Elizabeth became an arbiter of standards and taste, since few matched
her experience in foreign courts. She was also sly enough to make Henry
Adams think her the most intelligent woman in the capital. With some
assurance she told guests that Mrs. Rutherford Hayes was well fitted for
her official position, a remark the President appreciated, for others poked
fun at Lemonade Lucy's drabness, abstinence, and religious zeal. Bright
and attractive, Elizabeth habitually deferred to her outgoing and chatty
"Mr. Bancroft" and happily left the management of their affairs to him.
She shared his anti–women's rights stand and, unlike some of her younger
friends, never felt sorry either for her own position or for that of her sex.
A woman was like "a lily among the thorns," in Bancroft's words, and
even though republican institutions made them "less conspicuous," yet
they were "redeemed" into "the full dignity of [their] nature." Domestic
equality, after all, was more valuable than "an occasional ascendency in
political affairs." Elizabeth had no such aspirations, and while the mysterious maladies that had once kept her away from Berlin in European spas
disappeared, she played her role cheerfully.[7]

In the summer, Washington became uninhabitable, and the Bancrofts escaped its heat, humidity, and dust by moving to Newport. The
transportation of great amounts of luggage, as well as servants, horses,
and two carriages, involved logistical details Bancroft did not relish, and
they became burdensome with the years. For Elizabeth the trip also be-

came more difficult when her health worsened once more. But once the couple were installed in their cottage, the sea air revived her spirits, and they enjoyed the congenial company of Alexander Agassiz, and the less congenial friendship of Thomas Wentworth Higginson. Bancroft rode horseback, tended his gardens, dealt with the voluminous mail, and wrote. Life in Newport had a European tinge, Henry James once noted; business was remote. But the problems of the world would not keep away, and one summer during Bancroft's absence the Washington house was burglarized, silver disappeared, nor did the thrifty thief neglect a piece of ham and several bottles of wine.[8]

The interest in gardening was aesthetic, not a nostalgic longing for a life close to the soil. The historian remembered too well childhood hardships and the uncertain vagaries of nature. Directing a very large staff in Washington and Newport and enjoying the fruits of other people's labor expressed a love for natural beauty hemmed in, shaped, and civilized by the work of man. The gardens also were one more thing to do well, and Bancroft proudly relished compliments for his Washington hyacinths, which bloomed more beautifully than those in public gardens, and for his Newport roses. On the latter's significance he was almost poetic; roses were the reflections of the sun, the air, and the earth, their spotless beauty, exquisite perfume, perfect purity symbols of immortality, which taught "the lesson that the soul is a seed with wings." But he did not accord the same respect for God's creation of weeds; "kill them as fast as they show their heads" was the standing instruction to the gardeners.[9]

An unfriendly journalist would remember in these tranquil days the twists and turns of his political career, "changing his party colored coat with the facility of a harlequin." But Bancroft styled himself "the man of many years [who] can look before and after" sitting under the tree of life, its falling leaves "revealing a clearer vision of the eternal stars." That vision, based on "the large inductions of experience," added "to early intuitions," produced "a clearer conviction of a superior ordering of human affairs and the overruling influence of general laws." Not much changed for this faith-driven optimist except that he had ceased to fret about the evildoers of the world.[10]

The harshness beneath his genial exterior (a quality that a contemporary thought made Bancroft "a good hater both in life and history") remained, leaving the impression that he was always trying to be something he was not. He flattered politicians when there was nothing in it for him till the end of his life, and he was profusely complimentary toward women—at their feet, he once said, he worshiped all his life—

always the practitioner of pleasant deceptions. The "little vanities and frivolities," personal peculiarities, and intolerant demeanor did not escape notice and repelled visitors who expected something else. Utterly inflexible about his historical judgment, convinced that there could be no appeal from his decision, Bancroft sometimes reminded people of a schoolboy released from work, the sage of history and profound philosopher turning into a social punchinello.[11]

"A bilious, melancholic, nervous temperament," Bancroft thought, accounted for his personality. Instances of ill temper, intolerance, and exertion alternated with periods of gloom, introversion, and restlessness that no amount of activity could assuage. But over the years Bancroft had also acquired enough self-control to overcome his own propensities. Methodically he noted the day and hour when he set his watch, recorded riding conditions on Newport beaches, kept strict account of expenses and income, and supervised numerous household details while keeping abreast of scholarly publications. Financial shrewdness combined with thrift and careful management also paid off. The Bancrofts easily weathered a series of recessions and economic downswings by living strictly within an income that permitted leisurely existence, additions to the library, full-time secretaries, and charitable contributions.[12]

Arrogantly Bancroft defied the passing years. Horseback riding provided fresh air and relaxation, and if he was occasionally thrown into a ditch, it was only to rise and be about again. Haunted by fears of mental decay, he hoped to stave off the inevitable decline through vigorous exercise. The diary recommended "find time for exercise or will have to find time for illness." Holding true to that injunction, he was never ill. When a Newport neighbor inquired whether it was prudent to ride at his age, Bancroft replied that it would be imprudent not to.[13]

Yet more and more his thoughts turned to the days in Worcester, the pranks on the river, the wild boy he had been, and the wild man many thought he became in manhood. The lessons of those days, Bancroft assumed, carried him onward. "I was trained to look upon life here as a season for labor," and he never lost that sense. He would not have wished for himself the fate of Prescott, who died soon after the publication of *Philip II,* passing away, Bancroft said, "like a great commander who falls in the hour of victory, when the heat and the contest and the dangers of the day are over." For there were still projects to complete, new ones to begin. Incessant writing and revising were the order of the day. But he also knew his limits. "Being more than four score years old I know the time for my release will come," he wrote to a friend in 1882. "Conscious of being near the shore of eternity I await without impatience and without dread the beckoning of the hand which will summon me to rest." That too had been a lesson learned in childhood.[14]

He did not become a more regular churchgoer, testily maintaining, "I am not an Episcopalian, I am a Congregationalist." When a friend sent a pamphlet listing one hundred reasons for believing in Christ's divinity, Bancroft responded by defining his own infinitely simpler theology, based on belief in God's perfection and by extension in the perfection of all His works. When the Unitarian Club of Boston elected him a member, Bancroft declined. "I was brought up a congregationalist, and am not willing at this time of life to adopt any other name." The forms of outward religion mattered little; faith counted, and that he had always kept.[15]

That faith also sustained his definition of the thinker's role in a democratic society. The preacher, steward of public morals, had always been the man of letters, guardian and mentor of the public mind. Out of politics and untainted by current transient concerns, Bancroft took an Olympian view and felt entitled, on the basis of his own experience, to outline an agenda for other intellectuals. They had to follow popular wisdom (as distinct from class wisdom), "applaud the people," and deal with "the grandeur of simplicity" as opposed to preoccupation with "costly . . . useless and often trivial details," guiding along "the increasing moderation of the American mind." As "heralds of rightful liberty," the intellectuals remained the servants of the masses, dealing with "glorified representations of the infinite." Knowledge was valuable only as it furthered the general good. A democratic republic had no use for aesthetes who removed themselves from the marketplace; scientific achievements, railroads, factories, mechanical inventions, industrialization counted as well as spiritual contributions, for all brought man and nature closer together and furthered the harmony of the universe.[16]

With the Civil War over, Bancroft like many others looked forward to a period of national regeneration when a new spirit of moral purpose would infuse the united nation based on free labor. But promises went unfulfilled and sharp sectional animosities, political corruption, personal shortcomings, and a general malaise made abolition of slavery the only substantial achievement of the carnage. To arrest the sense of degeneracy Bancroft renewed his old calls for a moral revolution, to be led by men of letters fulfilling their duty in a society unfortunately still individualistic. He intended to remind them that the individual suffered from depravity, that events were subordinate to law, and that salvation lay in the belief that "there is something in man greater than himself."[17]

His plea came against a background of growing disillusionment and

discontent. An economic depression hovered over the nation, and renewed cries for reform extended into all fields of human activity. Nothing remained the same. A man born in 1800 knew change, of course. But
after 1870, the pace accelerated and affected more facets of life. As he
gathered materials for his new historical projects, Bancroft noticed the
low esteem in which government was held, the charges of corruption
and bargaining, which bewildered onlookers interpreted as signs that the
traditional rules were giving way. Conflict over economic opportunities,
the expansion of railroads, the trials of agriculture, and the power of
labor created a sense of dislocation to which Bancroft responded in the
remaining years of his life.

Concern with the present had filtered into the tenth volume of the
History, which unfriendly critics called a citizen's breviary. Published in
1874, its subject, the conclusion of peace with Great Britain, focused on
the involvement of European powers in the American struggle, and the
interplay among English conditions, Old World politics, and colonial
fortunes. Although forty years divided the tenth volume from the first,
Bancroft's basic outlook, method, and preconceptions remained intact.
The multilevel narrative, a complicated, subtly drawn, chronologically
arranged framework, served as vehicle for a theory of human development and captured the drama of the past. The message of the tenth
volume had also shaped its predecessors—the dangers to which an individualistic society was peculiarly prone and the obligations of Americans
to rise above their own depravity.[18]

By emphasizing once more the inevitability of historical developments, the volume clarified the limits of human freedom and the extent
of individual achievements. Speculations about paths not taken were irrelevant, the work implied. "It is useless to ask what would have happened if the eternal providence for a moment suspended its rule," for
events always occurred as they were meant to. The divine plan was
inexorable in its unfolding, the product of "the infinite love which
founded all things and the infinite justice which carries all things forward in continuous progression." To people puzzled by their inability to
resolve contemporary problems, this consolation provided the assurance
that, in the end, all would turn out for the best.[19]

Emphasis on historical laws diminished the dangers of depravity and
individualism. Bancroft never made clear what those laws were, or how
they operated, but their axiomatic existence expressed itself in historical
generalizations and illustrative judgments. "The fortunes of a nation are
not under the control of a blind destiny," nor were they necessarily

subject to the vagaries of human nature. "Freedom is of all races and of all nationalities, it is in them all older than bondage and ever rises again ... for the rights of man spring from eternal law ... and by their own indestructibility prove their lineage as the children of omnipotence," which also illustrated the effect of overwhelming forces impinging on human actions.[20]

Had it been otherwise, the outcome might have been dismal indeed, for the volume also fleshed out the instances of human depravity, short-sightedness, or unrestrained individualism. Bancroft noted the greed of states suddenly freed from the imperial yoke, the selfishness of military figures, a pervasive and dangerous "love and exercise of individual liberty," personal interests, profiteering, the ambition and petty desires of small minds, get-rich-quick schemes, and cheating. But what mattered was the growing realization that "for success the liberty of the individual must know how to set to itself bounds." "America had seated anarchy deeply in the very source of legislation," and recovery "lay through humiliation and sorrow." But the "people was superior to its institutions, possessing that vital force which goes before organization and gives to it strength and form." They were ultimately willing to set themselves bounds which, a few years later, culminated in the Constitution.[21]

The *Literary World* considered this just the reminder the nation needed; it lauded the volume for its contribution to the national consciousness. Bancroft had not only provided "the story of events" but also familiarized readers with "the principles, moral and political, involved in the Revolution in all its stages." The work "helps us to know what our country is."[22]

Other critics were less charitable. Among them was the *Historical Magazine,* soon to go out of business, which pronounced Bancroft "a literary coxcomb" who sacrificed worth for effect, writing with "a finical obscurity of style." "Saturated with the droppings of Prussian royalty," the author had wasted forty years on puny volumes destined to molder "among the unused and uncared for curiosities of American historical literature." Friend Henry Adams (privately) thought Bancroft "a compiler ... the subjects he treats deserve scientific analysis and it will be a disgrace to let such a work out as the measure of our national scholarship." The *History* had "proportions but not ... completeness" and never really reached its subject, due to Bancroft's lack of "extraordinary gifts." Had he not decided to write history he would have left no mark on the world. Publicly Adams's commentary was mixed. The volume was improved by the absence of the spirit of Jackson, and time had tempered—"if only slightly"—Bancroft's ardent faith in the "abstract virtues of democracy," but he still "showed the lack of a judicious mind." Too bad, Adams implied, that the book would "inevitably and permanently affect the ultimate judgment of mankind on the great period here described." The review would do no harm, he told Bancroft, since no one would pay it much attention.[23]

Neither Dawson nor Adams received a reply, for as soon as he finished Volume Ten, Bancroft decided to recast the entire work in a more compact form. The contrast between the knowable and glorious past and the uncertain present and future had always enhanced the *History's* popularity; a new edition might aid in resolving the unfolding crisis of conscience and make appropriate reading for the nation's centennial in 1876.

For months Bancroft labored, with Elizabeth's help, comparing his statements with later scholarship, cutting adjectives, and introducing some sobriety. "Simplicity and clearness" were his goals, a response to adverse comment on his tone and phraseology, if not his outlook. A year's work cut the ten volumes down to six, corrected details, but changed no interpretations. The man who for fifty years saw the past as a unity, its forces as constant, and their manifestations as part of an organized whole was not about to alter the structure of the narrative. "Each individual must have his place in the picture, but the background is the history of the race"—by 1876 that background was fixed.[24]

By the time the work was published, the preparations for the hundredth anniversary of the Declaration of Independence were in full swing. As if to counter a growing mood of questioning and doubt, tumultuous celebrations everywhere that year lauded past advances and traced progress in health, education, science, technology, agriculture, and standard of living. Enormous pride in the nation's achievements, graphically presented at the Philadelphia Exhibition, expressed smug contempt for the primitive life of the forefathers and satisfaction in recent changes. If the political demigods of yesteryear compared favorably with the clay-footed mortals of the 1870s, that did not mar the occasion.

The centennial year was also the year of Moody and Sankey's campaign to decrease the population of hell by revivalism; the brand of salvation in Bancroft's Centenary Edition was only a pale version of theirs. But the salvation the *History* had preached since 1834 was an integral part of the finished product. The intellectual foundation on which this many-volumed sermon rested had weathered numerous contradictions and was not to be refashioned in the face of sordid political scandals, fallen hopes, and general uncertainty. On the contrary, a framework that assumed as staunchly as in the past the certainty of providential guidance, the transitory significance of the individual, the progress and immortality of the race, was more in demand than ever.

On the eve of the Civil War Bancroft had examined the document whose anniversary was being celebrated in 1876. In 1860 he was sure that the Declaration of Independence "was steadily prepared in the convictions of all the people just as every spire of grass is impearled by the dews of heaven and assists to reflect the morning sun." This typically Bancroftian construction—a historical generalization illustrated by a metaphor—led to a restatement of democratic philosophy, to prove that "the many are more sagacious, more disinterested, more courageous than the few." This in turn preceded another generalization—that the people "had grown weary of atrophied institutions, and longed to fathom the mystery of public life. Instead of continuing a superstitious reverence for the sceptre and the throne, as the symbols of order, they yearned for a nearer converse with the eternal rules of right as the generative principles of social peace." The chapter's final sentence read, "All the colonies, as though they had been one individual being, felt themselves wounded to the soul when they heard and could no longer doubt that George the Third was hiring foreign mercenaries to reduce them to subjection."[25]

The few who considered this mélange of facts, suppositions, metaphors, insights, and philosophy intolerable were to be disappointed with the new edition. Bancroft's motto was "live and learn," and he styled himself "simply a searcher after truth." But he had long ago learned enough and was certain that he had found the truth. The artistry of the literary conventions, the effort to enliven the action, arouse suspense, and keep the reader's attention, were all legitimate means of communication. Language clothed assumptions; since the latter remained the same, so did the words used to express them. As a result the chapter on the Declaration in Volume Eight reappeared in the fifth volume of the Centenary Edition, virtually unchanged.[26]

On the lower level of the narrative, excisions led to greater precision, without affecting the superstructure. A sentence which in 1834 read that Roger Williams's "wrong had not clouded his accurate understanding, in the capacious recesses of his mind he had revolved the nature of intolerance, and he, and he alone, had arrived at the great principle which is its sole effectual remedy," in 1876 became the more manageable "a fugitive from English persecution, he had revolved the nature of intolerance and had arrived at its only effectual remedy, the sanctity of conscience." But the grand interpretations, such as that "the voice of the majority was the voice of God and the issue of Puritanism was popular sovereignty," remained unaltered.[27]

The success of the edition in sales and receipts proved that Bancroft had not lost his touch and that the public taste remained what it had been in 1834. Younger historians, like Henry Adams and Henry Cabot Lodge, may have had reservations, but the new set sold eighteen thousand copies in 1876 and four years later was still selling at an annual rate of ten thousand. Royalties in the first year of publication alone amounted to $11,500. The fact that the volumes sold well (which did not necessarily mean that they were read) showed their hold on the public. The historical profession had changed, but not the popular passion for what the *History* represented. While that passion did not extend to what Richard Hildreth called "the undress portraits" of American antecedents, neither did it crave "the thin, shining bubble so assiduously blown up by so many windy mouths" (Hildreth's presumed reference to Bancroft and others). Influential and less influential segments of that public were not ready to be told that their ancestors were robbers, racists, or hypocrites, and debunking was not the fashion of the day. To touch "the chord of public feeling with accuracy and power" (Bancroft's words) was a great achievement; and the *History* did so.[28]

No sooner did the Centenary Edition appear than Bancroft started on his next project—a two-volume history of the writing and adoption of the federal Constitution. For many nineteenth-century Americans there was a direct line between 1776, 1781, and 1787. This was the process Bancroft set out to document, presenting the Declaration of Independence, the Articles of Confederation, and the Constitution as progressive steps in the popular willingness to rein in individual liberty.

But this was not the only reason for more books on a subject that had already received serious attention. In 1854 George Ticknor Curtis, no friend of Bancroft's, published his own account, to describe "the foundations on which national liberty and prosperity were then deliberately settled," a sentiment Bancroft in 1876 fully shared, though he thought little of Daniel Webster, to whom Curtis paid homage. Bancroft disagreed even more with Herman von Holst's *Constitutional and Political History of the United States.* Where Bancroft saw unanimity, von Holst found only divisions. The latter sarcastically criticized the Declaration of Independence's dangerously crude theories and lampooned the faith in special dispensations, that "pharisaical self righteousness which is one of the most characteristic traits of the political thought of the masses of the American people." Maintaining the separate identity of thirteen states

within one framework—for Bancroft the great achievement of the constitutional convention—for von Holst outdid the mysteries of the Trinity, by making thirteen one while leaving one thirteen. A whole chapter
in von Holst derided worship of the Constitution and the pitfalls of "a
system of politics based on absolute principles" which led to "idealistic
doctrinarianism and demagogism" and the perversion of democracy "in
the minds of the masses into the equal capacity of all men to decide on
political questions of every kind"—precisely what Bancroft the philosophical democrat had been saying since 1834.[29]

Nor did Bancroft consider sufficient another interpretation of the
Constitution written a decade earlier and dedicated to him "in memory
of old friendship and as a slight homage to genius." Orestes A. Brownson, rejecting "pure individualism and pure socialism," wrote a more
agreeable book, asserting that nations were individuals writ large, that
each realized a providentially given idea—in the case of the United
States, popular sovereignty without despotism and individual freedom
without anarchy. These were Bancroftian slogans, but this "sort of public atonement," while pleasing, was irrelevant to current concerns. The
same was true of Richard Hildreth's account, which treated the Constitution as the victory of conservatives in the struggle between property
and freedom.[30]

Bancroft's purpose was entirely different. In those hard days of growing unemployment, social cleavages, and labor unrest, he wrote to justify
the federal government's do-nothing approach, reaffirming the old
states' rights school and providing it historical legitimation. In 1831
Bancroft had announced his faith in natural laws which controlled the
market, currency, and the price of labor and goods; now as the 1870s
drew to a close he repeated his belief in a self-regulating economy, in the
harmony between labor and capital, and in the equality of opportunities
in a country where, under divine guidance, no one wanted equality of
outcome. While the Yale social scientist William Graham Sumner concluded that complicated public issues could not be "decided by reference
to a general political dogma, or a moral principle or a text of Scripture,"
Bancroft implied that the Constitution certainly embodied the first two
standards and came as close to the third as any human document could.
The answer to problems of intention and meaning, as well as the need
for an infallible guide of conduct, became the focus of his work.[31]

Bancroft's final contribution to national consciousness was the definition of an immutable yardstick by which to judge progress. The very
assumption that such a yardstick was necessary reflected the bewilder-

ment of a thinker who always assumed that everything changed for the better. When the 1870s presented contrary evidence, he responded by demanding more consistent implementation of a government instrument already perfect. The man who had once daringly placed his trust in popular common sense, who had claimed that the voice of the majority was the voice of God, finished his days relying on artificial contrivances to compensate for human shortcomings.

Adopting the language of the day, Bancroft claimed to write the history of the most important and also the final American reform that produced the supreme law of the land, which in turn became the source of stability in a unique society. In the eighteenth century "the principle of individuality" had developed "the most perfect liberty in thought and action" and had produced a community "composed of separate, free and constantly moving atoms, ever in reciprocal action, advancing, receding, crossing, struggling against each other and with each other." Aware of the destructive potential this development entailed, but still supremely individualistic, restless, and risk taking, the Americans found their ultimate safeguard in the constitutional framework.[32]

Bancroft had always stressed the conservative character of American democracy. In its government, "all sufficient powers are so plainly given that there is no need of striving for more by straining the words in which they are granted beyond the plain and natural import." This arrangement satisfied social and individual needs, allowed individualism to reign but hedged it in on all sides. Wide distribution of authority and strict accountability assured respect for individual rights. Therefore, Bancroft noted with satisfaction, "the gates of revolution are shut, and barred and bolted down"; no further upheavals of the European sort need plague the United States.[33]

How did this come to pass? "The wheels of providence" governed the totality of nations as they did individuals "and the centuries move as they are ordered." The divinely ordained process of reform was the product of clashes between the party of the past and the party of the future, between conservatives and radicals. In the 1780s the nationalists and antinationalists, federalists and confederalists, were the identifiable forces; the outcome of their struggles defined the final form of the Constitution. Its authors, great reformers and pragmatists, balanced the desirable against the attainable in a series of compromises that ignored both those who wanted only the status quo and the party of the ideal. Rejecting "a revolt against the past" and impossible attempts to institutionalize the kingdom of heaven on earth, men like James Madison pushed moderate objectives and the people concurred.[34]

This concept structured the volumes around the history of the three factions that shaped the Constitution. Against the background of fluid social and economic conditions in the aftermath of war, Bancroft presented Samuel Adams and Patrick Henry as leaders of an older, outdated radical tradition that refused to move with the times. At the other extreme were Alexander Hamilton and Robert Morris, devoted to far-reaching changes that outdistanced both the possible and the desirable. George Washington and James Madison, the middle-of-the-roaders, resolved the clash between the two extremes and saved the nation.

To sustain this thesis required selective quotation, judicious juggling of the evidence, and, in rare instances, plain distortion. In order to allow for resolution of the dialectic and to buttress his case, Bancroft muted sharp differences and slightly altered the views of the participants. He also imputed a high degree of amicability, resignation, understanding, and acceptance to all concerned. Selectivity and biased documentation that sustained the narrative were legitimate scholarly methods, not falsifications of the record.

A case in point, one among many, was the account of the South Carolina ratification debate. The arguments of both sides involved conflicting interests—fear of oppressive navigation acts, slavery, and friction between the upper counties dominated by Charleston and the lower ones dreading new inequalities. Bancroft allowed various factions to make their cases, but presented those opposed to the Constitution in a less favorable light. Additions to quotations from Rawlins Lowndes informed the reader that this opponent of the Constitution had also opposed the Declaration of Independence, had sought British protection while governor of the colony, and had demanded the maintenance of slavery. He belonged to a group Bancroft dubbed "the malcontents" representing "selfish interests." Its members wanted a worthless paper currency, disliked the North, feared eastern domination, and ascribed mistaken goals to the War for Independence. Yet they too were Americans, amenable to persuasion which the equally reasonable federalists—in this case Cotesworth Pinckney—amply provided. The latter—"that purest spirit of patriotism and union"—carried the day in 1788, when South Carolina ratified the Constitution by a vote of 149 to 73, and the malcontents "promised as good citizens to accept the results."[35]

Selfish "malcontents" were also present in the Virginia debate, ranging from more "moderate" ones, like Richard Henry Lee, to extremists like Patrick Henry, who "exceeded . . . [themselves] in vehemence," raised the specter of emancipation, and threatened an end to paper money. Worst of all, in Bancroft's view, was their demagogic fear of endangered liberties. But they were like a "cavalry that tries in vain to break the ranks of infantry" and the outcome was never in doubt. In Virginia too, the defeated party acquiesced in the decision of the majority, while the victors "were careful not to ruffle their opponents by exultation."[36] Although Bancroft provided plenty of evidence to show how economic and personal interests motivated the views of the federalist leaders, his presentation made them appear moderate and calm; and he ignored the blatantly antidemocratic opinions of some. To show that Hamilton was on the right track, Bancroft quoted the *Federalist Papers* selectively and toned down the New Yorker's broad vision of a national government, thus bringing him much closer in line with the final outcome.

Admittedly "a friend to the protection of manufacturers," Hamilton nonetheless argued that by supporting the Constitution the states protected themselves against excessive tariffs. He battled "the fiercest resistance that selfish interests could organize." Internal political squabbles racked New York, which stood to gain the most from an efficient government. But while the leaders fought, "all the while the people of the state were drifting toward union." The opponents of the Constitution published "inflammatory tracts," while its defenders "commented with severe wisdom." Clinton, the anticonstitutionalist, subsequently moderated his views, while Hamilton, miraculously, became almost a proponent of states' rights.[37]

While Bancroft documented antifederalist selfishness, he handled diplomatically less creditable issues that favored the federalist arguments—as in the case of Shays's rebellion. A few paragraphs expressed Bancroft's sympathy with the suffering farmers but also his satisfaction that order was ultimately maintained. Greedy lawyers and barbarous indebtedness laws drove naturally law-abiding people to the verge of revolt. But the "real causes" of this insurrection were the failures of Massachusetts and of the central government to meet their obligations. The farmers took to arms not because the state was too weak to enforce its authority but because Congress had not paid its debts. The text did not mention Samuel Adams's suggestion of sharp retaliation or the fears the insurrection aroused everywhere or contemporary accounts that ascribed the outbreak to an overly democratic society with a weak executive and a citizenry contemptuous of authority. Such evidence might have cast doubt on the assertion that "by calm meditation and friendly councils" the "negation of the self" led to triumph over "a conflict of interests, passions, hesitancies and wills."[38]

Bancroft devoted the final chapters to the meaning of the Constitution in light of its history. Since he was not a lawyer, he confined himself to general judgments in favor of limited government, substantive states' rights and "rigid consistency"—as opposed to "craving after untried experiments." Above all, he reminded his readers they lived under a conservative arrangement. "America, being charged with the preservation of liberty, has the most conservative polity in the world, both in its government and in its people," and nothing should change that. Specifically the Constitution explicitly denied both the state and federal governments the right to issue paper money. The protection of domestic manufacturers by imposts was always incidental to raising revenue. The Supreme Court was subordinate to the Constitution, and its opinions, when at variance, were void. Bancroft interpreted restrictively the controversial meaning of "the general welfare" clause, and had little to say on the delicate balances between the local and central governments, except to emphasize how essential they were.[39]

Issues of the post–Civil War era fell outside the scope of the volume, but Bancroft took a stand on a number of controversies. The expansion of federal power during the war was a necessary aberration not to extend into peacetime. The Constitution did not sanction a third term for Grant, a possible step toward a monarchy, subverting the republic. Nor did the document legitimate expansion beyond reasonable geographical borders; Cuba and Santo Domingo's "tropical influences" were alien to the national heritage. Bancroft, who had once lauded the United States as the best poor man's country, now wished to exclude the Chinese, who did not conform to existing patterns. Maintenance of the Constitution required a community of will, shared values, and beliefs. While Bancroft believed that Congress had no right to legislate on religious opinions, it could deal with practices subversive of the social order—such as polygamy. The Mormons were free to believe what they wished, but not to practice their faith.[40]

When a New York journalist inquired whether the Constitution required any changes, Bancroft replied unequivocally: "I know of none, if any change is needed it is in ourselves that we may more and more respect that body of primal law," the mainstay of the republican order. The historian had come a long way since the Preface to the first volume of the *History* had lauded the Constitution for being "not a dead letter, unalterably fixed," but "an instrument with the capacity for improvement, adopting whatever changes time and the public will may require, and safe from decay, so long as that will retains its energy." By 1882, convinced that the public will no longer functioned, Bancroft urged society to conform to the document, without tailoring it to current needs. The philosophical democrat ended his intellectual odyssey a fervent upholder of institutions to guide sinful man and society. In the America of the 1880s, trust in "the people" was a dangerous gamble.[41]

Nothing else would do in a period which held politicians in low esteem, when both parties engaged in internecine warfare rather than furthering the public's good, and appeals to principle had given way to passionate harangues catering to prejudices. Presidents were no longer men of vision but weak partisans, and Congress was the scene of buffoonery, selfishness, and narrow visions. Labor unions with large memberships had replaced the pliable Workingmen Bancroft remembered, while the cities he had once described as extended villages had become teeming urban centers.

Some reviewers in 1882 shared his hope that the Constitution would be the mainstay of social order. One magazine approved, although chiding Bancroft for ignoring secondary sources—by stressing the trees, the historian obscured the forest and rhetoric replaced instruction. The *Literary World* credited his historical innovations but snidely suggested that one of his secretaries wrote them up. *Harper's* found minor faults, yet praised the author's "gentler and more urbane judgments of men and motives" that left him "more chastened in his estimates of conflicting political principles." The volumes' "sedateness and elevation of thought, and a ripeness and mellowness of tone" seemed a marked improvement.[42]

Other readers were less impressed and accepted neither his remedies nor his account of the past. Henry Cabot Lodge took the historian to task for his "Jeffersonian republicanism," and for failing to show how "narrow unreasonable and averse to the difficult work of reconstruction" the demoralized and confused nation was in 1782. By fixing his eyes "on the lofty and far seeing views of the comparatively small minority, led by the illustrious handful of men who thought continentally," Bancroft could say of 1787 "one desire prevailed for a closer connection, one belief that the only opportunity for its creation had come." Lodge by contrast agreed with John Adams, who said that "the constitution was extorted from the grinding necessity of a reluctant people." Henry Adams found Bancroft unreadable, although the appendices were vastly entertaining.[43]

Bancroft did not respond, for no sooner were the volumes out than he sat down once more to revise the entire *History*. This would be "the Author's Last Revision" because—at the age of eighty-two—he still hoped to bring the narrative down to the originally promised date, 1834.

A long correspondence with historians led to corrections of detail; slaughtered adjectives and condensations reduced the twelve books to six. Rearrangements and emendations lessened the eulogistic tone of the original, and judgment of controversial figures, among them the revolutionary generals, mellowed. But if the style changed slightly, the theory did not. Even with prose muted, no one could mistake the authorship, since Bancroft had no intention of abandoning his early self-imposed criteria. He never doubted "the right of history to pronounce opinions" even if he was content "to leave events as they sweep onward to speak their own condemnation and praise." Yet events of course never spoke for themselves, they spoke through the author, and the condemnation and praise were his, as they had been through all the previous editions and revisions.[44]

Devotion to setting the record straight, as well as the feeling that younger historians were resurrecting buried myths, drove Bancroft on. Failing eyesight and shorter working hours slowed down the work but did not quench the desire to appear before the public with yet another essay to clinch an argument once and for all. The *Magazine of American History* published an article to prove the continuity of democratic instincts in Virginian colonial history, and a description of an incident in the life of Alexander Hamilton revealed that friendship with Henry Cabot Lodge (Hamilton's biographer) had not softened Bancroft's hostilities. For the *Ledger* there were short pieces on Washington, whose glory remained untarnished and who, Bancroft still maintained, "all his life trod near the most advanced ideas." The *Century* printed papers on Henry Clay and John Adams, and other publications too enhanced their moral and intellectual tone with his writings.[45]

Once disputes over details had aroused Bancroft's passion; in these days of greater tranquillity only monetary policies were worrisome enough to call for forceful public statements. In an appropriate ending to a public career that began with an assault on the United States Bank, Bancroft in 1883 set out to combat dangerous divergences from the natural laws of economics. While he had long ceased to view corporations as bastions of aristocratic greed and had watched the postwar accumulation of wealth in a few hands with remarkable complacency, his hard-money policies remained the same. "Return to specie payment" was his last political slogan; "until that event occurs our glorious constitution lies bleeding." Nothing short of a holy war was involved when the Supreme Court, regrettably, rendered incorrect judgments upon "the truths of political and economic sciences."[46]

The third legal tender case that aroused Bancroft to action dealt with the right of Congress to empower the secretary of the Treasury to issue United States notes and make them legal tender. Several decisions in the 1870s declared such wartime measures valid. The question raised by *Juillard* v. *Greenman* with which Bancroft dealt enlarged the scope of the debate. Could notes issued in time of war be redeemed in gold by the Treasury, and when reissued under the acts of 1878 constitutionally be legal tender in payment of private debts? Relying upon John Marshall's concept of the implied powers, the Supreme Court ruled that Congress could issue paper currency and argued that the prohibition against the emission of bills of credit and against making anything but gold and silver legal tender applied only to the states. Under its power to borrow, Congress had broad authority to establish a national currency in paper or in coin.

That judgment took the historian by surprise. He had been watching the case attentively and was present while *Juillard* v. *Greenman* was being argued. Dinner with the chief justice the night before the decision convinced Bancroft that the outcome would coincide with his views. The volumes on the Constitution, he thought, provided all the historical ammunition necessary to steer the Court in the right direction. When it turned out otherwise, Bancroft blamed "prepossession and pride of opinion." A letter to the chief justice informed the Court of his intention to combat the decision in public—"in this I am sure you and your associates know how loyal I have always been to the Supreme Court."[47]

The *Plea for the Constitution, Wounded in the House of Its Guardians* was a cry on behalf of a world that no longer existed. Had it been written fifty years earlier the Democrats would have turned it into an effective campaign document; in 1886 its terminology and arguments were out of date. Trying to prove that "the immortal framers" intended to withhold from the federal government the power to emit the promise of money as legal tender, Bancroft used the history of colonial currency, the opinions of Washington, Madison, Oliver Ellsworth, and others, as well as the records of the Philadelphia convention, to prove that the Supreme Court indulged "in the language of revolution" when it asserted that "the United States has powers as a sovereign government." "At home we are states in union," Bancroft cried, and the government had only those powers delegated to it. The decision was "in flagrant antagonism to the constitution of the United States" and a threat to "free institutions and well defined government throughout the world." The United States was a capitalist, not a socialist country, made up of the industrious classes, poor and rich, as distinguished from speculators and visionaries, whom the Supreme Court seemed to back. The Court also violated the inherent moral order of the universe that governed relations between money and labor. "I am pleading the cause of industry, the cause of labor, the cause of the poor," Bancroft continued in the vein of his now forgotten stump oratory, "for the welfare of society, in which the interests of various classes need not clash." The decision was unconstitutional in the most profound sense, "the candle must be lighted every time at [that] primal light which must be observed in vestal purity." The Constitution was kin to Newton's law of gravity, valid not because Sir Isaac pronounced it, but because it was true. Both expressed "that superior ordering of human affairs and the overruling influence of general laws."[48]

He swayed neither the Court nor the public. In 1886 the needs of the American economy were different, and at least one lawyer produced a counterargument dismissing much of Bancroft's evidence as irrelevant. To a few kind friends identification of hard-money policies with the essence of democracy was unanswerable, compact, logical and conclusive, the expression of a master who recalled the nation to the simplicity of truth, and the sole safety of righteous dealings. But the case was determined, and Bancroft knew it. In what remained of his life he turned once more to history—safer, less controversial, and with consequences more durable than the work of such mortals as the justices of the Supreme Court.[49]

Private sorrows and family difficulties in the last years of Bancroft's life marred his immersion in the past. The death of brother Tom at the age of ninety-two was another reminder of mortality; for years Bancroft had cared for his older sibling, albeit at a distance, sending money and books for this one son of Aaron Bancroft who never learned to fend for himself. Of his sisters, only Lucretia remained, and she was far away in Europe, supervising her niece's children, leading a wandering existence, separated from her husband and relying on Bancroft's generosity, in her case freely given. The widowed John continued to drift from occupation to occupation, also dependent on his father for financial help. The only time he showed some sense, Bancroft thought, was in the choice of his second wife. Hester Jones, a teacher, a more forceful and determined woman than Louisa, took good care of Wilder and Pauline, and managed a husband who had never been able to manage himself. Bancroft enjoyed the grandchildren's visits in Newport and Washington, and occasionally traveled to Milton, where they lived.

George, Jr., remained a source of endless trials. When his daughters needed dowries, he turned to his father, who had lost none of his antagonism toward the younger son. Sarah married Jules Rousillon, a respectable if grasping French bureaucrat, who also expected money from a rich grandfather-in-law. The younger daughter, Suzanne, was about to contract an unsuitable marriage, and for once father and grandfather agreed—the marriage never took place. In 1884 she arrived in Washington. Melting away Bancroft's suspicions, she became a close companion, accompanying him everywhere, as adept with housekeeping tasks as in presiding over formal occasions. The introduction of this accomplished and pretty young woman to society was a success, and the delighted grandfather wrote to friends that "a sunbeam has entered my window," marveling how his incompetent and bungling son could be the father to such perfection. Her uncle John thought otherwise; his children disliked Suzanne, and one unwelcome aspect of her arrival was yet another quarrel between Bancroft and his older son. Meanwhile Elizabeth's health deteriorated; frequently indisposed, she lingered in her bedroom, heavily dosed with drugs, unable to sleep at night, an invalid till the end of her life.[50]

While Suzanne flourished and Elizabeth's life was ebbing away, George, Jr.'s, reached a low point. He had been drinking heavily and became violent. His disorderly behavior prompted French relatives to place him in a mental institution. George considered himself eminently sane, interpreted this institutionalization as a plot, and assumed that his father could secure his release. This Bancroft refused to do, nor would he provide further funds in answer to George's raving letters. But he did supervise the French property and for five years dealt with his son's debts and bills, while leaving the correspondence with George to his secretaries.[51]

In February 1886 Elizabeth's situation worsened, and on March 15 she died, leaving her husband alone after forty-eight years of marriage. Her "perfect acceptance of the divine ordering" and the "holy death scene" which attended her demise soothed and pacified the distraught husband, who prided himself on his total acceptance of "the grand laws of nature." Letters of condolence were a further reminder of his loss; Varina Davis affectionately recalled the happier days of antebellum Washington, while others stressed Elizabeth's womanly virtues and the role she played in her husband's life. With Sandy's help, Bancroft made preparations for interment in Worcester, with a special car reserved for the funeral party. Elizabeth was buried in the quiet rural cemetery where so many of Bancroft's relatives rested, among them his first wife, Sarah, and his daughters, Louisa and Susan Jackson. His own remains would join them.[52]

In Washington life became more subdued. For a year and a half Suzanne remained at home to keep Bancroft company, but then married Charles Carroll, her grandfather settling a handsome dowry and showing the generosity he never extended to her father. Bancroft now overcame his anti-Catholic scruples, for Carroll was a papist—but an acceptable one, with the proper lineage and money. To have a granddaughter marry into one of Maryland's most illustrious families, with a signer of the Declaration of Independence among its members (although a bastard—which Bancroft did not know), was the kind of social status he craved. Suzanne's departure left a void, and for a while only the trusted Herman remained to look after him, but the house soon filled up again when John and his family moved to Washington. In spite of his still vigorous constitution, Bancroft aged—"I find I am growing very old," he noted in his diary, "and must begin to take farewell of the world."[53]

Such gloomy thoughts were not in character for the bustling old man, whose relish for life remained unabated. There was much to enjoy, for honors and adulation came his way from friends, fellow historians, visiting dignitaries, and humble folk. Bancroft could not attend the unveiling of his portrait at Cornell University, but Moses Coit Tyler sent a full account of the ceremony. Less welcome was the rising crime rate. A series of burglaries in Washington and Newport, in the course of which plate and clothing disappeared, was a sign of the times, but the losses were bearable. More difficult to explain was the suicide of Clover Adams (a relative by marriage), although Bancroft had by now learned to accept death with equanimity. A drawing comparing Bancroft to a thriving tree sent by a group of children from Florence, Alabama, was an apt description of the gray-haired and white-bearded gentleman seen riding daily along the Potomac River.[54]

Curiosity about Worcester and a desire to revisit the graveyard where his body would someday rest drove Bancroft to his hometown. Except for a short visit at the time of Elizabeth's funeral, Bancroft had neglected the place of his birth for forty years. Few who had once been his playmates now remained. But everyone knew the great historian, and his arrival became an occasion for yet another celebration. Bancroft attended a session of the American Antiquarian Society of which his father had been a founder, saw a new Free Public Library, and on Main Street revisited the family's last home. Old Isaiah Thomas's house still stood, as did the congregational society building where Aaron Bancroft preached.

Even the pillory remained in place, and Bancroft recalled how as a child he had seen a man punished for blasphemy. When the elderly and by now stooped gentleman appeared at a concert of the Worcester County Musical Association, his presence brought a standing ovation. The city had changed enormously; a growing population and new factories effaced the sleepy New England village Bancroft recalled. All for the good, he told his hosts, the late difficulties notwithstanding; the library showed the increasing intelligence of the people, industry meant more jobs and livelihood, and no one suffered anymore for religious doctrines.

The American mind had become more moderate, Bancroft thought, as he embarked on yet another project—the history of the James K. Polk administration. Few issues were more heatedly debated, in the course of his lifetime, than the annexation of Texas and the Mexican War, or were more momentous for the nation's future. Most members of the generation who were directly involved were dead, but Bancroft thought that the issues they grappled with demanded a fairer assessment. In order to provide one, he began an extensive correspondence with Mrs. James Polk and his old friend J. G. Harris. The final words could not be left to Ben. Perley Poore, who charged that Polk was fraudulently elected; or to Abby Sage Richardson, who called the Mexican struggle a war of conquest; or to professional historians likes James Schouler, assembling evidence to prove "a lying instigation," "a palpable fraud," the "signal triumph for slave propagation" in the addition of Texas to the Union. Schouler also had sharp words to say on the score of "the rapacity of our annexationists," to Bancroft gross misrepresentations.[55]

Invitations from Tennessee encouraged the undertaking, and Bancroft journeyed to Nashville to examine the material preserved in the former President's house. Well received, he gloried in attention and bestowed diplomatic compliments everywhere—there is no more North and South, he told his hosts, we are all one people. At Fisk the black students were asked "to rise in the dignity of [their] souls," while the local historical society heard Andrew Jackson placed next only to George Washington in national importance. In one newspaper interview Bancroft claimed to have gained Polk the presidential nomination at the Baltimore convention, which few believed. But it did not matter. This stately and dignified celebrity made good copy, and for a week the state's newspapers recorded his excursion.[56]

The result was another mass of notes and more Polk documents, including the President's diary. For a while Bancroft worked hard, and even reread back issues of the *Bay State Democrat* to refresh his memory.

Those events seemed even more important than the Civil War. The North won in 1865 (Bancroft thought) largely because of steps he and Polk had taken back in 1846, and the nation ought to appreciate their achievements.[57]

Nothing came of this project, however, except revision of an article in *Appleton's Cyclopedia,* which called the period of Polk's administration "perhaps the greatest in our national history, certainly one of the greatest." A host of other projects also petered out—including a Shakespeare biography and an essay on John Milton, one of those heralds of rightful liberty. Bancroft's last published book was the once aborted Martin Van Buren campaign biography, which appeared in 1889, bringing him little fame and even less income. The work was what it had been at the time of its writing—a hastily assembled document, better left forgotten.[58]

That Bancroft thought otherwise was yet another testimonial to his efforts to square the record with posterity. The current generation needed reminders of "those days of vehement conflict between the power of the people and interests embodied against that power," when principled, moderate, frank, and public-spirited men like Van Buren (and himself) were in office, and their election (later interpretations notwithstanding) "seemed friendly to the harmony and perpetuity of the union." An account of the 1837 depression blamed "the American paper system" for all its hardships, while the narrative concentrated on rehashing the battles against monopolies, moneyed institutions, European aristocratic codes, favoritism, and legislative interference. Several swipes at Henry Clay also showed that Bancroft's loyalties remained intact.[59]

But in 1889 the Whig Party was dead and buried, the Democracy was a new alignment, and few cared to read this antiquated political eulogy. Its cool reception was a disappointment the author blamed on his publishers and insufficient advertising, not understanding that readers just did not care.

More consequential and disturbing were changes in the discipline of history, moving away from what it had been in the days of Sparks, Irving, and Prescott. Bancroft did not grasp what the new historians were up to in their vaunted comparison between history and science, their stress on methods, exactness, accuracy, and training. None of this, he thought, was new; he had been calling history a science as far back as anyone could remember. And as for accuracy and exactness, that too had been his goal, even if footnotes sometimes floundered and quotations were not as precise as Herbert Baxter Adams liked. He appreciated the younger men's stress on training and scholarly endeavor, but these, while valuable, were always of secondary importance. What mattered was experience, live acquaintance with the affairs of men, firsthand contact with the conduct of the state, which no seminar could teach. And all that precision and accuracy resulted only in dry and boring books that no one, including himself, enjoyed.[60]

In a belated effort of recognition, the two-year-old American Historical Association elected Bancroft its president in 1885, extending homage to a man the rest of the country (if not all of its historians) considered the dean of the profession. When he rose to address its meeting, the mixed audience he faced reflected the state of the craft, for in addition to historians, university teachers, and other scholars, government officials, church leaders, and the curious filled the hall. They heard what they expected—a philosophical disquisition on the nature of American history and the makings of a free society, with praise for the conservative constitutional safeguards that would keep it so. This was philosophical history in action—the broad sweep, the grand generalization, the musings of an old man on the past. The Adamses and Franklin Jamesons snickered. But the audience was receptive for the reassurance of the message and its stately tone.

The relevance of that message receded with the years, and objections to his style downgraded Bancroft's historical standing. His declining reputation reflected the professionalization of the discipline, the vagaries of fashion, and, most important, the shifting self-image of Americans. In a sense Bancroft became the victim of his own success, forever wrongly identified with a Whiggish interpretation of history that celebrated the progressive march of liberty without bemoaning the fate of the losers. His work became first a classic that everyone knew about but none read, and ultimately a historical document, revealing the supposed delusions of a century that found the *History* palatable. Ideological changes also shoved Bancroft aside; few bothered to inquire what he had to say, since his conclusions seemed so obvious; and as those conclusions became unacceptable, so did the volumes that embodied them.

Yet the *History* remains full of meaning and content. It was one of the first to reconstruct the past from the bottom up, and its author brilliantly combined detailed analysis with a multilayered narrative structure that captured both the immediate and long-range meaning of events. The historian in effect tackled problems confronting any Americans curious about their antecedents. All this was ignored by newer schools of scholars who prided themselves on having avoided all of his mistakes, only to substitute some glaring ones of their own, but ones more in tune with the times.[61]

Visitors to H Street after 1889 noted that the historian often confused his facts, forgot the identity of his callers, and drifted off in the middle of conversation. Senator George F. Hoar of Massachusetts enjoyed a chat about history, Aaron Bancroft, and Unitarian theology, but after a while realized that the old man had forgotten his visitor's name. While work continued as before, keeping the secretaries occupied with correspondence, hours devoted to jottings on Cornwallis, Napoleon, Talleyrand, and Shakespeare grew shorter. Robert Winthrop came from Boston only to find Bancroft thinking that he was talking to Winthrop's long-dead brother Francis, also a member of the Harvard class of 1817. In the fall of 1890, after his last trip to Newport, Bancroft returned to Washington with a persistent cold that no amount of medication (in which he did not believe) or exercise (in which he did) could cure. Doctors began to frequent the house that winter, while the patient joked with his son, chafed at the confinement, and resigned himself to fate. On January 15, 1891, he lost consciousness, dying two days later. In accordance with his wishes, John took his father's body for interment in Worcester.[62]

Bancroft would have enjoyed what followed. President Benjamin Harrison ordered all the flags in the capital to fly at half-mast during the funeral, and the cities through which the cortege passed would do the same. A memorial service at St. John's church, opposite the White House, attracted the President and most of the cabinet, justices of the Supreme Court, members of the diplomatic corps, as well as army and navy officers, senators and congressmen, and representatives of scholarly societies. No remarks or eulogies were heard, Bancroft having left strict instructions on that score. As the choir sang, Chief Justice Melville W. Fuller, Justice Stephen J. Field, Admiral Rogers, and Ainsworth Spofford of the Library of Congress, among others, bore the casket out of the church. Even the German Kaiser remembered to send a wreath. It was just this kind of solemn pomp Bancroft relished, with its blatant reminders of mortality, and the satisfaction of survival.

"The nations of the civilized world mourn the death of Bancroft without having to ask each other who he was," one editorial said, while the New York Sun's long article described his crowded life and great achievements. The Independent called him the creator of American historical literature, and newspapers all over the nation, as well as in Europe, carried the news of his death. In faraway Cairo, the major Egyptian weekly noted his passing.[63]

In 1899 a bill in the House of Representatives would have set up a bronze statue in his memory. Referred to the Committee of the Library, it died a quiet death. Bancroft would have approved—the less the government did the better. And his proper monuments, he liked to think, were the state of California and the *History*. But another development, years later, would have pleased him immensely. In 1965 a new Polaris submarine was named in honor of the former secretary of the navy. The destructive capacity of this mighty engine would have astounded the not always pacific Bancroft, but he would have approved. That the United States had to be strong enough and remain what God had intended her to be, the one shining beacon of freedom in the world, was one of his cherished beliefs.[64]

A NOTE ON THE SOURCES

George Bancroft always knew that he would become a subject of curiosity to future scholars. Frugal and methodical, he saved all his papers and was also honest enough not to dispose of embarrassing documents. Late in life he went to the trouble of arranging his correspondence and filling in some gaps. The result is a voluminous record of a long and varied life, ranging from important diplomatic and political dispatches to food, clothing, and gardening bills. At various stages of his life he also kept a diary, and guest and legation books record the range of his other occupations. Bancroft's widespread connections also put him in contact with many important figures of nineteenth-century American history, and as a result most major American libraries contain some of his letters. The Historical Society of Pennsylvania, the Library Company of Philadelphia, the Phillips Exeter Academy in New Hampshire, the Maryland Historical Society, as well as the American Antiquarian Society in Worcester, are among the institutions possessing collections that throw light on various facets of Bancroft's life. The Bancroft-Bliss papers, as well as the papers of Andrew Johnson, in the Library of Congress provide additional documentation.

The bulk of the material related to Bancroft's life is divided among the Massachusetts Historical Society, the New York Public Library, Cornell University Library, and, to a lesser extent, the Harvard University Archives. Unless otherwise noted, the material cited in the notes is located at the Massachusetts Historical Society.

The most important published collections of documents are Mark Anthony de Wolfe Howe, *The Life and Letters of George Bancroft*, 2 vols. (New York, 1908); John Spencer Bassett, ed., "The Correspondence of George Bancroft and Jared Sparks," *Smith College Studies in History*, 2 (January 1917); Worthington C. Ford, ed., "The Correspondence of George Bancroft and Martin Van Buren," Massachusetts Historical Society, *Proceedings*, 62 (January 1909). Lists of Bancroft's published writings can be found in Robert H. Canary, *George Bancroft* (New York, 1974), 133–135, and in Russel B. Nye, *George Bancroft, Brahmin*

Rebel (New York, 1944), from which this study departs in many ways.
  The following abbreviations have been used in annotation:

CUA—Cornell University Archives
HUA—Harvard University Archives
MHS—Massachusetts Historical Society
NYPL—New York Public Library Manuscripts Collection
CUMR—Cornell University Microfilm Reels

SOURCE NOTES

Foreword

1. George S. Boutwell, *Reminiscences of Sixty Years in Public Affairs* (New York, 1902), 249; Gordon Milne, *George William Curtis* (Bloomington, Ind., 1956), 61; Donald Emerson, *Richard Hildreth,* (Baltimore, 1946), 116.
2. N. P. Trist to George Bancroft, September 30, 1840.
3. *Hampshire Gazette,* October 8, 1834; George William Curtis, *Orations and Addresses* (New York, 1894), I, 327; George Bancroft, *History of the United States* (Boston, 1866), IX, 258, 500.
4. R.W.B. Lewis, *The American Adam* (Chicago, 1958), 1; John Hildebidle, *Thoreau* (Cambridge, Mass., 1983), 12, 142; Bancroft, *History,* IX, 257, 473.
5. George Bancroft, "Williamstown Oration, 1835," *Literary and Historical Miscellanies* (New York, 1855), 434.
6. George Bancroft, *History of the United States* (Boston, 1866), VIII, 4th edition, 119.
7. Bancroft, *Miscellanies,* 501–502.
8. Bancroft, *History,* VIII, 116; "Progress of Mankind, 1854," *Miscellanies,* 505–506; George Bancroft, *History of the Formation of the Constitution* (New York, 1883), II, 366; George Bancroft to Edward Everett, December 29, 1834.

I. *The Minister's Son*

1. George Bancroft to Samuel A. Eliot, September 24, 1822; Bancroft, Ship Diary, August 2, 1822. On the encounter with Byron and Goethe, see Bancroft, Diary, October 12, 13, 1819, May 21, 22, 1822; George Bancroft to Samuel A. Eliot, May 29, 1822.
2. George Bancroft to Andrews Norton, September 18, 1822.
3. Franklin P. Rice, ed., "Town records of Worcester for the year 1783," *Collections of the Worcester Society of Antiquity,* 4 (1882); Alonzo Hill, *Dis-*

course Delivered at the Interment of the Reverend Aaron Bancroft (Worcester, 1839); Aaron Bancroft, *Sermon at Worcester at the Termination of Fifty Years in the Ministry, January 31, 1836* (Worcester, 1836).

4. See William Lincoln, *History of Worcester* (Worcester, 1862); Caleb A. Wall, *Reminiscences of Worcester* (Worcester, 1877); Franklin P. Rice, *The Worcester Book, Diary of Noteworthy Events* (Worcester, 1884).

5. Population figures are in Lincoln, *History of Worcester,* 259.

6. Charles W. Akers, *Called Unto Liberty: A Life of Jonathan Mayhew 1720–1766* (Cambridge, Mass., 1964), 41–42; Elam Smalley, *The Worcester Pulpit* (Boston, 1851), 63–64; W. S. Barton, *Epitaphs from the Cemetery of Worcester Common* (Worcester, n.d.).

7. Lincoln, *History of Worcester,* 166–167. See also Samuel A. Eliot, *Heralds of a Liberal Faith* (Boston, 1910), II, 20–31; Samuel S. Green, *Gleanings from the Sources of History of the Second Parish* (Worcester, 1883); and "Beginnings of the Second Parish," *Proceedings of the Worcester Society of Antiquity,* 16 (1899); Smalley, *Worcester Pulpit,* 226–249.

8. Eliot, *Heralds of a Liberal Faith,* I, 131–140.

9. Lincoln, *History of Worcester,* 157–158, 184.

10. Seymour Van Dyken, *Samuel Willard* (Grand Rapids, Mich., 1972), 101; Christopher Columbus Baldwin, *Diary 1829–1835* (Worcester, 1901), 176.

11. For a fuller exposition, see Aaron Bancroft, *The Doctrine of Immortality* (Worcester, 1819); *Nature and Worth of Christian Liberty* (Worcester, 1816); *The Leaf as an Emblem of Human Life* (Worcester, 1818).

12. Aaron Bancroft, *Sermon Preached Before the Grand Lodge of Free and Accepted Masons* (Worcester, 1793); *Sermon Preached Before the Worcester Auxiliary Society for Meliorating the Condition of the Jews* (Worcester, 1824); "The Office of Reason in the Concern of Religion," *The Liberal Preacher,* 1, (1828), 9–18.

13. Van Dyken, *Willard,* 114, quoting from Samuel Willard, *Compleat Body of Divinity.*

14. Wall, *Reminiscences of Worcester,* 131–143; Lincoln, *History of Worcester,* 166–167. Madame Salisbury was difficult to satisfy and the first parish dearly wished that she had joined her husband in the second. Eventually she became a Baptist.

15. Horace Daniel, ed., "Letter of Lucretia Chandler to Her Daughter," *Proceedings of the American Antiquarian Society,* 14 (1900). See also "Sketch of the Chandler Family in Worcester," *Proceedings of the Worcester Society of Antiquity,* 19 (1903); Poem of George Henry Davis, March 12, 1862, CUMR; Lucretia Farnum to George Bancroft, Dec. 12, 1876; George Bancroft to Oliver Wendell Holmes, January 19, 1885, in Mark A. de Wolfe Howe, *The Life and Letters of George Bancroft* (New York, 1908), II, 304.

16. For the parental influence, see letters exchanged between Eliza, Lucretia, and George later in their lives, CUMR. George Bancroft to William B. Sprague, January 28, 1863, reprinted in William B. Sprague, *Annals of the American Unitarian Pulpit* (New York, 1865), VIII, 138–140.

17. Lucretia Bancroft to George Bancroft, August (n.d.), 1822; Daniel, ed., "Letter of Lucretia Chandler to Her Daughter."

18. Lincoln, *History of Worcester*, 166–174; Wall, *Reminiscences of Worcester*, 131–143. At one time Bancroft even preached at the Brattle Street Church. Aaron Bancroft to Timothy Newell, April 16, 1784, Smith-Carter papers, MHS; Baldwin, *Diary*, 240, 278.

19. The published sermons collected in book form were Bancroft's contribution to the controversy surrounding the English Unitarian Thomas Belsham's pamphlet on the history of American Unitarianism, which accused the heralds of the new faith of trimming their views for self-protection.

20. *American Antiquarian Society Transactions*, 1 (1820), 30, reprinted the petitions, list of signatures, committee accounts of activities in New England; Nathaniel Paine, *An Account of the American Antiquarian Society* (Worcester, 1876).

21. Aaron Bancroft, *Sermon at Worcester* (Worcester, 1836), 32–33.

22. Ellery B. Crane, "Shays' Rebellion," *Proceedings of the Worcester Society of Antiquity* (1881); Hill, *Discourse*, 15; *Historical Magazine*, 6 (May 1862), 158; Smalley, *Worcester Pulpit*, 241.

23. Aaron Bancroft, "Lessons from Nature," May 25, 1828, in Smalley, *Worcester Pulpit*, 266.

24. Aaron Bancroft, *An Essay on the Life of George Washington* (Worcester, 1807), Preface and 527–532. Judging Marshall's work to be too expensive and complicated "for the unlettered portion of the community," Bancroft designed his to be a model not only for the less educated classes but also for their political leaders. The same themes informed Bancroft's eulogy on Washington, delivered February 22, 1800.

25. For general interpretations of ministerial responses, see Donald M. Scott, *From Office to Profession* (Philadelphia, 1978); Alan E. Heimert, *Religion and the American Mind* (Cambridge, Mass., 1966).

26. Aaron Bancroft, "Sermon, The Office of Reason in the Concerns of Religion," *The Liberal Preacher*, 1 (1828), 15.

27. Aaron Bancroft, "Sermon, Importance of Salvation," *The Liberal Preacher*, 3 (1830), 161–168.

28. Aaron Bancroft, "The Office of Reason in the Concerns of Religion," *The Liberal Preacher*, 1 (1828), 13; *Duties Enjoined by the Fourth Commandment* (Worcester, 1817).

29. *The Reports of the American Unitarian Association* (Boston, 1831), 12–31; *Semi-Centennial of the American Unitarian Association* (Boston, 1875).

30. Aaron Bancroft, *Sermon Before His Excellency, Caleb Strong, May 27, 1801* (Boston, 1801). For the general context, see Paul Goodman, *The Democratic Republicans of Massachusetts* (Cambridge, Mass., 1964); Van Beck Hall, *Politics Without Parties, Massachusetts 1780–1791* (Pittsburgh, 1972); James M. Banner, *To the Hartford Convention: The Federalists and the Origins of Party Politics in Massachusetts 1789–1815* (New York, 1970); David Hackett Fisher, *The Revolution of American Conservatism* (New York, 1965).

31. The published Worcester Town Records contain numerous references to Aaron Bancroft's educational interests as do many of his sermons.

32. Aaron Bancroft, "Sermon on Female Duties and Trials," *The Liberal Preacher*, 2 (August 1828), 27, 28, 33; Smalley, *Worcester Pulpit*, 272.

33. George Bancroft to William B. Sprague, January 28, 1862; Lucretia Bancroft to George Bancroft, August (n.d.) 1822, also Lucretia Farnum to George Bancroft, June 1, 1868, January 27, 1886, and Jane Gerhardi to George Bancroft, August 7, 1843.
34. George Bancroft to Whitelaw B. Reid, December 9, 1859.
35. Sprague, *Annals of the American Pulpit,* VIII, 139.
36. Charles H. Bell, *Phillips Exeter Academy in New Hampshire* (Exeter, N.H., 1883); Laurence M. Crosbie, *The Phillips Exeter Academy* (Exeter, N.H., 1923); "Exercises at the Centennial Celebration of the Founding of the Phillips Exeter Academy, June 20 and 21, 1883" (Exeter, N.H., 1884); Robert Middlekauf, *Ancients and Axioms* (New Haven, Conn., 1963).
37. Nathan Parker to Aaron Bancroft, October 10, 1811, in Howe, *Life and Letters of George Bancroft,* I, 20–22.
38. Ibid., 21, 22; Frank H. Cunningham, *Familiar Sketches of the Phillips Exeter Academy* (Boston, 1883); "Order of Exercises for Exhibition," August 18, 1813, for Bancroft's participation at the end of his second year at the academy.
39. Arthur E. McGuinness, *Henry Home, Lord Kames* (New York, 1970), 58–118.
40. Henry Ware, *Memoir of Nathan Parker* (Boston, 1835); Eliot, *Heralds of a Liberal Faith,* 159–163; Sprague, *Annals,* VIII, 411–416. See also Nathan Parker, *Sermon Preached February 15, 1826* (Portsmouth, N.H., 1826).

II. *Harvard*

1. Hamilton Vaughan Bail, *Views of Harvard, A Pictorial Record to 1860* (Cambridge, Mass., 1949).
2. On John Thornton Kirkland, see Josiah Quincy, *Figures from the Past* (Boston, 1926); Samuel A. Eliot, *Heralds of a Liberal Faith* (Boston, 1910), 75–89; Samuel E. Morison, *Three Centuries of Harvard College 1636–1936* (Cambridge, Mass., 1936). For George Bancroft's impressions, see George Bancroft to Whitelaw Reid, July 12, 1880; George Bancroft to Charles W. Eliot, July 4, 1871. Kirkland's papers at the HUA contain his sermons.
3. George Bancroft to Charles W. Eliot, July 4, 1871, and to Whitelaw Reid, July 12, 1880. On college life under Kirkland, see Artemas Bowers Muzzey, "College Life under President Kirkland," *Harvard Register,* 3 (March 1881); Andrew Peabody, "Harvard College Half a Century Ago," ibid., 1 (January 1880).
4. John Thornton Kirkland, "Literary Institutions," *North American Review,* 8 (December 1818), 191–193, written mostly by Edward Everett, fully reflected Kirkland's views. For his early political views, see "Letters from President Kirkland to President Quincy," Massachusetts Historical Society, *Proceedings,* 17 (1879–1880), 111–117.
5. John Thornton Kirkland, "A Discourse in Commemoration of John Adams and Thomas Jefferson, October 30, 1826," *Memoirs of the American Academy of Arts and Sciences,* 1 (1833), vi, xii, xvi, xxx.
6. Francis Parkman, *A Discourse Occasioned by the Death of the Reverend John Thornton Kirkland* (Boston, 1840); Alexander Young, *Discourse on the Life*

and Character of the Reverend John T. Kirkland (Boston, 1840); Peabody, *Reminiscences,* 9–17; "The State of Learning in the United States," *North American Review,* 9 (September 1819).

7. Harvard College Records, VII (April 1814), HUA; Andrews Norton to John Thornton Kirkland, January 1, 1816, HUA; Papers of the Corporation, 1810–1820, HUA.

8. *Laws of Harvard College for the Use of the Students* (Cambridge, Mass. 1816); L. F. Stowe, *The College Curriculm in the United States* (New York, 1907); Anna Haddow, *Political Science in American Colleges, 1636–1900* (New York, 1939); George P. Schmidt, *The Old Time College President* (New York, 1930), 108–145.

9. On the definition of insanity, see "Intelligence and Remarks," *North American Review,* 5 (September 1817), 437.

10. Three hundred letters from Stephen Salisbury, Jr., to his parents giving an excellent picture of the life of the class of 1817 are housed in the American Antiquarian Society Archives. A portion was reprinted in American Antiquarian Society, *Proceedings* (April 1910) XX. See also George Bancroft to George F. Hoar, May 12, 1884; George Bancroft to Stephen Salisbury, Jr., September 23, September 30, 1884; and the scattered references to Bancroft in College Papers, Volumes VII and VIII, HUA.

11. George Bancroft to John Jay, July 26, 1884. On the larger issue of student unrest, see Steven J. Novack, *The Rights of Youth, Student Unrest and American Higher Education 1798–1815* (Cambridge, Mass., 1977).

12. George Bancroft to A. T. Rice, March 17, 1885.

13. "Records of the Class of 1817," HUA, and Papers of the Corporation, 1814–1817, HUA.

14. For moral philosophy, its relationship to Unitarianism, and its impact on Harvard's curriculum, see Daniel Walker Howe, *The Unitarian Conscience; Harvard Moral Philosophy 1805–1861* (Cambridge, Mass., 1970), 27–44. See also Gladys Bryson, *Man and Society: The Scottish Inquiry of the Eighteenth Century* (Princeton, N.J., 1945).

15. "Notices of Professor Frisbie," in Levi Frisbie, *Miscellaneous Writings,* Andrews Norton, ed. (Boston, 1823), xxiv; "Review of Levi Hedge's Elements of Logick," *North American Review,* 4 (1816), 86.

16. Peabody, *Reminiscences,* 37–40; Levi Hedge, *Elements of Logick: A Summary of the General Principles and Different Modes of Reasoning* (Boston, 1816); Howe, *Unitarian Conscience,* 31–71; Ezra Stiles Gannett, "Obituary for Levi Hedge," *Christian Examiner,* 34 (1844).

17. John Gorham Palfrey, *Discourse on the Life and Character of Henry Ware Sr.* (Cambridge, Mass., 1845); Eliot, *Heralds of a Liberal Faith,* I, 40–49; Peabody, *Reminiscences,* 2–7.

18. Levi Hedge, *Elements of Logick* (Boston, 1821), 178.

19. Frisbie, *Miscellaneous Writings,* 6; Levi Frisbie, "Review of Adam Smith's The Theory of Moral Sentiments," *North American Review,* 8 (March 1819); Andrews Norton, "Review of Levi Frisbie's Inaugural Address," *North American Review,* 6 (January 1818).

20. Frisbie, *Miscellaneous Writings,* 88. Frisbie's disapproval of Paley's utilitarian motive for virtue seeped into Bancroft's thought; see George Bancroft to

Andrews Norton, July 18, 1821, in Mark de Wolfe Howe, *The Life and Letters of George Bancroft* (New York, 1908) I, 112.

21. Frisbie, *Miscellaneous Writings*, 92, 204.

22. Sprague, *Annals of the American Pulpit*, VIII, 430–435; Peabody, *Reminiscences*, 73–78; Andrews Norton, "A Defence of Liberal Christianity," *The General Repository and Review*, 1 (January 1812), 1–25; and his poems in *The General Repository and Review*, 1 (April 1812), 342–344.

23. Andrews Norton, *Inaugural Discourse, August 10, 1819* (Cambridge, Mass., 1819), 18, 30, 32, 39. Class of 1817, student papers, HUA, reveal that the student repeated almost verbatim what he had been taught.

24. See Bancroft's copybooks for samples of Andrews Norton's poems, in HUA; George Bancroft to Justin Winsor, August 4, September 20, 1880; and Justin Winsor, *Memorial History of Boston* (Boston, 1880) IV, where George Ripley summarized the controversy in a fashion which Bancroft thoroughly approved, since it was not derogatory to Norton.

25. Lucretia Farnum to George Bancroft, January 13, 1886; John Chandler Bancroft to Aaron Bancroft, April 30, 1818, as transcribed into George Bancroft's copybook; essay of 1815, on the meaning of death, in HUA. See also the death scene described in Alonzo Hill, *Discourse* (Worcester, 1839), 22–23.

26. 1815 exercise and theme book, Student Notebooks, class of 1817, HUA and CUMR.

27. George Bancroft, "The Influence of Enthusiasm on Happiness," Student Notebooks, class of 1817, HUA. For Kirkland's approval, see George Bancroft, Diary; and John T. Kirkland, Diary, 1816, HUA. Howe, *Unitarian Conscience*, 163.

28. Bowdoin Prize Oration, in "Prize Essays of the Class of 1817," HUA.

29. Cazneau Palfrey, "John Snelling Popkin," *Harvard Register*, 2 (November 1880); Peabody, *Reminiscences*, 40–46. Andrew Peabody, "The Study of Greek and Latin Languages," *Harvard Register*, 3 (January–July 1881); Henry K. Oliver, "Reminiscences of Harvard Sixty Years Ago," *Harvard Register*, 1 (June 1880); Frisbie, *Miscellaneous Writings*, 27–41.

30. Joseph G. Cogswell, "On the Means of Education," *Blackwood's Edinburgh Magazine*, 4 (1819), 546–553, 639–649. Sidney Willard, "The State of Learning in the United States," *North American Review*, 9 (September 1819), 240–259.

31. "The Tendency of Homer's Iliad," *Christian Disciple*, 5 (October 1817), 327–329; "On Greek Literature," *Monthly Anthology and Boston Review*, 6 (May 1809), 309–330, 394–399. See also Carl Diehl, *Americans and German Scholarship 1770–1870* (New Haven, 1978).

32. "Student Essays and Prize Orations for the Class of 1817," HUA.

33. George Bancroft, Bowdoin Prize Essay, HUA.

34. Hedge, *Elements of Logick*, 149. William Enfield, *Institutes of Natural Philosophy* (Boston, 1824).

35. George Bancroft to George F. Hoar, May 12, 1884.

36. Willard Phillips, "Byron's Poems," *North American Review*, 5 (May 1817), 98–110. "Mr. English's Grounds of Christianity Examined," *General Reposi-*

tory and Review, 4 (1813), 304–305.

37. "Mr. Everett's Defence of Christianity," *Christian Disciple,* 2 (1814), 370; "The Faery Queen of Spencer," *North American Review,* 5 (September 1817), 305; Frisbie, *Miscellaneous Writings,* 17–26.

38. See Terence Martin, *The Instructed Vision, Scottish Common Sense Philosophy and the Origins of American Fiction* (Bloomington, Ind., 1961); Robert E. Streeter, "Association Psychology and Literary Nationalism in the North American Review, 1815–1825," *American Literature,* 17 (1945); Lewis P. Simpson, *The Man of Letters in New England and in the South* (Baton Rouge, La., 1973).

39. Frisbie, *Miscellaneous Writings,* 20; George Bancroft, Student Diary, and Bowdoin Prize Essay, HUA. Library charging lists for 1817–1818 HUA disclose Bancroft's reading in these years. See also Lewis P. Simpson, ed., *The Federalist Literary Mind* (Baltimore, Md., 1962).

40. George Bancroft, Harvard College Essays, April 22, 1815; George Bancroft to Lucretia Bancroft, April 21, 1821.

41. Edward Everett, "The Works of Maria Edgeworth," *North American Review,* 8 (October 1823), 383–389; Theophilus Parsons, "Memoirs of Richard L. Edgeworth," ibid., 11 (October 1820), 436–438; "Review of Leonora, A Novel," *Monthly Anthology and Boston Review,* 3 (August 1806). Lists of library users in HUA show Willard, Sparks, and others reading Scott and Edgeworth. See also Frisbie, *Miscellaneous Writings,* 20–22.

42. "Review of Scott's Lay of the Last Minstrel," *Monthly Anthology and Boston Review,* 3 (October 1806), 546–550; "Review of Walter Scott's Rokeby," *General Repository and Review,* 4 (July 1813), 107–127; "Memoir Relative to the Highlands," *American Monthly Magazine and Critical Review,* 4 (November 1818), 1–13; "Review of Rob Roy," ibid., 2 (April 1818), 456–469. See also George B. Orians, *The Influence of Walter Scott upon American Literature before 1860* (Urbana, Ill., 1919); and G. Harrison Orians, "The Romance Ferment after Waverley," *American Literature,* 3 (January 1932), 408–431.

43. George Bancroft, Bowdoin Prize Essay, HUA.

44. Boston *Advertiser,* August 20, 1817; George Bancroft, "Second English Oration," student papers, HUA. See also Albert Matthews, *Harvard Commencement Days 1642–1916* (Cambridge, Mass., 1916).

45. George Bancroft, "Second English Oration," HUA; Arthur Perry to George Bancroft, April 23, 1875, January 10, 1887.

46. For reading lists, texts, and notes on Coleridge, read "superficially," see HUA, George Bancroft reading lists, November 1817.

47. George Bancroft, Notebooks 1817–1818, HUA.

48. On moral philosophy and its influences, see Douglas Sloan, *The Scottish Enlightenment and the American College Ideal* (New York, 1971); Sydney Ahlstrom, "The Scottish Philosophy and American Theology," *Church History,* 24 (September 1955); D. H. Meyer, *The Instructed Conscience: The Shaping of the American National Ethic* (Philadelphia, 1972).

49. Frisbie, *Miscellaneous Writings,* 11, 23. Bancroft carried several copies of the address to Europe.

III. *Innocent Abroad*

1. George Bancroft, reading lists, November 1817–April 1818, HUA. On the meager knowledge about Germany, see George Bancroft to Horatio S. White, May 10, 1883.

2. George Hillard, ed., *Life, Letters and Journals of George Ticknor* (Boston, 1877), I, 73; Anna Ticknor, ed., *Life of Joseph Cogswell as Sketched in His Letters* (Cambridge, Mass., 1879). See also Orie Long, *Literary Pioneers* (Cambridge, Mass., 1935), for additional letters, and Thomas W. Higginson, "Harvard and Göttingen," *Harvard Graduates Magazine*, 6 (September 1897).

3. George Bancroft to John Thornton Kirkland, January 17, 1819; George Bancroft to Henry C. Lodge, June 12, 1877. See also Orie Long, "Attitude of Eminent Englishmen and Americans toward Werther," *Modern Philology*, 14 (December 1916); Henry A. Pochman, *German Culture in America* (Madison, Wis., 1957), 59–66.

4. "Letter from Germany," *North American Review*, 3 (July 1816); "Notice of the University of Goettingen," ibid., 5 (January 1818); Emma G. Jaeck, *Mme de Stael and the Spread of German Literature* (New York, 1915). See also "Selections from the University Library of Biblical Literature Reprinted," *General Repository and Review*, 1 (January 1812); Edward Everett, "Review of Goethe's Life," *North American Review*, 4 (January 1817).

5. Harvard College Library reading lists, March–April 1818, HUA; Bertha Reed, *The Influence of Solomon Gessner upon English Literature* (Philadelphia, 1905), 97.

6. Records of Overseers, VI, June 25, 1818, HUA. The Saltonstall money usually went to prospective divinity students.

7. George Bancroft to Aaron Bancroft, October 20, 1820; George Bancroft, Diary, September 30, 1818. For other students, see David B. Tyack, *George Ticknor and the Boston Brahmins* (Cambridge, Mass., 1967), 32–36; William R. Taylor, *Cavalier and Yankee: The Old South and American National Consciousness* (New York, 1961), 38–51.

8. Margaret Fuller, *Writings*, Mason Wade, ed. (Boston, 1941), 424; George Bancroft to Andrews Norton, December 31, 1818; George Ticknor to Ellery Channing, November 16, 1816, in Hillard, ed., *Life, Letters and Journals of George Ticknor*, I, 119.

9. Samuel A. Eliot to George Bancroft, October 22, 1818; Francis W. Greenwood to George Bancroft, April (?), 1819; George Bancroft to Andrews Norton, March 21, 1819; George Bancroft to Edward Everett, August 4, 1818.

10. Aaron Bancroft to George Bancroft, October 10, 1818; Lucretia Bancroft to George Bancroft, [n.d.] 1819; John Bancroft to George Bancroft, July 7, 1819; Eliza Bancroft to George Bancroft, October 23, 1819; Aaron Bancroft to George Bancroft, September 27, 1820.

11. On Mrs. Samuel Perkins, see Francis W. Greenwood to George Bancroft, August 30, 1819.

12. Philip Rahv, ed., *Discovery of Europe* (Boston, 1947), xviii, 166, 57; George Bancroft, "An Incident in the Life of John Adams," *Century Magazine*, 4

(July 1887); Foster Rhea Dulles, *Americans Abroad* (Ann Arbor, Mich., 1964).

13. George Bancroft to Andrews Norton, August 6, September 5, 1818; Edward Everett to George Bancroft, August 13, 1818; Orie W. Long, *Frederic Henry Hedge: A Cosmopolitan Scholar* (Portland, Me., 1941).

14. For the university and how it appeared to Americans, see Reginald H. Phelps, "The Idea of a Modern University—Goettingen and America," *Germanic Review,* 29 (1954), 175–190; *Der Göttingen Student* (Göttingen, 1813); *Gesetze für die Studieren auf der Georg Augusta Universität* (Göttingen, 1814–1816); George Benecke, "Abschiedswort," *Nachricht von den Feierlichkeiten* (Göttingen, 1812).

15. George Bancroft, Diary, September (?) 1818, quoted in Mark de Wolfe Howe, *Life and Letters of George Bancroft* (New York, 1908), I, 37–38; also George Bancroft, "Schiller's Minor Poems," *North American Review* 16 (October, 1823), and "Goethe's Werke," *North American Review* 19 (October 1824).

16. Bancroft, Diary, April 5, 1819; Howe, *Life and Letters,* I, 58; George Bancroft to Lucretia Bancroft, November 25, 1818.

17. George Bancroft to Edward Everett, August 4, 1818, September 12, 1818; George Bancroft to Andrews Norton, September 5, 1818; Edward Everett to George Bancroft, October 14, 1818.

18. George Bancroft to Aaron Bancroft, October 3, 1818.

19. George Bancroft to Jane Bancroft, August 18, 1818; George Bancroft to Edward Everett, September 12, 1818.

20. George Bancroft to Edward Everett, September 12, 1818. Letter of introduction in Howe, *Life and Letters,* I, 33.

21. Bancroft, Diary, March 28, 1820; George Bancroft to Andrews Norton, October 26, 1818; George Bancroft to John Thornton Kirkland, January 17, 1819.

22. George Bancroft to John Thornton Kirkland, January 17, 1819.

23. Carl Diehl, *Americans and German Scholarship 1770–1870* (New Haven, 1978), 79–91, presents a different interpretation.

24. Bancroft Notebooks, Göttingen years, NYPL; George Bancroft to John T. Kirkland, July 6, 1819.

25. Tyack, *George Ticknor,* 43; George Bancroft to Andrews Norton, July 10, 1819, March 18, 1820.

26. George Bancroft to Andrews Norton, August 19, 1820. Detailed notebooks are in NYPL. Bancroft took notes in English, translating as he went along, leading to such sentences as "Ireland in 1800 by Pitt with England was politically united," Heeren's ethnography notebooks, 217. See also George Bancroft to Andrews Norton, October 3, 1818; to John Kirkland, April 2, 1821; Diary, December 3, 1821.

27. George Bancroft to Andrews Norton, July 10, October 17, 1819, June 1, 1820; to John Kirkland, February 22, 1819; to Abiel Holmes, December 6, 1818.

28. George Bancroft to Andrews Norton, March 21, May 1, 1819; to Levi Frisbie, April 13, 1821.

29. George Bancroft, Diary, March (?), 1819; George Bancroft to John T. Kirkland, September 17, 1820, in Howe, *Life and Letters,* I, 84–86.
30. George Bancroft to Andrews Norton, December 31, 1818, January 9, 1819; to John T. Kirkland, January 15, 1820.
31. George Bancroft to Andrews Norton, February 7, 1820, March 9, 1820; Diary, March 1819, December 3, 1821; to John T. Kirkland, April 2, 1820, November 5, 1820.
32. George Bancroft to Jane Bancroft, April 14, 1819; Diary, April 11, 1820; to Andrews Norton, August 19, 1820.
33. Aaron Bancroft to George Bancroft, May 13, 1819, September 27, 1820; Mary Bancroft to George Bancroft, March 12, 1819; Samuel A. Eliot to George Bancroft, August 30, 1819, December 31, 1819; Francis W. Greenwood to George Bancroft, August 30, 1819.
34. George Bancroft to Andrews Norton, January 17, 1819; to John T. Kirkland, January 15, 1820.
35. George Bancroft, Student Notebooks, NYPL. For Johann G. Eichhorn on the Scriptures and his influence, see Jerry W. Brown, *The Rise of Biblical Criticism in America* (Middletown, Conn., 1969).
36. George Bancroft, Diary, March 1819, and Student Notebooks; Long, *Literary Pioneers,* 122–123; George Bancroft to Edward Everett, August 1, 1819. See also George Bancroft to Andrews Norton, October 17, 1818; to John T. Kirkland, January 17, 1820, in Long, *Literary Pioneers,* 115.
37. Bancroft, Notebooks on Heeren, NYPL; Arnold Herman Ludwig Heeren, *Geschichte des Studiums der Classischen Litteratur seit dem Wiederaufleben der Wissenschaften* (Göttingen, 1797–1801); George P. Gooch, *History and Historians in the Nineteenth Century* (London, 1913).
38. George Bancroft to Andrews Norton, December 31, 1818. See also Notes on Dissen's course and the dismissal of Adam's *Roman Antiquities* in it, NYPL.
39. George Bancroft to John T. Kirkland, November 5, 1820; Diary, December 3, 1820. The articles he would write in the next decade, commonplace, inaccurate, and vastly overrated, were among the first on the subjects to be published in the United States. Russel B. Nye, *George Bancroft* (New York, 1944) lists most of them.
40. George Bancroft to Lucretia Bancroft, March 11, 1819.
41. George Bancroft, Diary, February 27, 1819.
42. George Bancroft, Diary, August 30, 1818, October 2, 1818, October 12, 13, 1818, Howe, *Life and Letters,* I, 38–39, 44–46, 67–69.
43. George Bancroft, Diary, September 2, 1820; to Joseph Chandler, September 16, 1820. The thesis and defense are reproduced in CUMR.
44. George Bancroft to John T. Kirkland, September 17, 1820; to Andrews Norton, January 9, July 10, 1819.
45. George Bancroft to Aaron Bancroft, October 3, 1819; John Bancroft to George Bancroft, January 7, 1820; Aaron Bancroft to George Bancroft, May 19, 1820.
46. George Bancroft to Aaron Bancroft, October 20, 1820; George Bancroft to Lucretia Bancroft, October 3, 1820. See also Kirkland Letter Books, May

12, 1821, HUA, where $1,000 is transferred to London via Frederick Paine.

47. George Bancroft, Diary, December 3, 1820; to John T. Kirkland, November 5, 1820; to Edward Everett, December 28, 1820.

48. George Bancroft to Edward Everett, December 28, 1820; Diary, December 19, 1820, January 2, February 1, 1821.

49. George Bancroft to Andrews Norton, November 5, 1820, July 18, 1821; Diary, September 3, October 2, November 5, November 13, 1820.

50. George Bancroft to Edward Everett, August 1, September 25, November 4, 1819, December 28, 1820; to Levi Hedge, March 6, 1821; Long, *Frederic Henry Hedge*, 13–15.

51. George Bancroft to John T. Kirkland, November 5, 1820; to Edward Everett, April 2, 1821, and to Levi Hedge, March 6, 1821, in Long, *Frederic Henry Hedge*, 8–11.

52. For Hedge's evaluation, see ibid., 12, 14–15; also William R. Hutchison, *The Transcendentalist Ministers* (Boston, 1965), 46–47.

53. George Bancroft to John T. Kirkland, July 26, 1819, November 5, 1820.

54. Howe, *Life and Letters,* I, 96–97; George Bancroft to Levi Hedge, March 6, 1821; Diary, Weimar, March 7, 1821; to John T. Kirkland, March 24, 1821; to Levi Frisbie, April (?), 1821.

55. George Bancroft to John T. Kirkland, May 6, 1821; Diary, May 6, 1821; Suzanne Storrow to George Bancroft, January 4, 1822.

56. Tyack, *George Ticknor,* 63; George Bancroft to John T. Kirkland, August 17, 1821; Diary, June 24, July 1, 1821.

57. George Bancroft, Diary, August, 1821.

58. George Bancroft, Diary, August 6, 8, 1821; Samuel A. Eliot to George Bancroft, August 7, 1821. See also Frederick Paine to George Bancroft, October 8, 1819, August 6, June 7, 1820.

59. George Bancroft, Diary, August 8, 12, 14, 16, 1821; to Andrews Norton, August 16, 1821; to John T. Kirkland, August 17, 1821. See also Howe, *Life and Letters,* I, 114–116.

60. See Pierre M. Irving, *The Life and Letters of Washington Irving* (New York, 1962), II, 51; George Bancroft, Diary, May 7, 30, June 20, July 4, 1821.

61. George Bancroft to John T. Kirkland, August 17, 1821, in Howe, *Life and Letters,* I, 116–121.

62. George Bancroft to John T. Kirkland, August 17, 1821, ibid.

63. George Bancroft to Andrews Norton, April 2, 1820; Diary, April 3, 1820. For the letters from John, see CUMR; see also Convers Francis to George Bancroft, November 2, 1820.

64. "Resolutions," George Bancroft, Diary, September 10, 1821.

65. George Bancroft, Diary, September 19, 24, October 4, 6, 12, 1821. Frederick Paine to George Bancroft, September 22, 1821.

66. George Bancroft to Andrews Norton, October 13, 1821, in Howe, *Life and Letters,* I, 123–128; George Bancroft, Diary, October 13, 27, 1821.

67. George Bancroft, Diary, October 12, 28, 1821; to Samuel A. Eliot, October 12, 1821; to Andrews Norton, October 13, 1821. See also George Bancroft, Diary, October 19, 21, 23, 28, 1821.

68. Ibid., undated fragment, either October or November 1821.

69. Ibid., October 29, 30, 1821; see also Howe, *Life and Letters,* I, 130–131.
70. George Bancroft, Diary, November 26, 1821.
71. Ibid.
72. Ibid., December 21, 22, 1821, January 5, 1822.
73. Ibid., December 21, 1821, January 1, 5, 1822.
74. Ibid., January 1, 3, May 21, 1822; George Bancroft to John T. Kirkland, February 10, 1822; to Samuel A. Eliot, May 29, 1822.
75. George Bancroft to Andrews Norton, February 9, 1822; to John T. Kirkland, February 10, 1822; to Aaron Bancroft, February 19, 1822.
76. George Bancroft, Diary, October 29, 1821; to Samuel A. Eliot, January 7, 1822; to Andrews Norton, March 5, 1822.
77. Samuel A. Eliot to George Bancroft, February 2, May 27, 1822; Thomas Searle to George Bancroft, April 16, 1822.
78. George Bancroft to Andrews Norton, October 13, 1821, March 5, 1822; Andrews Norton to George Bancroft, December 29, 1821; George Bancroft to Samuel A. Eliot, April 15, 1822.
79. Dulles, *Americans Abroad,* 1.
80. George Bancroft to Andrews Norton, July 18, 1821, March 5, 1822.
81. Joseph Cogswell to Mrs. Samuel Prescott, January 17, 1818, in Ticknor, ed., *Life of Joseph Cogswell,* 78; George Bancroft to Andrews Norton, July 18, 1821; to John T. Kirkland, May 6, 1821.

iv. *Floundering*

1. George Bancroft to Samuel A. Eliot, April 2, 1823.
2. George Bancroft to John T. Kirkland, August 2, 1822; John T. Kirkland to George Bancroft, August 10, 1822.
3. Norton's letter is lost, but see George Bancroft to Andrews Norton, September 18, 1822.
4. George Bancroft to Samuel A. Eliot, April 2, 1823, May 10, 1823; to Andrews Norton, September 18, 1822.
5. George Bancroft to Samuel A. Eliot, September 24, 1822, in Mark de Wolfe Howe, *Life and Letters of George Bancroft* (New York, 1908), I, 160.
6. On the general problems of men of letters, see David Levin, *History as Romantic Art* (Stanford, Calif., 1959); David B. Tyack, *George Ticknor and the Boston Brahmins* (Cambridge, Mass., 1967).
7. Tyack, *George Ticknor,* 129; George Bancroft to Samuel A. Eliot, September 24, 1822.
8. On early Unitarianism, see Paul Frothingham, *Boston Unitarianism* (New York, 1890); William R. Hutchison, *The Transcendentalist Ministers* (New Haven, 1959); John C. Meyer, *Church and State in Massachusetts* (Cleveland, 1938); Conrad Wright, *The Beginnings of Unitarianism in America* (Boston, 1955).
9. George Bancroft to Samuel A. Eliot, September 24, 1822, Howe, *Life and Letters,* I, 161.
10. George Bancroft to Samuel A. Eliot, September 24, 1822, full text in MHS.
11. George Bancroft to Aaron Bancroft, January 3, 1822; George Bancroft,

"German Literature," *American Quarterly Review,* 4 (September 1828), 172–173.

12. The brightest ordained preached a few sermons, then left, for example, Jared Sparks, Edward Everett, John Gorham Palfrey, and Emerson.

13. Bancroft's sermons are in the MHS and the American Antiquarian Society.

14. "Sermon," 1823, MHS.

15. George Bancroft, "He Went his Way Rejoicing," MHS. See also Samuel S. Green, "George Bancroft," American Antiquarian Society, *Proceedings,* 7 (April 29, 1891). For a different reading, see Russel B. Nye, "The Religion of George Bancroft," *Journal of Religion,* 29 (1939).

16. James E. Cabot, *A Memoir of Ralph Waldo Emerson* (Cambridge, Mass., 1887), 90, quotes Ralph W. Emerson to John B. Hill, March 12, 1822.

17. George Bancroft to Samuel A. Eliot, May 10, 1823, in Howe, *Life and Letters,* I, 163.

18. Samuel A. Eliot to George Bancroft, May 27, 1822.

19. For the reform attempts, see Robert A. McCaughey, *Josiah Quincy 1772–1864* (Cambridge, Mass., 1974), 138–142; Samuel E. Morison, *Three Centuries of Harvard College* (Cambridge, Mass., 1936); Tyack, *George Ticknor,* 85–128.

20. George Bancroft to Samuel A. Eliot, September 24, 1822, in Howe, *Life and Letters,* I, 161.

21. George Ticknor to Samuel A. Eliot, February 1, 1823, in Anna Ticknor, ed., *Life of Joseph G. Cogswell* (Cambridge, Mass., 1874), 135; John Spencer Bassett, *The Middle Group of American Historians* (New York, 1917), 141–146; George Bancroft to Samuel A. Eliot, May 10, 1823; Records of Harvard Corporation, 1823, HUA.

22. George Bancroft to Samuel A. Eliot, December 3, 1822; Andrew Ritchie to George Bancroft, April 24, 1823.

23. George Bancroft to Samuel A. Eliot, December 3, 1822.

24. Bancroft, Library readings lists for 1822–1823, HUA; Harvard University Faculty Records, April–May 1823, HUA.

25. George Bancroft to Samuel A. Eliot, December 3, 1822, May 10, 1823; Howe, *Life and Letters,* I, 168.

26. George Bancroft to Samuel A. Eliot, December 3, 1822, May 10, 1823.

27. See George Bancroft, Diary, n.d., 1822.

28. Jared Sparks to George Bancroft, March 3, 1823; Nathan Parker to George Bancroft, March 16, 1823.

29. George Ticknor to Samuel A. Eliot, October 29, 1822; February 1, 1823; Joseph G. Cogswell to E. Cogswell, January 19, 1823, in Anna Ticknor, ed., *The Life of Joseph Cogswell* 133–137; George Bancroft to Samuel A. Eliot, May 10, 1823. The choice of Round Hill, away from large metropolitan centers, aimed to avoid the complications resulting from Harvard's proximity to Boston.

30. Joseph Cogswell to Elisha Ticknor, June 6, 1818, Cogswell, Diary, May 28, 1818, in Ticknor, ed., *Life of Cogswell,* 80, 81.

31. George Bancroft, "The Object of Liberal Education," n.p., NYPL.

32. George Bancroft and Joseph Cogswell, *Prospectus of a School to Be Established*

at Round Hill (Cambridge, Mass., 1823), 7, 9–10; Bancroft and Cogswell, *Some Account of the School for the Liberal Education of Boys* (Northampton, 1826), 9, 5, 8; Samuel A. Eliot to George Bancroft, August 26, 1823.

33. George Bancroft to John T. Kirkland, October 1, 1823. George Bancroft to Samuel A. Eliot, December 3, 1822; May 10, 1823. On Northampton, see Richard D. Hathaway, *Sylvester Judd's New England* (University Park, Pa., 1981), 109–118.

34. *Names of Students Attending the Round Hill School until 1831* (Newport, 1852), *Round Hill Boys and Instructors Album* (n.p.n.d.), Ticknor, ed., *Life of Joseph Cogswell,* Appendix B; Lately Thomas, *Sam Ward, King of the Lobby* (Boston, 1965), 15–16; Joseph Cogswell to George Bancroft, December 21, 23, 1823; George Bancroft to Samuel A. Eliot, December 28, 1823; Catherine Prescott to George Bancroft, January 25, 1824.

35. On daily life, see Thomas G. Appleton, *A Sheaf of Papers* (Boston, 1875) 1–47; Susan Hale, ed., *Life and Letters of Thomas Gold Appleton* (New York, 1885), 23, 37; Maude H. Elliott, *Uncle Sam Ward,* (New York, 1938), 14–19; Sarah Forbes Hughes, ed., *Letters and Recollections of John Murray Forbes* (Boston, 1910), 43–52; Thomas, *Sam Ward,* 5–24, 43–52; Louise Hall Tharp, *The Appletons of Beacon Hill* (Boston, 1973), 112–123.

36. George Bancroft to Jeremiah Day, March 19, 1828; Jeremiah Day to George Bancroft, March 25, 1828.

37. George Bancroft to Jared Sparks, August 27, 1825, in John S. Bassett, "The Correspondence of George Bancroft and Jared Sparks," *Smith College Studies in History,* II (1917), 99. Joseph Cogswell to C. S. Davies, November 28, 1823; Joseph Cogswell to Joseph Davies, March 23, 1828, in Ticknor, ed., *The Life of Joseph Cogswell,* 144–145, 160; also John S. Bassett, "The Round Hill School," American Antiquarian Society, *Proceedings* 27 (April 1917), 18–62; "Round Hill School, Flourishing Conditions and Import," *Hampshire Gazette* (Northampton), May 2, 1827; "Life at Round Hill by a Student," *Hampshire Gazette,* June 23, 1872; Lemuel Shattuck, "The Centenary of the Round Hill School," Massachusetts Historical Society, *Proceedings,* 57 (December 1923–January 1924), 205–211.

38. Catherine Prescott to George Bancroft, April 13, 1824. For Bancroft's educational practices, see George Bancroft to Theodore Sedgwick, September 25, December 6, 1826, in Sedgwick Papers, MHS; and George Bancroft to Nathan Appleton, November 17, 1826, January 27, 1828, in Appleton Papers, MHS.

39. Aaron Bancroft to George Bancroft, November 29, 1824; Joseph Cogswell to George Bancroft, October 4, 1824. See also George Bancroft to Theodore Lyman, March 14, 1824; Theodore Lyman to George Bancroft, March 21, 1824, Lyman Papers, MHS.

40. George Bancroft to Jared Sparks, September 13, 1824; Jared Sparks to George Bancroft, September 16, 1824, in Bassett, "The Correspondence of George Bancroft and Jared Sparks," 84–87.

41. Jonathan Dwight, Jr., to George Bancroft, March 6, 1826; Sarah Dwight to George Bancroft, March 7, 24, 26, April 16, 1826; George Bancroft to Sarah Dwight, May 3, 1826, CUMR.

42. George Ticknor to George Bancroft, May 11, 1826. See also Catherine Prescott to George Bancroft, May 22, 1826.

43. George Bancroft to Sarah Dwight, August 30, September 17, November 28, December 6, 26, 1826, CUMR.

44. George Bancroft to Sarah Dwight, May 3, June 15, July 19, October 26, November 7, December 26, 1826; Sarah Dwight to George Bancroft, May 1, 1826, CUMR.

45. George Bancroft to Sarah Dwight, September 4, 1826, January 4, 8, 1827, CUMR.

46. George Bancroft to Sarah Dwight, June 15, October 17, November 14, December 6, 1826; Sarah Dwight to George Bancroft, September 26, 1826, CUMR. See also Aaron Bancroft to George Bancroft, January 31, 1827.

47. Anna Ticknor to George Bancroft, January 4, 1827; George Ticknor to George Bancroft, February 1, 1827; Thomas Searle to George Bancroft, February 12, 1827; George Bancroft to John T. Kirkland, August 6, 1827; John T. Kirkland to George Bancroft, August 7, 1827.

48. George Bancroft, *Poems* (Cambridge, Mass., 1823). For possible influences, see Howe, *Life and Letters,* I, 164–166; Russel B. Nye, *George Bancroft* (New York, 1944), 64–65; Percy Matenko, "The Goethe, Schiller and Byron Translations of the Saaling Album," *Modern Language Quarterly,* 6 (1945); Andrew Schiller, "A Letter from George Bancroft," *New England Quarterly,* 33 (1960).

49. George Bancroft to John T. Kirkland, November 4, 1823; Thomas Searle to George Bancroft, October 10, 1823; N. C. Frothingham to George Bancroft, March 3, 1824; Henry Cabot Lodge, *Early Memories* (New York, 1913), 314.

50. Edward Everett, "Heeren's Reflections on the Politics of Ancient Greece," *North American Review,* 18 (April 1824), 390–401; George Bancroft to Edward Everett, July 31, 1824, August 23, 1825.

51. George Bancroft to Edward Everett, November 16, 1827; to John T. Kirkland, February 3, March 5, 1828; to Lemuel Shaw, October 13, 1834. Later Bancroft hoped to do the same for his *History* in the common schools; see George Bancroft to Horace Mann, June 9, 1839 in Horace Mann Papers, MHS.

52. John T. Kirkland to George Bancroft, May 1, 1826; George Ticknor to George Bancroft, January 5, 1828; J. K. Kingsley to George Bancroft, April 22, 1829; George Bancroft to Edward Everett, April 19, 1829.

53. George Bancroft to John T. Kirkland, February 3, 1828; George Ticknor to George Bancroft, March 24, 1828; George Bancroft to Charles W. Eliot, July 4, 1871.

54. Tyack, *George Ticknor,* 129. See also Andrews Norton, "Byron," *North American Review,* 12 (October 1825), 300–359; John Clive, *Scotch Reviewers: The Edinburgh Review 1802–1815* (Cambridge, Mass., 1957); William Charvat, *The Origins of American Critical Thought* (Philadelphia, 1936).

55. For Bancroft's views see George Bancroft, "Mrs. Hemans's Poems," *North American Review,* 24 (April 1827), 446–447, 463; George Bancroft, "Dwight's Travels," *American Quarterly Review,* 6 (September 1829), 214–216.

56. The series of articles on German literature, politics, theology, drama, and poetry is partially listed in Robert H. Canary, *George Bancroft* (New York, 1974).

57. George Bancroft, "Dwight's Travels," *American Quarterly Review,* 6 (September 1829), 215–216; "Mrs. Hemans's Poems," *North American Review,* 24 (April 1927), 443, 463; "Saxe Weimar's Travels in North America," ibid., 28 (January 1829), 254.

58. Andrews Norton, "Dr. Franklin," *North American Review,* 7 (September 1818), 289–323; Francis Gray, "An Address," ibid., 3 (September 1816), 289–305; Richard H. Dana, Sr., "The Sketch Book," ibid., 9 (September 1819), 322–356; R. H. Dana, Sr., "The Sylphs of the Season," ibid., 5 (September 1817), 365–389; "Magnalia Christi," ibid., 6 [new series] (1829), 255–272.

59. For this attitude see George Bancroft, "Mrs. Hemans's Poems," *North American Review,* 24 (April 1827), 446–447; "Goethe's Works," ibid., 19 (October 1824), 304–305. Many of these articles were reprinted in George Bancroft, *Literary and Historical Miscellanies* (New York, 1855).

60. George Bancroft to Jared Sparks, July 10, 12, 29, November (?) 1824; in Bassett, "The Correspondence of George Bancroft and Jared Sparks," 80–89.

61. Jared Sparks to George Bancroft, July 20, September 16, November 23, 1824, February 17, 1825; Jared Sparks to George Bancroft, October 30, 1826; George Bancroft to Jared Sparks, November 2, 10, 1826; Jared Sparks to George Bancroft, November 10, 1826; George Bancroft to Jared Sparks, December 5, 6, 1826; Jared Sparks to George Bancroft, December 18, 1826, all in Bassett, "The Correspondence of George Bancroft and Jared Sparks," 81–125. See also George Bancroft, "Greek Lexicography," *North American Review,* 24 (January 1827), 142–155.

62. George Bancroft to Jared Sparks, March 10, November 14, December 6, 1826, in Bassett, "The Correspondence of George Bancroft and Jared Sparks," 108, 120–122, 123; Bancroft, "German Literature," *American Quarterly Review,* 2 (September 1827), 176.

63. George Bancroft, "German Literature," *American Quarterly Review,* 2 (September 1827), 179, 180. George Bancroft, "Early American Poetry," ibid., 2 (December 1827), 509.

64. George Bancroft to Jared Sparks, November 14, 1825, in Bassett, "The Correspondence of George Bancroft and Jared Sparks," 103–105; Bancroft, "German Literature," *American Quarterly Review,* 3 (March 1828), 157–158.

65. Bancroft, "German Literature," *American Quarterly Review,* 4 (September 1828), 158, 162.

66. George Bancroft to Jared Sparks, November 14, 1825, in Bassett, "The Correspondence of George Bancroft and Jared Sparks," 104; Bancroft, "German Literature," *American Quarterly Review,* 2 (September 1827), 171, 176–177.

67. Ibid., 176.

68. Ibid., 177; Bancroft, "German Literature," *American Quarterly Review,* 4 (September 1828), 158–159.

69. George Bancroft to Sarah Dwight, November 28, 1826, October 15, 1828, April 14, 1829, April 5, 1830; see also John Davis to George Bancroft, January 29, 1826; George Bancroft to Edward Everett, April 19, 1829.

70. George Bancroft to John T. Kirkland, August 6, 1827, in Howe, *Life and Letters*, I, 177–178; George Bancroft to Jared Sparks, November 14, 1825, February 3, March 10, 1826, October 4, 1829, in Bassett, "The Correspondence of George Bancroft and Jared Sparks," 104, 108, 138–139.

71. George Ellis, "The Round Hill School," *Educational Review*, 1 (April 1891), 341; *Account of Testimonial Dinner for Joseph Cogswell by Round Hill Scholars, December 1, 1864;* Appleton, *A Sheaf of Papers*, 1–47; Elliott, *Uncle Sam Ward*, 19; Susan J. Lesley, *Memoirs of Mrs. A. J. Lyman* (Boston, 1886).

72. George Bancroft to Sarah Bancroft, August 12, 1827; William H. Prescott to George Bancroft, November 10, 1826; J. M. Wainwright to George Bancroft, December 26, 1829; Robert Walsh to George Bancroft, March 24, 1830; Timothy Walker to George Bancroft, August 28, December 8, 1830.

73. John Davis to George Bancroft, December 25, 1826.

74. George Bancroft to Edward Everett, May 4, 1825.

75. For sample, see William Chamberlain, *Address at Windsor* (Windsor, Vt., 1826); David L. Child, *Oration before the Republicans of Boston* (Boston, 1826); Benjamin Gleason, *Oration* (Boston, 1826); William Hunter, *Oration* (Providence, R.I., 1826); Solomon Lincoln, Jr., *Oration* (Hingham, Mass., 1826); Charles Phelps, *Oration* (Brattleboro, Vt., 1826).

76. George Bancroft, *Oration at Northampton, July 4, 1826* (Northampton, Mass., 1826), 15–17, 19.

77. Ibid., 19, 20, 21, 22.

78. Ibid., 22.

79. George Bancroft to Sarah Dwight, July 1, September 17, 1826; Jared Sparks to George Bancroft, July 31, 1826; Levi Lyman to George Bancroft, July 5, 1826; Thomas Searle to George Bancroft, July 31, 1826; George Bancroft to Edward Everett, July 27, 1826; George Ticknor to George Bancroft, August (?) 1826; George Bancroft to Edward Everett, December (?) 1826. For the similarity to Edward Everett's Fourth of July address in Cambridge, see Edward Everett, *Oration at Cambridge* (Boston, 1826); also Irving H. Bartlett, *Daniel Webster* (New York, 1978), 83–85.

80. George Bancroft to Jared Sparks, December 5, 1826, in Bassett, "The Correspondence of George Bancroft and Jared Sparks," 122; George Bancroft, "Early American Poetry," *American Quarterly Review*, 2 (December 1827), 507, 508; George Bancroft, "Joseph II of Austria," *North American Review*, 31 (July 1830), 1; "German Literature," *American Quarterly Review*, 4 (September 1828), 168; "Works of Goethe," *North American Review*, 19 (October 1824), 306.

81. George Bancroft to Jared Sparks, March 10, 1826; November 11, 1827; December 6, 1830, in Bassett, "The Correspondence of George Bancroft and Jared Sparks," 106–108, 130–131, 142. George Bancroft to John T. Kirkland, August 6, 1827; "Works of Goethe," *North American Review*, 19 (October 1824), 308; "Early American Poetry," *American Quarterly Review*, 2 (December 1827), 508.

v. *Politics and the Past*

1. Boston *Atlas,* November 27, 1832; George Bancroft to Sarah Dwight, October 26, 1826, CUMR.

2. Edward Everett to Alexander H. Everett, September 25, November 15, 1828, Everett Papers, MHS; Edward Everett to George Bancroft, September 11, 1828; George Bancroft to Edward Everett, November 30, 1828; to Samuel A. Eliot, March 7, 1824. On the factions of the Democratic Party, see David Henshaw, *Remarks upon the Bank of the United States* (Boston, 1831); Henry Orne, *Reply of Colonel Orne to the Attacks of Mr. Nathaniel Greene, David Henshaw and Others in the Boston Statesman* (Boston, 1829); "William Ingalls," *Memorial Biographies* (Boston, 1880), I, 328–336.

3. John Davis to George Bancroft, June 27, 1830; William M. Sloane, "George Bancroft," *Century Magazine,* 11 (1887), 473–487.

4. George Bancroft, "The Economy of Athens," *North American Review,* 32 (April 1831), 367. For early efforts by others to master the Workingmen rhetoric, see Alexander H. Everett, *America* (Philadelphia, 1827), 340, 358, 359; Levi Lincoln, *Message of His Excellency the Governor, January 5, 1831* (Boston, 1831); Levi Lincoln, *Speech of His Excellency, the Governor, May 25, 1831* (Boston, 1831); Edward Everett, "Two Lectures to the Workingmen Delivered 1830–1831," *Orations and Speeches* (Boston, 1851), I, 283–328; Ronald Formisano, *The Transformation of Political Culture* (New York, 1983), 253–255. On Bancroft's local connections in Northampton, see Richard D. Hathaway, *Sylvester Judd's New England* (University Park, Pa., 1981), 119, 145–146, 148.

5. John Davis to George Bancroft, June 27, 1830; Joseph G. Cogswell to George Bancroft, February 2, 1830; George Ticknor to George Bancroft, March 19, 1831; Alexander H. Everett to George Bancroft, March 26, 1831.

6. Henry Dwight to George Bancroft, December 24, 1830; George Bancroft to Edward Everett, June 22, 1830; also Henshaw, *Bank of the United States.* On the banking debate, see Arthur M. Schlesinger, Jr., *The Age of Jackson* (Boston, 1946), 74–87, 103–114; James R. Sharp, *The Jacksonians Versus the Banks* (New York, 1970), 1–49; Bray Hammond, *Banks and Politics in America* (Princeton, N. J., 1957).

7. George Bancroft, "Report of the Committee on Ways and Means," *North American Review,* 32 (January 1831), 22, 23.

8. Ibid., 52–53, 55. Compare with Henry Dwight to George Bancroft, December 24, 1830; William Dwight to George Bancroft, January 3, 1831; Theodore Dwight to George Bancroft, February 24, 1831.

9. Alexander H. Everett to George Bancroft, July 3, 1831; George Bancroft to Edward Everett, August 30, 1831.

10. Robert Walsh to George Bancroft, March 2, 7, 1832; George Bancroft to Martin Van Buren, January 10, 1832 (misdated), in Worthington Chauncey Ford, "Van Buren-Bancroft Correspondence," Massachusetts Historical Society, *Proceedings,* 42 (1909), 381–382. William H. Prescott to George Bancroft, April 10, 1831, George Ticknor, *William H. Prescott* (Boston, 1864), 336–337.

11. George Bancroft to Sarah Bancroft, May 5, 10, 1831, CUMR.

12. Ibid., George Bancroft to Martin Van Buren, January 10, 1832, in Ford, "Van Buren–Bancroft Correspondence," 382.

13. For Bancroft's banking activities, see Harry N. Scheiber, ed., "Some Documents on Jackson's Bank War," *Pennsylvania History,* 30 (January 1963); Harry N. Scheiber, "A Jacksonian Radical as Banker and Lobbyist: New Light on George Bancroft," *New England Quarterly,* 37 (September 1964); Harry N. Scheiber, "The Commercial Bank of Lake Erie, 1831–1843," *Business History Review,* 40 (Spring 1966).

14. Sarah Bancroft to George Bancroft, December 16, 1831; George Bliss to George Bancroft, November 4, 8, 1831; George Bancroft to Leonard Case, November 24, 1831; to Edward Everett, January 7, 1832.

15. See Jane Gerhardi to George Bancroft, May 14, 1831; George Bancroft to Sarah Bancroft, December 27, 1831; Sarah Bancroft to George Bancroft, November 4, December 28, 1831, January 4, 1832; Lucretia Bancroft to George Bancroft, January (n.d.) 1832, CUMR.

16. George Bancroft to Sarah D. Bancroft, January 9, 19, 1832. For negotiations in the capital, see Leonard Case to George Bancroft, December 30, 1831; Robert Walsh to George Bancroft, October 5, 1831; Sarah Bancroft to George Bancroft, December 26, 28, 1831.

17. William Dwight to George Bancroft, January 10, 1832; Sarah Bancroft to George Bancroft, January 10, 11, 1832; William Dwight to George Bancroft, January 11, 1832, CUMR.

18. Aaron Bancroft to Sarah Bancroft, January 12, 1832; Lucretia Bancroft to Sarah Bancroft, January 15, 1832; George Bancroft to Sarah Bancroft, January 14, 15, 16, 1832, CUMR.

19. George Bancroft to Sarah Bancroft, December 25, 27, 28, 1831, January 11, 17, 23, 25, 1832, CUMR.

20. William Dwight to George Bancroft, January 16, 18, 19, 1832; Sarah Bancroft to George Bancroft, January 27, 1832; George Bancroft to William Dwight, January 18, 1832, CUMR.

21. Lucretia Bancroft to George Bancroft, February 17, 1832; George Bancroft to Sarah Bancroft, March 3, 15, April 17, 1832; Sarah Bancroft to George Bancroft, March 5, 1832, CUMR.

22. George Bancroft to Sarah Bancroft, January 18, 1832, in Mark de Wolfe Howe, *Life and Letters of George Bancroft* (New York, 1908), I, 200–202.

23. See an anonymous pamphlet written later by a disgruntled Whig, *To George Bancroft, Secretary of the Navy* (Washington, 1846), 1–2.

24. For his early work on the history and early contacts used, see the vast correspondence in Bancroft Papers, 1832–1834, MHS. See also, Richard C. Vitzthum, "Theme and Method in Bancroft's History of the United States," *New England Quarterly,* 41 (1968).

25. George Bancroft to Edward Everett, October 23, 1833; George Bancroft to Sarah Bancroft, January 18, 1832. The latest, and most perceptive, evaluation of Bancroft's *History* is Richard C. Vitzthum, *The American Compromise* (Norman, Okla. 1974), 3–76.

26. Joseph Story to George Bancroft, April 26, 1832; James Savage to George

Bancroft, May 25, 1834; William H. Prescott to George Bancroft, January 13, 1833; John Davis to George Bancroft, December 25, 1834.

27. George Bancroft, *History of the United States* (Boston, 1837), I, 460–469; also George Bancroft to Jared Sparks, August 22, 1834, quoted in Schlesinger, *Age of Jackson,* 370.

28. Bancroft, *History,* I, 1–4.

29. John B. Derby, *Political Reminiscences* (Boston, 1835), 158; John Davis to George Bancroft, March 13, 1835; Henry Ware, Jr., *Sober Thoughts on the States of the Times* (Boston, 1835), 35, 40; Charles Sumner, "The Americans," *North American Review,* 46 (January 1838), 106–126; "The March of Anarchy," *New England Magazine,* 7 (November 1834), 409–410; "Mobs," *New England Magazine,* 7 (December 1834), 475; Boston *Courier,* October 3, 1834.

30. Alexander H. Everett, *The Conduct of the Administration* (Boston, 1832), first published in the Boston *Daily Advertiser;* "Mobs," 475; Boston *Courier,* October 3, 1834; James Walker, *Sermon* (Boston, 1828), 16.

31. For early reviews, see Edward Everett to George Bancroft, October 5, 1834, Howe, *Life and Letters,* I, 205–207; Edward Everett, "Bancroft's History of the United States," *North American Review,* 40 (January 1835); "Bancroft's History of the United States," *American Quarterly Review,* 16 (1834); also Arnold H. L. Heeren to George Bancroft, September 1, 1835, Howe, *Life and Letters,* I, 209–210; John Davis to George Bancroft, April 2, 1835, Howe, *Life and Letters,* I, 210–211. Russel B. Nye, *George Bancroft* (New York, 1944), 102–104.

32. Frederick Robinson, "Oration Delivered on July 4, 1834," in Joseph Blau, *Social Theories of Jacksonian Democracy* (New York, 1947), 322; Edward Everett, *Oration in Cambridge* (Boston, 1826), 28; also Schlesinger, *Age of Jackson,* 267–268.

33. Bancroft, *History,* I, 152, 251, 310, 348, 403. For the method involved and comparison to those of other historians, see David Levin, *History as Romantic Art* (Stanford, Calif., 1959).

34. See for example, the luck of the early mariners, their navigational skills, and the will of Heaven, also the early problems of Virginia and the cunning of Providence. Bancroft, *History,* I, 115–116, 138.

35. George Bancroft, "Review of Graham's History," *American Quarterly Review,* 12 (December 1832), 426, 427; also Bancroft, "Clarke and Force," *North American Review,* 46 (April 1838), 475–487.

36. Bancroft, *History,* I, 367–368, 387–391.

37. Ibid., 386, 389.

38. For the transition, see ibid., 306, 308, 310; see also 433–439, 443.

39. See ibid., 390, 433. For the context of Bancroft's anti-individualist orientation, see Yehoshua Arieli, *Individualism and Nationalism in American Ideology* (Cambridge, Mass., 1964).

40. Bancroft, *History,* I, 266, 267, 277, 299, 310–311.

41. Ibid., 362–367.

42. Ibid., 158, 232, 234.

43. Ibid., 460, 461, 462, 463.

44. On the Democratic Party, see Richard Hildreth, *Despotism in America* (Boston, 1840; reprinted New York, 1970), 13; Edward Everett Hale, in Howe, *Life and Letters,* I, 214; Arthur B. Darling, *Political Changes in Massachusetts, 1824–1848* (New Haven, 1925), has misled Schlesinger, *Age of Jackson,* 144–148, and Nye, *George Bancroft,* in the belief that Bancroft's entrance into the party coincided with its radicalization and led to a Bancroft and Morton hegemony. See also Formisano, *Transformation.*

45. See Boston *Statesman,* September 18, 1826, January 15, 1828; June 17, 1828; September 4, 6, 1828; October 4, 1828; *Morning Post,* September 28, 1833.

46. Marcus Morton to William Parmenter, February 21, 1829; to D. Ingham, March 4, 5, 30, 1829; to David Henshaw, February 7, 1830; to John C. Calhoun, February 5, 1830, March 7, 1831; to Pliny Merrick, March 10, 1830; to Moses Stuart, March 7, 1831, Morton Papers, MHS.

47. Marcus Morton to James Harrington, February 13, 20, 1834. See also Marcus Morton to John C. Calhoun, March 9, 1831; to John K. Simpson, August 9, 1831; to Charles G. Greene, February 25, 1832; to Nathan Willis, March 15, 1832; to Committee on Arrangements, January 3, 1833; to Isaiah Hill, February 2, 1833; to Mathew Cobb, March 4, 1833; to John K. Simpson, February 13, 1834; to Levi Woodbury, November 10, 1834, all in Morton Letterbooks, MHS.

48. Samuel Whitcomb, Jr., *An Address Before the Workingmen's Society of Dedham, September 7, 1831* (Dedham, Mass., 1831), 3–4, 21–23. On the Workingmen, see Nathan Fine, *Labor and Farmer Parties in the United States 1828–1920* (New York, 1961); Edward Pessen, "The Workingmen's Movement in the Jacksonian Era," *Mississippi Valley Historical Review,* 43 (December 1956); Edward Pessen, *Jacksonian America, Society and Politics* (Homewood, Ill., 1969); Schlesinger, *Age of Jackson,* 146–158; Formisano, *Transformation,* 222–244.

49. Robinson, "Oration," in Blau, *Social Theories,* 327; Schlesinger, *Age of Jackson,* 153–155; Robert Rantoul, Jr., *Oration at South Reading July 4, 1832* (Salem, 1832), 1, 24, 36; *Oration Delivered Before the Gloucester Mechanics Association* (Salem, 1833).

50. Darling, *Political Changes,* 97–100, 102, 113–114; Formisano, *Transformation,* 224–231.

51. Amasa Walker, *Oration at Staughton, July 5, 1830* (Boston, 1830); *Address Before the Young Men of Boston* (Boston, 1833), 5, 28–29. See also James Phinney Munroe, *A Life of Francis Amasa Walker* (New York, 1923); J. R. Commons, *History of Labour,* (New York, 1918), I, 295–299.

52. Boston *Statesman,* November 18, 1831; Boston *Advocate,* November 1, 12, 1832. On anti-Masonic views of the National Republicans, see Boston *Atlas,* August 9, 1833. See also Boston *Advocate,* November 5, 6, 12, 1832; Boston *Atlas,* September 20, 1833. For the National Republicans and Edward Everett's long flirtation with the Anti-Masons, see Edward Everett to Benjamin F. Hallett, December 24, 1832; Benjamin F. Hallett to Edward Everett, February 10, 1833; Edward Everett to Anti-Masonic Committee, March 12, 1833; to Benjamin F. Hallett, October 5, 1835, November 11, 1835, Febru-

ary 17, March 8, 1836, Edward Everett Papers, MHS. The break between Everett and the Anti-Masons came in 1836—see Edward Everett to A. H. Everett, October 29, 1836.

53. Henry Dwight to George Bancroft, August 27, October 25, 1833; Edmund Dwight to George Bancroft, September 8, 1834; William H. Prescott to George Bancroft, March 16, 1833; C. E. Forbes to George Bancroft, October 2, 1833; Alexander H. Everett to George Bancroft, October 11, 1833.

54. George Bancroft to Edward Everett, July 11, 25, 1834. See also Alexander H. Everett to George Bancroft, August 5, September 17, 1834.

55. George Bancroft, "Communication," Convention of Literary and Scientific Gentlemen, New York, October 1830, *Journal of Proceedings* (New York, 1831).

56. Frederick Robinson, *Oration Delivered Before the Trade Union of Boston* (Boston, 1834), 22; John D. Eldredge to George Bancroft, September 30, 1834.

57. George Bancroft to the Workingmen of Northampton, October 1, 1834, Boston *Courier,* October 22, 1834. See also "Committee to George Bancroft," September 25, 1834. For a different reading, see Schlesinger, *Age of Jackson,* 162–164.

58. The second letter appeared in the *Hampshire Gazette,* October 8, 1834.

59. George Bancroft, "Slavery in Rome," *North American Review,* 39 (October 1834), 415, 416, 417, 426; reprinted in George Bancroft, *Literary and Historical Miscellanies* (New York, 1855). The speech occasioned a minor flap for its assault on Brutus. Margaret Fuller, Boston *Daily Advertiser,* November 27, 1834; Robert N. Hudspeth, *Letters of Margaret Fuller* (Ithaca, N.Y., 1983), I, 228.

60. Benjamin F. Hallett to George Bancroft, November 2, 1834; Anti-Masonic Convention Resolutions, October 14, 1834; in Bancroft Papers, MHS; William Wait to George Bancroft, October 15, 1834; Alexander H. Everett to George Bancroft, October 16, 19, 1834; Samuel Drake to George Bancroft, October 22, 1834. See also Jared Sparks to George Bancroft, November 21, 1834; George Bancroft to Marcus Morton, October 17, 1834, Bancroft Papers, MHS; Marcus Morton to George Bancroft, December 18, 1834 (Morton Letterbooks); J. Paulding to George Bancroft, November 21, 1834.

61. George Bancroft to the Public, October 22, 1834; Darling, *Political Changes,* 126–129.

62. On Buckingham's opinion, see Samuel Drake to George Bancroft, October 22, 1834; Boston *Atlas,* October 24, 31, 1834.

63. Boston *Atlas,* February 27, March 3, 4, 15, 18, April 5, June 3, 1834.

64. Boston *Atlas,* November 3, 5, 1834; Workingmen satires in Bancroft Papers, MHS. Everett also had to overcome anti-intellectual attitudes similar to those that plagued Bancroft. See Paul Frothingham, *Edward Everett,* (Boston, 1925), 135.

65. George Bancroft to Edward Everett, November 17, 1834; *Morning Post,* November 17, 1834; Boston *Atlas,* November 4, 1834; Howe, *Life and Letters,* I, 212–214.

66. On election results, see Boston *Courier,* November 17, 1834, in Howe, *Life and Letters,* I, 212.

67. George Bancroft to Alexander H. Everett, November 17, 1834; Boston *Courier,* November 17, 1834; Northampton *Courier,* October 14, 1834; John Davis to George Bancroft, April 17, 1835.

68. George Bancroft to Martin Van Buren, November 17, 1834; to Edward Everett, November 17, December 28, 1834. But until 1835 Bancroft still thought he had left all bridges open. See George Bancroft to Edward Everett, December 29, 1834, February 7, 1835.

VI. *Democracy in Theory and Practice*

1. George Bancroft to Edward Everett, July 11, 1834, January 8, 1835. For an earlier version of this self-definition, see George Bancroft, "Early Colonial History," *American Quarterly Review,* 12 (September 1832), 426–429.

2. John Davis to George Bancroft, March 8, 1835; George Bancroft, Williamstown Oration, 1835, reprinted in George Bancroft, *Literary and Historical Miscellanies* (New York, 1855), 421; George Bancroft, "On the Progress of Civilization," *Boston Quarterly Review,* 1 (October 1838), 394, 396, 400. Hubbard Winslow, *Oration* (Boston, 1838), 17; Benjamin F. Hallett, *Oration* (Boston 1838), 8, 10, 45. For other readings of Whig and Democratic ideology, see Ronald P. Formisano, *The Transformation of Political Culture* (New York, 1983); Daniel Walker Howe, *The Political Culture of the American Whigs* (Chicago, 1979). See also response to Bancroft's Deerfield oration in *Franklin Mercury,* March 3, 1835; Margaret Fuller to Frederic H. Hedge, March 6, 1835, in Robert N. Hudspeth, *Letters of Margaret Fuller* (Ithaca, N.Y., 1983), I, 225–228.

3. Lucretia Bancroft to George Bancroft, December 21, 1836, in Mark de Wolfe Howe, *Life and Letters of George Bancroft* (New York, 1908), I, 219; Orestes A. Brownson, "Grund's America," *Boston Quarterly Review,* 1 (April 1838), 166; "Bancroft's Oration in Springfield," *American Monthly Magazine,* 2 (September 1836), 304–305; Arthur B. Darling, *Political Changes in Massachusetts* (New Haven, 1925), 199; "Radicalism," *New England Magazine,* 8 (February 1835), 144; James H. Lanman, "Social Disorganization," *American Monthly Magazine,* 2 (December 1836), 583. See also Orestes A. Brownson to George Bancroft, September 25, 1836.

4. Theophilus Parsons, *Address* (Boston, 1835), 10–11, 15–16; *New England Magazine,* 9 (October 1835), 303–304; Boston *Courier,* October 22, 1834.

5. George Bancroft to Edward Everett, June 25, 1835; George Bancroft, "Prescott's Ferdinand and Isabella," *Democratic Review,* 2 (May 1838), 160; George Bancroft to Martin Van Buren, February 23, 1840; George Bancroft, "Graham's History," *American Quarterly Review,* 12 (December 1832), 428–429.

6. Bancroft, *Hartford Address* (Hartford, 1840), 11. Undated fragment, MHS. See also George Bancroft to Sylvester Mudd, October 1, 1834.

7. Orestes A. Brownson, "Thoughts on Unity, Progress and Government," *Boston Quarterly Review,* 1 (April 1938), 193.

8. Williamstown Oration, in Bancroft, *Miscellanies,* 409, 413, 424.

9. Ibid., 415, 425, 434; *Hartford Address,* 2–3, 4; George Bancroft, *Springfield*

Oration (Boston, 1836), 8–10, 17; also "On the Progress of Civilization," *Boston Quarterly Review,* 1 (1838), 389–407.

10. George Bancroft, *History of the United States* (Boston, 1837), II, 246, 239, 195, 176, 323, 160.

11. Hubbard Winslow, *Oration Delivered July 4, 1838* (Boston, 1838), 19, 12–13, 14; also Robert C. Winthrop, "Free Schools and Free Government," *Addresses and Speeches* (Boston, 1852).

12. Williamstown Oration, Bancroft, *Miscellanies,* 424; *History,* II, 160, 176. There is no evidence, in Bancroft, either for or against a paternalistic government, which to Formisano and Daniel W. Howe is an issue dividing Whigs and Democrats.

13. Williamstown Oration, *Miscellanies,* 422, 430. See also Bancroft, *Hartford Address,* 4, 11; *Springfield Oration,* 10.

14. Williamstown Oration, *Miscellanies,* 423.

15. Bancroft, *Springfield Oration,* 4, 6, 8; *Hartford Address,* 4–5. See also Bancroft, *History,* II, 145–146, 191.

16. Bancroft, *Williamstown Oration,* 410, 411; Bancroft, "William E. Channing," *Miscellanies,* 439, 440. See also Bancroft, "Progress of Civilization," *Boston Quarterly Review,* 391–392. On the Whig view, see Winslow, *Oration,* 9–12.

17. For the Whig view of poverty, see Jonathan M. Wainwright, *Sermon Before His Excellency, John Davis, Governor, January 7, 1835* (Boston, 1835), 17; Winslow, *Oration,* 16–17; John W. Yeomans, *Sermon Before His Excellency, Levi Lincoln, Governor, January 1, 1834* (Boston, 1834). For Kirkland's view, see John T. Kirkland, *Discourse on the Death of George Cabot* (Boston, 1823).

18. George Bancroft to the Public, Boston *Courier,* October 22, 1834. Bancroft, "William E. Channing," *Miscellanies,* 436–437, 439, 441.

19. Harriet Martineau, *Retrospect of Western Travel* (London, 1838), II, 83, Charles Crowe, *George Ripley* (Athens, Ga., 1967), 58–60; George Bancroft to Ralph W. Emerson, February 29, 1836; Thomas Carlyle to George Bancroft, June 13, 1838; to Ralph W. Emerson, June 15, 1838, Charles F. Norton, ed., *The Correspondence of Thomas Carlyle and Ralph Waldo Emerson, 1834–1872* (Boston, 1883), I. Later he changed his mind and thought the French eclectics were overrated (Bancroft papers, NYPL). When asked to contribute financially to the commemoration of Carlyle, Bancroft sent one dollar. George Bancroft to Cupples, Upham & Co., May 19, 1885.

20. Bancroft, *History,* II, 145–146, 338, 379–382. On the problems of Lockean epistemology, see Cameron Thompson, "John Locke and New England Transcendentalism," *New England Quarterly,* 35 (1962), 435–457. The assault on Locke could, however, also tally with conservative views. See Benjamin R. Curtis, *Address at Deerfield* (Greenfield, Mass., 1832), 20–21.

21. See George Bancroft to R. W. Emerson, February 29, 1836; Crowe, *Ripley,* 12, 135; Mason Wade, *Margaret Fuller* (New York, 1940), 66, 108; also A. S. Ladu, "Emerson, Whig or Democrat," *New England Quarterly,* 13 (September 1940), 419–422; George Bancroft, "Holmes's Emerson," *North American Review,* 140 (February 1885), 134.

22. Ralph W. Emerson, "The Naturalist," *The Early Lectures,* S. E. Whicher and R. F. Spiller, eds. (Cambridge, Mass., 1959), I, 76. For Emerson on history

and on Bancroft, see A. R. Caponigri, "Brownson and Emerson, History and Nature," *New England Quarterly*, 18 (1945), 368–390; Joel Porte, ed., *Emerson in His Journals* (Cambridge, Mass., 1982), 294, 324.

23. Emerson, "The Uses of Natural History," *Early Lectures*, I, 20, 24. See also "The Naturalist," ibid., 81, 82.

24. Marvin Meyers, *The Jacksonian Persuasion* (Stanford, Calif., 1957), 2. See also Porte ed., *Emerson in His Journals*, 294, where Bancroft is classed with those who fear individualism.

25. Emerson, "George Fox," *Early Lectures*, I, 168, 175, 180, 182; George Bancroft to Ralph W. Emerson, February 29, 1836.

26. Bancroft, *History*, II, 326, 330, 331, 333, 337, 338, 341, 342. See also Alexander H. Everett to George Bancroft, January 11, 1842; "Transcendentalism," Boston *Morning Post*, August 31, 1838.

27. Bancroft, Williamstown Oration, *Miscellanies*, 420, 422, 424, 428, 430–431. Election figures in Formisano, *Transformation*, Appendix II, 351: Davis 57.7%, Morton 24.8%, Anti-Masons 13.9%, others, 3.4%.

28. Marcus Morton to George Bancroft, September 9, October 29, 1835; Orestes A. Brownson, "Democracy and Reform," *Boston Quarterly Review*, 2 (October 1839), 488–489. Bancroft's analysis tallies in part with that of Formisano, who shows that new voters were more important in swelling Democratic ranks than members of splinter groups.

29. William H. Prescott to George Bancroft, June 17, 1835; Charles G. Greene to George Bancroft, September 16, 1835.

30. Worcester *Republican*, September 30, 1835; *Hampshire Republican*, October 21, 1835; Boston *Statesman*, October 17, 1835; Marcus Morton to George Bancroft, September 9, October 29, 1835.

31. George Dickinson to George Bancroft, January 27, February 4, 23, March 1, May 11, 1835; J. R. Commons, *History of Labour* (New York, 1918), I, 318; Boston *Courier*, November 19, 1835; also Formisano, *Transformation*, 224–244, 253–255.

32. Boston *Transcript*, November 9, 1835; Formisano, *Transformation*, 254; Paul R. Frothingham, *Edward Everett* (Boston, 1925), 126–129; Marcus Morton to J. D. Pearce, October 10, 1835. Morton had 25,227 votes, Everett 37,555, others 1,901.

33. Orestes A. Brownson to George Bancroft, September 25, 1836; Mason A. Green, *Springfield, 1636–1886* (Springfield, Mass., 1887), 433–438; George Bancroft, *Springfield Oration, July 4, 1836* (Boston, 1836), 4, 5, 8–9, 30–31, 34–35.

34. On reaction to speech, see numerous letters in Bancroft Papers, MHS; Lucretia Bancroft to George Bancroft, September, 12, 1836.

35. David Henshaw, *Address, July 4, 1836* (Boston, 1836).

36. Marcus Morton to J. D. Pearce, June 6, 1836; to Martin Van Buren, June 16, 1836.

37. On Bancroft's congressional campaign, see Green *Springfield*, 438–439. Bancroft's diary (MHS) in these months shows efforts to assimilate more radical rhetoric than he earlier employed, but he used none of these slogans in his own electioneering.

38. Benjamin F. Hallett, *Oration, July 4, 1836* (Boston, 1836), 10, 42, 47.

George Bancroft to Orestes A. Brownson, September 21, 1836, in H. F. Brownson, *Orestes A. Brownson's Early Life* (Detroit, Mich., 1898–1900), I, 179–181.

39. Lucretia Bancroft to George Bancroft, May 18, 1837.

40. Francis Baylies, *Speech Before the Whigs of Taunton, September 13, 1837* (Taunton, Mass., 1837), 4, 6.

41. Arthur M. Schlesinger, Jr., *Orestes A. Brownson, A Pilgrim's Progress* (New York, 1963), 67–68; Robert Rantoul, Jr., *July 4, 1837, Oration* (Worcester, Mass., 1837), 20, 40, 71, 72.

42. Bancroft, *History*, II, 454, 455, 456, 468, 1.

43. Ibid., 128, 145, 2, 59, 139–150.

44. Ibid., 457, 459, 460.

45. Ibid., 344, 346, 350.

46. Condolence letters in Bancroft Papers, MHS.

47. Mary Bancroft to George Bancroft, July 6, 1837; George Bancroft to Mary Bancroft, July 25, August 8, 1837; George Bancroft to Louisa Bancroft, August 8, 1837; John Davis to George Bancroft, July 6, 1837; Henry Dwight to George Bancroft, September 21, 1837.

48. Bunker Hill Meeting in Darling, *Political Changes,* 206–208; Theodore Sedgwick to George Bancroft, September 14, 1837; Martin Van Buren to George Bancroft, September 14, 1837; David Henshaw, *Remarks Upon the Rights and Powers of Corporations* (Boston, 1837), 9, 10, 11; George Bancroft, *History of the United States* (Boston, 1837), I, 390.

49. Francis Baylies, *Speech . . . Taunton,* 14, 16; *To the Electors of Massachusetts: An Address October 4, 1837* (Worcester, 1837), 33; *To the Independent Voters of Middlesex County,* October 4, 1837; Marcus Morton to George Bancroft, September 17, 1837; William Marcy to George Bancroft, September 25, 1837.

50. William Parmenter to George Bancroft, October 12, 1837; William Marcy to George Bancroft, October 12, 31, 1837; Henry Dwight to George Bancroft, October 6, 21, 1837.

51. Seth Thomas to George Bancroft, November 2, 1837; George Ripley to George Bancroft, September 20, November 6, 1837; Crowe, *George Ripley,* 130–133; Lucretia Bancroft to George Bancroft, November 12, 1837. For party reorganization, see Formisano, *Transformation,* 258–259.

52. *Address of the Democratic State Committee of Massachusetts, Worcester, September 20, 1837; The Advocate,* November 1, 1837. The 1837 election results: Whigs 60.3%, Democrats 39.4%.

53. See large correspondence related to struggle over collectorship in Bancroft Papers, MHS, and Morton Letterbooks, MHS. For party factionalism, see also Abraham Lansing, *Brief Remarks in Reply to an Article in the Boston Morning Post on March 11, 1837* (Boston, 1837).

54. Some problems associated with the job can be traced in J. B. Derby, *Political Reminiscences* (Boston, 1835); W. H. Prescott to George Bancroft, January 12, 1838; *Refutation by His Friends of the Calumnies Against David Henshaw* (Boston, 1844); Benjamin R. Curtis to George Ticknor, January 14, 1838, in Benjamin R. Curtis, Jr., ed., *A Memoir of Benjamin R. Curtis* (Boston, 1879), 81.

55. Benjamin F. Hallett to George Bancroft, January 6, 8, 1838; William Parmenter to George Bancroft, January 8, 1838; Samuel Clesson Allen to George Bancroft, January 29, 1838; Marcus Morton to George Bancroft, February 3, 1838. For Washington's effort to help David Henshaw, see Seth Thomas to George Bancroft, January 29, 1838.

56. Undated report of Harris to George Bancroft, early 1838, in Bancroft Papers, MHS, came after Bancroft had accepted the job. See also extensive correspondence in January-February 1838 file, Bancroft Papers, MHS.

57. For the courtship, and problems with children, see extensive correspondence in April-July 1838 file, Bancroft Papers, MHS. Elizabeth's early letters are preserved in Bancroft-Bliss Correspondence, Library of Congress.

58. Levi Woodbury to George Bancroft, March 22, April 16, July 9, 1838. On aid to Henshaw, see *Refutation by His Friends.*

59. Henry Gilpin to George Bancroft, April 27, July 20, 1838. For the support Bancroft enjoyed from the Henshaw-Greene people, see Boston *Morning Post,* September 21, 1838, March 12, 1839, October 5, 1839.

60. Boston *Atlas,* October 26, November 9, 17, 1838. That Bancroft's method was attracting independent voters, see Richard Hildreth, *Report of Whig Committee, Proceedings of a Great Whig Meeting of the Citizens of Boston, October 10, 1838* (Boston, 1838). Asked to sign a petition in Kneeland's favor, Bancroft refused. See Ellis G. Loring to George Bancroft, June 13, 1838. The same cautious attitude also led to Bancroft's fence mending with Calhoun; see John C. Calhoun to George Bancroft, April 14, 1838.

61. Financial difficulties can be traced in the July 1838-March 1839 files, Bancroft Papers, MHS.

62. Levi Woodbury to George Bancroft, August 31, 1839. See also George Bancroft to Levi Woodbury, June 1, 1839; George Bancroft to Henry Gilpin, June 22, October 14, 1839; William Dwight to George Bancroft, June 29, 1839; Henry Dwight to George Bancroft, June 14, 19, July 9, 1839.

63. Levi Woodbury to George Bancroft, September 9, October 20, 1839. For another interpretation of Bancroft's activities on behalf of the Michigan bank, see Harry N. Scheiber, "George Bancroft and the Bank of Michigan 1837-1842," *Michigan History,* 44 (March 1960), 82-90.

64. Benjamin Hallett, *Oration Delivered July 4, 1839* (Worcester 1839), 30, 19. For local effect of the law, see Green, *Springfield,* 439-440. See also John P. Tarbell, *Oration Before the Democratic Citizens of the Northern Part of Middlesex County* (Lowell, Mass., 1839); Seth J. Thomas, *Address Delivered Before the Democratic Citizens of Plymouth County* (Boston, 1839).

65. Edward Everett to Robert C. Winthrop, October 28, 1839; Daniel Henshaw to George Bancroft, October 4, 1839; Arthur M. Schlesinger, Jr., *The Age of Jackson* (Boston, 1946), 256-257. For election results, see Formisano, *Transformation,* 298-299; Whigs 49.7%, Democrats 50%.

66. J. M. Niles to George Bancroft, November 25, 1839; Levi Woodbury to George Bancroft, November 21, 1839; E. D. Beach to George Bancroft, November 13, 1839.

67. *Hampshire Gazette,* October 8, 1834. The *North American Review* article on slavery in Rome (1834) expressed the same spirit, which swiftly evaporated in the face of Democratic difficulties. In the *History* Bancroft traced slavery

to climatic differences to explain why it did not flourish in the North, thus absolving the South of moral inferiority to the North.

68. Angelina Grimké to George Bancroft, n.d., filed correctly in 1838 folder, Bancroft papers, MHS; Joshua Leavitt to George Bancroft, June 20, 1839; Carl Follen to George Bancroft, October 23, 1837.

69. J. G. Harris to George Bancroft, January 25, 1839; George Bancroft to Andrew Jackson, June 25, 1839. On Jane's estate, see letters in the Bancroft Papers, MHS. For other nonabolitionist views, see the review of the Duke of Saxe-Weimar's travels in the United States, where Bancroft criticized the Duke for being too partial to slaves, George Bancroft, "Saxe-Weimar's Travels," *North American Review,* 28 (January 1829), 242, 249. If a mulatto woman fared better in Europe (as the Duke claimed), this meant (according to Bancroft) not greater tolerance "to a tinge of negro blood but a less delicate sense of the nature of conjugal relations."

vii. *The Popular Will*

1. Thomas Wentworth Higginson, *Carlyle's Laugh and Other Surprises* (Boston, 1919), 107. The Bancroft Papers, MHS, detail social activities, as do the biographies of the period's leading political and intellectual figures.

2. George Bancroft to Joseph T. Buckingham, November 20, 1840, in Mark de Wolfe Howe, *Life and Letters of George Bancroft* (New York, 1908), I, 235. For cooperation on historical research, see extensive correspondence in the Bancroft papers, MHS.

3. Orestes A. Brownson, "Introductory Statement," *Boston Quarterly Review,* 3 (January 1840), 14–15. Martin Van Buren to George Bancroft, March 18, 1840, in Worthington Chauncey Ford, "Van Buren-Bancroft Correspondence," Massachusetts Historical Society, *Proceedings,* 42 (1909), 385; George Bancroft, *Hartford Oration* (Hartford, 1840), 2, 16; J. M. Niles to George Bancroft, November 25, 1839.

4. *Bay State Democrat,* November 8, 1839; "The Progress of Redemption," ibid., November 15, 1839; "The Result," ibid., November 22, 1839.

5. Ibid., August 16, 1939; "Americus," ibid., August 23, 1839. See also ibid., September 20, 27, October 25, November 1, 8, 1839.

6. Governor Morton's address to the legislature quoted in Orestes A. Brownson, "Answer of the Whig Members," *Boston Quarterly Review,* 3 (April 1840), 241–242, 249, 250, 252, 253. See also letters of support in Bancroft Papers, MHS.

7. Charles J. Bullock, *Historical Sketch of the Finances and Financial Policy of Massachusetts from 1780 to 1905* (New York, 1907), 40–41.

8. J. G. Harris to George Bancroft, February 19, March 27, 1840; Alexander H. Everett to George Bancroft, March 20, 1840.

9. On Whig activities, see *Constitution and By Laws of the Harrison Club of Boston, April 3, 1840* (Boston, 1840), 1; also Whig Association, *Massachusetts Defrauded in Relation to the Public Lands* (Boston, 1840); R. G. Gunderson, *The Log Cabin Campaign* (Lexington, Ky., 1957).

10. J. M. Niles to George Bancroft, March 10, May 21, June 1, 1840; Levi

Woodbury to George Bancroft, March 10, 1840; F. M. Leland to George Bancroft, March 14, 1840; Alexander H. Everett to George Bancroft, March 17, 1840.

11. Richard A. Abbott, *Cobbler in Congress: The Life of Henry Wilson, 1812–1875* (Lexington, Ky., 1972), 14–18, 19; Mason A. Green, *History of Springfield, 1636–1886* (Springfield, Mass., 1886), 442–443.

12. Bancroft, *Hartford Oration,* 14. See also Jonathan B. Mann, *An Appeal to the Loco Focos* (Boston, 1840), 10–11.

13. Green, *Springfield,* 441; Bancroft, *Hartford Oration,* 16; Henry Gilpin to George Bancroft, June 17, 1840.

14. Howe, *Life and Letters,* I, 231–233, 234; A. Alden to George Bancroft, July 6, 1840; George Bancroft to Committee of Arrangements, July 10, 1840; Washington *Globe,* September 29, 1840; *National Intelligencer,* July 9, 1840; Gunderson, *Log Cabin Campaign,* 175. Thirty towns requested Webster's services for that day.

15. George Bancroft to Committee on Arrangements, July 10, 1840; *Proceedings of the Democratic Legislative Convention, March 1840* (Boston, 1840), 9–10; George Bancroft to Martin Van Buren, November 2, 1840, in Ford, *Correspondence,* 386–387.

16. *Bay State Democrat,* July 19, 1840; George Bancroft to Committee of Arrangements, July 19, 1839, July 10, 1840. Bancroft Papers, MHS, document his activities and statements. Even Prescott's *Ferdinand and Isabella* was drawn into the campaign, in support of hard-money policies. See William H. Prescott to George Bancroft, April (?) 1840. For a sample of party unity, see Charles G. Greene and Benjamin F. Hallett, *The Identity of the Old Hartford Convention Federalists* (Boston, 1840).

17. Orestes A. Brownson, "The Laboring Classes," *Boston Quarterly Review,* 3 (July 1840), 370, 375, 395; see also Hugh Marshall, *Orestes A. Brownson and the American Republic* (Washington, D.C., 1971), 22–26; Arthur Schlesinger, Jr., *Orestes A. Brownson: A Pilgrim's Progress* (New York, 1963), 112–114, 302–303; Charles Sumner to William Whewell, October 17, 1840; Edward L. Pierce, *Memoir and Letters of Charles Sumner* (Boston, 1877–1893), II, 167–168. See also "Loco-focoism as displayed in the Boston Magazine against schools and ministers, and in favor of robbing children of the property of their Parents," Albany *Evening Journal,* August 25, 1840.

18. George Bancroft to W. H. McAllister, August 15, 1840. On early support of the *Boston Quarterly Review,* see Levi Woodbury to George Bancroft, November 21, 1839.

19. *Bay State Democrat,* editorial, September 9, 1840; Gunderson, *Log Cabin Campaign,* 232; Levi Woodbury to George Bancroft, September 28, 1840.

20. William H. Prescott to George Bancroft, September 30, 1840; Benjamin F. Hunt to George Bancroft, October 3, 1840; Edward Everett to George Bancroft, February 15, 17, 1840.

21. E. D. Beach to George Bancroft, October 2, 1840; George Bancroft to Martin Van Buren, November 2, 1840, in Ford, *Correspondence,* 387. Election results: Whigs 55.7%, Democrats, 43.3%.

22. Martin Van Buren to George Bancroft, November 20, 1840; George Ban-

croft to Martin Van Buren, December 3, 1840, in Ford, *Correspondence,* 388–389.

23. George Bancroft, *History of the United States* (Boston, 1840), III, 397, 398.

24. George Bancroft to Levi Woodbury, draft, February 1841, February 22, 1841. For the long debate and maneuvers surrounding the resignation, see Bancroft Papers, MHS. See also George Bancroft to Martin Van Buren, December 3, 1840, February 23, 1841, in Ford, *Correspondence,* 388–390.

25. For Bancroft's financial dealings see letters and fiscal documents in the MHS files.

26. Trustees and William Dwight to George Bancroft, November 16, 1840; William Dwight to George Bancroft, November 23, December 14, 31, 1840; May 17, 29, 1841; January 27, February 16, 1841; George Bancroft to Trustees of Dwight Estate, January 23, 1841; Henry Dwight to George Bancroft, April 13, 1841; George Bancroft to Dwight Trustees, April 19, 1841; to William Dwight, April 1, 17, 1841; to Henry Dwight, April 22, 1841; William E. Sill to George Bancroft, May 3, June 17, October 25, 1841.

27. Edmund Dwight to George Bancroft, April 15, 1842; George Bancroft to Dwight Trustees, February 21, 1842; to Edmund Dwight, April 8, 12, 1842; to Franklin S. Haven, April 14, 1842.

28. Levi Woodbury deposition in case of *Bancroft* v. *Dwight,* filed November 17, 1842; Elizabeth Bancroft to George Bancroft, December 13, 17, 1842. See also Franklin Dexter to George Bancroft, December 12, 1842.

29. George Bancroft to Trustees of Dwight Estate, March 31, 1843; to Edmund Dwight, February 14, 1843; Edmund Dwight to George Bancroft, February 20, 1843; Dwight Trustees to George Bancroft, April 31, 1843.

30. Alexander H. Everett to George Bancroft, October 15, 1841; Marcus Morton to George Bancroft, March 4, 1841; *Bay State Democrat,* November 17, 1841. Election results of 1841: Whigs 50.4%, Democrats 46.3%.

31. Platform, *Bay State Democrat,* June 3, 1842; George Bancroft, *Address at Cambridge, September 28, 1842.* Compare *Address of the Democratic Members of the Massachusetts Legislature to Their Constituents and the People at the Close of the Session for 1841* (n.p., 1841).

32. Robert Rantoul to George Bancroft, September 13, 1842; Worcester County Committee to George Bancroft, October 15, 1842; Marcus Morton to George Bancroft, November 8, 1842; George Bancroft to Martin Van Buren, November 23, 1842; in Ford, *Correspondence,* 394-395.

33. Election results of 1842: Whigs 46.6%, Democrats, 47.9%, Liberty Party 5.4%.

34. George Bancroft, "Progress of Civilization," *Boston Quarterly Review,* 1 (October 1838), 402; George Bancroft, *Literary and Historical Miscellanies* (New York, 1855), 499-500.

35. George Bancroft to Elizabeth Bancroft, December 25, 31, 1842; George Bancroft to Martin Van Buren, January 12, 1843, in Ford, *Correspondence,* 397; Henry Gilpin to George Bancroft, December 12, 1842.

36. *Review of the Proceedings of the Massachusetts Legislature for 1843, by the Whig Minority* (Boston, 1843); *Address of the Whig Members of the Senate and the House of Representatives* (Boston, 1843).

37. George Bancroft to Sarah Bancroft, January 13, 17, 1832; William Lyon McKenzie, *The Life and Times of Martin Van Buren* (Boston, 1846), 295. These remarks formed a portion of Bancroft's letter to the Workingmen; see *Hampshire Gazette,* October 8, 1834.

38. George Bancroft, *History of the United States,* II, 193–194; III, 401–413. See also George Bancroft, "Slavery in Rome," *North American Review,* 34 (October 1834), 413–437, where the emphasis was on the political, social, and economic costs of bondage to the slave owners.

39. Bancroft, *Miscellanies,* 437, 515. For contemporary attacks, see *George Bancroft, Secretary of the Navy and the Traducer and Eulogist of General Andrew Jackson* (Washington, 1846), 4. On Bancroft's troubles with the abolitionists, see also Benjamin F. Hallett to George Bancroft, March 22, 1845.

40. *Review of the Proceedings of the Legislature for 1843 by the Whig Minority,* 5; *Address of Whig Members,* 16.

41. Marcus Morton to George Bancroft, January 9, 15, 1843; John Dunforth to President John Tyler, April 20, 1843 (copy in Bancroft Papers); John A. Bolles to George Bancroft, May 6, 1843. Bancroft was elected VP of the Boston Lyceum, May 19, 1843.

42. On party manipulations, see Charles M. Wiltse, *John C. Calhoun, Sectionalist 1840–1850* (New York, 1968), 98, 144–145; Isaac O. Barnes to John C. Calhoun, January 27, 1843; "Correspondence Addressed to John C. Calhoun, 1837–1849," American Historical Association, *Annual Report* (1929), 181–182. One local Calhoun supporter was Brownson. See Orestes A. Brownson, "Bancroft's History," *Boston Quarterly Review,* 4 (October 1841). On Tyler strength, see Foster Hooper to George Bancroft, July 11, 1843.

43. *Address of the Whig Members,* 42, 47.

44. George Bancroft to Martin Van Buren, November 23, December 9, 1842, February 16, May 10, 23, 1843, in Ford, *Correspondence,* 394–396, 398–399, 402–403, 404–405. Darling, *Political Changes,* 302–310; Boston *Atlas,* August 29, 1843; Marcus Morton to George Bancroft, September 12, 1843; Benjamin F. Hallett to George Bancroft, August 28, 1843; Foster Hooper to George Bancroft, July 11, 1843; Green, *Springfield,* 454–455; *Bay State Democrat,* December 23, 1843.

45. George Bancroft to Martin Van Buren, June 6, June 22, July 18, September 28, 1843, in Ford, *Correspondence,* 406–412, 413–415.

46. George Bancroft to Martin Van Buren, June 6, 1843, in Ford, *Correspondence,* 406.

47. George Bancroft to Martin Van Buren, September 1, 1843, in Ford, *Correspondence,* 413.

48. On Calhoun's local support, see Lemuel Williams to John C. Calhoun, September 6, 1843, in J. Franklin Jameson, ed., "The Correspondence of John C. Calhoun," American Historical Association, *Annual Report* (1899), II, 874–878; George Bancroft to Martin Van Buren, September 14, 1843, in Ford, *Correspondence,* 414, and other letters in Bancroft Papers.

49. Martin Van Buren to George Bancroft, February 25, July 3, 1844; Silas Wright to George Bancroft, April 8, 1844; John Garraty, *Silas Wright* (New York, 1949), 244–245; John L. O'Sullivan to George Bancroft, April 15, 23, 1844; George Bancroft to John L. O'Sullivan, April 18, 1844.

50. George Bancroft to Martin Van Buren, March 28, April 22, 1844, in Ford, *Correspondence,* 421–422, 424–425. George Bancroft to Marcus Morton, May 4, 1844; Marcus Morton to George Bancroft, May 5, 1844.

51. Marcus Morton to George Bancroft, May 5, 1844; William Parmenter to George Bancroft, May 6, 1844; George Bancroft to Martin Van Buren, May 2, 1844, in Ford, *Correspondence,* 426. John L. O'Sullivan to George Bancroft, May 10, 1844; William B. King to George Bancroft, May 12, 1844.

52. Silas Wright to George Bancroft, May 2, 6, 1844; Martin Van Buren to George Bancroft, May 8, 1844; William Parmenter to George Bancroft, May 1, 1844. See also Garraty, *Silas Wright,* 256–267.

53. George Bancroft to Elizabeth Bancroft, May (?) 1844; George Bancroft to Martin Van Buren, May 21, 23, 1844, in Ford, *Correspondence,* 428-430.

54. George Bancroft to Martin Van Buren, May 24, 1844, in Ford, *Correspondence,* 430.

55. George Bancroft to James K. Polk, July 6, 1844; Garraty, *Silas Wright,* 278; Samuel S. Green, "George Bancroft," *American Antiquarian Society Proceedings* (April 1891), 244–245. The convention and its results have been often examined; see Charles M. Wiltse, *John C. Calhoun* (Indianapolis, 1951), and Charles G. Sellers, *James K. Polk* (Princeton, N.J., 1957).

56. Bancroft, "William E. Channing," *Miscellanies,* 437, 438, 440; *History,* III, 2, 35, 76; also George Bancroft to Martin Van Buren, September 6, 1844, in Ford, *Correspondence,* 432.

57. Bancroft, *History,* III, 397, 399.

58. Green, *Springfield,* 456-457; Charles G. Greene to George Bancroft, June 4, 1844; J. G. Harris to George Bancroft, June 15, July 17, 1844; J.S.C. Knowlton to George Bancroft, July 5, 1844. See also Alonzo Lewis and James R. Newhall, *History of Lynn* (Boston, 1865), 414–415; James Phinney Munroe, *A Life of Francis Amasa Walker* (New York, 1923), 12–13; Roy F. Nichols, *Franklin Pierce* (Philadelphia, 1931), 131.

59. George Bancroft to James K. Polk, July 6, 1844.

60. Charles Sumner to George Bancroft, July 31, 1844, Edward L. Pierce, *Memoir and Letters of Charles Sumner* (Boston 1877-1893), II, 310; also Isaac Davis to George Bancroft, August 20, 1844; William J. Hawes to George Bancroft, August 30, 1844. The Pittsfield *Sun* predicted the demise of "that same old coon . . . the disease was found to be Polk fever," in Bancroft Papers, 1844 file, MHS. According to the Northampton *Democrat,* September 17, 1844, even the *Indiana State Sentinel* endorsed his candidacy.

61. George Bancroft to Committee on Arrangements, August 15, 1844, outlines his Texas vision and campaign agenda. See also campaign issues and slogans in *Bay State Democrat,* October 25, 31, November 1, 2, 4, 1844. For the origins of the idea that slaves might escape to South America, see Whitfield J. Bell, "The Relation of Herndon and Gibbon's Exploration of the Amazon to North American Slavery, 1850–1855," *Hispanic American Review,* 19 (1939), 394–503.

62. For events in Rhode Island, see Arthur M. Mowry, *The Dorr War* (Providence, R.I., 1901); George M. Dennison, *The Dorr War, Republicanism on Trial, 1831–1861* (Lexington, Ky., 1976); Marvin E. Gettleman, *The Dorr Rebellion 1833–1849* (New York, 1973).

63. The prolonged involvement of the Massachusetts Democracy with the Dor-
    rites can be traced through Alexander H. Everett to the editor, *The New Age,*
    November 8, 1841, in Dennison, *Dorr War,* 47; Gettleman, *Dorr Rebellion,*
    178–179; Henry B. Anthony, *The Dorriad and the Great Slocum Dinner*
    (Providence, R.I., 1870). For Bancroft's invitation to attend, see Committee
    of Correspondence to George Bancroft, August 2, 1844, also published in
    Mobile (Alabama) *Register.* See also Charles T. Congdon, *Reminiscences of a
    Journalist* (Boston, 1880), 114–115.
64. George Ticknor Curtis, *Merits of George Bancroft and Thomas Dorr as They Are
    Politically Connected* (Boston, 1844), 28–39, published during the campaign,
    reprinted Bancroft's letter. *Niles Register,* September 14, 1844, also quoted
    Bancroft. The Whig Norfolk *American* article was reprinted in the *Bay State
    Democrat,* October 15, 1844.
65. George Bancroft to Committee of Correspondence, September 12, 1844;
    "To the Friends of the Bay State Democrat," *Bay State Democrat,* September
    24, 1844. His sister assumed, correctly, that Bancroft disapproved of the
    behavior of Democrats in Rhode Island; see Jane Gerhardi to George Ban-
    croft, July 11, 1842.
66. George Bancroft to Elizabeth Bancroft, October (?), 1844.
67. Curtis, *Merits,* 32, 35, 36. See also *To George Bancroft, Secretary of the Navy,
    the Traducer and Eulogist of General Andrew Jackson* (Washington, D.C.,
    1846), 4; *George Bancroft: The Story of His Characteristic Treachery and Fraud*
    (Boston, 1846). Joseph Buckingham came to Bancroft's defense in the Bos-
    ton *Courier,* praising his efforts to prevent the misuse of his *History.* On the
    Whig uses of history, see George Ticknor Curtis, *The True Uses of Revolu-
    tionary History: Oration Delivered July 5, 1841* (Boston, 1841), 7, 14, 28.
68. Martin Van Buren to George Bancroft, September 10, 1844; Elizabeth Ban-
    croft to George Bancroft, September 18, 1844; George Bancroft to Eliza-
    beth Bancroft, September 25, 1844. Speech at Poughkeepsie in *Bay State
    Democrat,* September 25, 1844.
69. For Bancroft's optimism, see Charles Sumner to George Sumner, July 1, 31,
    1844, Pierce, *Charles Sumner,* II, 309–311. On Bancroft's involvement, see
    John Fairfield to George Bancroft, August 1, 1844; *Bay State Democrat,*
    September 24, 27, 30, October 1, 5, 10, 11, 12, 1844. Even Benjamin
    Hallett cooperated; see *Niles Register,* September 14, 1844. For one recorded
    instance of Bancroft's oratorical style, see Congdon, *Reminiscences,* 63-64.
70. *Bay State Democrat,* November 12, 1844. Whigs 51.8%, Democrats, 40.8%,
    Liberty Party 7.2%.

VIII. *Manifest Destiny*

1. George Bancroft to Marcus Morton, November 23, 1844; Marcus Morton
   to George Bancroft, November 26, 1844; George Bancroft to John Bragg,
   December 25, 1844.
2. For the background and history of Bancroft's Harvard reform proposals and
   relations with president Josiah Quincy see Bancroft Papers, MHS, December 1843 memoranda; George Bancroft to Jared Sparks, June 4, 1829; to
   Edward Everett, June 20, July 11, 1834; also George Bancroft and Linus

Child, *Report on Diminishing the Cost of Instruction at Harvard College* (Boston, 1845); John C. Gray, *Minority Report on the Same Subject* (Boston, 1845); Josiah Quincy, *Speech Before the Board of Overseers, February 25, 1845* (Boston, 1845); Robert McCaughey, *Josiah Quincy* (Cambridge, Mass., 1974). The question became a campaign issue later in the fall; see Elizabeth Bancroft to George Bancroft, September 23, 1845; John A. Bolles to George Bancroft, September 24, 1845.

3. John Bragg to George Bancroft, December 6, 1844; George Bancroft to Department of Treasury, December 3, 10, 1844.

4. William Parmenter to George Bancroft, January 8, 29, 1845; Jared Sparks to George Bancroft, February 4, 1845; Benjamin F. Hallett to George Bancroft, January 19, 1845; Marcus Morton to George Bancroft, January 27, 1845; William H. Marcy to George Bancroft, January 4, 1845; John Fairfield to George Bancroft, February 13, 1845; George Bancroft to James K. Polk, January 1, 1845; James K. Polk to George Bancroft, January 30, 1845; George Bancroft to Martin Van Buren, January 22, 1845, trace cabinet rumors and requests for aid.

5. George Bancroft to Martin Van Buren, February 11, 1845, in Worthington C. Ford, "Van Buren-Bancroft Correspondence," Massachusetts Historical Society, *Proceedings,* 42 (1909), 437; Benjamin F. Hallett to George Bancroft, February 13, 1845; Marcus Morton to George Bancroft, February 28, 1845.

6. See Charles G. Sellers, *James K. Polk, Continentalist* (Princeton, N.J., 1957), 182, for appointment problems. See also George Bancroft to Elizabeth Bancroft, February 15, 20, March 2, 1845; John Garraty, *Silas Wright* (New York, 1949), 333–361.

7. Martin Van Buren to George Bancroft, March 7, 1845, in Ford, *Correspondence,* 439–440.

8. George Bancroft to Marcus Morton, March 10, 1845.

9. George Bancroft to Elizabeth Bancroft, March 6, 1845.

10. Leonard White, *The Jacksonians* (New York, 1954), 230; William H. Prescott to George Bancroft, March 15, 1845; Theodore Parker to George Bancroft, May 26, 1845; Boston *Times,* March 13, 1845; New York *World,* March 8, 1845. The story that Bancroft defined himself as an antislavery man was a post–Civil War invention. See Samuel Swett Green, "George Bancroft," American Antiquarian Society, *Proceedings,* 7 (April 1891), 245.

11. See Theodore Parker to George Bancroft, September 2, 1846, for a belated condolence letter that called her "a transcendental baby." Elizabeth Bancroft to George Bancroft, September 14, 17, 19, 22, 1845; Jacob Bigelow to George Bancroft, October 1, 1845; Thomas Davis to George Bancroft, October 17, 1845.

12. Elizabeth Bancroft to George Bancroft, October 22, 23, 24, 1845; Henry Gilpin to George Bancroft, October 24, 1845; Eliza Davis to George Bancroft, November 5, 1845.

13. John A. Weisse's school reports for John Chandler and George, March, October, November 1845; George Bancroft to Bancroft Gerhardi, April 17, 1846; to William Dwight, April 18, 1846; to Lucretia Farnum, May 8, 1846.

14. On Louisa's problems see correspondence in Bancroft Papers, MHS and CUMR.

15. John A. Weisse to George Bancroft, August 6, 1846; George Bancroft to John A. Weisse, August 11, 1846. In the summer, the children were disposed of, usually in Hingham. See Charles Francis Adams, *Autobiography* (New York, 1916), 195; John Chandler Bancroft to George Bancroft, October 31, 1842, June 24, 1843.

16. Marcus Morton to George Bancroft, March 14, 1845; Charles G. Greene to George Bancroft, March 17, 21, 1845; John A. Bolles to George Bancroft, March 22, 1845; Benjamin F. Hallett to George Bancroft, March 22, 1845; Pliny Merrick to George Bancroft, March 24, 1845.

17. See letters of complaint in March, April, and May 1845 file, Bancroft Papers, MHS.

18. Franklin Haven to Robert J. Walker, March 31, 1845; to George Bancroft, April 1, July 29, 1845; George Bancroft to Franklin Haven, July 25, 1845; to Isaac Wright, April 5, 12, 1845; to Charles G. Greene, April 10, 18, 1845; William Parmenter to George Bancroft, April 15, 1845.

19. See extensive correspondence in May-August 1845 files, Bancroft Papers, MHS. For the problems created for Hallett later, see Charles T. Congdon, *Reminiscences of a Journalist* (Boston, 1880), 137–138.

20. George Bancroft to A. Loring Cushing, February 17, 1846. The vast correspondence relevant to these problems extended until August 1846. One indication of Morton's problems is in Polk's diary, February 2, 1846, in James K. Polk, *Polk: The Diary of a President,* Allan Nevins, ed. (London, 1929), 47.

21. Sarah Henderson to George Bancroft, June 16, 1845; Catherine Garrettson to George Bancroft, February 28, 1845; William C. Bryant to George Bancroft, March 5, 6, 1845; John O'Sullivan to George Bancroft, March 16, April 19, 23, May 2, 1845.

22. See *To George Bancroft, Secretary of the Navy, the Traducer and Eulogist of General Andrew Jackson* (Washington, D.C., 1846), 4, 8, 9.

23. Charles Oscar Paullin, *History of the Naval Administration 1775–1911* (Annapolis, Md., 1968), 221, 227, 233; Henry B. Hibben, *History of the Navy Yard in Washington* (Washington, D.C., 1890), 82, 87; Harold and Margaret Sprout, *The Rise of American Naval Power 1776–1918* (Princeton, N.J., 1944); Howard I. Chapelle, *The History of the American Sailing Navy* (New York, 1949); Charles Oscar Paullin, *Naval Administration, 1842–1861* (U.S. Naval Institute, n.p., 1907). For a possible source of Bancroft's naval reform suggestions, see William S. M. Ruschenberger, *Hints on the Reorganization of the Navy* (New York, 1845). See also *Congressional Globe,* January 28, 1846, 263; February 16, 1846, 374; March 8, 1846, 449; March 30, 1846, 572; April 9, 1846, 609.

24. Northampton *Democrat,* December 16, 1845. See also Robert G. Albion, "The Naval Affairs Committees, 1816-1947," U.S. Naval Institute, *Proceedings,* 78 (1952). Other newspaper clippings, December 1846 file, Bancroft Manuscripts, MHS, comment favorably on Bancroft's annual report.

25. *To George Bancroft, Traducer,* 9. See also Paullin, *History of the Naval Administration,* 227–237.

26. *To George Bancroft, Traducer,* 9. See also Peter Karsten, *The Naval Aristocracy* (New York, 1972), 284.

27. Park Benjamin, *The United States Naval Academy* (New York, 1900), 150–151; Mahon S. Tisdale, "A Cruise Through the First Academic Journal," U.S. Naval Institute, *Proceedings,* 50 (March 1924), 352, 353; George Bancroft to Board of Philadelphia Naval Asylum, June 13, 1845; Board to George Bancroft, June 25, 1845; John L. O'Sullivan to George Bancroft, May 23, 1845. For antecedents, see F. M. Brown, "A Half Century of Frustration," U.S. Naval Institute, *Proceedings,* 80 (1954).

28. Tisdale, "Cruise," 355; *Niles Register,* July 19, 1845; Karsten, *Naval Aristocracy,* 69. William Chauvenet, *History and Origins of the United States Naval Academy* (n.d., n.p. [October, 1860]), 3. See also Henry F. Sturdy, "The Founding of the Naval Academy," and "The First Academic Staff," in U.S. Naval Institute, *Proceedings,* 61 (1935).

29. Chauvenet, *History,* 10–11. See also *Plan and Regulations of the Naval School* (Washington, D.C., 1846).

30. Brooklyn *Eagle,* September 8, 1846. For reaction of one of the first students, see letters of William N. Jeffers to Anne H. Brewster in Elihu S. Riley, "Early Days of the Naval Academy," *The United Service* (February 1905).

31. George Bancroft, "Commemoration of Andrew Jackson," *Literary and Historical Miscellanies* (New York, 1855), 470–471.

32. Ibid., 446, 462–463. See also George Bancroft, "Polk biography," unpublished fragment, NYPL Bancroft Ms, 26–27, 32, 47, 49.

33. The effort to make Jackson a national, rather than merely Democratic, hero informed Bancroft's commemorative address, which left out party labels.

34. On preparation for the address and audience reactions, see Roger B. Taney to George Bancroft, June 24, 1845; Louis McLane to George Bancroft, June 15, 1845; William S. Waite to George Bancroft, June 12, 1845; Lucien B. Chase, *History of the Polk Administration* (New York, 1850), 25; *Niles Register,* June 28, 1845.

35. Bancroft, *Miscellanies,* 444, 463, 466.

36. Ibid., 465, 470. Compare George Bancroft, "On the Progress of Civilization," *Boston Quarterly Review,* 1 (October 1838), 395.

37. Bancroft, *Miscellanies,* 464–465.

38. Ibid., 447, 462–463.

39. Ibid., 480.

40. James Schouler, *History of the United States Under the Constitution* (New York, 1889), IV, 499; also Sellers, *Polk,* 213; for accounts of this meeting.

41. Eugene McCormac, *James K. Polk* (Berkeley, Calif., 1922), 374–375.

42. Bancroft's views on Oregon appear in George Bancroft, *Acceptance Speech, August 14, 1844;* George Bancroft to William Sturgis, August 25, 1845; Edward Everett to George Bancroft, November 10, 17, 1845; George Bancroft to Edward Everett, November 14, 1845; to Louis McLane, December 12, 1845.

43. George Bancroft to William Sturgis, August 25, 1845; Bancroft, "Polk biography," 48. For Bancroft's cabinet views, see Polk, *Diary,* August 26, 1845, p. 4., August 27, 1845, p. 5; Sellers, *Polk,* 250–251; George Bancroft

to Louis McLane, June 10, July 23, 1845; to William Sturgis, June 11, 1845.

44. George Bancroft to Commodore Robert Stockton, June 2, 15, 1845; George Bancroft to Commodore David Conner, July 11, December 10, 1845. See also George Bancroft to Henry Wikoff, May 12, 1845; to Samuel Hooper, June 28, 1845.

45. George Bancroft to David Conner, August 30, 1845; David Conner to George Bancroft, September 3, 11, 1845, quoted in David Pletcher, *Awkward Years in American Foreign Relations,* (Columbia, Mo., 1962), 260; William Kemble to George Bancroft, August 29, 1845, September 3, 1845; John D. Bradford to George Bancroft, August 17, 1845. See also David Conner to George Bancroft, October 20, 1845.

46. George Bancroft to Commodore John D. Sloat, June 24, October 17, 1845. For Polk's views in September 1845, see Polk, *Diary,* September 16, 1845, pp. 9–10.

47. George Bancroft to Louis McLane, March 29, 1846. See also David Conner to George Bancroft, March 19, April 9, 1846; Polk, *Diary,* February 16, 1846, pp. 52–53; February 28, 1846, pp. 58–59.

48. George Bancroft to Louis McLane, March 29, 1846. For Polk's views, see Polk, *Diary,* March 28, 1846, pp. 65–68.

49. McCormac, *James K. Polk,* 405; George Bancroft to John Van Buren, April 13, 1846.

50. George Bancroft to I. M. Holmes, May 16, 1846; to Samuel Hooper, June 10, 1846. See Bancroft Papers, NYPL and MHS for further correspondence in these months. For the cabinet meeting, see Polk, *Diary,* May 13, 1846, pp. 89–93.

51. William H. Prescott to Thomas Aspinwall, July 15, 1845; to George Sumner, August 15, 1845, in Roger Wolcott, ed., *The Correspondence of William H. Prescott, 1833–1847* (Boston, 1925), 547–550; John Davis to George Bancroft, May 9, 1845; John Weiss, *Life and Correspondence of Theodore Parker* (New York, 1864), 78; also *Niles Register,* December 20, 1845.

52. William Hogan to George Bancroft, May 28, 1845.

53. George Bancroft to Charles Sumner, January 13, 1846.

54. See Polk, *Diary,* December 22, 1845, 34.

55. George Bancroft to Samuel Hooper, June 22, 1846. See similar pronouncement in Bancroft, *Miscellanies,* 468–470.

56. George Bancroft to Samuel Hooper, June 2, 1846; to Commodore John D. Sloat, July 12, 1846; House Executive Session Documents, 30th Congress, first session, Number 60, 238; Sellers, *Polk,* 424–425; Bancroft's orders to Kearney, Sloat, Tompkins, June 3, 8, 20, July 12, 1846, House Executive Session documents, 237–245. George Bancroft to Commodore John D. Sloat, June 8, 1846. These and other letters are partly reprinted in T. W. Hittell, "George Bancroft and His Services to California," *California Historical Society Reprints* (San Francisco, 1893).

57. See Constance McLaughlin Green, *Washington, Village and Capital 1805–1878* (Princeton, N.J., 1962), 178–200; William H. Prescott to Susan Amory Prescott, April 3, 5, 1846, in Wolcott, *Correspondence,* 588–591;

Polk, *Diary,* February 6, 1846, p. 48; April 1, 1846, p. 69, for a few of Bancroft's social activities.

IX. *The Court of St. James's*

1. For the appointment, see James K. Polk, *Polk: The Diary of a President,* Allan Nevins, ed. (London, 1929), August 2, 1846, p. 135; Mark de Wolfe Howe, *Life and Letters of George Bancroft* (New York, 1908), I, 292; George Bancroft to Louis McLane, June 23, 1846; Brooklyn *Eagle,* September 8, 1846.
2. George Bancroft to James K. Polk, October 4, 1846; John A. Garraty, *Silas Wright* (New York, 1949), 373.
3. George Bancroft to George W. Greene, September 18, 1846; John Appleton to George Bancroft, September 19, 1846; Caleb Cushing to George Bancroft, October 6, 1846. See also quotation from *Journal of Commerce,* in John Romeyn Broadhead to George Bancroft, October 18, 1846.
4. Marcy's quote in Leonard D. White, *The Jacksonians* (New York, 1954), 230–231. For departure arrangements see Bancroft Papers, MHS. On the poor educational progress of his sons, see John A. Weisse to George Bancroft, November 1846, school report.
5. George Bancroft to James K. Polk, November 3, 1846, in Howe, *Life and Letters,* II, 3. On settling in, see letters and diary in Elizabeth Davis Bliss Bancroft, *Letters from England* (New York, 1909). Other letters by Elizabeth to William and Alexander are in Bancroft-Bliss Papers, Library of Congress.
6. For reports on politics, see Stephen Hoyt to George Bancroft, November 16, 1846; Edward Everett to George Bancroft, December 15, 1846; Lucretia Farnum to George Bancroft, December 24, 1846; John Appleton to George Bancroft, December 25, 1846.
7. For instructions from Buchanan, see James Buchanan to George Bancroft, October 6, 1846, in John B. Moore, ed., *The Works of James Buchanan* (Philadelphia, 1909), VII, 92–93. See also James Buchanan to George Bancroft, December 24, 1846, May 9, September 29, 1847, July 28, 1848, June 29, 1849. For the postal convention, see James Buchanan to George Bancroft, July 27, 1847, January 8, 9, 1849. For cultivation of parliamentarians and members of the Board of Trade, see George Bancroft to James K. Polk, June 3, 1847; to Robert Walker, August 17, 1847. Copies of all of Bancroft's official dispatches to Washington are in NYPL.
8. Elizabeth Bancroft to William Bliss, December 19, 1846, November 14, 1847, to Isaac P. Davis, January 2, 1847, recount a fraction of the couple's social activities, all in Bancroft, *Letters from England,* 43–56.
9. Elizabeth D. Bancroft to Mrs. William W. Story, March 23, 1847; to William D. Bliss, May 16, 1847; to Isaac P. Davis, January 2, 1847, in Bancroft, *Letters,* 43–56, 85, 104–109.
10. George Bancroft to Isaac P. Davis, November 17, 1846.
11. Elizabeth Bancroft to Isaac P. Davis, February 21, 1847; to Mrs. W. W. Story, March 23, 1847; to Isaac P. Davis, April 25, 1847; to Mrs. Sarah Polk, December 2, 1846, in Bancroft, *Letters,* 77–88, 91–96, 28–33; George Bancroft to William H. Prescott, September 15, 1848, in Howe, *Life and Letters,* II, 35.

12. Elizabeth Bancroft to her sons, January 1, 1847; to Isaac P. Davis, January 2, 1847, in Bancroft, *Letters,* 37–60.

13. Elizabeth Bancroft, "Diary," November 1, 4, 6, 1846; to Isaac P. David, January 2, 1847; to William Bliss, January 1, 1847, in Bancroft, *Letters,* 43–56, 37–43. See also for similar sentiments, George Bancroft to James K. Polk, October 20, 1848; to Hezekiah Niles, May 26, 1848; to James Buchanan, May 16, 1848; to Frank Blair, September 12, 1848.

14. George Bancroft to James K. Polk, October 20, 1848, in Howe, *Life and Letters,* II, 39.

15. George Bancroft to Hezekiah Niles, May 26, 1848; to James Buchanan, March 24, April 14, May 16, 1848; to Frank Blair, September 12, 1848. George Bancroft to Edward Everett, March 10, 1848, in Howe, *Life and Letters,* II, 30–34. See also on reaction to Chartism, Elizabeth Bancroft to Isaac P. Davis, April 10, 1848, in Bancroft, *Letters,* 175–178.

16. For English reaction to the Mexican War, see Frederick Merk, *The Monroe Doctrine and American Expansionism, 1843–1849* (New York, 1968), 163, where London *Times* is quoted.

17. James Buchanan to George Bancroft, December 29, 1846, February 25, June 14, September 29, 1847; Marcus Morton to George Bancroft, February 27, 1847. See also Lucretia Farnum to George Bancroft, January 27, 1847.

18. See David P. Crook, *American Democracy in English Politics 1815–1850* (Oxford, 1965).

19. George Bancroft to James K. Polk, December 3, 1846, January 4, 19, 1847; to James Buchanan, February 3, 1847.

20. George Bancroft to James K. Polk, May 14, June 3, November 18, 1847; to James Buchanan, May 18, 1847.

21. George Bancroft to James K. Polk, December 3, 1846, November 18, 1847. See also George Bancroft to William H. Prescott, August 17, 1847; to James Buchanan, August 17, October 18, 1847; to Charles G. Greene, November 3, 1847.

22. See George Bancroft to Lord Palmerston, August 31, September 15, 1847; Lord Clanricade to John Romeyn Broadhead, September 31, 1847; John R. Broadhead to George Bancroft, September 13, 14, 22, 1847; George Bancroft to Lord Clanricade, September 25, 1847, October 5, 1847; Richard Rush to George Bancroft, October 9, 1847; George Bancroft to James K. Polk, October 10, 1847; to William C. Bryant, November 3, 1847; to Charles G. Greene, November 3, 1847; to James Buchanan, November 3, 18, 1847.

23. George Bancroft to James K. Polk, October 10, 1847, February 11, 1848; to James Buchanan, October 18, 1847; to Earl of Auckland, March 23, 1848; to Robert K. Walker, April 1, 1848.

24. George Bancroft to James Buchanan, October 18, 1847; to William C. Bryant, November 3, 1847; to James K. Polk, November 18, 1847.

25. George Bancroft to James K. Polk, January 4, 19, 1847; to James Buchanan, February 3, 1847; to William H. Prescott, March 3, 1847.

26. On Irish relief, see George Bancroft to Lord Kildare, July 13, 1847; to A. Fiske, July 29, 1847.

27. Naturalization issue discussed in Samuel F. Bemis, ed., *American Secretaries of*

States and Their Diplomacy (New York, 1927), I, 335; James Buchanan to George Bancroft, December 18, 1848; also John B. Moore, *American Diplomacy* (New York, 1905), 178.

28. James Buchanan to George Bancroft, December 18, 1848, in John Bassett Moore, ed., *Works of James Buchanan* (Philadelphia, 1909), VIII, 264. See also further correspondence in Bancroft Papers, MHS and NYPL.

29. Eliza Davis to Louisa Bancroft, February 20, 1847; William Bliss to John Chandler Bancroft, June 13, 1847. Correspondence about and with the children in CUMR.

30. George Bancroft to Alexander Bliss, January 4, 1847. Letters from Switzerland in MHS and CUMR.

31. See deed of sale for Cleveland lands, July 1, 1847; George Bancroft to Samuel Hooper, September 30, December 3, 1847, January 27, 1848; Samuel Hooper to George Bancroft, October 1, December 30, 1847, March 23, 1848; George Bancroft to Cashier of Merchants' Bank, October 1, 1847; to Prosper Wetmore, December 4, 1847.

32. George Bancroft to Elizabeth Bancroft, April 12, 13, 1847. On historical research, see correspondence in Mark de Wolfe Howe, *Life and Letters of George Bancroft* (New York, 1908), II, as well as MHS.

33. Interview with the king in 1847 in Howe, *Life and Letters,* II, 65–69; George Bancroft to Elizabeth Bancroft, December 29, 1847, in Howe, *Life and Letters,* II, 76.

34. George Bancroft to Elizabeth Bancroft, December 20, 21, 1847, January 1, 1848, in Howe, *Life and Letters,* II, 69–74, 79.

35. See E. N. Curtis, "American Opinions of French Nineteenth Century Revolutions," *American Historical Review,* 29 (January 1924), 249–270; Arthur J. May, *Contemporary American Opinions of Mid Nineteenth Century Revolutions in Central Europe* (Philadelphia, 1927).

36. Charles Sumner to George Sumner, April 18, 1848, in Pierce, *Memoir and Letters of Charles Sumner,* III, 37. Also George Ticknor to Charles Lyell, April 5, 1848; to George Curtis, April 22, 1848; to George S. Hillard, July 17, 1848; to Prince John of Saxony, July 30, 1848, all in George S. Hillard, ed., *Life, Letters and Journals of George Ticknor* (Boston, 1880), III, 230–236. That Bancroft was aware of these misgivings, see George Bancroft to Elizabeth Bancroft, April 22, 1848, in Howe, *Life and Letters,* II, 91.

37. George Bancroft to Edward Everett, March 10, 1848, and to James Buchanan, March 24, 1848, in Howe, *Life and Letters,* 30–33.

38. George Bancroft to Edward Everett, March 10, 1848, in Howe, *Life and Letters,* II, 32; George Bancroft to James Buchanan, March 24, 1848, and to William H. Prescott, September 15, 1848, in Howe, *Life and Letters,* II, 33–37.

39. George Bancroft to James Buchanan, March 10, April 14, 1848; to James K. Polk, July 29, 1849. See also George Bancroft to Samuel Hooper, May 4, June 16, 1848.

40. See George Bancroft to Joseph Cogswell, July 4, 1848; to James Buchanan, July 25, 1848; to Edward Everett, March 9, 1848; to James K. Polk, December 24, 1848; to William C. Bryant, November 3, 1848. Benjamin Hallett and

the Democratic National Convention thought likewise. See Richard Rush to James Buchanan, August 8, 1848, in Moore, ed., *Works,* VIII, 161–162.

41. George Bancroft to Elizabeth Bancroft, April 20, 22, 23, 1848; to Robert Walker, March 24, 1848; to James Buchanan, March 24, 1848; to Lucretia Farnum, May 5, 1848.

42. George Bancroft to Elizabeth Bancroft, April 23, 1848, in Howe, *Life and Letters,* II, 91. George Bancroft to Edward Everett, March 10, 1848; to William D. Bliss, September 22, 1848; to James Buchanan, March 24, 1848, all in Howe, *Life and Letters,* II, 30–33, 37–38. There were even rumors in Boston that Bancroft drew up the French constitution. See William D. Bliss to George Bancroft, May 2, 1848.

43. George Bancroft to Elizabeth Bancroft, February 4, 11, August 6, 1849 in Howe, *Life and Letters,* II, 95–98. See also George Bancroft to John Davis, June 15, 1849.

44. George Bancroft quoted in Howe, *Life and Letters,* II, 97; George Bancroft to William D. Bliss, September 22, 1848, ibid., 37.

45. William F. Butler to George Bancroft, June 10, 1848.

46. Lucretia Farnum to George Bancroft, June 18, July 5, 1848; George Bancroft to Marcus Morton, July 31, 1848; to James K. Polk, August 5, 1848.

47. George Bancroft to William H. Prescott, September 15, 1848; to William D. Bliss, September 22, 1848.

48. George Bancroft to John Mason, December 29, 1848; to Samuel Hooper, October 20, 1848; to Lewis Cass, October 20, 1848. See also Edward Everett to George Bancroft, October 30, 1848. Bancroft was wily enough to renew his ties with Caleb Cushing at this time. See George Bancroft to Caleb Cushing, June 23, 1848.

49. David Donald, *Charles Sumner and the Coming of the Civil War* (New York, 1967), 178.

50. James Buchanan to George Bancroft, July 28, 1848, in Moore, ed., *Works,* VIII, 140–141. See also extensive correspondence in Bancroft Papers, MHS, on the conduct of negotiations.

51. James Buchanan to George Bancroft, December 11, 18, 1848; George Bancroft to James Buchanan, December 15, 1848, January 8, February 5, 1849; to John Davis, February 23, 1849; James K. Polk to George Bancroft, January 5, 1849.

52. Bancroft himself probably saw to the publicity given to some of his activities in the Washington *Union.* See James Buchanan to George Bancroft, January 9, 1849, in Moore, ed., *Works,* VIII, 279.

53. George Bancroft to John Davis, May 4, 1849; to Samuel Hooper, April 5, May 4, 1849; to William C. Bryant, May 4, 1849; to John Davis, May 4, 1849; to Lord Grenville, May 5, 1849.

54. George Bancroft to John Davis, March 9, 1849; to Louisa Bancroft, April 16, 1849; Eliza Davis to George Bancroft, Jr., January 10, 1849. On financial matters, see also George Bancroft to Samuel Hooper, May 25, 1849; Thomas O. Handy to George Bancroft, May 16, 1849.

55. George Bancroft to Samuel Hooper, May 25, 1849; to John Davis, June 22, 1849; Lord Palmerston to George Bancroft, September 15, 1849.

x. *The Scholar as Gentleman and Citizen*

1. On Bancroft's early moving plans, see Charles Sumner to Elizabeth Bancroft, April 23, 1845, in Edward L. Pierce, *Memoir and Letters of Charles Sumner* (Boston, 1877–1893), III, 53.

2. George Bancroft to Elizabeth Bancroft, April 11, 1847; George Hillard, ed., *Life, Letters and Journals of George Ticknor* (Boston, 1880), II, 235.

3. William H. Prescott to George Bancroft, December 20, 1852, George Ticknor, *Life of William H. Prescott* (Boston, 1864), 355. See also Charles Sumner to John Bigelow, March 17, 1851, in John Bigelow, *Retrospections of an Active Life* (New York, 1905–1913), I, 113.

4. See Joel H. Ross, *What I Saw in New York* (Auburn, N.Y., 1852), 18, 66.

5. *Semi-Centennial Celebration of the Founding of the New-York Historical Society* (New York, 1854), 55; George Bancroft, *Literary and Historical Miscellanies* (New York, 1855), 494; Pierce, *Memoir and Letters of Charles Sumner,* III, 6; also William H. Prescott to George Bancroft, January 8, 1850; Rufus Rockwell Wilson, *New York, Old and New* (Philadelphia, 1909), II, 235.

6. See Alfred S. Roe, "The Homes and Haunts of George Bancroft," *New England Magazine,* 23 (October 1900), 161–180; also Oliver Dyer, ed., *The History of the Battle of Lake Erie and Miscellaneous Papers* (New York, 1891), Introduction; "George Bancroft in Society, Politics, and Letters," *Century Magazine,* 11 (January 1887); Philip Hone, *The Diary,* Allan Nevins, ed. (New York, 1927), II, 881, 911.

7. The large correspondence about gardening and household details is in the Bancroft Papers, MHS.

8. George Templeton Strong, *The Diary,* Allan Nevins and Milton Halsey Thomas, eds. (New York, 1952), II, 20, 335. See also Stewart Mitchell, *Horatio Seymour of New York* (Cambridge, Mass., 1938), 85; George B. Lodge to Anna C. Lodge, August 31, 1847, Henry C. Lodge, *Early Memories* (New York, 1913), 319.

9. Parke Godwin, *A Biography of William Cullen Bryant* (New York, 1883), II, 125. On Thackeray's impression of Bancroft, see Eyre Crowe, *With Thackeray in America* (London, 1893), 37–38.

10. Margaret Clapp, *Forgotten First Citizen, John Bigelow* (Boston, 1947), 56; Charles Crowe, *George Ripley* (Athens, Ga., 1967), 229, 231; George Ripley to George Bancroft, July 4, 1853, February 22, 1855; George Bancroft to George Ripley, March 5, 1853.

11. Strong, *Diary,* II, 117, 440–441, on New York gossip.

12. George Bancroft to Washington Irving, May 30, 1855, May 7, 1859; Washington Irving to George Bancroft, n.d., 1856, n.d., 1857, M. Irving, *Life and Letters of Washington Irving* (New York, 1864), IV, 208, 209, 230, 281. See also "George Bancroft on Washington Irving," *Living Age,* 65 (June 1860), 620–621; George Bancroft to William H. Prescott, January 8, 1856; O. W. Holmes, *Life and Letters of Ralph Waldo Emerson* (Boston, 1884); George Bancroft, "Holmes' Life of Emerson," *North American Review,* 140 (February 1885). For Bancroft on Emerson, see also James C. Derby, *Fifty Years Among Authors* (New York, 1884), 328.

13. James Phalen to George Bancroft, April 7, 1853; Dudley Bean to George Bancroft, January 20, 1851; William H. Paine to George Bancroft, April

10, 1853. See also B. J. Lossing, *History of New York City* (New York, 1884), II, 664. George Bancroft to Moses H. Grinnell, January 20, 1855, in Mark de Wolfe Howe, *Life and Letters of George Bancroft* (New York, 1908) II, 120–121.

14. For income and dividends see extensive correspondence during this decade in Bancroft Papers, MHS.

15. George Bancroft to William H. Prescott, November 24, 1854; to Boivin Firm, October 29, 1853; to Hippolyte Vezian, January 4, 1854; to Pollard and Barry, March 30, 1854; to F. M. Sauli, n.d., 1854.

16. On family difficulties, see George Bancroft to Elizabeth Bancroft, September 4, 1854; to Lucretia Farnum, December 31, 1855; Eliza Davis to George Bancroft, February 4, 1855; Lucretia Farnum to George Bancroft, March 8, May 22, 1855; Clara Gerhardi to George Bancroft, May 27, 1855; Thomas Bancroft to George Bancroft, December 23, 1855; John Chandler Bancroft Davis to George Bancroft, July 17, 1856. On Louisa's death, see condolences in Bancroft Papers, MHS.

17. On John Chandler and George Jr., see letters in CUMR.

18. George Bancroft to George Bancroft, Jr., January 9, 1854; John C. Bancroft to George Bancroft, May 21, 1856, CUMR.

19. George Jr.'s temporary exile and escapades in CUMR.

20. George Bancroft, Jr., to George Bancroft, August 23, 1854; William Babcock to George Bancroft, August 25, 31, December 27, 1854; James Walker to George Bancroft, January 19, 1855, CUMR.

21. John Chandler Bancroft to George Bancroft, December 13, 1854, CUMR; William Dwight to George Bancroft, June 4, 1855; William H. Prescott to George Bancroft, November 30, 1855; John Chandler Bancroft to George Bancroft, February 7, May 1, 1856. On his financial debacle, see correspondence in CUMR and MHS.

22. George Bancroft, Jr., to George Bancroft, May 20, June 2, August 5, 1856, CUMR.

23. John Chandler Bancroft to George Bancroft, June 24, July 8, 1857.

24. George Bancroft, Jr., to George Bancroft, February 11, 1858, CUMR.

25. George Bancroft to George Bancroft, Jr., April 28, 1858, CUMR.

26. George Bancroft, Jr., to George Bancroft, July 24, August 15, 1858; John Chandler Bancroft to George Bancroft, September 11, 23, 1858.

27. George Bancroft to George Bancroft, Jr., August 19, 1858. For efforts to break the marriage, see George Bancroft to Augustus C. Dodge, October 25, 26, 1858, and to Henry Benbow, May 17, 1859; Augustus C. Dodge to George Bancroft, November 30, 1858; George Bancroft, Jr., to George Bancroft, September 11, 1858, March 13, 1859.

28. John Chandler Bancroft to George Bancroft, April 25, May 8, June 6, 19, 1860; George Bancroft to E. Bendenmann (lost); for response, see E. Bendenmann to George Bancroft, July 3, 1860.

29. George Bancroft to Elizabeth Bancroft, in Howe, *Life and Letters,* II, 113.

30. Bancroft, *Miscellanies,* 501, 504; George Bancroft to George Ripley, September 12, 1857.

31. Strong, *Diary,* II, 199, 333; Bancroft, *Miscellanies,* 503–505; Howe, *Life and Letters,* II, 120.

32. See Crowe, *Thackeray,* 38-39; Earl Wesley Fornell, *The Unhappy Medium* (Austin, Tex., 1964), 25, 28, 104–105.
33. For Bancroft's belief in populated planets, see Bancroft, *Miscellanies,* 509–510. See also Howard Kerr, *Mediums and Spirit Rappers and Roaring Radicals* (Urbana, Ill., 1972).
34. George Bancroft to Simon Draper, December 16, 1851; to Augustus Shell, June 17, 1850; William B. Marcy to George Bancroft, October 20, 1850.
35. George Bancroft, *History of the United States* (Boston, 1852), IV, 12.
36. Ibid., 12, 15, 55, 5, 13.
37. Ibid., 4, 5.
38. Ibid., 9.
39. Ibid., 10.
40. Ibid., 4, 12, 13, 15.
41. Ibid., 7.
42. Ibid., 8. See also George Bancroft, *History of the United States* (Boston, 1834), I, 4, 5. On exaggerated individualism, which Bancroft feared, see Porte, ed., *Emerson in His Journals,* November 1842, 294.
43. Bancroft, *History,* IV, 12, 13; George Bancroft, *History of the United States* (Boston, 1852), V, 270, 291, 313.
44. Bancroft, *Miscellanies,* 490; George Bancroft, *History of the United States* (Boston, 1854), VI, 528.
45. Ibid., 514, 515; Bancroft, *Miscellanies,* 486–487. Bancroft, Perry Monument Address, reprinted in *Inauguration of the Perry Statue at Cleveland on the 10th of September, 1860* (Cleveland, Ohio, 1861), 45.
46. See, e.g., George Ticknor to Sir Edmund Head, December 20, 1852; to Sir Charles Lyell, May 23, 1854; Hillard, ed., *George Ticknor,* II, 285, 287. George Bancroft to William H. Prescott, November 24, 1854; to Henry Power, November 26, 1854.
47. Theodore Parker, *A Sermon Preached at the Music Hall in Boston, June 18, 1854* (Boston, 1854), 9–10, 31; Henry Steele Commager, *Theodore Parker* (Boston, 1936), 209–213.
48. Bancroft, *Miscellanies,* 486.
49. George Bancroft to Elizabeth Bancroft, May 11, June 4, 1854. See also George Bancroft to Elizabeth Bancroft, June 25, 29, July 2, 1856.
50. George Bancroft to Elizabeth Bancroft, March 7, 10, 16, 17, 21, April 5, 7, September 16, 20, 23, October 5, 1855. See also George Bancroft to Elizabeth Bancroft, June 6, 14, 1857.
51. George Bancroft to Lewis Cass, June 15, 1858. See also for similar views: Edward Everett to George Bancroft, January 14, 1856; Brantz Mayer to George Bancroft, October 8, 1856; George Bancroft to Lord Montague, October 14, 1856; George Bancroft to John Smith Preston, November 6, 1858. For impressions of the South, see also George Bancroft to Elizabeth Bancroft, May 28, 29, June 11, 1858.
52. Franklin Pierce to George Bancroft, June 30, 1852; George Bancroft to William Forney, July 5, 1852; William Forney to George Bancroft, July 8, 1852; C. H. Palmer to George Bancroft, July 27, 1852; John Davis to George Bancroft, November 4, 1852.

53. George Bancroft to William Marcy, September 24, 1856, in Howe, *Life and Letters,* II, 122–125. See also George William Curtis's complaint that Bancroft praised heroes but was himself a time server. "Men write history, and forget they are living it." See Gordon Milne, *George William Curtis* (Bloomington, Ind., 1956), 91.

54. George Bancroft to William Marcy, September 24, 1856, Howe, *Life and Letters,* II, 122–125.

55. Ibid., 124. See also Bancroft, *Miscellanies,* 514, 515.

56. George Bancroft to James Buchanan, February 21, 1857; George Bancroft to William H. Marcy, December 20, 1856.

57. George Bancroft to James A. Mason, July 24, 1857, in Howe, *Life and Letters,* II, 126–128. For Dred Scott, see Don E. Fehrenbacher, *The Dred Scott Case* (New York, 1978).

58. George Bancroft to James A. Mason, July 24, 1857, in Howe, *Life and Letters,* II, 127.

59. George Bancroft to Stephen A. Douglas, December 3, 1857; to Elizabeth Bancroft, May 28, June 11, 1858. See also William Forney to George Bancroft, February 18, 1858; George Bancroft to John B. Haskins, February 18, 1858.

60. Stephen A. Douglas to George Bancroft, February 11, 15, 1858; George Bancroft to Stephen A. Douglas, February 13, 1858; J. N. Morris to George Butler, February 9, 1858; John Haskins to George Bancroft, February 11, 1858; John Chandler Bancroft to George Bancroft, March 8, 1858. See also New York *Tribune,* February 12, 13, 1858; Philip S. Foner, *Business and Slavery: The New York Merchants and the Irrepressible Conflict* (Chapel Hill, N.C., 1941), 149–152; and numerous letters in Bancroft Papers, MHS.

61. George Bancroft to Lewis Cass, June 26, 1858.

62. George Bancroft, *History of the United States* (Boston, 1858), VII, 21, 83, 29, 295, 301, 302, 355.

63. Ibid., 51, 81, 312.

64. Stephen A. Douglas to George Bancroft, April 11, 1859; George Bancroft to Stephen A. Douglas, April 19, 1859; Glyndon Van Deusen, *William H. Seward* (New York, 1967), 290.

65. George Bancroft to James A. Mason, July 24, 1857; H. C. Duncan to George Bancroft, December 7, 1859; Lucretia Farnum to George Bancroft, January 15, 1860; Samuel Hooper to George Bancroft, January 24, 1860; William P. Miles to George Bancroft, February 6, 1860. See also George Bancroft to William P. Miles, January 31, 1860.

66. George Bancroft to Thomas C. Amory, November 28, 1860.

XI. *The Furnace of Affliction*

1. George Bancroft, *History of the United States* (Boston, 1860), VIII, 119.

2. George Bancroft, *History of the United States* (Boston, 1852), V, 292, 335, which also formed the theme for his *History of the United States* (Boston, 1858), VII.

3. Bancroft, *History,* VIII, 118.

4. Ibid., 248–249; George Bancroft, *Literary and Historical Miscellanies* (New York, 1855), 484. See also George Bancroft to Reverdy Johnson, January 2, 1868, in Mark de Wolfe Howe, *Life and Letters of George Bancroft* (New York, 1908), II, 185. For the similarity of this interpretation to the Whig uses of history, compare Benjamin R. Curtis, *Address at Deerfield, Mass.* (Greenfield, Mass., 1832), 17, 22–23.

5. George Bancroft, *Address at the Perry Monument* (1860), reprinted in *Inauguration of the Perry Statue at Cleveland on the 10th of September, 1860* (Cleveland, Ohio, 1861), 45.

6. George Bancroft to Dean Milman, August 15, 1861, in Howe, *Life and Letters,* II, 136, 137. See also George Bancroft to Elizabeth Bancroft, February 9, 11, 1861.

7. William D. Bliss to Alexander Bliss, December 18, 1860; in Bancroft-Bliss Papers, Library of Congress; William Howard Russell, *My Diary North and South* (London, 1863), I, 20–21, 29–30. See also Edward Everett to George Bancroft, March 22, 1861; Stewart Mitchell, *Horatio Seymour of New York* (Cambridge, Mass., 1938), 216, 226.

8. John Chandler Bancroft to George Bancroft, January 14, May 23, 1861; Lucretia Farnum to George Bancroft, January 20, March 24, 1861; Wilder Dwight to George Bancroft, February 4, 1861.

9. George Bancroft, "The Place of Lincoln in American History," *Atlantic Monthly,* 15 (June 1865), 763–764; George Bancroft to Dean Milman, August 15, 1861, in Howe, *Life and Letters,* II, 138.

10. For his definition of "the people," see George Bancroft, *Memorial Address on the Life of Abraham Lincoln* (Washington, D.C., 1866), 25, 34, 36–37.

11. George Hillard, ed., *Life, Letters and Journals of George Ticknor* (Boston, 1880), II, 433–434; Lucretia Bancroft to George Bancroft, July 26, 1861. See also George Frederickson, *The Inner Civil War* (New York, 1965), for the context of this anti-individualist position.

12. George Bancroft to Dean Milman, August 15, 1861, in Howe, *Life and Letters,* II, 133–143. On the conspiracy thesis, see Thomas J. Pressley, *Americans Interpret Their Civil War* (Princeton, N.J., 1954); Edward Everett, "The Question of the Day, July 4, 1861," *Pulpit and Rostrum,* 21–22 (August 1, 1861), expressing similar views.

13. George Bancroft, *Oration Delivered in April 1865* (New York, 1865), 5; Bancroft, *Memorial Address,* 11; Bancroft, "Place of Lincoln in American History," *Atlantic Monthly,* 15 (1865), 759, 760, 761.

14. Bancroft, "Place of Lincoln in American History," 762; Bancroft, *Oration, February 22, 1862,* (New York, 1862) 111, 115; Bancroft, *Oration April 1865,* 3; Bancroft, *Memorial Address,* 14, 15, 24.

15. George Bancroft to Dean Milman, August 15, 1861. For views of members of the Century Association, see George Templeton Strong, *Diary,* Allan Nevins and M. H. Thomas, eds. (New York, 1952), III, 139.

16. George Bancroft to Elizabeth Bancroft, September 21, 25, 30, 1861.

17. George Bancroft to Abraham Lincoln, November 15, 1861; Abraham Lincoln to George Bancroft, November 18, 1861; Abraham Lincoln, *The Collected Works,* Roy Basler, ed. (New Brunswick, N.J., 1953), V, 25–26. See also *New York Times,* November 8, 1861.

18. George Bancroft to Elizabeth Bancroft, December 12, 16, 17, 19, 1861; to Lucretia Farnum, January 5, 1862.
19. George Bancroft to William H. Seward, January 28, 1862; see also George Bancroft to Salmon P. Chase, January 28, 1862.
20. Bancroft, *Oration, February 22, 1862,* 103, 105, 107, 108, 109, 111, 112; see also Bancroft, "Letter to the Voters, October 18, 1862," *To the Voters of Massachusetts* (Boston, 1862), 9; George Bancroft to William H. Seward, February 7, 1862.
21. See Basil Leo Lee, *Discontent in New York City 1861–1865* (Washington, D.C., 1943), 160–161; *The Caucasian,* March 15, 1862; New York *Tribune,* February 24, 1862; George Bancroft to Abraham Lincoln, April 18, 1862.
22. Wilder Dwight to George Bancroft, February 25, 1862; George Bancroft to John P. Hale, March 17, 1862; William S. Wait to George Bancroft, March 30, 1862. Other favorable reactions in Bancroft Papers, MHS.
23. Jack Lindeman, ed., *The Conflict of Convictions* (Philadelphia, 1968), 55.
24. George Bancroft to William H. Seward, February 4, 1862.
25. William Dwight to George Bancroft, June 2, 3, August 2, September 5, 13, 1862; David A. Dwight to George Bancroft, October 2, 1862; George Bancroft to John Andrew, November 18, 1862. On Sandy's experience, see letters exchanged with his mother, in Bancroft-Bliss Papers, Library of Congress, and their letters in "Civil War and Reconstruction," University of Illinois, Historical Survey Collections.
26. George Bancroft, Jr., to George Bancroft, March 12, 1861; George Bancroft to George Bancroft, Jr., October 24, 1864, August 14, 1865. George Bancroft, Jr., to George Bancroft, November 11, 1863; March 25, 1867. For Bancroft's adamant opposition to the marriage and extensive correspondence with George Jr., see CUMR.
27. George Bancroft to John Bigelow, March 25, 1862; John Bigelow to Edward Laboulaye, August 18, 1862, John Bigelow, *Retrospections of an Active Life* (New York, 1909), I, 533.
28. George Bancroft to Salmon P. Chase, August 9, 1862, in Howe, *Life and Letters,* II, 153; George Bancroft to Samuel Hooper, October 2, 1862.
29. George Bancroft to Alexander Bliss, July 17, 28, 1862, in Benjamin P. Thomas and Harold M. Hyman, *Stanton: The Life and Times of Lincoln's Secretary of War* (New York, 1962), 212; George Bancroft to William H. Seward, August 27, 1862, in Frederic Bancroft, *The Life of William H. Seward* (New York, 1900), 336.
30. Bancroft, *Letter to the Voters,* 8, 10–11.
31. Bancroft, *Memorial Address,* 38; Bancroft, "Place of Lincoln in American history," 764.
32. George Bancroft to John Bigelow, January 20, March 6, 1863, in Bigelow, *Retrospections,* I, 597.
33. Strong, *Diary,* III, 321.
34. George Bancroft, *Address Delivered in New York, April 20, 1863* (New York, 1863), 9; compare to Frederickson, *Inner Civil War,* 53–56.
35. Strong, *Diary,* III, 339. On draft riots, see Adriane Cook, *The Armies of the Streets* (Lexington, Ky., 1974).
36. Strong, *Diary,* III, 290, 292; Frederick S. Cozzens to FitzGreene Halleck,

January 24, 1864, in Nelson F. Adkins, *FitzGreene Halleck* (New Haven, 1930), 347. See also Frederick S. Cozzens to Gulian C. Verplanck, February 3, 1864, in Robert W. July, *The Essential New Yorker, Gulian C. Verplanck* (Durham, N.C., 1951), 265–266; "Editor's Easy Chair," *Harper's,* 29 (June–November, 1864), 132; "Editor's Easy Chair," *Harper's,* 28 (December 1863–May 1864), 708–709.

37. See *Gratitude to General Grant, Proceedings Held at Union Square June 1864* (New York, 1864).

38. There is no evidence for the assertion—Robert H. Canary, *George Bancroft* (New York, 1974), 100—that Bancroft actively campaigned for Lincoln in 1864.

39. George Bancroft to Andrew Johnson, December 16, 1864, in Papers of Andrew Johnson, Library of Congress.

40. George Bancroft to Reverdy Johnson, January 2, 1868, in Howe, *Life and Letters,* II, 186; George Bancroft to Samuel S. Cox, January 28, 1865, ibid., 157–158. See also Charles Sumner to George Bancroft, February 28, 1865.

41. On the funeral proceedings, see *Obsequies for Abraham Lincoln in the City of New York* (New York, 1866); also Lloyd Lewis, *Myths After Lincoln* (New York, 1929), 139.

42. George Bancroft, *Oration at the Obsequies for Abraham Lincoln* (New York, 1865), 10, 12, 13; also, Bancroft, *Memorial Address,* 3, 4.

43. Bancroft, *Memorial Address* 35, 43–45, 48, 50; George Bancroft, "The Place of Lincoln in American History," *Atlantic Monthly,* 762–763, 764. For favorable reactions to the address, quoting lost letters, see Elizabeth Bancroft to William Bliss, April 26, 1865, in Bancroft-Bliss Papers, Library of Congress.

44. Bancroft, *Oration April 1865,* 12.

45. George Bancroft to Andrew Johnson, April 26, 1865. See also George Bancroft to Reverdy Johnson, January 2, 1868.

46. George Bancroft to Andrew Johnson, April 26, August 18, November 9, 1865. See also on the fortunes of the Democratic Party, Irving Katz, *August Belmont* (New York, 1968); and Eric L. McKitrick, *Andrew Johnson and Reconstruction* (Chicago, 1960).

47. George Bancroft to Andrew Johnson, November 9, 1865. Bancroft's help with the speech was a secret only to later historians: see William A. Dunning, "A Little More Light on Andrew Johnson," Massachusetts Historical Society, *Proceedings,* 39 (1905), 395. At least one person knew, since Elizabeth told Bigelow; see Bigelow, *Retrospections,* IV, 486. On the speech, see Lawanda Cox and John H. Cox, *Politics, Principles and Prejudices 1865–1866* (London, 1963), 131; Michael Les Benedict, *A Compromise of Principles* (New York, 1974), 132.

48. George Bancroft to Andrew Johnson, December 1, 1865.

49. On preliminaries to the speech, see correspondence in Bancroft Papers, MHS and NYPL.

50. George Bancroft, *Memorial Address,* 4, 23, 50, 51. Some newspapers forgot about Lincoln, and titled their reprint "God in History"; see Philip Kinsley, *The Chicago Tribune* (Chicago, 1945), II, 35.

51. On the local and international furor that followed, see George Bancroft to Charles Francis Adams, March 13, 1866; Bigelow, *Retrospections,* IV, 186–187.

52. George Bancroft to Elizabeth Bancroft, February 12, 1866; Howard K. Beale, ed., *The Diary of Gideon Welles* (New York, 1960), II, 43; Orville H. Browning, "Diary" (Illinois Historical Society, 22, Collections, Lincoln Series, II), 61; Howe, *Life and Letters,* II, 159; Charles Sumner to George Bemis, March 15, 1866, in Pierce, *Memoir and Letters of Charles Sumner,* IV, 270.

53. See Arnold Blumberg, "Bancroft's Eulogy of Lincoln and British Reactions," *Lincoln Herald,* 57 (Winter 1965), 151–157; Arnold Blumberg, "George Bancroft, France and Vatican Diplomacy," *Catholic Historical Review,* 50 (1964), 475–493; clippings of English newspapers and other responses in Bancroft Papers, MHS.

54. Charles Sumner to George Bancroft, Sunday, December (?) 1865, January 21, February 13, 1866; George Bancroft to Charles Sumner, January 29, 1866.

55. George Bancroft, *History of the United States* (Boston, 1866), IX, 257–258, 5. See also George Bancroft to Andrew Johnson, September 30, 1866; to Robert C. Winthrop, September 30, 1866. "Inward law" expression appears in Bancroft, *Address at the Perry Monument,* 45.

56. Bancroft, *History,* IX, 47, 48, 257–260, 271–272, 276, 282–283.

57. Ibid., 499, 501, 60.

58. "Miscellany," *Historical Magazine,* 11–12 (September 1867), 192.

59. The most extensive argument in favor of impartiality is in Bancroft, *History,* VIII, 118–120.

60. "Mr. Bancroft as a Historian," *Southern Review,* 4 (July 1868), 202–231. See also Henry Dawson, "Review of George Bancroft's History of the United States, Volume IX," *Historical Magazine,* 11–12 (March 1867), 187–193; also "President Reed of Pennsylvania," *Southern Review,* 1 (April, 1867), 501.

61. Colonel Samuel Swett, *Defense of Timothy Pickering against Bancroft's History* (Boston, 1859) 3, 5; Octavius Pickering, *Life of Colonel Timothy Pickering* (Boston, 1867), Appendix.

62. George Bancroft, *Joseph Reed, An Historical Essay* (New York, 1867), 1, 4, 38, 47, 58, 59. For the entire controversy, see correspondence in Bancroft Papers, MHS; Bancroft, *History,* IX, 229, 105–107; William B. Reed, *President Reed of Pennsylvania, A Reply to Mr. George Bancroft and Others* (Philadelphia, 1867).

63. "Mr. Bancroft as a Historian," *Southern Review,* 4 (July 1868), 208–209.

64. See William B. Reed, *Rejoinder* (Philadelphia, 1867), 112–113. See also "President Reed," *Southern Review,* 1 (April 1867), 501; "Mr. Bancroft," *Historical Magazine* 11–12 (February 1867), 102–105; "Joseph Reed," ibid., (July 1867), 54; Benjamin Rush, *William B. Reed of Chestnut Hill: Expert in the Art of the Exhumation of the Dead* (London, 1867), 3, 4, 5, 6, 7; J. G. Johnson, *A Criticism of Mr. William Reed's Aspersions on the Character of Dr. Benjamin Rush* (Philadelphia, 1867).

65. George L. Schuyler, *Correspondence and Remarks upon Bancroft's History of the Northern Campaign of 1777* (New York, 1867), 36, 46, 47; Timothy C. Amory, "Memory of John Sullivan," Massachusetts Historical Society, *Proceedings* (December 1866), 394–5, 406, 433, 436.

66. Bancroft, *Joseph Reed,* 59; Friedrich Kapp to George Bancroft, May 22, 1867; George Bancroft to William H. Seward, May 8, 1867.

67. Bigelow, *Retrospections,* IV, 78–79.

68. George Bancroft to George L. Schuyler, December 28, 1866; George Schuyler, *Correspondence and Remarks* (New York, 1867), 45–46; Bancroft, *Joseph Reed,* 4. For a recent evaluation of the dispute, see John F. Roche, *Joseph Reed* (New York, 1957), 56–57, 104–105.

xii. *Bismarck's Berlin*

1. George Bancroft to Elizabeth Bancroft, April 23, 1848, in Mark de Wolfe Howe, *Life and Letters of George Bancroft* (New York, 1908), II, 91. George Bancroft, "Address at the Perry Monument," *Inauguration of the Perry Statue at Cleveland* (Cleveland, Ohio, 1861), 45.

2. George Bancroft to Andrew Johnson, February 11, 1867, May 18, 1867. See also John Bigelow, *Retrospections of an Active Life* (New York, 1909), IV, 486.

3. George Bancroft, "Address at the Perry Monument," 42; George Bancroft to Baron Gerolt, May 19, 1867.

4. Karl F. Neumann to George Bancroft, June 4, 1867; George Bancroft to Baron Gerolt, May 19, 1867.

5. George Bancroft to William H. Seward, July 27, 28, 30, August 1, 8, 1867, NYPL. See also George Bancroft to Elizabeth Bancroft from Spain, July 8, 10, 12, 14, 17, 20, 25, 1867, Bancroft Papers, MHS.

6. George Bancroft to William H. Seward, July 1, 1867, NYPL.

7. The events surrounding this meeting can be reconstructed through letters in CUMR.

8. George Bancroft to Louisa Denny Bancroft, October 25, 1867; to John Chandler Bancroft, January 17, June 18, December 12, 1868.

9. Bancroft's relations with his sons during his European stay are traceable in Bancroft Papers, MHS and CUMR.

10. Otto zu Stolberg-Wernigerode, *Germany and the United States of America during the Era of Bismarck* (Philadelphia, 1937), 90–91, 94–95; George Bancroft to William H. Seward, August 29, September 10, 1867, NYPL. See also George Bancroft to Charles Sumner, January 21, 1868; to Carl Schurz, February 17, 1868, Bancroft Papers, MHS.

11. See, e.g., George Bancroft, Diary, August 17, 1867, February 18, 1873; to William H. Seward, August 29, 1867; to Frederica Davis, December 13, 1867, NYPL.

12. George Bancroft to George Ripley, January 17, 1868; to Frederica Davis, April 23, 1868.

13. George Bancroft to Frederica Davis, December 27, 1867, in Howe, *Life and Letters,* II, 183. Also George Bancroft to Frederica Davis, January 1, 1868; to George Ripley, January 17, 1868.

14. Bancroft, Diary, November 6, 30, 1869, July 23, October 6, 1871, January 15, 1874; George Bancroft to Frederica Davis, April 23, 1869, May 2, 1871, on Wagner.

15. George Bancroft to John Jay, January 4, 1872.

16. Bancroft's early naturalization negotiations are traceable in Bancroft Papers, NYPL and MHS. See also Stolberg-Wernigerode, *Germany and the United States,* 100-101; Frederick Van Dyne, *A Treatise on the Law of Naturalization of the United States* (Washington, D.C., 1907), 466–468.

17. George Bancroft to William H. Seward, January 21, 24, 1868, May 26, 29, 1868, NYPL; to Andrew Johnson, January 24, 31, February 9, 1868, Library of Congress.

18. John G. Gazley, *American Opinion of German Unification 1848–1871* (New York, 1926), 229–231. Letters critical of the treaty reprinted in Charles Munde, *The Bancroft Naturalization Treaties* (Würzburg, 1868), 59, 63. For an early criticism, see Thomas Hilgard to George Bancroft, May 18, 1868.

19. Munde, *Naturalization Treaties,* 67–68, 82, 153, 154.

20. Congratulatory letters from Andrew Johnson, William H. Seward, and Charles Sumner, letters soliciting support for his achievements and favorable articles in the *Hamburger Borsenhalle* and the *Frankfurter Zeitung* in Bancroft Papers, MHS.

21. George Bancroft to Samuel Osgood, May 5, 1868.

22. George Bancroft to H. W. Watts, April 4, 1869. On moves to ingratiate himself with Grant, see letters in Bancroft Papers, MHS and NYPL.

23. Newspaper clippings and copies of letters to Washington in NYPL. See also Gazley, *American Opinion,* 424, for New York *World,* September 16, 1870, February 9, 1871.

24. For Bancroft's impressions of Bismarck, see George Bancroft, Diary, August 17, 1867. See also George Bancroft to Frederica Davis, December 13, 1867, in Howe, *Life and Letters,* II, 178-179; George Bancroft to William Astor, January 3, 1968; to Hamilton Fish, October 8, 23, 1869; Otto zu Stolberg-Wernigerode, "Bismarck and His American Friends," *Virginia Quarterly Review,* 5 (July 1929), 397–410.

25. George Bancroft to Otto von Bismarck, September 30, 1870; to William H. Seward, September 10, 1867; George Bancroft to Reverdy Johnson, January 2, 1868, in Howe, *Life and Letters,* II, 187; George Bancroft to Countess Andrassy, October 27, 1868; to Hamilton Fish, September 27, 1869. See also George Bancroft, unpublished sketch of Bismarck's character, NYPL; Henry Blumenthal, "George Bancroft in Berlin, 1867–1874," *New England Quarterly,* 27 (June 1964).

26. Sidney Whitman, ed., *Personal Reminiscences of Prince Bismarck* (New York, 1903), 285, 34, 120.

27. Count Bismarck to John Motley, September 19, 1869, in John L. Motley, *Correspondence* (New York, 1900), 311–312.

28. George Bancroft to Otto von Bismarck, December 11, 1867; to William H. Seward, November 1, 1867; Otto von Bismarck to George Bancroft, December 14, 1867.

29. George Bancroft to Christian E. Detmold, February 7, 1868; to Carl

Schurz, February 17, 1868; to George P. Marsh, January 16, 1868; to J.C.B. Davis, May 2, 1870.

30. Gazley, *American Opinion*, 230–231; George Bancroft to Andrew Johnson, January 21, 1868; to William H. Seward, December 24, 1868. See also Stolberg-Wernigerode, *Germany and the United States*, 102.

31. George Bancroft to William H. Seward, August 29, 1867, September 15, November 20, November 29, 1868, NYPL.

32. George Bancroft to John Chandler Bancroft Davis, August 2, 1870. See also Bancroft Papers, NYPL.

33. George Bancroft to John A. Dix, December 29, 1868, January 11, 1869; to George P. Marsh, July 16, 1869.

34. Gideon Welles, *Diary*, Howard K. Beale, ed. (New York, 1960), II, 511, 512; Orville H. Browning, *Diary* (Illinois Historical Society, 22, Collections), 235, 238; Stolberg-Wernigerode, *Germany and the United States*, 105.

35. George Bancroft to Hamilton Fish, October 18, 1870; to Elizabeth Bancroft, July 3, 15, 16, 1870. See also Lawrence D. Steefel, *Bismarck, the Hohenzollern Candidacy and the Origins of the Franco-Prussian War of 1870* (Cambridge, Mass., 1962).

36. George Bancroft to Hamilton Fish, August 7, 1870; to Baron von Thiele, August 10, 13, 1870; Baron von Thiele to George Bancroft, August 11, 1870.

37. George Bancroft to Lucretia Farnum and George H. Davis, July 27, 1870.

38. George Bancroft to Frederica Davis, September 4, 1870; to Mrs. Hamilton Fish, December 11, 1870; to J.C.B. Davis, September 5, 1870. For another example of this Manichaean bent, see George Bancroft to Friedrich Kapp, April 7, 1871.

39. George Bancroft to Hamilton Fish, September 12, 21, 29, 1870; to J.C.B. Davis, September 5, October 12, 1870.

40. George Bancroft to Elihu Washburne, August 30, September 10, 1870; to Hamilton Fish, September 11, October 8, 1870.

41. On aid to stranded Germans, see extensive correspondence with Elihu Washburne, Bancroft Papers, NYPL; Hamilton Fish to George Bancroft, October 12, 1870. See also Elihu Washburne, *The Franco-Prussian War and the Insurrection of the Commune* (Washington, D.C., 1878); and *Recollections of a Minister to France 1869–1877* (New York, 1887); also Allan Nevins, *Hamilton Fish* (New York, 1936), 400–410; Henry Blumenthal, *A Reappraisal of Franco-American Relations, 1830–1871* (Chapel Hill, N.C., 1959).

42. Victor Hugo, *L'Année terrible* (Paris, 1872), 73–74. For a bitter assault on Bancroft, see Joseph Aaron, *Alsace Lorraine: A Monument to Grant* (New York, 1885); Gazley, *American Opinion*, 393.

43. Bancroft's dispatches are in NYPL.

44. George Bancroft to J.C.B. Davis, October 12, 1870.

45. George Bancroft to Friedrich Kapp, April 7, 1871; to Christian E. Detmold, May 2, 1871; John L. Motley to George Bancroft, November 30, 1870; Bigelow, *Retrospections*, IV, 418.

46. George Bancroft to Hamilton Fish, November 12, December 15, 1873.

47. George Bancroft to Samuel Osgood, February 21, 1868, in Howe, *Life and*

Letters, II, 203–204; George Bancroft to Samuel Osgood, December 24, 1871, in Howe, *Life and Letters,* II, 262-263.

48. George Bancroft to Frederica Davis, March 8, September 4, 1870; to Hamilton Fish, May 25, 1874; to George Ripley, November 22, 1871.

49. George Bancroft to Hamilton Fish, January 31, May 25, September 24, 1870, April 10, 1871, October 23, 27, December 1, 1873, March 30, 1874.

50. George Bancroft to Hamilton Fish, September 2, November 20, 1871, March 18, June 17, 1872, May 26, 1873. For Bancroft's anti-Catholic prejudices, see Arnold Blumberg, "George Bancroft, France and Vatican Diplomacy," *Catholic Historical Review,* 50 (1964), 475–493; Mary Philip Trauth, "The Bancroft Dispatches on the Vatican Council and the Kulturkampf," *Catholic Historical Review,* 40 (1954), 178–190.

51. Nevins, *Hamilton Fish,* 518–566, discusses the steps which led to the agreement and Davis's role.

52. George Bancroft to Hamilton Fish, December 19, 1871. The entire issue is ably examined in James O. McCabe, *The San Juan Water Boundary Question* (Toronto, 1966). See also extensive correspondence in Bancroft Papers, NYPL.

53. McCabe, *San Juan Water Boundary,* 127.

54. See extensive correspondence relevant to these problems in Bancroft Papers, NYPL and Bancroft Papers, MHS.

55. George Bancroft to Lucretia Farnum, May 29, 1873.

56. George Bancroft, Diary, April 27, 1872; George Bancroft to Mrs. Hamilton Fish, January 3, 1874.

57. See Bancroft Diary 1872–1873, NYPL. For letters and newspaper clippings about the trip, see Bancroft Papers, MHS.

58. George Bancroft to Hamilton Fish, August 2, 12, 1873; to Department of State, October 6, December 15, 1873.

59. Richard Lepsius to George Bancroft, June 16, 1874.

XIII. *Reflections on the Past and Present*

1. *Literary World,* 22 (January 31, 1891), 40; *Harper's Weekly,* 35 (January 24, 1891).

2. George Bancroft, quoted in Mark de Wolfe Howe, *Life and Letters of George Bancroft* (New York, 1908), II, 278.

3. Henry Adams, *The Education of Henry Adams* (Cambridge, Mass., 1961), 243; J. L. Gilder, *Authors at Home* (New York, 1902), 21; see also numerous references in Ward Thoron, ed., *Letters of Mrs. Henry Adams, 1865–1883* (Boston, 1936) and Harold D. Cater, *Henry Adams and His Friends* (Boston, 1947).

4. *Public Opinion,* 5 (October 6, 1888), 569. For honors that came his way, see the many letters in Bancroft Papers, MHS. On Stevenson, see Richard Bartlett, *The New Country* (New York, 1974), 334.

5. Sarah Chandler to George Bancroft, July 26, 1889; Isaac Hughes to George Bancroft, January 13, 1887. For other evidence of these activities, see Bancroft Papers, MHS.

6. Thoron, ed., *Mrs. Henry Adams,* 254, 373; Rutherford Birchard Hayes, *Diary and Letters,* Charles Richard Williams, ed. (Columbus, Ohio, Ohio State Historical Society), I (1922), 126, III (1924), 461, 643. See also George Bancroft to Samuel Tilden, October 18, 1885; Samuel J. Tilden, *Letters and Literary Memorials,* John Bigelow, ed. (Freeport, N.Y., 1971), 700; Allan Nevins, *Grover Cleveland* (New York, 1932), 2; George Frederick Howe, *Chester A. Arthur: A Quarter Century of Machine Politics* (New York, 1934). For other White House contacts, see letters in Bancroft Papers, MHS.

7. Hayes, *Diary and Letters,* IV (1925), 235. For women's rights, see George Bancroft, "Progress of Mankind," *Literary and Historical Miscellanies* (New York, 1855), 499–500. On Elizabeth see also Harriet S. Blaine Beale, *Letters of Mrs. James G. Blaine* (New York, 1908), I, 189, 276, 297, 301–302, 305, 309.

8. *The Critic,* 6 (October 2, 1886). See also Van Wyck Brooks, *New England: Indian Summer 1865–1915* (New York, 1940), 66–78.

9. George Bancroft to Miss Bruen, January 11, 1883; to John Ryan, May 1, 1885.

10. Henry Tuckerman, "George Bancroft," *Magazine of American History,* 25 (1891), 229; George Bancroft to Oliver W. Holmes, January 19, 1885, in Howe, *Life and Letters,* II, 301–305; George Bancroft, *A Plea for the Constitution, Wounded in the House of Its Guardians* (New York, 1886), 87.

11. Tuckerman, "Bancroft," *Magazine of American History,* 229; Henry Cabot Lodge, *Early Memories* (New York, 1913), 316; George E. Ellis, "George Bancroft," Massachusetts Historical Society, *Proceedings,* 6 (February, 1891), 295.

12. George Bancroft to Oliver W. Holmes, January 19, 1885, in Howe, *Life and Letters,* II, 303.

13. Ibid., 282. See also Francis Parkman to George Bancroft, October 27, November 19, 24, 1878, in Wilbur R. Jacobs, ed., *Letters of Francis Parkman* (Norman, Okla., 1960); Henry Adams to Elizabeth Cameron, October 10, 1887, in Jacob C. Levenson, ed., *Letters of Henry Adams* (Cambridge, Mass., 1982), III, 83; Henry Adams to John White Field, June 4, 1885, ibid., II, 614.

14. Tuckerman, "Bancroft," *Magazine of American History* (1891), 230; George Bancroft, "William H. Prescott," *Historical Magazine,* 3 (March 1859), 69; George Bancroft to S. Austin Allibone, May (?) 1882, quoted in Samuel Swett Green, "George Bancroft," American Antiquarian Society *Proceedings,* 7 New Series (April 1891), 248.

15. Howe, *Life and Letters,* II, 310; Green, "Bancroft," 252; George Bancroft to S. Austin Allibone, August 29, 1887, in Howe, *Life and Letters,* II, 311. See also George Bancroft to Henry H. Edes, April 30, 1888.

16. George Bancroft, "Lowell, Our Ablest Critic," *Literary World,* 16 (June 18, 1885), 217–218; also Bancroft, "Holmes's Life of Emerson," *North American Review,* 140 (February 1885), 133, 134.

17. George Bancroft, *History of the Battle of Lake Erie* (New York, 1891), 243.

18. George Bancroft, *History of the United States* (Boston, 1874), X, 592–593.

19. Ibid., 86; also 366.

20. Ibid., 345, 366.

21. Ibid., 139, 593, 422, 424–425.

22. "Bancroft's History of the United States, Volume X," *Literary World,* 5–6 (September 1874), 57.

23. "Bancroft's History of the United States, Volume X," *Historical Magazine,* 23 (March 1875), 233, 234; Henry Adams to Henry Cabot Lodge, June 2, 1872, in Cater, *Henry Adams and His Friends,* 65; [Henry Adams], "Bancroft's History of the United States, Volume X," *North American Review,* 120 (April 1875), 424–432.

24. George Bancroft, *History of the United States,* Centenary Edition (6 vols., Boston, 1876), I, v–vi. On Elizabeth's editorial role, see George Ripley to Moses Coit Tyler, January 3, 1875, in Jessica Tyler Austen, *Moses Coit Tyler, 1835–1900* (Garden City, N. Y., 1911), 88–89.

25. George Bancroft, *History of the United States* (Boston, 1860), VIII, 248, and Centenary Edition, V, 165; also Bancroft, *History,* VIII, 248, 249, and Centenary Edition, V, 165–166. Robert Winthrop to George Bancroft, February 11, 1880; George Bancroft to Lucretia Farnum, January 3, 1881. See, for example, Hildreth's sarcastic rewriting of one such sentence, Donald E. Emerson, *Richard Hildreth* (Baltimore, 1946), 165.

26. George Bancroft to S. R. Crocker, November 22, 1875; to John T. Short, March 3, 1881. See also George Bancroft to Roswell Smith, November 17, 1884.

27. George Bancroft, *History of the United States* (Boston, 1837), I, 367, 462, and Centenary Edition, I, 286, 372.

28. Emerson, *Hildreth,* 139; Bancroft, *Battle of Lake Erie,* 244.

29. George Ticknor Curtis, *History of the Origin, Formation, and Adoption of the Constitution of the United States* (New York, 1860), I, v; Herman von Holst, *The Constitutional and Political History of the United States* (Chicago, 1876), I, 31, 69, 72, 75.

30. Orestes A. Brownson, *The American Republic: Its Constitution, Tendencies and Destiny* (New York, 1866), 5; Orestes A. Brownson to George Bancroft, October 21, 1866, in H. F. Brownson, *Orestes A. Brownson's Later Life* (Detroit, 1900), 465; also Arthur M. Schlesinger, Jr., *Orestes A. Brownson: A Pilgrim's Progress* (New York, 1963), 261; Richard Hildreth, *History of the United States* (New York, 1876), III.

31. Morton Keller, *Affairs of State* (Cambridge, Mass., 1977), 238.

32. George Bancroft, *History of the Formation of the Constitution* (New York, 1883), I, 211; II, 323, 324.

33. Ibid., II, 322, 329, 330, 331.

34. George Bancroft to Robert Winthrop, August 1, 1876; Bancroft, *Formation of the Constitution,* I, 4.

35. Ibid., II, 283, 285–294, 339, 341.

36. Ibid., 283, 300, 301, 306, 315, 316.

37. Ibid., 337, 338, 341, 339.

38. Ibid., I, 266, 274–275; II, 366.

39. Ibid., 134–137, 203, 208, 322, 327, 329, 330.

40. George Bancroft to William Bliss, June 8, 1882. See also Morrison R.

Waite to George Bancroft, January 17, 1879, in Bruce R. Trimble, *Chief Justice Waite* (Princeton, N. J., 1938), 244–245; George Bancroft to Edmund Gosse, May 30, 1885; to John C. Hurd, December 22, 1881; to B. T. Sage, February 8, 1882.

41. Howe, *Life and Letters,* II, 300; George Bancroft, *History of the United States* (Boston, 1834), I, Preface.

42. "Bancroft's History of the Formation of the Constitution," *Literary World,* 13 (1882), 175–176; "Editor's Literary Record," *Harper's,* 65 (1882), 473, 474. See also "Bancroft's History of the Formation of the Constitution," *The Critic,* 2 (May 20, 1882), 136; J. Franklin Jameson, "Bancroft's History of the Formation of the Constitution," *Historische Zeitschrift,* 51 (1884), 189–190.

43. Henry Cabot Lodge, "Bancroft's History of the Formation of the Constitution," *Atlantic Monthly,* 50 (August 1882), 275, 276, 277; Henry Adams to Henry Cabot Lodge, October 31, 1882, in Worthington C. Ford, ed., *Letters of Henry Adams* (New York, 1930), II, 342.

44. George Bancroft, *History of the United States: Author's Last Revision* (New York, 1883), I, iv, v. This was also perceived by reviewers. See "Editor's Literary Record," *Harper's,* 66 (April 1883), 797; 67 (August 1883), 474; 68 (February 1884), 482–483.

45. On Washington, see undated diary note, 1880s, Bancroft Papers, MHS. See also George Bancroft to Moses Coit Tyler, September 24, 1887; to Austin Scott, February 18, 1885; to George H. Moore, March 21, 1885; to Robert Winthrop, February 28, 1885.

46. George Bancroft to Justin Morrill, April 15, 1885; to W. R. Gibbons, September 25, 1886. Even Goethe got into the act of opposing paper money— see George Bancroft to W. O. Milduer, August 26, 1875.

47. George Bancroft to Morrison R. Waite, May 6, 1884; see also private memoranda, March 7, 1884; and other diary notations for the year reflecting his discomfort in opposition to the Supreme Court.

48. Bancroft, *A Plea for the Constitution,* 7, 8, 60, 61, 68, 71, 72, 74, 75, 87.

49. See Richard C. McMurtie, *Observations on Mr. Bancroft's Plea* (Philadelphia, 1886), and correspondence in Bancroft Papers, MHS.

50. George Bancroft to Mary Perkins, February 14, 1885.

51. The deposition document (1883), Bancroft Papers, MHS, details George's alcoholism and deliriums. See also extensive correspondence on the subject in CUMR.

52. George Bancroft to Austin Scott, July 17, 1886; to Baron Alvensleven, March 20, 1886; Varina Davis to George Bancroft, March 23, 1886; Lucretia Farnum to George Bancroft, April 9, 1886.

53. Bancroft, Diary Note, 1887, in Howe, *Life and Letters,* II, 306. For further material on John Chandler Bancroft, see CUA and Elizabeth Swinton, "John Chandler Bancroft," *Worcester Art Museum Journal* (1982–1983).

54. Clippings of New York *Daily Tribune,* December 3, 1887; and the *Cornell Sun* (1887), in Bancroft Papers, MHS. Florence, Alabama, Academy to George Bancroft, February 22, 1887.

55. George Bancroft to J. G. Harris, August 30, 1887; George Bancroft to Sarah

Polk, January 9, 18, 1886; Ben. Perley Poore, *Reminiscences of Sixty Years in the National Metropolis* (Philadelphia, 1886), 326; Abby Sage Richardson, *The History of Our Country* (Cambridge, Mass., 1875), 375; James Schouler, *History of the United States* (New York, 1889), IV, 482–499, 519.

56. On Nashville trip, New York *Herald,* April 19, 1887; Washington *Post,* April 19, 1887; Nashville *Evening Telegram,* April 18, 1887; Nashville *Banner,* April 18, 1887; Nashville *Daily American,* April 18, 19, 20, 23, 1887; Nashville *Weekly American,* April 20, 1887; Nashville *Union,* April 22, 1887; Knoxville *Daily Sentinel,* April 22, 1887; Chattanooga *Daily Times,* April 22, 1887; also Anson and Fanny Nelson, eds., *Memorials of Sarah Childres Polk* (New York, 1892), 207–213, 260–261.

57. Scraps for the Polk biography, a fairly complete draft, and some correspondence on the subject are among Bancroft's papers in the NYPL.

58. Bancroft's revisions shaped the "James K. Polk" article in *Appleton's Cyclopedia of American Biography,* V, 55. Correspondence about Shakespeare, Milton, and others in Bancroft Papers, MHS. At least one reviewer, however, was impressed with the very feat of publishing at the age of eighty-nine. He called Bancroft "the Hotspur of historians who kills some six or seven dozen Scots before breakfast, washes his hands and cries out 'Fie upon this quiet life, I want work.' " "Martin Van Buren," *Harper's,* 79 (October 1889), 183.

59. Bancroft, *Martin Van Buren*, 179, 191, 201.

60. On the final vision of history, see George Bancroft to Daniel Coit Gilman, March 6, 1881; to Roswell Smith, November 17, 1884; to Austin Scott, February 18, 1885; to George H. Moore, March 21, 1885; to Moses Coit Tyler, September 24, 1887.

61. For later low esteem of Bancroft because of his bias, see Ray Allen Billington, ed., *The Reinterpretation of Early American History* (San Marino, Calif., 1966), 152–153, 114–115, 185–188; J. R. Pole, "The American Past, Is it Still Usable?", *Journal of American Studies,* 1 (April 1967), 63–78, where the answer, as far as Bancroft goes, seems to be no. Yet not everyone rejected him: see Michael Kammen, ed., *What Is the Good of History: Selected Letters of Carl L. Becker* (Ithaca, N.Y., 1973), 298. Another set of historians uses Bancroft to flesh out the supposed nineteenth-century rebellion against history. See David W. Noble, *Historians Against History* (Minneapolis, 1965), 18–36. For Bancroft's relationship to some of his successors and presumed lack of interest in intellectual history, see Robert Allen Skotheim, *American Intellectual Histories and Historians* (Princeton, N.J., 1966), 15–20. For a sympathetic effort to understand the inner workings of the *History,* from which, however, this study departs in many ways, see Robert H. Canary, *George Bancroft* (New York, 1974). Another sympathetic account is Bert James Loewenberg, *American History in American Thought* (New York, 1972), 239–257. See also John Higham, *Writing American History* (Bloomington, Ind., 1970); David Levin, *In Defense of Historical Literature* (New York, 1967), and his masterly *History as Romantic Art* (Stanford, Calif., 1959). For more favorable assessments of Bancroft as historian, see Daniel Boorstin, *The Americans: The Colonial Experience* (New York, 1958), 375; Edmund S. Morgan,

The Birth of the Republic, 1763–1789 (Chicago, 1956), 158. When the American Historical Association in 1948 asked its council to name the greatest dead historians of the United States, Bancroft's name was among the top five.

62. Robert Winthrop, "George Bancroft," Massachusetts Historical Society, *Proceedings*, 6 (February 1891); George F. Hoar, *Autobiography of Seventy Years* (New York, 1903), 206; Austen, *Moses Coit Tyler*, 259.

63. *The Independent*, January 22, 1891, 12; other editorials reprinted in *Public Opinion*, 10 (January 24, 1891); also Boston *Advertiser*, January 19, 1891; *Al Mokattam* (Cairo), 1891.

64. Boston *Globe*, March 21, 1965.

INDEX

About the Author

Lilian Handlin is coauthor of *Abraham Lincoln and the Union* (Boston, 1980) and of *A Restless People* (New York, 1982). A graduate of Queens College and Brown University, she received her Ph.D. at the Hebrew University of Jerusalem, where she was an instructor in the Department of History.